Introduction to Human Communication

Introduction to Human Communication

James W. Gibson
University of Missouri, Columbia

Michael S. Hanna
University of South Alabama

 WCB Wm. C. Brown Publishers

Book Team

Editor *Stan Stoga*
Developmental Editor *Jane F. Lambert*
Production Editor *Renee A. Menne*
Designer *Christopher E. Reese*
Art Editor *Mary Swift*
Photo Editor *Laura Fuller*
Visuals Processor *Amy L. Saffran*

Wm. C. Brown Publishers

President *G. Franklin Lewis*
Vice President, Publisher *Thomas E. Doran*
Vice President, Operations and Production *Beverly Kolz*
National Sales Manager *Virginia S. Moffat*
Group Sales Manager *Eric Ziegler*
Executive Editor *Edgar J. Laube*
Director of Marketing *Kathy Law Laube*
Marketing Manager *Carla Aspelmeier*
Managing Editor, Production *Colleen A. Yonda*
Manager of Visuals and Design *Faye M. Schilling*
Production Editorial Manager *Julie A. Kennedy*
Production Editorial Manager *Ann Fuerste*
Publishing Services Manager *Karen J. Slaght*

WCB Group

President and Chief Executive Officer *Mark C. Falb*
Chairman of the Board *Wm. C. Brown*

Copyedited by Stephen Shepherd

The credits section for this book begins on page 467, and is considered an extension of the copyright page.

Brief Table of Contents

Table of Contents

Preface

This book is concerned with the scope and specifics of human communication, which is a marvelously complex and exciting process. It is also concerned with the total person and with all of the tools and intellectual skills that each person brings to the communication act.

The process of human communication is central to our existence. The qualities exhibited as people communicate separate humans from other species. Communication defines friends, enemies, lovers, students, teachers, employers, and leaders, and it defines any of a myriad of different roles. This unique human act of communication transmits roles and personalities.

The skills and understanding shown in communication behavior determine relations with other people and with society. Communication skills can be improved through education and practice. Effective communicators understand the elements of communication and how they can be used more effectively.

You are capable of being a more effective communicator if you understand more about the process of human communication. As you learn about that process in this book, you'll learn the principles and guides that will assist you in improving your daily interpersonal and public communication behavior.

Effective communication does not just "happen." It is a product of understanding and of being willing to practice and to improve communication behavior. Those two matters, understanding and practice, are essential in order to improve your communication. *You* must assume the responsibility for putting into daily practice those elements of communication that are discussed in the following chapters.

This book goes beyond the average communication text; instead, it is a true survey approach to communication. Some of the significant differences between this survey approach and the average text are the chapters on mass communication, cross cultural communication, critical thinking, and organizational communication. The "It's More Fun to Know" boxes, which are found in every chapter, are another unique feature. These boxes present interesting and thought-provoking communication research. We also cover the traditional topics of interpersonal communication, public speaking, group communication, listening, and verbal and nonverbal communication. Therefore, the approach to this introductory survey blends theory and skills for a comprehensive, balanced text that newcomers to the field of communication will enjoy.

This book is divided into five sections. Part I, "Preliminary Concerns," builds a conceptual base for understanding the variety of interactions that comprise private, group, and public communication. Chapter 1 introduces "symbolic interactionism," the perspective from which this book was written, and it presents several other models that are fundamental to understanding communication. Chapter 2 examines the individual as communicator, especially on the evolution of the self and to improve confidence and communication by modifying self-concept. Chapter 3 examines listening, and it explains how to improve skills in active, empathic, and other kinds of listening in order to become a better communicator. Chapter 4 concerns the theories of verbal messages, and it suggests specific methods to improve the use of language. Chapter 5 explores the various elements of nonverbal communication, and it relates many techniques for sending and receiving these messages.

In Part II, the background information from the previous five chapters is used to approach "Interpersonal Communication Settings." Chapter 6 introduces the interpersonal event and explains the contexts of interpersonal communication and the essential factors in relationship development. Chapter 7 brings the interpersonal relationship into greater focus by providing the fundamental principles and by suggesting skills for increasing relationship satisfaction. Chapter 8 explains how to emerge successful from interviews by explaining the features common to all interviews, and it gives specialized knowledge for employment and for performance appraisal interviews.

Part III explores the "Analysis and Larger Communication Contexts." Chapter 9 concerns critical thinking and suggests ways to monitor your own reasoning and the reasoning of others, in order to avoid fallacies and to gain acceptance for your ideas. Chapter 10 focuses on group communication and teaches two essential skills in every complex organization: leadership, and effective participation. Chapter 11 stresses the most important aspects of organizational communication: how an organization evolves, what its communication functions are, and how it influences an individual's communication behavior.

Part IV, "Public Communication Settings," focuses on the processes involved in preparing to speak publicly. Chapter 12 looks at the preliminary concerns, such as communication apprehension, the speaker's attitude, and the role of the thesis within the message structure. Chapter 13 leads you through the steps of audience analysis and speech organization, and it reveals the secrets of effective delivery. Chapter 14 focuses on the major elements of the informative speech, while providing the techniques both for presenting ideas clearly and for increasing audience retention of material. Chapter 15 concerns the persuasive speech; it illustrates the most important concepts with easy-to-understand models in order to gain acceptance for your ideas.

Part V, "Communication Across Boundaries," examines how communication principles extend to media and intercultural settings. Chapter 16 discusses the influence of media on social agendas, world knowledge, and consumer needs, and it also considers the impact of the media on the individual. Chapter 17 looks at intercultural communication in the 1990s, and it teaches the skills needed to communicate across cultural and national boundaries.

The purpose of this book is to expose you to a basic understanding and awareness of the role of human communication in modern society. As we build on that understanding, we look at the variety of settings and communication behaviors that define our individuality. Throughout, the book focuses on **symbolic interaction** as the key element of human communication. Our lives are affected by the way that we react to the use of language and the feelings, attitudes, values, and impact that language has on us. Our language—our symbol system—is central to our lives and our responses, and that is the unique message of this book.

Acknowledgments

We would like to express our appreciation to the following reviewers for their comments and suggestions:

- Leonard Barchak, McNeese State University
- Elizabeth Faries, Western Illinois University
- Kenneth D. Frandsen, University of New Mexico
- Doris Gillard, Bowie State University
- Monte Koffler, North Dakota State University
- Sandra Ragan, University of Oklahoma
- Mary Ruth Rang, University of Dayton
- Frank Trimble, University of North Carolina–Wilmington

Introduction to Human Communication

Part I

Preliminary Concerns

Understanding human activity means understanding the processes of human communication. The unique activity that distinguishes us from other members in the animal kingdom is our ability to develop and utilize symbols. Our communication symbol systems are both verbal and nonverbal, and they transmit meaning and stimulate reaction from those people who receive them. The response of others is not always what we desire because listeners' reactions to words are affected by their previous language experiences that are unique to that individual. Thus, our primary concern must be with the way that people react to what we say.

We must concern ourselves with the nature of the people we talk to and their feelings about what we say. We must put "symbolic interaction" at the center of our communication concern. If the cycle of talk and listening is complete we create commonness.

This section will introduce you to several models of the communication process and discuss the role of communication in your lives and its part in the general function of society. The major focus of this section of the book will be upon the "self," your development of a personal concept, and the part that communication plays in image construction. The symbolic interaction process of using a common language to exchange experience and interact with different realities is the premise of this book. As humans, our reality is created and changed by the language we use and by our reactions to the symbols we exchange with others.

The symbolic interaction is both verbal and nonverbal. We listen to sounds (messages), and we observe the transmission of other thoughts (messages) sent nonverbally. We listen with both our eyes and our ears.

As you read this section on "Preliminary Concerns," you will come to understand the broad base for the variety of interactions that make up private, group, and public communication. The principles of communication and symbolic interaction cut across the settings in which we communicate. The initial chapter on the communication process and communication models will help you to better understand this process.

Chapter 1

Communication Process and Models

Outline

When you finish reading this chapter you will be able to:

1. Define several key terms that describe the communication process.

2. List, describe, and explain key features of the symbolic interactionist perspective on human communication.

3. Draw, label, and explain the component parts of a process model of communication.

4. Explain several reasons or benefits of formally studying communication.

Objectives

affective	ideology	science
art	interpersonal	semantic noise
channels	communication	source
communication	intrapersonal	stimulus field
contexts	communication	symbol
decoder-receiver	language	symbolic interaction
encode	messages	"to mean"
feedback	noise	

Key Terms

Introduction

When Bill Jackson got up the morning of January 10, he remembered the assignment from his communication professor on the previous day. "Keep a list of all the communication events that occur in your life between the time you awaken and the time you arrive in this class tomorrow."

"Piece of cake," thought Bill. "Communication is my first class in the day."

Despite being the first class of the day, Bill's communication's list turned out to be a surprisingly long one for him. He awoke when the radio began to play rock music at 6:30 A.M. He threw on some clothes, tossed his books and papers into a backpack imprinted with a picture of a dog and the words, "Party Animal," and went through the door, listening for the "click" of the lock behind him. He barely grunted at Tom (What's his name?) as he passed through the lobby of his dorm. He raced by some vending machines, selected a chicken-salad sandwich and a carton of milk. On the way out the door he picked up a copy of the student newspaper and noticed that the basketball team was playing an "away" game that night.

Carillon bells began to chime the hour just as Bill entered the main academic quadrangle on campus. He ignored the "keep off the grass" sign, hopped over a low wire fence, and cut diagonally across the lawn. About halfway across the lawn he heard his name called out: "Bill! Bill!"

Turning, Bill saw that Helen Stamish was running to catch up with him. Her red scarf was easy to see, even at that hour of the morning. He could tell that she was rushing to class this morning, too.

"Hi," she said. "Are you ready for class this morning?"

"Well, I don't have anything written down, but I sure have a lot of communication events to talk about." Bill smiled as he realized that Helen's approach provided him a rich source of additional messages to report to his class.

In the classroom, Bill decided that some of the writing on the chalkboard represented the remnants from yesterday's psychology lecture. "Psychology," he said aloud to no one in particular, "must have been quite a lecture, judging from the board."

Professor Jameson entered the room, straightened her books at a small table, placed her notes on a lectern, spoke quietly to one of the students in the front row, and then began: "Good morning, ladies and gentlemen."

Consider the enormous number of communication events in Bill's first morning hour. It reminds us that ours is a communication-based existence. Every day we exchange messages from the moment we awaken in the morning until the moment we go to sleep at night. Communication behavior (i.e., message exchange and interpretation) binds us together as human become possible, while the symbolic interactionist perspective provides a coherent framework for its study.

Definitions of Important Terms

Symbol

A **symbol** is something that represents something else. That is, a symbol represents or takes the place of, or points to ideas, or objects, or events.[3] A symbol can even represent a feeling or an emotion. For example, the word, "car," refers to a physical object. You can see and touch a car. But you can't observe an **affective** state, because affect arises from feelings or emotions. When you say or write the word, "joy," for example, you are referring to an affective state. We can use our symbols in this way because we agree, as a speech community, that the symbols refer to, or represent, some part of our shared experience. They mean something to all of us.

"To Mean"

People make symbols mean something to each other. In technical terms, **to mean** implies an agreement between two or more people that they will recognize what they represent by a sign or symbol. Thus, if you say the word, "chair," your roommate understands that you "mean" a certain object in the room.

Language

Language is a system of signs and symbols, a body of words and the rules for their use, that ties people together into a speech community. Language is our primary message system. As far as we know, only humankind has evolved a language.

Language allows us to think about the past, to plan for the future, to imagine a dream, and to think about a different county or a far away continent. Language makes it possible for us to feel love, to cry at a tender moment in theatre, and to delight in a memory. For better or worse, the human ability to exchange and interpret such sophisticated and complex messages sets us apart from other creatures. Each message exists in its own verbal and nonverbal signs and symbols. When we interact we exchange those signs and symbols; thus, the name, *Symbolic Interaction.*[4]

Ideology

The symbolic interactionist perspective imposes upon us a certain **ideology.** We are taking a particular point of view, which is combined with a set of rules for acting and a set of assumptions for viewing the world. An ideology helps us to come to grips with the most diverse and complex of all human studies.

IT'S MORE FUN TO KNOW

Touch

Females touch more because touch is considered appropriate for a female. Women also touch more appropriately. Men initiate touch less and use more talk without touch because they know less about how to touch.

See Stanley E. Jones, ''Sex Differences in Touch Communication,'' *Western Journal of Speech Communication*, 50:3 (Summer 1986), pp. 227–241.

Comment . . .
Touching tends to be more of a female behavior. We expect women to touch more and, when men do touch, they often do not do it appropriately. This is a more intimate form of communication, and women are more successful and more likely to use it than men.

Communication, Art, and Science

For most of recorded history, people have thought of communication as an art. Indeed, Aristotle defined *rhetoric* as "the art of discovering all the available means of persuasion." **Art** can be defined to mean the disposition or modification of a thing by human skill. Thus, persuasion can be called an art. But communication study is also a science. It is a **science** when we try to discover some systematically arranged body of facts or truths about communication that shows the operation of general laws governing our communication behavior.

Because our discipline is both art and science, textbook writers and teachers sometimes have difficulty developing a coherent and comprehensive course of study that can be completed in a single curriculum term. Therefore, much that is interesting and useful from more than twenty-three centuries of study has to be left out. That fact creates the problem of choosing what information to use, and what information to exclude from this text. Even

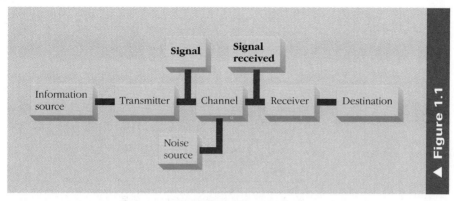

Figure 1.1

so, this book contains seventeen chapters of material, although your instructor may not ask you to read them all!

Communication Models

While still teaching at the University of Missouri, the late B. Aubrey Fisher began to think about how to organize the broadly diverse studies of communication. His influential book, *Perspectives on Human Communication*[5] describes four ideological points of view. One of these points of view is the symbolic interactionist perspective, which is the primary view of this text. Fisher argued that the perspective a person takes imposes certain basic assumptions on that person. Those assumptions control what we can examine and ultimately control our interpretations.

Another helpful model was introduced in 1949 by Claude Shannon and Warren Weaver[6] in their book entitled *Mathematical Theory of Communication.* They presented the model in figure 1.1.

Shannon and Weaver described communication as a linear and sequential phenomenon. Notice how the model focuses our attention on the components. Also, notice that the components occur in a sequence that begins at the information source. A transmitter sends a signal through a channel. An important component of the model is the noise source, which may introduce noise into the channel. The receiver picks up or "collects," the received signal and conducts it to its destination.

This model encourages us to ask questions about message transmission. It also encourages questions about message fidelity and message effect. ("What's the best way to get a message across from source to receiver?" "Are there ways to control sources of noise?" "If we can't control the sources of noise, are there ways to control for the effects of noise in the receiver?")

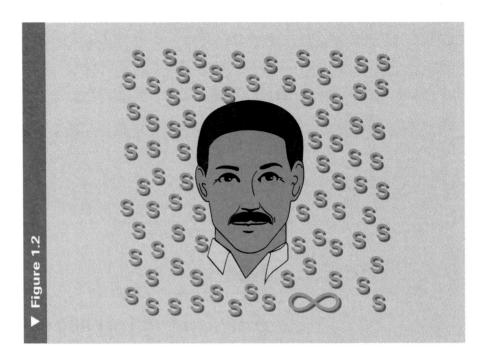

Nothing in the model, however, points to what occurs inside people. You can see that this omission makes an enormous difference. For instance, the distinction between sender and receiver blurs when you begin to think about a person's psychology. If you study the psychology of the participants, you discover that a communicator is always at the same moment both a sender and a receiver of messages.

This means that communication success requires at least two people to share experiences and goals. In turn, it follows that communication scholars would develop an interest in **interpersonal communication** and that schools would begin to devise courses in interpersonal communication.

Since communication occurs inside people, **intrapersonal** concerns become important to the study of communication. So it seems important to devise studies of what is going on *inside* a person engaged in communication behavior.

From this psychological perspective, people exist inside a **stimulus field.** They are changed by the stimuli they receive. For example, as you read this sentence, the sentence has some impact on you. Similarly, when the breeze softly touches your skin, that stimulus also has an impact on you. People select certain stimuli to attend. Thus, we can *choose* future responses. In this way, information is always filtered through the people (see figure 1.2).

Notice how the psychological perspective encourages us to emphasize the filters, or mental processes, of communicators. This change in focus can

We learn who we are and how to manage our relationships through symbolic interaction.

be important to communication study because we are encouraged to study selective perception and to focus on how people assign (rather than receive) meanings to the stimuli that they perceive. It also encourages us to think about the communication event as a two-way phenomenon, rather than one way.

The symbolic interactionist perspective not only gives us all of the benefits of the psychological perspective, but it also locates communication in the human activity of role taking and assigning, rather than inside the individual.

Symbolic interactionists believe that the self is built-up through social interaction. The *mind,* the *self,* and the *society* are each a function of talk. Therefore, communication occurs through the creation of shared significant symbols, thus meaning is socially derived. Human beings define themselves, others, and the things in their world by a process of negotiation. We talk to each other, we exchange symbols, and we discover "the truth" by doing these things.

A basic assumption throughout this book is that social activity is only possible through the role-taking process. First, we learn, then we "take on" our role behaviors by discovering directly or by imagining what others think, and what they think of us. By this method we learn how "it is supposed to be" and how "we are supposed to behave."

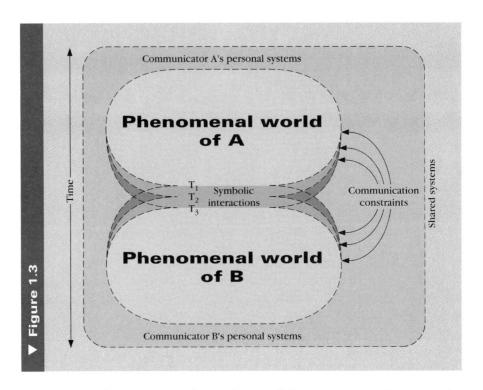

▼ Figure 1.3

This book projects the evidence of this perspective. For example, chapter 2 relates how an individual's self-concept evolves and how it can be changed as a function of talk. Chapter 4 describes the relationship between language and experience, and how our learned ways of using language control our drawing of inferences. Chapter 8 argues that a relationship exists between our observations and the inferences drawn from them; namely, inferences about such things as feelings and wants. Chapter 11 describes organizations as cultures, and argues that successful communication in organizations depends upon our skills of role assigning and role taking within those cultures.

From this point of view, the communication process exists in time as a shared system. People exist independently, but within a shared system. Therefore, communication occurs when people exchange symbols, and when they create and share the meaning of their experiences. Figure 1.3 illustrates a symbolic interactionist model of the communication process.

This model, like all models, is both limited and limiting. It imposes an ideology upon us. For example, it does not include any mention of channels. However, the model focuses attention on some things that other models virtually ignore. For example, this particular model focuses a good deal of attention on time.

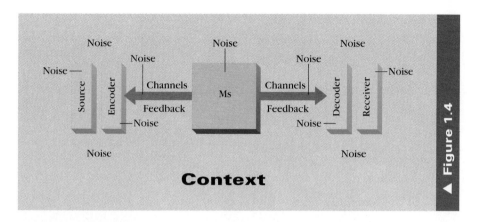

▲ Figure 1.4

Context

To illustrate why the limits imposed by models are important, we can turn to a different field that uses them. If you wanted to test the aerodynamic effectiveness of an automobile design, you would build a clay model of the car, put it into a wind tunnel, and study the flow of smoke blown over the model. You could consider alternative shapes in order to decrease the drag coefficient, but the model would not let you study such things as the best weight-to-power ratio for the car. You would need a different model for those other studies.

Some students have found it helpful to approach their study of communication by examining various models of the communication process. This procedure helps them to conceptualize the process and to examine how the components relate. Although we have already described two of these, we would like to describe just one more model. It is called a process model. If you study it, you will learn some important terms commonly used in communication studies, and you will learn how the components of the communication process interact.

A Process Model

The Shannon and Weaver model presented earlier was a one-way model. While communication scholars found the model useful (it called attention to and explained a good many things about the communication process), they were also frustrated by its limitations. Subsequently, variations on the Shannon and Weaver model began to appear in textbooks. Figure 1.4 illustrates one such model.

This model shows communication as a two-directional process. In a communication event, both the sender and the receiver share responsibility for the success of the communication event. Messages flow in both directions, and the communication event includes components that do not appear in a one-way model.

Figure 1.5

A **source** originates an idea and translates, or **encodes** the idea so that it can take shape and have substance. The English language is a code. So is a facial expression or a gesture.

Once the source-encoder has developed the idea, it must go through **channels,** which are the pathways through which messages are sent. Notice that both terms are plural. For instance, a channel might be a telephone line, a radio wave, or even this printed page. When speaking before an audience, sound waves carry speech, and light waves carry the speaker's gestures and the visual aids. Therefore, a communicator chooses among a large number of channels to carry ideas to a receiver.

Any information sent becomes **messages.** Again, notice the plural form. More than one message is sent, including some unintended messages. Moreover, it is impossible in human communication to send only *one* message! The words comprise the verbal portion of the message, and the facial expressions, gestures, bodily posture, and phrasing (i.e., the way you say those words) constitute the nonverbal portion of the message. When combined, the words and the nonverbal messages say more than the words alone.

The **decoder-receiver** works on the incoming messages by sorting out and interpreting the words and the nonverbal messages.

The communication event occurs in a **context,** which includes such features as light, space, temperature, furniture, electronic equipment, the number of people, and the purpose of the people assembled. The context enhances some interpretations and inhibits others. Thus, context becomes an important element in understanding the communication process.

The idea of feedback that occurs in figure 1.4 is a new one, when compared to the other concepts in the model. **Feedback** refers to messages that the receivers send to a source. For example, in a public speech, the glances, nods, and smiles of the audience work as feedback. These messages tell the speaker who is listening and enjoying the event. Feedback can take a long time, or it can take a short time and occur at the same moment that a message is sent. Thus, the message exchange can be an instantaneous transaction. When this occurs the communication event involves each participant in an instantaneous and mutually beneficial message exchange where the distinction between source and receiver is blurred and indistinguishable. We are, at the same moment, both sender and receiver.

From a learning point of view, **noise** becomes the most important part of the communication process. Noise includes anything that interferes with the success of the message exchange. Noise can be either physical (i.e., in the channel, or some impairment in the encoder or decoder) or it can be psychological.

To illustrate, suppose you are talking on the telephone when suddenly you hear loud static on the line. This is physical, or channel noise. Psychological, or semantic, noise would be your decision about the gender of a person named Leslie. Suppose you determine that Leslie is a woman, so you write "Ms. Leslie Nielsen." Later you discover that Leslie Nielsen is a man.

Any distortion that occurs when your use of language differs from that of another person is called **semantic noise.** If your use of language causes you to bring a different meaning from the one the speaker intended, then semantic noise has interfered with the message exchange.

One good way to learn about semantic noise is to answer some questions about the drawing in figure 1.5. Working alone, answer the following three questions:

1. Who are these people?

2. What do you think they're doing?

3. Where do you think they are doing it?

Now compare your answers with the answers of your classmates. How do you account for the differences in response to the same stimulus material found in the sketch? The answer, of course, is that people project themselves onto the messages they receive. The more ambiguous the messages, the more this projection phenomenon occurs. Each person distorts messages so they conform to personal expectations; therefore, each person introduces semantic noise into the communication process. What began in 1949 as a mechanistic model has therefore evolved into a symbolic interactionist model.

Meaning

Meaning is not contained in words. Rather, meaning is generated when people use words. For example, when you speak to a friend, your words become mere physical vibrations in the air column that surrounds your friend.

Your friend must decide what you mean. To accomplish this feat, your friend processes your verbal statements and the nonverbal messages that surround them. Processing the meaning occurs within your friend as he or she applies conceptual filters.

A filtering system allows you to notice some things and to eliminate other things from your attention. No one can process all of the available information at a particular moment in time and space. Therefore, our filtering system selects information and helps us to arrive at a meaning.

To illustrate this point, try to focus your immediate attention on your own weight. Can you feel your weight resting on a chair or on a place where you are standing? That information was always present, but it was not important enough to notice until you focused your attention. In other words, you had previously filtered that information out of your consciousness in favor of other information. If you were constantly aware of your weight resting against the floor or against the chair, then that awareness would begin to create "attention" problems for you.

Similarly, typographers think about something they call "x-height." The height of the lower case letter x in a particular font is the x-height. That information is important in typography because it controls the readability of the type face. Subsequently, when you read, you pass your eye along a line of type, while noticing the extensions of letters (i.e., the letter forms) above and below the x-height. Some fonts are easier to read than others because of the extensions. Look closely at a line of type on this page. Notice how far the letter *t* rises above the x-height. Now notice the difference between the *t* and the *l* and study the descenders, the tail on the *q* or the *y*.

The x-height information that you have just made a conscious effort to study was always there, but you filtered it out. The features of particular letter forms go unnoticed until your attention is directed to them. These features are enormously important to your ability to read the lines in this book. In fact, they help you to see the groupings of letter forms, rather than the letters themselves. But it would be a terrible inconvenience if you had to be consciously aware at all times of such information.

F O R E X A M P L E Y O U C O U L D N O T R E A D T H I S line of type easily. You had to study the line for individual letters, then determine where the spaces "should" have occurred between them.

Th isli neo fty peisa lsod if ficultt orea dfort hes ame reason. We have violated the expectations you have about letter forms. You had to look for the particular information that you would otherwise take for granted.

Thus, when you apply your conceptual filters, you selectively perceive certain information and you discard other information. That filtering process is common to each of us, but *how* we filter information is unique to each of us. No one else on Earth can do it in quite the same way you do, because no one else has had your exact same experiences. Thus the meanings you derive from the messages that you receive are unique to you. The meanings may be similar, but they are never the same as the messages intended by someone else.

The idea of having a conceptual filter is useful. It focuses attention on what is going on inside each of us as we process the billions of pieces of information that surround us at any given moment.

In summary, although various models are used throughout this book, it takes a symbolic interactionist approach to the study of communication. This choice seems useful for two reasons. First, it will help to avoid presenting a mixture of ideas that lack theoretical consistency or unity. Second, the symbolic interactionist perspective focuses on the relationships among communication, the self, and the choices of behavior as we exchange ideas. This focus will be most useful.

About the Rest of the Book

In chapter 2, "The Individual as Communicator," takes a much closer look at how the self evolves, and how it controls our communication behavior. From a Symbolic Interactionist Perspective, we are formed out of talk. We create our own minds, our society, and our selves. Fortunately, we can also change ourselves.

Chapter 3, "Listening," examines how a more effective listening behavior can begin the process of changing the self, not only for ourselves, but also for others. The skills of active and empathic listening are described in detail. Clearly, better listening means better communication.

Chapter 4, "Verbal Messages," examines language usage. It discusses how meaning is negotiated and describes some of the errors that are "built into" our language. It also discusses some specific suggestions in order to use language more effectively.

Nonverbal messages may be more important than words.

However important our language may be, some scholars believe that our nonverbal message systems are even more important. Chapter 5, "Nonverbal Messages," examines how gestures, posture, facial expression, clothing, use of space, and other non-language based forms of expression can influence people for better or for worse. We don't have to send out conflicting and confusing nonverbal messages. And we can learn how to "read" the nonverbal messages other people send more accurately.

Chapter 6, "The Interpersonal Event," describes and examines dyads and groups as the contexts in which interpersonal communication can occur. Here, too, trust and self-disclosure are essential to relationship development.

Chapter 7, "The Interpersonal Relationship," focuses on those interpersonal communication skills that allow you to manage your relationships.

An "agenda" is introduced for talking about relationships, and suggestions are made about how to increase your satisfaction from your relationships. You will also see how to reduce frustrations and how to control damaging conflicts that arise from misperceptions, and so forth.

Chapter 8, "Interviewing," concerns a particular kind of interpersonal communication event. This chapter studies those features that are common to all interviews, regardless of kind. At least six kinds of interviews occur in our lives, and our success in each one requires some specialized knowledge. The two kinds of interviews you are most likely to encounter, the employment interview, and the performance appraisal interview are described in detail.

Chapter 9, "Critical Thinking," focuses on some of the common pitfalls of human thought. It suggests ways to monitor reasoning—and the reasoning of others—in order to gain acceptance for your ideas, as well as to avoid certain fallacies in thinking and reasoning. The materials and ideas in this chapter especially apply to group problem solving and to public speaking.

Chapter 10, "The Group Communication Event," concerns how you can provide leadership and be a more effective participant in groups, which are essential skills in every complex organization.

Life in our society tends to be a life in organizations. Chapter 11, "Organizational Communication," asks the following questions: How does an organization evolve? How does it influence an individual member's communication behavior? An organization is its communication. Therefore, knowing the functions of organizational communication and the kinds of communication behavior that provide leadership is essential.

Chapters 12, 13, 14, and 15 discuss public speaking and communication in a "one-too-many" setting. Chapter 12, "Preliminary Concerns," describes certain essential preliminary concerns in order to make an effective public presentation. Chapter 13, "Preparing and Delivering a Speech," asks the following questions: How do you do an audience analysis? How do you organize a speech for different effects? What are the secrets of effective delivery?

Chapter 14 discusses "Speaking to Inform," while chapter 15 discusses "Speaking to Persuade." These chapters teach you how to clarify your ideas in the listeners' minds and how to gain acceptance for your ideas.

Chapter 16, "Mass Communication," discusses how the mass media set our agendas, control our knowledge of the world, skew our information, create our needs as consumers, and create our realities of the world. But how? And equally important, what impact (if any) can one person have on the massive and powerful American mass media system?

Chapter 17, "Intercultural Communication," takes a look at how people from different cultures and different nations communicate amid contemporary high-technology communication and transportation systems. Through the 1990s and into the twenty-first century, the world will become smaller and smaller, and the need to communicate across cultural and national boundaries will become increasingly urgent.

Summary

When Bill Jackson got out of bed the morning of January 10 to record all the communication events that occurred in his life, he had no idea of the enormous complexity of his professor's assignment. He thought the task would be a simple one; clearly it was not. Bill's assignment was *only* to identify the communication events. As exemplified, the task of understanding human communication is much more complex than that.

Communication has absorbed scholars and thinkers from earliest history. It can be a fascinating area of study that is profoundly relevant. Communication is the essence of our human nature, and it is the basis for all human relationships. Our complex system of communication sets us apart from other creatures and allows us to evolve ourselves and our society.

Communication can be studied as an art or as a social science, and it can be studied from many perspectives and approaches. But whatever the perspective approach, our choices impose upon us an ideology that views the world from a particular perspective and sets rules for our actions in it. The basic assumptions of our selected ideology will control the things we observe and the things we seek to define.

The symbolic interactionist perspective viewpoint throughout this book provides a coherent and thorough way to view the complexities of human communication. Three basic assumptions flow from the symbolic interactionist perspective. First, the self evolves through message exchange. Second, communication occurs through creation of shared symbols. And third, the creation of shared symbols is only possible through role assigning and role taking. Thus, by talking with other people, we learn about ourselves and our world.

No other discipline seems as intensely personal, nor as immensely important, to us as this.

Discussion Questions

1. Make a careful list of the communication events that happen in your life during just one hour of the day. Bring it to the class and compare it with the lists made by others. Studies suggest that in some occupations people spend as much as 90 percent of their working time in communication. Estimate the amount of time you spend in communication each day.

2. President Woodrow Wilson was a university professor. He once said that the real intellectual life of undergraduate students does not occur in the classroom. Rather, it occurs in what they talk about and what they set before themselves as their favorite objects between classes and lectures. What would President Wilson think about today's undergraduate students?

3. Work with a small group of classmates and find one attitude, belief, or value that has not evolved from your communication experience.

References

[1]Roger Peters, *Mammalian Communication: A Behavioral Analysis of Meaning* (Monterey, CA: Brooks/Cole Publishing Company, 1980).

[2]Noam Chomsky, *Syntactic Structures* (Paris: Mouton, 1968). See, also, Peter Farb, *Word Play: What Happens When People Talk* (New York: Knopf, 1973).

[3]Suzanne K. Langer, *Philosophy in a New Key* (New York: Mentor Books, 1951), pp. 30–33.

[4]An excellent anthology of classic works on this subject is Jerome G. Manis and Bernard N. Meltzer, (eds.), *Symbolic Interaction: A Reader in Social Psychology,* 2d ed. (Boston: Allyn and Bacon, 1972).

[5]B. Aubrey Fisher, *Perspectives on Human Communication* (New York: Macmillan Publishing Co., Inc., 1978).

[6]Claude Shannon and Warren Weaver, *Mathematical Theory of Communication* (Urbana: University of Illinois Press, 1949).

The Individual As Communicator

When you finish reading this chapter you will be able to:

1. Define self-concept and explain how it affects personal perception.

2. Explain how people can feel more positive about themselves as communicators by modifying their self-concept.

3. Identify how communication becomes a major defining social experience.

4. Specify how communication affects primary societal expectations.

5. Describe how communication is a crucial element in participation activities.

6. Identify examples of introverted and extroverted behavior.

7. Explain the effect of expectations on personal behavior and self-concept.

active communication

communication passivity

extrovert

introvert

positive self-talk

self-awareness

self-concept

self-definition

self-trust

symbolic interaction

visualization

Introduction

Military intelligence officers know that one way to break the "spirit" of prisoners of war is to isolate them from their comrades. During the Vietnam War, one of the favorite Vietcong strategies was to ship prisoners to remote prison camps and shut them off from any contact with other American soldiers. If you ask a POW about the most frightening part of his capture, he will tell you about the solitary confinement. Admiral, then U.S. Senator, Jeremiah Denton, a prisoner of war during the Vietnam conflict, testified often to that fact.

Therefore, we are alone in the animal kingdom in our ability to reflect and to communicate those thoughts to others. We like some people and dislike others. We feel good about ourselves based on the comments of others. Without the exchange of ideas we could neither build our relationships nor develop our self-concepts.

This chapter will explore how our communication behavior defines us, defines the nature of individual communication, and defines the roles we and others play in society. All of these things result from our symbolic interactions—the exchange of messages.

Foundations of Individual Communication

Our study begins with how communication affects the ways we see ourselves. We are both senders and receivers of messages, and the ways we allow ourselves to send and to interpret messages help form how we think and feel about ourselves.

Development of Self-Concept

The world of words is crucial in how we define and feel about ourselves. One term that is especially important in this definition is **self-concept.** By self-concept we mean your ideas of what makes you similar to and different from others. Self-concept is "how we feel about ourselves," when we are compared to others. Self-concept is the sum of the perceptions and of the ideas and images that we have about ourselves. Self is the way we interpret and organize our reality in the world of language. Our self-concept is produced, in part, from our use and interpretation of words.

"Self as image" is one way of how you think about yourself. You think about yourself on the basis of your perceptions of how others see you. For example, you may be a good student. But do others think that is true? If they do, they may communicate that to you, perhaps by telling you that they think you are a "brain." That is the self-image you project. Their description of you in their talk helps to create your self-image. Not only do you believe in yourself as a student, but also through symbolic interaction that belief is confirmed by your peers. Thus, the language interaction process has operated to help you to define yourself. This is part of your self-concept.

Self arises from communication. It is through the sharing of ideas and feelings that you develop yourself and your concept of personal worth. Because communication is on-going, your concept of self is constantly being forged in a process. Based on what you hear and say daily, your self undergoes consistent modification. Today you may feel positive about your self because of what you have heard or because of the reactions of others towards you. However, if someone makes cruel or critical statements about you tomorrow, your self-concept may change slightly in response to those comments. The effect becomes even greater as we grow older because of the increased importance we give to the positive reactions from members of our social circle.[1] These dynamics affect your concept of self.

Self-Concept and Personal Perception

You probably know people who lack confidence. You may call them insecure. When such people make a decision, they may apologize for it or may be ready to change their minds because they lack confidence. If you asked them, "How do you feel about yourself?" they might answer, "I think I'm an OK person, but most of my friends are smarter and have more friends than I do." The message is clear. They do not think very positively about themselves, and they compare themselves unfavorably to others. People who are like this generally have a low self-concept. When they compare themselves to others, they believe that they are inferior. They engage in negative self-talk, and they do not have positive thoughts about themselves.

Language and Self-Concept

Personal use of language creates self-image and, in some cases, self-doubt. Remember that you are affected directly by the language that you use about yourself or the language that others use about you. Your perceptions result from reactions to symbols whether it's you or others who generate them. Your world of words shapes the way you see yourself and others. Therefore, it is not difficult to see that symbolic interaction is central to our lives.

Positive Self-Concept

The development of a more positive self-concept through communication is the product of the following elements:

1. *Reinforcement.* Reinforcement is a powerful force in modifying attitudes and behavior. When others make positive comments about us or our activities, we feel better. For example, suppose an acquaintance said, "I think the proposal that you made to change the library fine structure was one of the best ideas that I've heard this year." That positive statement describes you in that person's mind. It reinforces your self-concept as a "good" and "worthwhile" person.

You give and receive reinforcement. When you tell others how you feel about them or about how they behave, you provide reinforcement. The kind and frequency of reinforcement has a profound effect on people and the way they react to the world.

2. *Positive self-thought.* Most of us have heard the statement "Success breeds success." If we think good things about ourselves, more good things are likely to happen. This is an old and very well accepted idea.

Several years ago Norman Vincent Peale wrote the best selling book *The Power of Positive Thinking.*[2] Peale stated that if we think positive thoughts about ourselves, then those thoughts will become action and we will begin to think and act more successfully. Dr. Peale was writing about the development of a healthy self-concept. What he had to say about people and their attitudes toward themselves is useful in our study of human communication.

Believing in yourself is the premise of the first chapter in Peale's book. Peale and contemporary psychological writers like Wayne Dyer,[3] maintain that your success is more likely to occur if you believe you can succeed. For example, in Alcoholics Anonymous meetings members remind each other to talk and to think positively about themselves. "Don't sit on the pity-pot," says one. "Look at what you have accomplished," says another.

Similarly, one colleague gave advice to another recently that was consistent with the idea of positive self-talk. "If you want to be a full professor, you have to act like a full professor. You have to write, walk, and talk with confidence, even if you're not feeling it."

Physicians also know that surgical patients who listen to positive-thinking audiotaped messages while under anesthesia in the operating room recover from their surgery faster than those who do not hear the messages.[4]

Public communicators develop improved self-concepts about their skills as a result of positive experiences and self-talk. Early in his political career, Prime Minister Winston Churchill of Great Britain sat down in the House of Commons because he was such a miserable speaker. But later, after speaking and rallying the British

After a childhood of negative messages, many of us have difficulty thinking positively about ourselves. But we can try.

nation during World War II, he said that speaking to thousands of people was not much different from speaking to a few because he had grown accustomed to it.[5] From experience, Churchill learned that he could speak more effectively. Thus, he had developed a better self-concept, and he thought more positively about himself as a public speaker.

3. *Self-fulfilling prophecy.* This phenomenon is an application of what social cognition scholars call "expectancy effects." You get what you expect. And numerous studies verify that position.[6] That belief supports the concept of positive self-talk. Anticipation breeds success, and self-talk about personal success (expectancy) increases the opportunity for a favorable outcome.

The self-concept is the sum of all these small experiences. Churchill built his self-concept with positive self-talk. So can you. Allow the verbal artist that lives within you to flourish.

Modifying Self-Concept

The self can be changed but that change needs direction. The following steps will help you to modify your self-concept and to make it healthier and more positive.

Visualization

Our attitudes about ourselves come from two sources. The sources are our experiences and our feelings of adequacy or inadequacy. We can change our attitudes by the way we think about ourselves—if we visualize success, our chances for success increase greatly. Visualizing success is not a gimmick. It is a technique that has been used for years by athletic coaches, who have told their pole-vaulters, long jumpers, high jumpers, sprinters, and distance runners to "see" themselves making the jump or running the race prior to attempting it. For instance, they might see themselves moving their arms in a smooth rhythm, or see themselves gliding over the bar. Sports psychologists tell us that visualization is an important ingredient in personal success.

Hence, people need to see themselves as successes. When people expect positive things to happen, they often do. Similarly, when they expect the worst, it often happens. Therefore, expect the best and it is likely to happen.

Self-Trust

Self-Trust is a major ingredient in the human communication process. Nathaniel Branden believes that people must trust their own competence, trust themselves, and trust their own judgment. In his book, *The Psychology of Romantic Love,*[7] Branden contends that in order for people to be successful in loving relationships, they first must have a successful love affair with themselves. They must like themselves before they can love others.

Successful relationships are founded on the belief of self-worth. To relate effectively with others, you must believe that you are a deserving person and that you can contribute positively to your own life and to the lives of others. The following example is drawn from a common interpersonal situation.

Many people have problems in a romantic relationship. Look at the case of Charlie and Sue. After searching for years for the right person, Sue finally found the man of her dreams, Charlie. Both of them felt that overwhelming love and concern that she had always wanted. However, after a few weeks, Sue began to feel that she was not worthy of being loved by Charlie. She was constantly worried that something would go wrong with their relationship. She was obsessed by the idea that she was unlovable. So, to reassure herself, she asked, "Do you still love me?"

Despite Charlie's reassurances, Sue became very possessive of Charlie, all the while telling Charlie that she didn't deserve him. At the same time, Sue hunted for ways to manipulate Charlie in order to make him feel guilty, so that she could prepare to reject him before he could reject her. Finally, Charlie had had enough. He tired of the need for constant reassurance and the "guilt trips." He ended the relationship, and Sue was crushed. Her personal prophecy was fulfilled. She could not find another person who could love her!

Sue's poor self-concept resulted in the failure of her relationship. She thought so negatively that she translated those thoughts into actions and drove Charlie away. Her relationship could have been more successful if she had accepted the idea that she was a "good" person and deserved to be loved. If she had expressed her own love and had not tried to "smother" Charlie, their relationship may have continued. Sue had many opportunities to build her own and Charlie's self-concept. Sue could have said how happy that she was when they were together. Sue could have told Charlie how much that she liked his company and how much that she enjoyed the things that they did together. Overall, Sue needed to believe that it was okay to be loved. However, this was something that her self-concept said was not possible.[8]

Self-Concept and Communication Attitudes

People with poor self-concepts are less likely to be successful communicators. They often feel inadequate and they engage in behavior that validates a negative self-fulfilling prophecy. They also are less likely to be successful in most of the everyday activities that command their attention.

Communication is a learned human behavior. We learn a native language and learn how to engage in conversation. At a young age, we learn the conventions for one-to-one communication through interaction with family and then friends.

Interpersonal Settings

As we learn more of the rules of communication, we develop conversational skills. When we begin school our communication behavior expands to include one-to-several relationships. We talk in small groups with classmates. We get involved in extra-curricular activities with others. As our range of experience expands, we learn increasingly elaborate systems of personal behavior.

Public Communication

Occasionally, you may encounter a new type of communication setting: public communication. It may seem strange to you, although many of the characteristics are similar to conversational and small group communication. The prospect of a public communication experience may trouble you. You may underestimate the chances for your success. In many ways, it is an extension of the one-to-one and small group communication that you have had all your life. It, too, has rules but you learned the other rules and were successful.

Communication as a Defining Experience

Because you understand the principle of symbolic interaction, you know that language and communication are key to self-definition. It is important that you know the ways in which we develop that self-definition. Here are some techniques that you can use to define yourself more precisely and satisfactorily.

Self-Awareness

People need to be accurately aware of themselves, the perceptions others have of them, and how they feel about themselves. To have **self-awareness** makes it easier for you to understand and modify your self-concept and to heighten your self-esteem. Personal sensitivity is a key element in the development of self and in the development of interpersonal relations. Each of us should be sensitive to the ways that we affect others and sensitive to how we behave both verbally and nonverbally.

Communication is a mutual experience and activity that defines our uniqueness to others. What we say, verbally and nonverbally, creates impressions for others. Other people listen to our ideas and positions and decide whether we are interesting, intelligent, insightful, or amusing. What we say and do tells others what is going on inside our heads. It tells them what and how we feel. It is our way of establishing a common bond.

Self-Definition

Communication also helps us to define ourselves. Our success as communicators affects the way we see ourselves and how we feel about ourselves. The total of this is **self-definition.** For example, the people who are effective in expressing ideas and who often volunteer their feelings are more likely to become the centers of a conversation or to be the leaders of groups. As the attention of the group focuses on them, they become more confident of themselves. Other group members see them as leaders. Subsequently, group members ask them for their opinion, seek their friendship, and introduce them to their acquaintances. Their behavior as an effective communicator has established their leadership role in their social group.

Other people may be awkward in expressing even the simplest of ideas. They may fumble for ideas and words. These people may come to speak less because of their embarrassment about their impression. After a while, those periods of silence become longer. The person says little and eventually we consider them a "loner." They may have many good and attractive ideas. However, their problems in communication create the impression that they are inadequate because of their inability to express ideas effectively.

Most people fit somewhere between these extremes. Still, their role is determined largely by their communication skills. What you say, the way you

Your communication is your most defining experience.

This two-dimensional image causes us to perceive depth. It is an example of perceptual stability.

Figure 2.1

say it, and the frequency with which you speak sends many messages about you. *Your communication is your single most defining experience.* Only mankind can generate language, structure it, and use it to convey the entire span of emotions, thoughts, and decisions. This communication of aspirations and feelings provides us with unique characteristics. It is through this creation and transmission of language that each of us defines our individuality. Our societal roles are a product of what we say and the ways that others perceive our messages. Therefore, we define ourselves by our language and its impact. People interpret the words we use and form their impressions of us based on their understandings of these words. The matter of impression formation through language *is* **symbolic interaction** at work.

Perception Is an Active Process

We do not merely absorb what we experience in the world. Instead, we actively participate in creating our experiences. Our perceptions help to create "reality" for us. We do this by trying to maintain at least three kinds of consistency.[9]

First, we *structure* our perceptions by turning what we perceive into a form that is consistent with what we already know or believe about the world. For example, if there is a dark cloud on the horizon, if the day is unusually hot and muggy, and if the cloud on the horizon has the shape of a funnel, then based on the shape of the cloud and what you know and believe about the weather conditions, you would probably think that a tornado is approaching.

Second, we strive to give our perceptions *stability.* For example, when you look at figure 2.1 carefully you can see that the telephone poles are not all the same size. Even so, when you glance at the end, you experience the telephone poles as the same size and you determine that you are perceiving depth. Similarly, when you drive down the street, passing through the shadows of buildings and trees, the amount of available light changes, but you compensate, and you experience the light as stable.

Finally, as part of perception, we divide the continuing stream of sensations that we experience into meaningful events. We attribute *meaning* to that stream of sensations based on our past experiences and our current purposes. We infer attitudes and motives when we hear the statements of others. Because we cannot "see" attitudes, we arrive at conclusions based on our interpretations of words.

When Isaac says "Sowash University is a great place to go to school because it has outstanding athletic teams," you may conclude that Isaac's attitude toward education is warped. You base that on what he has said. It appears that Isaac measures the quality of a university by its athletic programs, not by its library, faculty, and student body.

Symbolic interaction affects us as receivers of messages. Our interpretation of words and their implications gives us a direction to our perceptions. In this case, our perception of Isaac probably is negatively affected in the symbolic interaction process. We interpreted his value system as unusual, based on the symbols he has used to express it.

Categories of Individual Behavior

The communication act expresses our interpretation of the world to others. We tell others what we are like as we make statements or react to events. People form judgments about us based largely on labels. Often we hear people described as "sophisticated," "vulgar," "well read," "intelligent," or "stupid." These descriptions typically arise from statements or verbal positions. Our language has a clear impact on the ways others feel about us, and, in many ways, it defines how we will feel about ourselves. Because language is one of our major means of self-identity, language is crucial in self-definition.

This section examines general behavior categories where people are placed based on their communication activity. The general behavior categories are extrovert, introvert, follower, and leader. A category system is a convenient type of "pigeon-hole." When we use categories we assess large groups of people together into a category under a single set of headings. Some people fit conveniently in a category, while others do not and fall on the category's fringes.

One way to categorize people is on the basis of appearance. We can term people "tall," "short," "average," "heavy," "thin," "attractive," "handsome," "pretty," or "homely." This is a simple set of classes based on the way we view each other. However, as mentioned, people rarely fall into one category. Thus, it is easy to see from these opinions why many different ways to categorize other people are necessary.

People can be classified into four general categories. The classification categories are rough indicators of individual behavior based on verbal activity. They are broadly based descriptions of personality. This approach uses personal language activity to develop a personal profile. It is another example of how we use *symbolic interaction* to describe and evaluate people. Our reaction to language becomes our classification of the person doing the talking.

The Extrovert

Extrovert is an easily misapplied label. We think of an extrovert as a loud person who always dominates conversations. The extrovert interrupts others and wants to be the center of attention. However, that stereotype is wrong because it focuses on the extreme. Each of us has elements of extroversion in our behavior. No one is a complete extrovert; it is a matter of degree. Perhaps we speak out when we feel that it is necessary and we disagree if the issue is important. Also, we enjoy being the center of attention when we tell about an amusing experience at a social gathering.

The activities we associate with extroversion are primarily communication behaviors. They involve language and the reaction of people to words. The nature of symbolic interaction helps define our personality and the way others perceive us. The language we use and the way we respond to the language of others is our way of stating our individuality. When you say that "I like to skydive," you are making a statement about yourself. You could expand on that preference by saying, "I also enjoy watching professional sports." These statements help to define you as a person. People who talk about themselves constantly may be strongly extroverted. Most of us, though, express our feelings, preferences, and amusement as part of "just being alive."

Extroversion is a matter of degree and situation. Most effective communicators are somewhat extroverted. They are people who enjoy speaking to others. They like to voice their opinions and to associate with others. Extroverts are not loud, self-centered, arrogant, or stupid. They say what is on their minds when they feel it is important. Extroverts do not feel that they are better or worse than anyone else. They simply enjoy talking and the company of other people. Their interest in sharing their ideas and feelings with

IT'S MORE FUN TO KNOW

Vague Messages

The assignment of the defense attorney is to develop and present "doubt." Messages which are designed to create doubt could be abstract or ambiguous. This study of defense attorneys reveals that vague and ambiguous speech are predictors of defense success.

See Michael G. Parkinson, "Verbal Behavior and Courtroom Success," *Communication Education*, 20:1 (January 1981), p. 31

Comment . . .

If you want to create confusion or doubt in the minds of your listeners, vague and unclear statements are the best route. This is the objective of a defense attorney when arguing that the prosecution's case is confusing and not acceptable. Communicators, generally, should not use this courtroom strategy since the goal in most situations is to be clear and understood.

others is a part of their personality and self-definition. Therefore, communication has helped them to define themselves.

The Introvert

An **introvert** has many stereotypes. To many people, an introvert is a silent, nonsocial person who is meek and spends the day reading books or avoiding contact with others. That stereotype of an introvert also suggests that the introvert is passive. This possibility is an extreme example. Some people do shun social contact, but they are a social minority. Many people, although quiet in large social settings, are very normal. However, for our purposes it is easier if the extreme example defines the class.

Contrary to popular opinion, introverts like to talk. The question may be a matter of with whom they wish to speak. Introverts may like to be with people, although they may be more "choosy" about their friends. Moreover, introverts may be interesting persons, although their general communication may suggest that fewer ideas interest them. They do not mix easily with others, and this lack of social contact is a result of their public or interpersonal communication.

An introvert may only exhibit introverted behavior in certain settings under specific conditions. While they may be publicly introverted, they may be privately extroverted. For example, at a company work meeting, Anne may say nothing and shun the spotlight. However, when Anne is at home or is with a group of her friends, she may talk a great deal and entertain others. A social "label" is applied as a result of observing the communication behavior of a person. We observe how often a person speaks and how vigorously they take and defend a position. We also note how interested they appear in the ideas or problems of others. From those observations, we conclude that they meet our standards for an extrovert or for an introvert. The result is that much of our definition of people is a reflection of their communication activity. Therefore, our communication *defines* how others perceive us.

Leaders

A leader provides direction, understands goals, and uses language to galvanize followers. Consider the following description of former President Ronald Reagan:

> *Ronald Reagan's adversaries, allies, and admirers agree that he is an effective communicator. . . . Reagan's success as a communicator is attributable to his understanding of the medium (television) that more than any other dominates our lives. . . . Better than any modern president, Reagan translated words into memorable televisual pictures.*[10]

Jamieson describes Ronald Reagan as a man who was able to communicate effectively through the electronic media. Reagan is a good example of a modern political leader whose communication skills contributed to his success and provided the basis of his administration. It is no surprise that people referred to him as "The Great Communicator."

Leaders master the art of communication and influence the minds and actions of others. Our great leaders touch lives through speech. Eric Hoffer once said, ". . . The preliminary work . . . can be done only by men who are, first and foremost, talkers or writers and are recognized as such by all."[11]

The spoken word is the force that moves people and society. Reagan inspired the United States during the 1980s, and Churchill's speeches held the British Empire together during World War II. Hitler inflamed millions with his tirades, and Franklin Roosevelt stirred the American public with his "fireside chats" before and during World War II. We know that the word *is* mightier than the sword. Spoken language influences people, and it can move even the harshest critic to agreement.

Communication also defines our leaders. The great leaders are often effective speakers and the less noted leaders may be mediocre ones. This observation is true even at the local level. We choose student body presidents or other officers because they communicate their ideas effectively to the student population. For example, they say, "Elect me and together we will stop any future tuition increases on this campus." Other students may have the same idea, but until they say it publicly and effectively it remains a private thought. On the other hand, a leader expresses the idea and attracts believers or converts disbelievers to the cause. Mayors, members of city councils, and city managers are leaders. They lead because they communicate effectively in order to define the future of the voters. Business people and educators are prominent individuals because they effectively express their ideas both privately and publicly. If a person is an effective communicator, the odds of that person becoming a leader increase greatly because *leadership is communication.*

Being an effective leader means communicating in a way that provides the speaker with an improved perception of self-worth. Sharing ideas and having those ideas accepted is a reinforcing experience.[12] Our elected officials cherish the opportunity to communicate with voters. A leader's self-worth is reinforced by direct and continuous contact with voters. Leaders need to remain "in touch" in order to execute plans and programs that must have popular support. That support is crucial to the positive perception of self that leaders must possess.

Followers

Most of us are followers. It would be impossible for leaders to exist unless there was a group that needed direction. We have seen how communication defines our leaders. In a different way, communication also defines a follower. The difference is the type of role and the expectations of that role in a follower's behavior. For example, leaders are highly assertive, while followers are not. A follower's social role is the management of tasks and opportunities, while a leader's is the statement of goals and the communication of direction. Here is an example of dialogue between a leader and a follower.

FOLLOWER 1: "Well, we have a problem. I don't have any idea how we can get more people to shop at our new store in the East Mall."

LEADER: "Here's a thought. Let's try a promotion where we give each person who purchases $10 in merchandise a gift certificate worth $3 on their next purchase. We could call it '3 for 10'."

FOLLOWER 2: "I don't believe that people will spend ten dollars just to get a gift certificate for three more dollars. That's not much of an incentive. I sure would want more of a reason to shop at the East Mall than that."

LEADER: "Let me try to explain what I had in mind. When people think they're getting a bonus, they're more likely to investigate. Why do you think car manufacturers have rebates and grocery stores use coupons? Yeah, people may be getting a little better deal on their groceries and cars, but the businessmen have larger sales. That leads to more profits. The same type of thing probably would happen here. What I'm suggesting is along the same line. See?"

FOLLOWER 1: "I guess you have a point. Why not use those ideas that have worked in other businesses in ours too? I like the approach and I guess the others will too when it's explained that way."

Followers are different from leaders because their communication tends to be *reactive*. They respond to the words and thoughts of others rather than initiate their own words or thoughts. The follower may be just as bright, may be as articulate, and may be as thoughtful as the leader. However, the follower is not as *outspoken*.

Many people have grown up learning how to be a follower. They were told that children should "speak only when spoken to" and that children should not challenge the ideas of other people. These children often grow up to be silent, meek, or reluctant to challenge the ideas of others. Their parents have prepared them to be followers by their advice and direction. Symbolic interaction—the message children receive about their expected behavior—shapes their lives.

However, followers are not created by environment alone. Generally, followers are less outgoing; they may see the flaw in ideas or designs but hesitate to offer an opinion. They may have a less positive self-concept than the leader, and that dimension of personality can make the difference between a leader and a follower.

Communication and Societal Expectations

Communication expectations and behavior play a key role in the ways that you are perceived. The use and misuse of language determine attitudes, actions, and expectations. Words and our responses to them affect most dimensions of our lives.

Our communication suggests our behavior and our attitude. Ours, therefore, is a society of *talk*.

Whether our background is urban or rural, ours is a world of talk. Speech creates perceptions and shapes our beliefs of right and wrong. Based on their communication, people are deemed honest or dishonest and attractive or unattractive. Even helplessness can be attributed to communication. For instance, although economic problems play a great part in the plight of homeless people in the United States, the homeless also learn helplessness from society at large. They are told that they will not be successful and, because of the self-fulfilling prophecy, they remain without homes and beg on the streets. Because of our societal communication, we see them, and they come to see themselves, as failures largely based on societal expectations.

Thus, communication shapes our perceptions, and those perceptions create our expectations. If we are told to expect an event, we await it. If a highly regarded person tells us that an unfortunate experience is inevitable, then we prepare for it. Our expectations and anticipations are largely the result of symbolic interaction.

For example, if you perceive someone to be marginally honest, you may expect him or her to commit some criminal act. If you hear that Henry was suspected of shoplifting and you then see Henry enter the store where you work, you watch him suspiciously. If other customers pick up merchandise and examine it carefully, you might consider them careful shoppers. If Henry does the same, the information that you have heard about him makes you consider his action differently. Your perceptions and expectations are woven together, and communication is important to that link. Its use causes you to view the world in different ways and to treat people differently. Communication *is* a controlling behavior and it *does* affect our actions. Our world is a reaction to language and to the symbols and reality that it creates for us.

Communication and Participation

Communication is the currency of participation. In most of society's activities, we judge and we are judged by the amount and quality of our communication. For example, "Beth is a quiet type." "Matt is a loudmouth and always has an opinion on everything." "Art is hard to understand when he

Our communication tells others what and who we are.

gets excited. He talks so fast!" "Mike wants to be the center of attention so he always makes jokes at the expense of others." These are just a few of the comments that we hear daily about our friends or acquaintances.

These statements identify the amount and type of communication participation by others. Also, they tell what people think about their friends or peers. Notice that all of the comments revolve around the "communication participation" of the person. If a person does not speak, then that is a negative feature. If they talk too much, then they are domineering or outspoken. Therefore, we try to strike a "balance" between talking too much and not talking enough.

Impressions are developed as a result of the exchange of language and ideas with other people. If you have a conversation with a new acquaintance, Cheryl, and she agrees with nearly everything you say, her verbal behavior creates an impression. If Cheryl disagreed with most of your statements, you probably would feel differently about her. We are symbolic interactionists and our reality is formed by our use and reaction to communication. That is how we are influenced and how we influence others. We make decisions about people based on their communication behavior.

Because communication is the instrument used to measure much of our self-worth, we must talk effectively and do it often enough to have an impact. However, we must balance that speech with the knowledge that too much talk will cause others to consider us domineering or self-centered. Communication frequency and style create impressions. We like people who contribute, but we do not like people who say too much. Likewise, we like people who have opinions, but we don't like people who insist that their way is the only way. People act on impressions and communication is our most often used impression-forming activity. It is important to remember that our communication tells others what and who we are.

Active Communication Participation

Active communication participation creates a positive impression for us. "Active" communicators let others know where they stand because they express their opinions. They agree or disagree. They participate in dialogue, and disagreeing over ideas may intrigue them. To them, speech is the most important element in relating to others. They enjoy talking, listening, and seeing the reactions of other people. Learn a lesson from these people. The next time you speak, remember: what you say and your attitude toward your listeners are two of the most important elements in developing a personal reputation. How often you speak and how you behave also help to define you.

Communication of Passivity

Passive people are those who say little or who "knuckle under" easily to the wishes or statements of others. It's easy to be a passive person. If you nod your head at most of the statements others make, you have taken the first step. If you hesitate to disagree with even highly controversial statements, people may think that you either do not have an opinion or are afraid to state it. When you decide not to state your opinion at a social or political meeting, you start to fall into the **communication passivity** category.

Society places a higher value on active rather than on passive behavior. An active person is a doer. In fact, many people believe that a passive person is lazy or lacks intelligence. Those impressions are the result of the frequency and quality of what passive people say. When people say nothing or have no opinion, it raises questions in our minds about their interests, motives, or competency. How many students take the time to express their opinions by voting in student government elections? Those who don't vote show passive behavior, which could be interpreted by their leaders as either apathy or as silent support. Without hearing the opinions of the nonvoting students, leaders could make some very unpopular decisions. Then the nonvoting students may feel powerless and helpless and become even more passive about voting. The result for both students and leaders is frustration and misunderstanding from a lack of information sharing and a negative evaluation of the other side.

Passive communication behavior conveys a message about us. If we are passive, other people may conclude that we do not care or are uninformed.

We have a responsibility to ourselves and to others about the conclusions drawn about us. We should tell them how we feel about issues and people and why we feel that way. Ignoring the chance for communication may support the old saying, "Silence is golden." But silence *is not* golden, and it may have tragic consequences.

Summary

Human communication helps define our individuality. The process and product of our use of language is symbolic interaction, and the ways we use and respond to language determine our reality.

No one thinks the same way, acts the same way, or speaks the same way. Individual speaking reveals our concerns, attitudes, and much about our self-concept. Subsequently, communication can help us to develop our self-concept and it can influence the way that we view ourselves. When people seek opportunities to communicate, their positive experiences help them to form a more constructive view of themselves.

The communication behaviors of leaders and followers influence their roles. Communication activity is the element that holds people and groups together. It is more responsible than any other single societal element for our roles and our expectations for ourselves and for others. Communication behavior defines people and their participation in society. It is a complex human behavior that provides people with a unique identity and social expectations.

Discussion Questions

1. Describe how you have used visualization in anticipating events. How can you apply that approach to your communication behavior?

2. What elements make a person self-aware? How do people with this characteristic differ from others?

3. How do your introverted friends differ from your extroverted friends? Which friends are roughly in the same category as you? Which category do you generally prefer?

4. Describe a person who has a high level of self-trust. How is that self-trust affected by communication behavior? How does it affect communication behavior?

References

[1]Leona L. Eggert and Malcolm R. Parks, "Communication Network Involvement in Adolescent's Friendships and Romantic Relationships," *Communication Yearbook 10* (1987). McLaughlin.

[2]Norman Vincent Peale, *The Power of Positive Thinking* (New York: Ballantine Books, 1987).

[3]Wayne W. Dyer, *You'll See It When You Believe It* (New York: William Morrow and Co., Inc., 1989).

[4]Study by United Medical and Dental Schools of Guy's and St. Thomas Hospitals, London, reported in *The Lancet,* and reviewed in *Boardroom Reports,* (January 1989).

[5]*British Orations from Ethelbert to Churchill* (London: J. M. Dent and Sons, Ltd., 1960), p. 359.

[6]See Leslie Zebrowitz McArthur, "What Grabs You? The Role of Attention in Impression Formation and Causal Attribution." *Social Cognition, The Ontario Symposium,* Volume I (eds.) E. Tory Wiggins, C. Peter Herman and Mark P. Zanna (Hillsdale, NJ: Lawrence Earlbaum Associates, Publishers, 1981), pp. 221–227.

[7]Nathaniel Branden, *The Psychology of Romantic Love* (Los Angeles: J. P. Tarcher, Inc., 1980, pp. 121–22), reprinted with permission of the publisher.

[8]Branden, pp. 121–22. (Used with permission of the publisher.)

[9]David J. Schneider, Albert H. Hastrof, and Phoebe C. Ellsworth, *Person Perception,* 2d ed. (Reading, MA: Addison-Wesley Publishing Company, Inc., 1979), pp. 2–7.

[10]Kathleen Hall Jamieson, *Eloquence in an Electronic Age* (New York: Oxford University Press, 1988), pp. 118–19. Used with permission of the publisher.

[11]Eric Hoffer, *The True Believer* (New York: Harper and Row, 1951), p. 129. Reprinted with permission of the publisher.

[12]Roderick P. Hart, *The Sound of Leadership* (Chicago: The University of Chicago Press, 1987).

Chapter 3

Listening

Outline

When you finish reading this chapter you will be able to:

1. Explain the process of listening..

2. Identify the role of attention in improving listening.

3. Cite the results of inadequate and ineffective listening.

4. Compare and contrast the basic types of listening behavior.

5. Explain how to improve personal listening performance.

Objectives

active listening	communication cycle	empathic listening
appreciative listening	comprehensive listening	naive listening
attention span	critical listening	

Key Terms

Introduction

Listening is our most common human behavior. Few waking moments pass when we don't listen. Listening is such a frequent and habitual part of our daily activity that we often take listening and the receiving portion of the communication cycle for granted. Effective listening is important in our lives and especially in our relationships with others. It is at the heart of symbolic interaction.

This chapter examines the nature of our listening process, our behaviors as we listen (or fail to listen), and the ways that we can improve our listening skills. Few of us make good use of our listening potential; instead, we have learned to "get by" at a low level of efficiency. Here is an opportunity to study and improve our listening, which involves such diverse activities as listening to daily music on the radio, to conversations with classmates, to dialogue when making purchases at the bookstore or listening to TV "soaps," and to discussions when helping a friend to deal with a problem.

Listening Defined

There are many definitions of listening. Listening is complex and some explanations of it can make it even more complex and confusing. Wolvin and Coakley offer a simple, yet thorough definition. They say listening is, "the process of receiving, attending to and assigning meaning to aural stimuli."[1]

This definition includes both verbal and nonverbal messages. Thus, listening involves music, the scream of a siren, the chirp of a bird, or the blast of a cannon just as much as it does listening to a conversation with your date, attending a public speech by the local mayor, or listening to a class lecture presented by your favorite professor. Whatever the event, people can either participate actively or passively. Whether they ask questions, make faces, act bored, or close their eyes, they can still receive and attend to the stimulus. But, the meanings we assign to that stimulus can be very different for each person. And here lies a problem. Symbols convey different meanings based on our individual experience with the symbol. Observable behaviors such as smiles, scowls, or nods can suggest the way that we feel about what we have heard.

When we talk to each other, we process both verbal and nonverbal messages. It is very difficult not to listen, just as it is very difficult *not* to communicate. We receive many messages, and we attend to some of them and assign a variety of meanings (ranging from useful to worthless) to those messages. We are listeners during most of the time that we are awake.

Listening and the
Communication Process

For communication, or *commonness,* to occur, listening must take place. The important elements in communication are a sender, a receiver, a message, and a channel. Consider listening and the **communication cycle.** We can use models to represent what occurs in an oral transaction. Here is an example:

SENDER—WITH A *MESSAGE* FOR THE—RECEIVER/LISTENER—WHO ATTENDS AND *INTERPRETS*—AND SENDS *FEEDBACK*

In this case, we have a full cycle of communication. It could be as simple as when you approach an attendant at a service station and report the total cost of your gasoline. The attendant hears you tell how many gallons of gas you pumped and the total cost. The two figures correspond roughly so the attendant gets ready to process the sale. He asks for your credit card or enough cash to cover the cost of the purchase. When you finish the purchase, you receive a receipt and your change (if you are fortunate). Then, he thanks you for your patronage.

All this happens in the task dimension of the communication event. At the same time, both you and the station attendant are monitoring each other's nonverbal messages and tone of each other's voice while trying to understand the relationship component of the event. For example, we know when others are being pleasant or unpleasant, and we know how we should respond to that pleasantness.

To illustrate, suppose the attendant does all those things that we've just said, but in this fashion. He stalks over to your car and bangs the gas cap on the car's roof when he lays it down. He shoves the pump nozzle into the gas tank with an audible metal-against-metal clang. When he hands you the receipt, you notice that he has a frown on his face. His tone seems hostile to you. He says, "Here" when he gives you the receipt and your change, and he turns away without saying "thanks." Such a performance seems out of place and unpleasant. You might wonder what was wrong with the attendant, or what caused his unpleasant behavior. In fact, you could be so offended by his behavior that you would no longer buy gas at that station.

In this example of purchasing gasoline, the listening behavior focuses on both the tasks involved and on the relationship issues when they seem important to us.

Listening is at the heart of receiver reaction. If people are not listening, they do not receive messages, thus adjustments are not made and actions fail to occur. When you see models of communication, remember that the receiver *is* the listener and that the circular process of communication cannot be complete without active and responsive listening. Therefore, listening is crucial to effective interpersonal exchange.

Improving Listening Skills

Most of us are not effective listeners. Compared to our potential, we are seriously inadequate. Since we spend much more time listening than we do speaking, our needs are clear. Our most important concern should be improving our listening skills and becoming more effective in our most common communication behavior.

Impact of Behavior

The way we approach listening situations dictates how effectively we perform. If our attitude is, "Make this very interesting and appealing to me," chances are that we will not become better listeners. It is our job to improve our attitude and resulting behavior as we work on becoming better listeners. We have to want to become a better listener. Ask yourself these questions:

1. Do I hope to learn something?

2. What is my general attitude toward listening to someone else speak?

3. What kinds of people "turn me off" and cause me to not want to listen?

4. Do I listen only to ideas that clearly have a valuable result for me?

5. Do some people make me want to listen?

6. What setting is best for me as a listener?

Most of us are not effective listeners. When compared with our potential, however, we are seriously inadequate.

The answers to these questions tell how you are behaving as a listener. They tell you whether you are interested in people and in what they have to say. Did the answers tell you that you seek situations where you have a chance to listen to someone else? Listening is an "other-directed" act. Listening is keyed to the sharing of symbols between sender and receiver. Effective listening happens when we have successful symbolic interaction.

When you are in a conversation with good friends, it means that you direct your attention to *their* description of a happy weekend instead of thinking about a test *you* will be taking later in the week. It keys on what someone else says. Thus, it is not "I" centered. Good listening puts us in other people's shoes. We try to appreciate the ball game they saw or the trip they took. We try to understand what they mean as they talk from their point of view. If what they say is vague, we should not turn them off. Instead, we should try to work even harder to understand why the game interests them or how the trip was exciting. We should try to find out why they think and feel the way they do. The key to good listening is developing the proper attitude. Once we admit to ourselves that paying attention to what others say is important and valuable, then we begin to become better listeners.

Situational Variables

The place, the time, and our mood all affect our listening efficiency. Last week a friend told a group of people about a problem that had occurred the previous day.

MARY: "And so I told him that unless he loaned his car to me to drive to work for the next week, our relationship was over. He did not seem to care. I don't understand why. He always seemed to be interested but suddenly he just 'shut me out.' Can anyone tell me what might have gone wrong?"

There was silence from the group. No one appeared to have an answer. Was there an answer? Did they care? Were they listening? Consider this variable. The group was sitting on couches in a large living room. It was 5:30 P.M. on Sunday afternoon, and Mary had been talking about her life for nearly twenty minutes.

Does this suggest what the problem might be? The time of day, the fatigue of Mary's friends, and her lengthy talking may have turned them off. The situational variables of *time and location* made listening to Mary difficult. Mary's friends may have been tired of hearing about her personal difficulties. They may have gotten hungry or just sleepy. Their *moods* may have affected their listening. In short, they were *not ready* to listen.

Listening to a conversation while loud music is playing is difficult. Sometimes we just stop trying. However, the other person continues to talk and is unaware that no one is listening. We look like we are listening; we nod our heads and smile, but we are not really listening because the situational variables have taken control. We cannot process both sounds at the same time, so we choose which sound will get our attention. In this case, it may be the music. To avoid hurting the other person's feelings, we act as if we are still listening. However, we could choose to work at listening, and we could concentrate on the person doing the talking. We must make choices and listening often forces us to choose which stimulus is most interesting or important to us. Sometimes it is possible that we simply cannot hear any other message, such as during a noisy athletic event. That situational variable of *setting* is out of our control. Therefore, we have to postpone our other conversations (talk later), or leave the setting, which is often not a likely choice during an exciting contest.

Why Study Listening?

Listening is at the heart of personal and corporate success. The personal failures and successes that we experience are partially attributable to our listening skills. We often fail to follow directions. We sometimes don't wait for the entire message, or we forget the main idea of the other person's message. We are sometimes late for meetings because we weren't listening when the group set the time. Have you ever missed a meeting because you *assumed* it would be at the usual time? When was the last time you neglected to listen carefully and then embarrassed yourself when something went wrong as a result of your lack of information?

Have you ever been in an unfamiliar area, asked for directions at a service station, and still could not remember when to make a left turn? Have you ever agreed to meet a friend at a specific time or place and one of you failed to show because of a misunderstood agreement? Or, have you ever blamed someone else for failing to provide you with enough data to do a job when you just did not listen to what they had previously explained?

In an article that discusses tension during the holiday seasons, Carol Rubin and Jeff Rubin say that listening is a key element in breaking a stalemate that can develop in communication problems during times of potential tension. They write about those familiar family arguments that take place during the Thanksgiving and Christmas seasons. They say the positive outcome of good listening is that, "Effective listeners identify with the other side and see the world from that perspective. They also listen between the lines, trying to focus not on positions but on underlying needs and feelings."[2]

Imagine the scene. Aunt Maude brings sweet potatoes for five people for Thanksgiving dinner. "You told me that just our two families would be here so I thought that would be enough." Maude did not realize that when you said two families you meant there would be ten people for the meal. "I guess I didn't make it clear and it was my fault," is an appropriate answer. Maude cannot see inside your head. She can't read your mind, but you can tell she is feeling bad and threatened. (The exchange of symbols was unproductive and now people have hurt feelings.) However, as a good listener, you can defuse the situation. You can pay attention to Aunt Maude's feelings and words. In this situation, no one gains by arguing over who is in the immediate family. Clear the air and get on with the Thanksgiving festivities.

This kind of communication problem could happen to you because people have many listening weaknesses. Those listening weaknesses often cause many of our personal and professional problems. We may perform a job incorrectly or miss a plane connection. We might leave an important document at home or forget a reunion. As more effective listeners, we can lead more productive and effective lives.

The value of listening can be illustrated in this way. Assume there are 200 million people in the United States. If each one of those people made one listening error during the next 365 days and the cost of that mistake was ten dollars, the expense to this country would be $2 billion.

Ten dollars is not an exaggerated price for a listening mistake. That figure includes jobs misdone, letters sent to the wrong people, advice needed but misgiven or heard, and missed objections raised by someone to a sales presentation. These situations illustrate the costs of not listening to people. A conservative calculation of the total yearly expense to the business world is $2 billion.

Corporations are becoming increasingly sensitive to the role that listening plays in their manufacturing and customer relations. A recent issue of *The Wall Street Journal* featured a front page article about General Motors new effort to improve listening within its company. The corporation identified poor communication, and particularly poor listening, as one of the *major* elements in the decline in quality and customer satisfaction with GM products.[3] In their book, *A Passion for Excellence,* Peters and Austin discuss what they call "naive listening" and its significance to such companies as Smith-Kline Beckman, Milliken and Company (the textile manufacturer), Apple Computer, and Westinghouse.[4] The term **naive listening** refers to what we would call "audience-centered" listening. That is listening that puts the business person in the shoes of the customer and forces them to react as a "first-time" user—nonexpert who we must lead through the steps, advantages, or process of the product or service.

This is customer-centered listening and the customer is the audience. These major corporations know that they must get the customer to talk and then they must listen to them. Information is the lifeblood of a successful corporation. When customers say that they need a new 15 inch widget, a new type of hammer, or a newer and softer sheet, successful corporations listen.

For these corporations, listening is at the heart of their operation. Companies that listen well succeed more often than those companies that do not. For years, MacDonalds and IBM have been known as companies that approach and listen to the concerns and preferences of their clients. Their willingness to listen to their customers is among the reasons why these companies have been so successful. In fact, effective listening is perhaps *the* primary reason why they have become household names.

If you must be a listener throughout your life, you might as well be a good one. Being a *good* listener means being able to adapt better than the poor listener in order to be successful.

Good listening is a way of life. Good listeners show an interest in other people. Listening is socially relevant because it helps to define how each of us reacts to others. Our impressions are formed largely by how we *think* others are listening and responding to us. We choose to listen to those things and to those people we find interesting, amusing, or challenging. Listening behavior defines the nature and scope of our reactions. It describes us as human beings. Listening behavior may shout our feelings and reactions to others far louder than anything we might say.

Roles of Listeners

The two roles that we play in listening—active listener and empathic listener—include most of our social, personal, and business listening. The way that we play these two roles helps to determine how much and what kind of information we will gain from others.

Active Listening

Active listening is a voluntary participation in the communication transaction by the receiver. Listeners have a responsibility to carry their share of the communication burden and active listening is their portion. Listeners involve themselves in the acquisition of information, in making decisions for themselves, or in the appreciation of sound or information. Active listening is a more self-centered type of listening in that the listener is working to clarify the received messages to gain the fullest possible meaning from the transaction. For a student, listening for personal interests involves such things as how to get a better grade, whether to skip class and go home early, or whether to attend a Friday afternoon lecture in a large room. For a businessperson, it involves whether to listen to a discussion on stress management or salary criteria by the head of your company division. Active listening helps us to learn material, to make choices, and, in general, to guide our lives. Here are some examples of active listening:

1. Listening to instructions about how to prepare a term paper for a class and asking a question to clarify a part of the assignment you don't quite understand.

2. Following along on some profit charts while listening to a discussion about the comparative advantages of saving money or investing in the stock market.

3. Listening to a report of the weather in the Caribbean just before traveling there on a vacation trip.

4. Listening to directions about how to prepare a recipe for blackened red fish.

5. Listening to a bank officer explain the procedure for getting an auto loan through the bank and providing feedback as a way for the bank officer to see that you're following along.

In each case, the listener has some self-interest in the information. You also could call this "self-interested" listening. There is nothing wrong with self-interest. Much of what we do is out of self-interest and it should be. It has positive potential outcomes for us. Self-interest in listening can be a strong motivator.

Empathic Listening

Empathic listening allows us to identify, to understand, and to reflect the feelings, needs, and intentions of another person. It is a form of active listening. Active listening describes the task and empathic listening refers to the relationship. We must be active listeners to listen empathically. Empathic listening also involves relationships, especially feelings. Words such as "teamwork" or "understanding" fit well with empathy.

A decision about whether someone close to you should continue dating another person fits into this category. "Should I continue to go out with Gordon?" "Are Linda and I right for each other?" You could listen empathically to friends' statements as you try to solve these problems. As you engage in empathic listening, you work as a member of a team with another individual in a problem-solving activity. You seek to understand their perspective on the problem and to try to incorporate the information so that they can use it for personal decision making. Empathic listening is listening to give advice or to help others make judgments.

Empathic listening involves the sharing of another's feelings. Here are some examples of empathic listening:

1. A coworker says, "Here's the way that Marilyn has been doing her job for the past week. Do you think I should fire her or just give her a reprimand?" (You now are given the information.) "What do you think?"

In this situation, they expect you to listen (empathically) and then to help make a decision. You must listen carefully and get all of the information in order to *help* them reach a decision.

2. "We have to get this soccer team organized. No one seems to want to come to practice, but they all want to play on the day of the game. How can I motivate more of the team members to come to practice on Wednesday?"

What are your suggestions? You have listened to the basic problem. Now, it is your role to help the coach to decide what motivational techniques to use in order to get a full team for practice. What does the coach want? He wants to have a successful soccer team. He also wants some support for his feeling that he is working hard at his job. He may be feeling frustrated. This is where the empathic element is important in listening. When you affirm his effort and understand his work and frustration, you become an empathic listener.

Types of Listening

We have many goals when listening to messages. These goals influence both how and why we listen. We listen either to talk or to listen to some other person's sound form. These goals are about the tasks and topics of our communication events and are also about relationship issues. In the task dimension, our most commonly used listening approaches are (1) comprehensive listening, (2) critical listening, and (3) appreciative listening. We will discuss each of these in turn, and then take up the matter of empathic listening. Understanding these approaches will help you to decide if the way you listen is the most appropriate to your own needs and to the intention of the sender in any given communication event.

Comprehensive Listening

Listening to understand the material presented is called **comprehensive listening.** It is one of the elemental steps in listening. We listen for comprehension many times each day. For example, we listen to understand the time and the weather forecast. We listen when someone provides us with directions on a job that they want us to complete. We listen to the details of an invitation to a party that we might want to attend. We listen to the gossip or news from our friends or network commentators. The list of examples for a single day's comprehensive listening is endless.

Comprehensive listening is the *base* on which other types of active listening rest. We must first understand material before we can make decisions about it. For example, understanding a "double wishbone suspension" and what it does is necessary before you can decide whether a Honda automobile is a better buy for your needs than a Hyundai.

Thus, understanding comes first, and that understanding comes from successful symbolic interaction. One person understands, decodes, and uses the symbols coming from another person.

Critical analysis follows almost immediately. Once you can understand how the "double wishbone suspension" operates, then you can decide if you really need it. Understanding and critical analysis can overlap so closely that they occur almost simultaneously. A typical day is full of situations in which we listen first to understand and then listen more carefully to apply critical standards. Imagine the following scenario:

> *Fred comes downstairs for breakfast. His Mother says,*
> *"Fred, I want to talk with you about your plans for this evening. If I understand correctly, you plan to go directly from school to Matt's house, stay there for dinner, and then go to the basketball game. Is that right?"*
> *Fred replies, "Yes."*
> *His mother then says, "Don't you think it would be wise to use some of that time after school to study for the math final and the English test you have the next day?"*
> *To this point, Fred has been listening, generally, for understanding. Now he starts to apply critical standards.*
> *He says, "No, I have that material cold. Besides, school shouldn't take up so much of my time. I deserve a little time off for fun."*

In this scenario, two types of listening are at work. First, Fred listened to *understand* what his Mother was saying. Second, he applied what he considered to be his standards. Thus, comprehensive listening comes first. It is not the only goal in listening, but it must occur if communication is to happen.

You can improve your comprehensive listening skills to understand. Paraphrase information in your mind as you hear it. Instead of just digesting a statement like "Become an informed citizen before you go to the polls," try this. Ask yourself: what is an informed citizen? How much should you know? What are the critical issues? How should you evaluate them? When you take those steps, you paraphrase the statement and apply it to your actions. Become an active participant by asking questions and following directions as you hear information. Ask questions about how you can become a better informed voter. This is one of the important steps in improving your comprehensive listening skill.

Critical Listening

Critical listening is the application of a set of standards to evaluate the ideas that we hear. Then we make value judgments about the content. When Maria

IT'S MORE FUN TO KNOW

Listening Skills

"Many employees do not seek to improve their listening abilities because they mistakenly believe they listen well." See Gary T. Hunt and Louis P. Cusella, "A Field Study of Listening Needs in Organizations," *Communication Education*, 32:4 (October 1983), p. 399.

Comment . . .

People operate under the assumption that they are good listeners, although they actually make many mistakes in listening each day. People would profit if they would study the principles of good listening and apply them in their everyday lives.

Critical listening habits that we apply in a formal situation can also be applied in less formal situations.

Sloan heard a presentation at the city council meeting about the advantages of releasing partially treated effluent into the nearby Big Watchasee River, she was doing critical listening.

Maria listened carefully as the representatives of the pipeline company outlined the cost efficiency and the environmental impact of their delivery system. She asked herself, "How much will this save? What effect will this discharge have on the water quality of the river? Are we merely disposing of our problem and asking others to clean up after us?" As Maria wrestled with answers to these questions, she listened critically. Her answers helped her to arrive at a sensible decision about the desirability of the proposed system.

Maria was not listening just for information. She was listening critically to the proposal. She listened to the proposal, applied what she considered to be critical standards, and then made a decision about the usefulness of the proposed plan. She concluded that the disadvantages of the proposal were far greater than the claimed advantages.

We must learn to listen critically to most of what we hear. "Don's Used Cars are the least expensive and best maintained in Pierpont." " When you

Questions for the Critical Listener

1. Is the claim nullified by modifiers? (e.g., Gargle mouthwash *helps* control bad breath.)
2. Is the claim complete? (e.g., Chevrolet gives you *more*.)
3. Is the claim truly unique? (e.g., *Only* Acme gasoline has this special additive for cleaning your fuel injectors.)
4. Is the claim really an advantage? (e.g., Mom's cake is the only really *moist* mix on the market.)
5. So what? (e.g., Secret is strong enough for a man, but made for a woman.)
6. Is the claim vague? (e.g., Slip into the *Corinthian leather* seats of this new luxury sedan.)
7. Is the claim scientifically sensible? (e.g., Use Brand *X* aspirin with the ingredients nine out of ten doctors recommend.)
8. Is the claim mere flattery? (e.g., You deserve a break today!) (e.g., You've worked hard. You deserve Cadillac status.)
9. Is the claim a rhetorical question? (e.g., Tired of someone else always being your boss?)

▲ Table 3.1

think about eating out, think first of the 'home cooking' at the 'Eatery' " are only two examples of messages that radio, television, and conversation push into our ears every day.

We cannot accept all statements as factual. Therefore, we have to develop our set of evaluative standards or criteria. Those standards might be questions that we ask ourselves. "Is this a reasonable claim or statement?" "How could it be the cheapest and still the best?" "Is 'home cooking' really the best or is that claim just a myth that has become part of our culture?" "Can this product or service deliver all that it claims?" "Would the advantages outweigh the disadvantages?" "Does this candidate have all the virtues his supporters claim?"

Maria applied critical standards like these when listening to the pipeline proposal. That critical process influenced her thinking about the plan. She would have been wrong just to accept the claims as truth. Instead, she had standards that helped her to evaluate critically the elaborate pumping system. Once she applied those standards, she could then decide if the plan's originators had a satisfactory solution. She also could decide whether it met her requirements for a resolution to the problem.

Consider the standards in table 3.1 as you listen critically.

Not all criteria will apply to every critical listening experience. You should choose the criteria that seem most appropriate to you and your experience. Determine your goal in listening. Probably you will listen *critically* in a setting where there is an attempt to influence your attitudes or feelings. However, there will be elements of critical listening in almost all communication situations.

Appreciative Listening

We engage in **appreciative listening** when we stimulate our minds, get enjoyment, and stir our senses by listening to the works of others. We listen to help us realize more of our need to be complete people (i.e., to understand music, culture, or history). When we listen to these things, we listen for appreciation or recreation. Small children who listen to their mother reading a bedtime story and the opera buff who listens to the singing of Luciano Pavorotti engage in appreciative listening. They are appreciating or enjoying information or culture, and they are becoming more complete people in the process.

Today, one of the most frequent objects of appreciative listening is music. Artists such as singers and musicians that range from rock and roll to popular, country, and classical music captivate the attention and affections of millions. People listen appreciatively and with enormous intensity to music. For some people, appreciative listening becomes one of the most significant forces in their lives. Appreciative listening is not a simple sidelight of the listening process. It is one of the most significant and moving categories of the three types of listening in the task dimension.

We can listen for several reasons at the same time. For example, we could listen to President Bush to comprehend his message and at the same time we could listen to his ideas. We could listen appreciatively to the way he uses language or modulates his voice. One type of listening would predominate, but not at the exclusion of the others.

Listening for comprehension, critical evaluation, and appreciation are all task dimension activities. However, it is clear that there is another kind of listening, too. Empathic listening, as previously mentioned, is a relationship-dimension activity. When we listen for the purpose of identifying with another person's experience (e.g., feelings and wants), we listen empathically. As you will see, better listening is both an attitude and a set of skills.

Effects of Poor Listening

Poor listening can be expensive and damaging. Previously, the potential cost of poor listening to American business and industry was presented. However, the cost also appears in the form of damaged interpersonal and public relations. Because we fail to listen well, we sometimes say the wrong thing, miss appointments, become embarrassed, or purchase the wrong product. Our failures in this phase of the symbolic interaction process are painful and frequent. In short, many of our daily mistakes occur because we fail to listen effectively.

For example, Carlos' flight left Columbus on TWA at 7:40 A.M. When he picked up his tickets from the travel agent, the agent said that he should check in with the airline no later than 7:10. Carlos asked his friend, Noell, how long it would take for him to drive to the airport. Noell said, "Oh, about 30 to 40 minutes on a normal day." On the day of his flight, Carlos got up early and left his apartment for the airport at 6:30 A.M. Because snow was beginning to fall, Carlos had some trouble getting up a hill near his apartment. Traffic was moving slowly; two cars had collided in a "fender-bender" accident. By the time Carlos arrived at the entrance to the airport parking lot, it was already 7:25. Subsequently, by the time he had parked his car and caught a shuttle bus to the terminal, his flight had left. There was no other plane to San Antonio from Columbus for seven hours.

What did Carlos fail to do and how would improved listening have solved his dilemma? (We can examine Carlos' experience for lessons about how to make our own listening behavior more effective). What problems, if any, does Carlos have in his listening behavior? How might better listening have prevented his problem?

Carlos heard his travel agent tell him about how far to check in in advance. He heard the symbols, but he ignored their implications. He failed to follow up. Carlos might have asked how long it would take him to get from the parking lot to the airline counter. We know that a passenger does not drive a car directly to the terminal desk and leave it. There must be time for parking and for traveling to the terminal itself. Carlos listened for comprehension, but he didn't critically analyze the implications of the information. An effective listener follows up on the information and requests additional information, such as the time needed to park a car and get to the check-in location.

However, Carlos' story does not end here. Noell had told him the travel time of 30 to 40 minutes applied on a good day. What happens on a bad day? Again, Carlos did not listen well in his 'comprehensive' role. How much time he needed if the weather was bad remained an unanswered question.

Finally, Carlos failed to listen to the weather forecast. It probably would have given him the information that he needed to plan. The likelihood of bad weather would have told him to allow for extra travel time.

The costs of ineffective listening result in daily personal inconvenience, frustration, and anger. We might fail to get a promotion, lose a sale, or be late for a date. We might even spend money at a restaurant, especially if we don't hear a friend say that it's inferior.

In general, poor listening damages our relations with others. On the other hand, effective listening can become one of our most important public behaviors. As exemplified, it was important in Carlos' case.

Positive Listening Behaviors

You can do many things to become a more effective listener. Some suggested activities to improve your listening skills follow.

1. Try to extend your attention span.

Most of us do not pay attention for a very long period of time. Since words flow from a speaker's mouth at around 140 to 160 words per minute, we need to hear as many words as possible. To interact with the words of another, we need to listen to all the words. We should be active and constantly involved in this symbolic interaction process. However, because our mind can process information so much faster than our speech patterns can process it, our **attention span** sometimes suffers. Our minds often stray to other matters. When we come back to listen to the speaker's words, we may be lost.

Paying attention is hard work. Try to focus your thoughts on the conversation of the next person you meet. Regardless of how hard you try, before long other thoughts will enter your mind. This results in some of that person's message being lost. You have no doubt noticed this happening to you in class, church, and even in conversations where you were sincerely interested.

School often encourages us not to pay attention. We know that information usually is repeated about three times. Although it will not be "word for word," the repetition will still be there. Look at the following excerpt from a classroom.

PROFESSOR DANIELS: "And the first role of electors is to cast votes for their candidate. Let me explain how this works. . . ."

PROFESSOR DANIELS (five minutes later): "So the electors represent the views and preferences of the voters within their states. When the electors cast their votes in the state capitol in January of the year following the election . . ."

PROFESSOR DANIELS (near the end of the class hour): "One of the main issues we've seen today is that electors are morally but not legally bound to vote for the presidential nominee they have been chosen to represent."

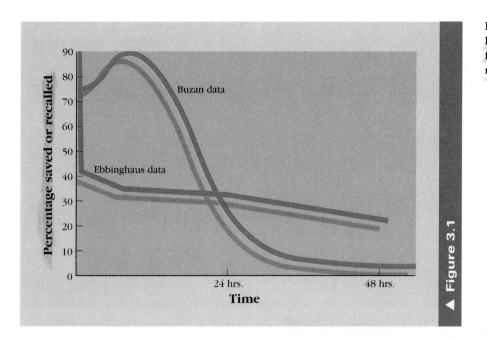

Forgetting curves. It is a lot easier to forget than to remember.

▲ Figure 3.1

The teacher's behavior invites us to ignore some of the class information. We know that we will hear much of it again to help us learn. We can be much better listeners if we work at getting the information the first time. Pay attention. We won't become passive receivers if we become interested. Extend your attention span and you will gain more information.

2. Listen for key points and main ideas.

Try to sort out the major ideas. Make a mental outline of the major points and sub-points. If the situation allows, take notes. If you can visualize the outline of the message, you are more likely to remember the main ideas and the details. It is similar to recalling the silhouette of a city skyline. If you can remember what the major buildings looked like at sundown, then that helps to trigger memories of other details, such as the narrowness of the streets, the sound of the traffic, the crush in the elevators, or the (in)efficient public transportation system.

After a few hours, most of what we hear will be forgotten. Therefore, it is very important that listeners remember the main ideas in order to retain the major part of the message. Listening for major ideas helps to insure that we at least remember the important thoughts. Figure 3.1 shows clearly how quickly we forget material.

It is easier to remember or to feel interest in materials that are in short or summarized form.

3. Keep an open mind.

It is easy to jump to conclusions or to shut out information that disagrees with our own beliefs. For example, people who believe that automatic weapons should not be sold to the public will have trouble listening to someone who argues that people have a right to purchase or to own any type of firearm. Despite the listener's attitude, there may be some merit in the ideas offered by the opponent to any type of gun control. The old argument that "you need to know the other side of the issue to be able to present your own" is important if we are listening critically or for comprehension.

How do you know your ideas are best if you do not listen to the other side? Be smart. Listen with an open mind. Avoid the closed-minded position that says, "Don't confuse me with facts; my mind already is made up."

4. Review and summarize major points.

You can mentally review and summarize a speaker's major points. You don't need to write them down. Ask yourself, "What were the main ideas?" and then summarize them in your mind. This is primarily a short review process aimed at helping you to repeat materials so that you are more likely to remember them later.

It is easier to remember or to be interested in materials that are in an abbreviated or summarized form. For example, network television provides "news briefs" between portions of one-hour or two-hour programs. The news stories presented are the most important ones of the day. As a listener, you can learn from this example observation. Review and summarize the major points of a conversation in your own mind. Repeat the material and you will remember most of it.

5. Pay attention to the messages that don't have words.

We send out more nonverbal messages than we do verbal ones. Furthermore, most of the messages about our feelings, our wants, our intentions, and our openness to others (etc.) are expressed nonverbally. An effective listener must become sensitive to the messages that don't have words.

Remember these questions. They will help you to listen more efficiently.

1. How does the speaker *feel*?

2. Are the speaker's feelings as important or more important than his ideas?

3. Does the speaker *want* something from me that he's not asking for with words?

4. Is the speaker signaling some *intention* to act that he's not stating openly?

5. How *open* is the speaker to feedback?

6. What relevant *image* does the speaker seem to have? How accurate does that image seem to be?

Following up on these questions with "why?" will help greatly in improving your critical listening skills. You will be *actively* involving yourself in the exchange by seeking more information.

Negative Listening Behaviors

Most of us probably have several behaviors that we consider undesirable, although we do not associate them with listening. Some things that we do every day emerge as major obstacles to becoming effective listeners.

Jumping to Conclusions

When we hear certain key or emotional words, we leap to a conclusion about the person or idea. Our experience with these symbols leads us to decide whether the idea is good or bad, interesting, or boring. We may conclude that the person talking is foolish, intelligent, or amusing. We often draw these conclusions based on incomplete information.

You can deal with this problem if you learn to be patient. It is easy for people to jump to conclusions. Most of us believe that we know what another person will say and we interrupt or jump to a conclusion. Often, however, our guess is wrong. We *assumed* that we knew the other person's intention based on how we felt. Remember the experience. "I know what you're going to say. There's no sense in studying for this test because ten students who didn't study last semester all got A's or B's." Your assumption was based on your feeling that the student would argue that studying for the course was a waste of time. That was your feeling, but it may not have been what the speaker intended to say. Remember, none of us is a mind reader. Wait until you hear what others have to say, then make a critical judgment.

An Army Captain greeted a group of graduating high school seniors by saying, "The Army promises a great career. I'd like to encourage you to become part of the team." Frank thought, "Fat chance. Most of us don't want that baloney and all the discipline that goes with it. I'm going to turn off this turkey right now before I listen to any more of that garbage!" What Frank did not know was what Captain Fuentes would say next. "But most of you have little interest in a life of considerable discipline or cannot accept the challenge this type of career demands. I understand and respect that view. I'd suggest that if you are suspicious of challenge, hard work, or rewards or advancement, then the Army or any other career probably is not for you." Frank had never expected to hear that message. He could not be patient. He had stopped listening because he believed that he could predict what he would hear next. He allowed his emotions to interfere with his ability to listen.

We cannot hear all of the information until we learn to hear the entire message. Being patient may mean biting your tongue in order to keep yourself from interrupting. Even so, it is better to be patient until you hear the other person's message. The outcome of listening to an entire message means that we base our conclusion on all of the information instead of on part of it.

Summary

Listening is essential to the communication cycle. We engage in critical, comprehensive, and appreciative listening each day. Listening is the centerpiece of symbolic interaction. Based on our experience with the language, we become interested, amused, stimulated, or bored with the ideas. We listen as empathic or active listeners. Listening has a substantial personal and professional value. It helps to define us, and it is an accurate indicator of our personal behavior and attitude. Many of our personal behaviors, such as jumping to conclusions and having a short attention span, contribute to our listening problems. Listening skills can be improved if we improve our attitude toward the listening process. We need to become more "other-directed" and to be certain that the setting for listening is satisfactory.

Discussion Questions

1. What are your most common listening problems? What steps could you take to reduce or eliminate them from your daily behavior?
2. What type of listening is most common for you? Cite an example of each type and explain why it meets the criteria for that type of listening.
3. Explain how listening is part of your communication cycle. Provide an example from a recent personal experience.

References

[1] Andrew D. Wolvin and Carolyn Gwynn Coakley, *Listening*, 3d ed. (Dubuque: Wm. C. Brown Publishers, 1988), p. 91.

[2] Carol Rubin and Jeff Rubin, "'Tis The Season To Be Fighting," *Psychology Today* 22:12 (December 1988), p. 38. Reprinted with permission of the publishers.

[3] *Wall Street Journal,* January 12, 1989, "GM Woos Employees by Listening to Them, Talking of Its 'Team'," pp. 1, 5.

[4] Tom Peters and Nancy Austin, *A Passion for Excellence* (New York: Warner Books, 1985), pp. 16–20.

Chapter 4

Verbal Messages

When you finish reading this chapter you will be able to:

1. Explain the major functions of language: to exchange messages in order to manage complexity.

2. List from memory, define and explain abstraction, categorization, generalization, and time-binding.

3. Define and explain signification, definition, polarization, reification, paradox, and stereotyping as problems in using language.

4. Describe the relationship between language and interactive style, and the relationship between language and credibility.

5. List and explain five choices that you can make to use language more effectively: simplicity, specificity, action, illustration, and comparison and contrast.

6. Differentiate between connotation and denotation.

abstraction	paradox	time-binding
connotation	polarization	Triangle of Meaning
definition	reification	▲ referent
denotation	self-fulfilling prophecy	▲ symbol
frame of reference	signification	▲ thought
inference	speech community	
language	stereotype	

Introduction

People underestimate the magic and the miracle of language. Yet, they do not often think about some rather astounding facts.

For instance, it is a fact that linguistic creativity is the birthright of all human beings. It is born into all babies, regardless of their status in life, their birth location on Earth, their kind of community, or their degree of intellect.

It is also a fact that the birthright of linguistic creativity is uniquely human. No other specie has developed a language, although it is clear that other animals do communicate.

Furthermore, it is a fact that all human beings can create sentences that have never been uttered before. They can't all paint portraits, compose music, build bridges, or jump over a fallen tree, but they all can commonly utter original sentences.

And finally, it is a fact that the potential for new sentences—sentences never uttered before by anyone at any time in history—is theoretically infinite.

You can begin to understand this infinite potential to create original sentences merely by performing a simple calculation. Suppose you know 500 nouns that name things (i.e., tree, Mary, dreams) and 500 verbs that tell action (i.e., run, paint, cry). If you know these words, and no other words, you can create 250,000 two-word sentences. If you know 1,500 nouns and 1,500 verbs, the number of possible two-word combinations is 2.25 million sentences. Most of these would seem meaningless, of course, but they would be grammatically correct. Beyond that, as time goes on, more and more of these combinations become meaningful. For example, there was a time when "airplanes fly" would have made no sense to anyone. "Input data" would have seemed a ridiculous idea just fifty years ago. Before Alexander Graham Bell invented the telephone, "Call me" meant something different from our current understanding of this combination.

Now, suppose that you increase the number of words in the combination to three: noun, verb, noun. Assuming 1,500 nouns and 1,500 verbs in the language, the formula would be $1,500 \times 1,500 \times 1,500$. The possible number of original sentences is now close to 3.4 billion.

This is more three-word sentences than could be spoken in a lifetime. Indeed, 150 words spoken per minute would require 1,300 years to speak them.

Yet, even with such a vast potential for original sentences, our language would still seem inadequate. English includes many words, more than 1,500 nouns and 1,500 verbs. It also includes adjectives, adverbs, articles, and pronouns. Therefore, the potential number of combinations is beyond measure and beyond comprehension, which prompts a couple of conclusions. First, the miracle of language is that it is infinitely creative, which allows us to invent whole worlds and realities for ourselves and our fellow human beings. The magic of the miracle is that we do this by using nothing more than arbitrary combinations of sounds. In short, we make and we change the world with words. Some say we also create ourselves with words.[1]

The second conclusion is that no one can learn all of the possible combinations of words. Yet, people still learn language. Hence, they must be learning some rules for the use of words.

The key idea in this chapter is that language is our major message system. Language makes it possible to name, to identify, and to define the objects and phenomena in our world. Language organizes our experience and allows us to test and to make judgments about that experience. Language makes it possible to construct meanings and to think hypothetically. Because of language, we can recognize alternatives, remember, and plan. Language makes it possible for us to conceive of ourselves and to pay attention to our own values, attitudes, and beliefs. Even so, language is often taken for granted and often little understood.

The General Nature of Language

Language is a body of words, plus the rules for their use, that ties people together into a speech community. As symbolic interactionists, we believe that language allows us to create and to share our meaning and experience. Language allows us to think about time and to transcend distance. Language gives rise to our culture, our experience of reality and our social system. But how does language work? How does language function? How can language be used more effectively?

The Functions of Language

The definition of language (i.e., a body of signs and symbols, plus rules for their use) suggests three important ideas. First, it suggests that language is composed of words. Second, it suggests that words are abstract. That is, words are not directly related to the things they represent or describe; they are arbitrary. And third, it suggests that the use of the words is governed by rules that tell us which ones are appropriate, how they go together, and how to understand them. Thus, language is our primary means of exchanging messages.

Managing Complexity

The primary function of language is to exchange messages in order to manage complexity. We use language to tell each other who we are and how we feel

A speech community is a group of people who use language in the same way.

about each other. We use language to tell each other how we experience the world of objects, phenomena, and events. We use language to create and to organize a world of past and present experiences and to anticipate future events and experiences. We use language to transmit our culture. Language imposes its rules and assumptions upon us, and determines what we will know and how we will know it.[2]

We learn all these things from our closest associates—our speech community. A **speech community** is a group of people who use language in the same way. They "understand" the rules and the words. Thus, they share a common orientation to the things outside themselves.

We can't share exactly what we think and feel because we are limited to our own frames of reference. A **frame of reference** is a psychological window through which we see the world. It evolves from symbolic interaction. It is based in language.

To illustrate, English employs a common sentence structure that imposes attribution. We say:

- ▲ "John dropped the ball."
- ▲ "Milton played the piano."
- ▲ "Lectron scored a touchdown."

In each of these sentences, language allows us to identify an actor, the action, and the object of the action. The form is so common that we often use it without realizing that it does not literally apply. So we say:

- ▲ "Communism threatens America."
- ▲ "Freedom builds democracy."
- ▲ "America protects the world."

Notice how this form is different from the usual Chinese construction.[3] And notice how the differences focus attention on different aspects of a situation. In northern China the usual form is *topic* and *comment*. So, for "John dropped the ball," a Chinese is likely to say "Ball-object dropping." That would translate: "As for the ball, [it *understood*] dropped." Attribution would be implied by the context, perhaps, but not intentionally. In sentence form, the subject would be separated from doing the action.

It simply doesn't occur to the Chinese to attribute the action to anyone, or to be concerned about the time of the action. That is not part of the language. The Chinese listener would understand the Chinese speaker, of course, and the two might very well be clear about who did what. But not necessarily. The Chinese *imply* attribution, but never assign it. In some ways it is similar to our own use of the passive voice. In English the construction would be something like: "As for the ball, [it] dropped." But the word, "it" would be understood, not spoken.

Because they have different language assumptions, a Chinese speaker does not understand ("see") the same event as the English speaker.

People create frames of reference out of words. These different frames of reference create different points of view and different positions. All these differences are based in language, and they are simply not possible without symbolic interaction. If the words or the sentence structure of a language does not allow something, then that "something" does not exist. Thus, the language we use *governs* the meanings we take from the world.

Language and Meaning

Remember when you were introduced to the concept of denotation and connotation? The teacher was trying to teach you about what language means. Therefore, it might be useful to review the lesson.

Denotation

Denotation refers to the meaning of a word that a speech community shares. It is the definition that you will find in a dictionary. For example, the word *car* may be defined as "an automobile; any wheeled vehicle; a means of transportation." We can use that word to name many examples, and we will agree readily that the naming is correct. We "know" what the word means. We agree to use the word in a certain way. But we still have a problem. Words do not "feel" the same to different people. Moreover, people use different words because of their feeling and texture.

To illustrate, *average,* and *mediocre* both refer to a middle ground, but you would not use the words synonymously. They connote different things to different people. So do words like *faith, belief, creed,* and *dogma.* These words share essentially the same referent, but they, too, lend different textures.

Both *inexpensive* and *cheap* refer to price. Which one suggests the better quality? Would you prefer to stay in a *cheap* hotel, or would you prefer to stay in an *inexpensive* one?

Connotation

Connotation is the personal meaning of a word. It is the affective associations that people bring to words. We can agree on the denotative meaning of *car* and use the word to refer to a thing, although each of us will have a private and personal understanding of the word, as well.

To illustrate, here's an actual conversation between father and daughter. Compare some possible connotative differences between a father and his daughter as they talk about cars. See how the connotative implications of the word influence the communication event.

"Daddy, I need your advice about a car. I mean, it's clear I am going to have to get one pretty soon, and . . ."

"Yes," interrupts father. "I agree that it's time. In fact, I was thinking you might like to have the Tercel."

What the father was thinking:	What the daughter may have thought:
▲ My Toyota Tercel would be good.	▲ I want a Toyota Celeca GT.
▲ It's already paid for and has low maintenance.	▲ It's sleek and fast and has a great radio.
▲ It gets thirty miles per gallon.	▲ It has an electronic everything.
▲ It's reliable transportation.	▲ It represents freedom and privacy.
▲ It's no hassle and relatively safe.	▲ It would make me feel powerful.
▲ It's inconspicuous and conservative.	▲ Boys would flock to my car.

From all of this, it seems clear that language does not "have" any meaning. The meaning of language is determined by the people who use it.

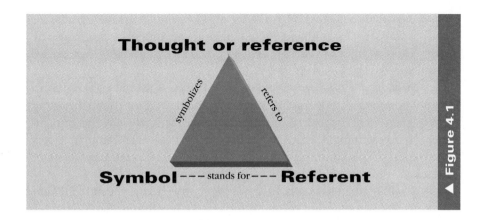

Figure 4.1

The Triangle of Meaning

Charles Ogden and I. A. Richards focused on just such a problem when they developed their **triangle of meaning** nearly seventy years ago.[4] The basic idea of this triangle is that people use signs and symbols to refer to objects, phenomena, and events. Figure 4.1 illustrates this triangle.

The **referent** at the lower right of the triangle is the subject of a communication event. For example, if you pronounce the word *shoe,* the referent would be the particular shoe that you have in mind, or it would be some generalized concept. A referent may be a person, an object, or an event. It may also be a feeling or something wanted. A referent is both the object of perception and that to which a symbol refers.

The **thought** at the top of the triangle represents human perception and interpretation of the referent. Feelings about a referent, experiences relating to the referent, and other perceptions may also be included. When you saw the *shoe* in the previous paragraph, you probably formed your own mental image of what *shoe* represented. Your image may have even been quite specific (i.e., an old pair of sneakers perhaps). The person that sits next to you in class probably also formed an equally specific, yet very different, image of what *shoe* meant (perhaps the memory of the discomfort from a poorly fitting shoe). The image is different because your neighbor's perception is based on a different set of life experiences, values, and current moods. Thus, the thought is the mental image that each person has of the referent.

The **symbol** in the left corner of the triangle is something that stands for something else. In this example, *shoe* is just a symbol that the English language has assigned to represent the things that we wear on our feet. The word *shoe* is not actually the referent. It exists to provide a way for us to understand what we are talking about without having to take our footwear off to show it to each other. Words, phrases, and sentences stand for thoughts and real objects. It is not possible to communicate thoughts and images directly (how would you show a specific shoe on the telephone?). Instead, we must translate them into symbols.

Symbols are arbitrary. Symbols do not have a natural connection to what they represent. For example, there is no natural reason to call that thing a *car.* There is no natural connection between the word *shirt* and the garment you are wearing. Rather, the symbols are convenient and arbitrary labels that we can use because we agree to. Without them we could not communicate.

Symbols are ambiguous. Every symbol is open to interpretation. There is no single, agreed upon meaning for words. To illustrate, suppose your friend says, "There's a good movie in town. Let's go see it." Your friend's idea of a good movie and your own idea of a good movie may not always agree. Even so, the words can be used within a range of agreed upon interpretations in our speech community.

Symbols are abstract. Symbols are removed from the things that they represent. Symbols are not the things they represent. Rather, symbols derive from our own translation of experience into thought, and then into language. John C. Condon explained abstraction as an act of selection. The selection occurs when we try to explain our experiences by choosing language. The process of perceiving and making sense of language is called **abstraction.**[5]

S. I. Hayakawa explained this abstracting process with a "ladder of abstraction."[6] As we climb higher and higher up the ladder, we change the view of an event in important ways. The process of abstracting also changes the language that we choose to describe that event. The higher the abstraction, the farther the symbol is removed from the referent. Thus, our language becomes much less precise and much more general. Hayakawa's sketch appears in figure 4.2. Begin reading it from the bottom.

We select the level of abstraction based on how well we know something or someone. In human relationships, the level implies the level of intimacy or knowledge that we have of the other people. Thus, we say *secretary* to refer to the woman who works in the outer office. We do not have to know her very well, and we can continue to maintain that level of relationship by continuing our use of the word. Now, suppose we say *Rita* instead of *secretary.* Three implications about our relationship to the secretary emerge.

First, the abstraction level that we choose identifies the relationship that we experience, as well as the behaviors that are appropriate to the relationship. Second, the level of abstraction that we choose in a relationship tells a lot about our understanding of the depth and intensity of that relationship.

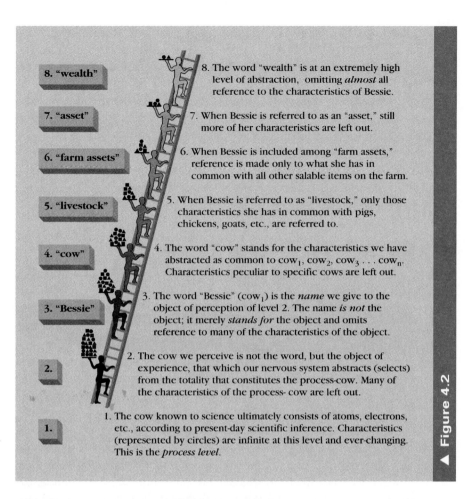

8. "wealth"

8. The word "wealth" is at an extremely high level of abstraction, omitting *almost* all reference to the characteristics of Bessie.

7. "asset"

7. When Bessie is referred to as an "asset," still more of her characteristics are left out.

6. "farm assets"

6. When Bessie is included among "farm assets," reference is made only to what she has in common with all other salable items on the farm.

5. "livestock"

5. When Bessie is referred to as "livestock," only those characteristics she has in common with pigs, chickens, goats, etc., are referred to.

4. "cow"

4. The word "cow" stands for the characteristics we have abstracted as common to cow_1, cow_2, cow_3 ... cow_n. Characteristics peculiar to specific cows are left out.

3. "Bessie"

3. The word "Bessie" (cow_1) is the *name* we give to the object of perception of level 2. The name *is not* the object; it merely *stands for* the object and omits reference to many of the characteristics of the object.

2.

2. The cow we perceive is not the word, but the object of experience, that which our nervous system abstracts (selects) from the totality that constitutes the process-cow. Many of the characteristics of the process- cow are left out.

1.

1. The cow known to science ultimately consists of atoms, electrons, etc., according to present-day scientific inference. Characteristics (represented by circles) are infinite at this level and ever-changing. This is the *process level.*

▲ Figure 4.2

If we call the secretary *Mrs. Schlecht,* we define the relationship as formal. If we call her *Rita,* we imply a different relationship. If we call her *sweetheart,* she will probably resent that you have gone too far in assuming or implying an inappropriate level of intimacy, depth, or intensity. Her frame of reference may view "sweetheart" as a degrading label when applied in a work environment or relationship.

Third, the level of abstraction that we choose in a relationship tends to be reflected by the other. So, the levels of abstraction we use become an important measure of the status of our relationships. The language levels may become more similar as their relationship grows more intimate. The continuing interaction tends to create more similarity in each person's frame of reference so that understanding comes more easily. If not, then one or both of the partners in that relationship could experience discomfort. This explains why Mrs. Schlecht would not appreciate our use of too familiar a term when we talk with her.

To summarize, the use of language is arbitrary and limiting. Our words cannot ever represent all of a thing. We cannot say all that might be said or convey everything that we feel, think, and perceive. Rather, we *symbolize* these things with words. Our representations are only as good as our choices of language for a particular situation or relationship.

When we talk with other people, we ask them to interpret our symbols. We ask them to fill in the details and to fill in all of our connotative overtones. They can't do it the same way we do because their frames of reference will be somewhat different from our own.

Language and Experience

The way we use language controls our experience of the world and of each other.

Symbols organize. When we use words we organize our experiences into categories. Each figure of speech (noun, pronoun, adjective, verb, adverb, and so forth) contributes to the categorization process in some way.

For example, a person might say *men.* By using that noun, a person organizes the world of experience into two categories. The first is *men;* the second is *not men.* If you modify the category with an adjective, you subdivide the category into two smaller categories. *Big men* includes every man who is big, and it excludes men who are small. Therefore, by using language we classify experience. We must. Otherwise, we could not manage the complexity of the world.

When we use symbols to organize our experience, we often generalize. To illustrate, consider the awful stereotype of women drivers. The stereotype is offensive because its comments about women drivers are generically applied to every woman. If not, we would have to specify which drivers are meant. Thus, we do not hear that "some women are lousy drivers and some women are wonderful drivers." Instead, we hear a sexist slur: "Women are lousy drivers."

Generalization is part of the language, and it underpins our reasoning processes. Without it we could not make categorical assertions. Without it we could not ever know anything "for sure." That might be a good thing, but it would also be a frustrating thing. Whether we like it or not, we must live with what has been called the "allness" assumption.

Symbols allow us to think hypothetically. Another feature of symbolic interaction is called **time-binding.** Our language is always in past, present,

The inferences people draw are intimately connected to their ways of using language.

or future tense. This feature of language makes it possible for us to tie ourselves to history; to understand ourselves as part of a process. The great benefit from this feature of language is that we can learn from the past. All of the wisdom from the trial and error of 3,000 generations is ours because we can bind ourselves to the past. Moreover, we can plan the future because of this language feature. We can think in terms of "what if?"

This feature of symbolic interaction also creates problems. For example, relationship management is made far more difficult because we can remember and anticipate. If we could not do this, we would be unable to carry a grudge. When a disgruntled friend demands that a friend take back something that was said, then bases the behavior on what the friend does, this is "time-binding" in the most damaging way possible. It's obvious that the friend cannot take back what was said.

Our wonderful ability to draw inferences is also part of thinking hypothetically. Every time we go beyond what can be observed directly, we are drawing inferences. If you say to your friend, "You look tired," then you are drawing an inference. If you make a judgment about something, as in the sentence, "This car is really beautiful," then you are drawing an inference. If you anticipate, as in "She will win the race," or "We're going fishing," then you are drawing an inference.

An **inference** is a guess. It is a judgment, based on observation, about the meaning of what has been observed. *The inferences people draw are intimately bound up in their ways of using language.*

The English language profoundly influences the inferences that English speakers can draw in at least six ways: signification, definition, polarization, reification, paradox, and stereotyping.

Figure 4.3

Signification

Signification is using language that points to something. It is the act of making something known by using either verbal or nonverbal signs and symbols. We signify something when we say *the baby,* or *that hammer,* or *Ellen's car.* If we say, "Please run to the grocery store for me," we signify both a thing (grocery store) and an action (run). The problem, of course, is that people often use the same words to signify different things, and thus get themselves embroiled in problems that might have been avoided.

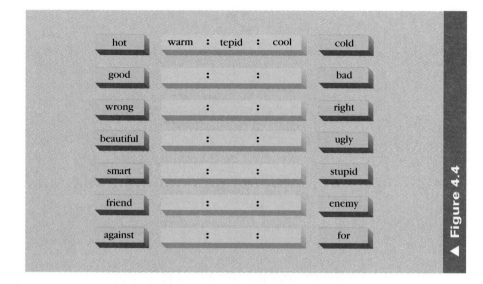

Definition

To define something is to mark its boundaries. Thus, **definition** means to mark the boundaries of some named thing. Definition allows us to divide the things defined and also to include and unify the things named. The problem is that we tend to assume that other people share our definitions of the named things.

Polarization

Another problem buried in language has been called polarization. **Polarization** occurs when we refer to the world as having only two values (e.g., good or bad, right or wrong). The world is not ever totally good or totally bad. A person is never totally right or totally wrong. But polarized language keeps us from finding those subtle shades of possibility between the extremes. Thus, when we think in polarized terms we create images in our heads like the high-contrast photograph in figure 4.3. Like the shades of gray in the photo, shades of meaning between the extremes are dropped out of our thinking.

If you spend a few moments trying to fill in the blanks provided between the pairs of words in figure 4.4, you will recognize the problem. We have given the first case to illustrate what you should do.

Without the words, we cannot think about the center of the continua. So, we experience the world in extremes and we overlook the truth because we do not have words to describe it.

Osgood, Suci, and Tannenbaum were concerned about our tendency to polarize when they conducted their research that led to the publication

IT'S MORE FUN TO KNOW

Self-Concept, Feeling, and Verbal Behavior

People who are socially insecure tend to ask more questions and provide fewer direct statements of information.

See Mark R. Leary, Paul D. Knight, and Kelly A. Johnson, "Social Anxiety and Dyadic Conversation: A Verbal Response," *Journal of Social and Clinical Psychology*, 5:1 (1987), pp. 34–50.

Comment . . .

Acquaintances and others who ask many questions but say little about themselves or provide general information probably are socially insecure.

of *The Measurement of Meaning*.[7] They discovered that this tendency to polarize exists in more than fifty of Earth's living languages. Therefore, they believe that the tendency to polarize the world is a universal problem.

Reification

We tend to think about abstractions as concrete things. When we do this, we reify those abstractions. **Reification** is treating a symbol as a real thing, an object that we can manipulate. Words like democracy, friendship, and love represent things, but the words are only symbols. "A friendship" is only a concept. To illustrate, put a three- or four-word description on the lines provided for each of the terms in the list.

A paradox

> ## This statement is a lie.

- ▲ abomination _____
- ▲ love _____
- ▲ barbarian _____
- ▲ cowardice _____
- ▲ capitalist _____
- ▲ communist _____
- ▲ friendship _____
- ▲ democrat _____

You could go through your dictionary, as we have, to discover a large number of such terms. If you reify any of these terms or terms like them, you risk clarity and agreement when you talk because you may be adding personal perceptions that someone else may not recognize.

Paradox

A **paradox** is any statement that seems inherently contradictory. For example, a road sign hanging above an Interstate Highway that says, "Disregard this sign" is a paradox.

Figure 4.5 is a paradox. If the statement is true, then it's false. If it is false, then it's true.

The child who engages his mother in this argument about supper is involved in paradox.

MOTHER: "Eat your spinach, Billy."

BILLY: "I don't like spinach."

MOTHER: "How do you know? You have never tasted it."

BILLY: "That's why I don't like it."

The problem in each of these examples occurs because a paradox has two levels of meaning. First, a statement asserts something at one level, then something different about itself at another level. And second, the assertions are contradictory. Paradoxes are common in everyday talk, and they can be damaging. Here are three more brief examples.

FATHER TO TEENAGE DAUGHTER: "It's not my business to say so, but I think you should abstain from sex until you're married."

TWENTY-FIVE-YEAR-OLD SON TO HIS FATHER: "Tell me how to be independent."

GIRLFRIEND TO BOYFRIEND: "I want you to surprise me."

Unless we learn to identify such paradoxes and to break out of their confines, we risk communication trouble.[8]

Stereotyping

To **stereotype** is to apply a fixed set of beliefs about a group or subgroup to an individual member of that group without acknowledging the individual's uniqueness. Although we are often told that stereotypes are damaging, we need our stereotypes to guide us through the world of unknowns. For example, you have a stereotype in your head of professors. That stereotype tells you how to interact with professors when you meet them for the first time. For example, your perception of the professor stereotype probably dictates that you address this person as "Dr." and that you don't step into this person's office until invited to do so. Stereotypes help to give us a *starting point* in new situations. Stereotyping can also get us into trouble.

Just after World War II, Wendell Johnson wrote the often-quoted lines, "To a mouse, cheese is cheese; that's why mousetraps work."[9] His idea was that we do not often question our expectations, and therefore we frequently miss the uniqueness in a situation. Because this is true, we set traps for ourselves that can get us into trouble.

Have you ever used sentences like these?

- ▲ "So, what did you expect? He's a man, isn't he?"
- ▲ "What did you expect? She's a woman, isn't she?"
- ▲ "Men are all after the same thing."
- ▲ "Women are all after the same thing."

These statements are problematic because they apply a set of general characteristics to an individual without acknowledging the individual's uniqueness. If we ignore the individual uniqueness of a person, we miss the opportunity for genuine communication. We limit our opportunities for new experiences.

When we take stereotyping too far, it can create a self-fulfilling prophecy. A **self-fulfilling prophecy** occurs when we let our expectations control our actions. It works like this: stereotyping creates the expectations, the expectations create the self-fulfilling prophecy, and then the prophecy comes true.

The following circumstance illustrates a self-fulfilling prophecy. Mike was absent from class the week that Sister Mary Leona taught her class about the mathematical concept of x. He had already decided that he was not "good" in mathematics before he had ever heard of Sister Leona. So he disliked studying his math, and he put off or completely avoided doing his mathematics homework. He surely was not going to try to read in his mathematics book while he was at home with the flu.

When Mike returned to school after his illness, he had missed another important mathematical concept—"unknown." He was so confused when Sister Leona gave him a sheet of problems to work that he concluded, again, that he was not "good" at math. Having concluded this, he decided to cheat. He got his older brother to help him with his homework. In effect, this meant that the older brother worked the problems for Mike. Mike turned in his paper, and Sister Mary Leona, a truly caring but overworked teacher, decided that he understood the concept of x. She continued her planned lesson sequence, and Mike was lost.

A self-fulfilling prophecy occurs when we let our expectations control our actions.

How to Use Language More Effectively

Here are some suggestions for using language more effectively. Remember, sometimes these suggestions may be inappropriate. In the final analysis, you must use your own judgment.

1. *Choose to expand your vocabulary.*
Your fluency and your credibility are closely tied to the number of words that you know how to use. There is strong support for each of the following arguments:

- ▲ The larger your vocabulary, the greater your control of imagery and the better your ability to manage the impressions you leave with others.
- ▲ The more words you know, the better able you are to manage your relationships.
- ▲ The greater the number of your feeling words, the richer your emotional range.
- ▲ The more words you know, the greater your ability to perceive the world accurately.
- ▲ The more words you know, the better your ability to express your attitudes and opinions.

Therefore, you can choose to expand your vocabulary. That's the first and most important step in learning to use language more effectively.

2. *Use language simply.*

Use simple words, simple phrases, and simple sentences. Listeners may be well educated and may have very sophisticated language skills. Still, people tend to limit themselves to the use of a few thousand words.

The advice to use simple language does not keep you from creating vivid images or using language powerfully or persuasively. Rather, it implies that you match your level of language usage to the least skillful of your listeners. You never have to sell out an idea to say it simply and clearly.

Table 4.1 (pages 88–89) was drawn from a longer sheet developed by the United States Navy to show that official writing can be simple and direct.

3. *Choose specific language.*

If you want someone to form an image, then you must give that person the materials needed to do it. Generalizations and abstractions do not conjure such images. What is needed is concrete language that's specific and to the point.

To illustrate this important concept, which is called *concretion* in English composition textbooks, compare these two columns:

General (abstract)	Specific (concrete)
▲ Corporation	▲ Exxon, IBM, General Motors
▲ Labor	▲ chopping wood, digging
▲ Labor union	▲ National Federation of Labor
▲ Organization	▲ Boy Scouts of America
▲ Tall	▲ six feet, seven inches

The general terms on the left do not relate vivid mental images. However, the column on the right is much more likely to do so.

4. *Choose action language.*

Receivers do better, whether reading or listening, when the sender uses the active voice. That is, let the subject of your sentences do the action of the verbs. If you follow this general suggestion about language usage, your receivers are more likely to draw accurate conclusions and vivid images.

Action language includes not only the active voice, but also short sentences, time words, and interrupted rhythms. You can feel the difference between the following two examples. Which one do you prefer?

Passive	Active
"Response latencies to the last four practice trials were averaged to establish a reaction-time covariate for each person. In order to examine the effects of extremity of self-perception along the industriousness dimension, each person's responses to the scale items tapping that domain were combined (after appropriate reversals) to create an additive index."[10]	"We averaged the response latencies in the last four practice trials. We wanted to discover each person's reaction time. We also combined each person's responses to particular items. We wanted to study what respondents thought of their own industriousness. So, it was necessary to create an additive index of this dimension."

Here, we have presented a sample of academic writing. Reader expectations in that context demand a less active language form. Nevertheless, you can compare and contrast your own response to the two samples. Which one do you prefer? (If you don't like either of these, it may be because of the complexity of the language used.)

5. *Choose to illustrate abstract ideas.*
People think about concepts in very predictable ways. First, they visualize a concrete image that makes sense to them. After that, they can handle more abstract concepts. Therefore, examples and illustrations help receivers to visualize ideas.

To verify the usefulness of illustrations, examine your own experiences. When you read a textbook or listen to a lecture, how do you respond to the examples? If your experience is like most other people's experiences, then you like those examples. They help you to understand abstract ideas because they are more vivid and clear.

6. *Employ comparison and contrast.*
Comparison and contrast (i.e., *analogy* and *antithesis*) add vividness and accuracy to language. Place one idea against another to show similarities and differences.

Use comparison and contrast for three purposes: (1) to make things clear and vivid, (2) to support or prove things, and (3) to make something abstract (justice, equality, goodness) more concrete.

To make a thing clear and vivid, compare it to something that is well known to the receiver. For example, you might explain the size of a newly developed electronic "micrometer" by comparing it to the thickness of a single human hair.

Simpler Words and Phrases

Official writing does *not* demand big words or fancy phrases. Write naturally—using the words with which you speak. Those words are usually small. The essence of English is in its small (often one-syllable) words. They save typing and reading time, and they make writing livelier and ideas clearer.

Instead of	Try
accompany	go with
accordingly	so
achieve	do, make
address	discuss
advantageous	helpful
apparent	clear, plain
appropriate	(omit), proper, right
ascertain	find out, learn
attached herewith is	here's
benefit	help
capability	ability, can
close proximity	near
comply with	follow
concerning	about, on
confront	face, meet
consolidate	combine, join, merge
current	(omit)
demonstrate	prove, show
designate	appoint, choose, name
develop	grow, make, take place
disseminate	issue, send out
echelons	levels
eliminate	cut, drop, end
encourage	urge
enumerate	count
equivalent	equal
evidenced	showed
exhibit	show
expend	pay out, spend
explain	show, tell
factor	reason, cause
failed to	didn't
feasible	can be done, workable
finalize	complete, finish
forfeit	give up, lose
function	act, role, work
herein	here
however	but
identical	same
impacted	affected, changed, hit
in addition	also, besides, too

in a timely manner	on time, promptly
in consonance with	agree with
indicate	show, write down
initiate	start
in order that	for, so
interface with	deal with, meet
in the course of	during, in
in view of	since
it is essential	must
justify	prove
legislation	law
limitations	limits
magnitude	size
methodology	method
monitor	check, watch
necessitate	cause, need
not later than	by
objective	aim, goal
obtain	get
operational	working
parameters	limits
permit	let
point in time	point, time
possess	have, own
prepared read	ready
prioritize	rank
procedures	rules, ways
programmed	planned
provided that	if
purchase	buy
reason for	why
reflect	say, show
relocation	move
remuneration	pay, payment
require	must, need
retain	keep
solicit	ask for
subject	the, this, your
subsequently	after, later, then
therefore	so
there is	(omit), exists
timely	prompt
transpire	happen, occur
until such time as	until
verbatim	word for word, exact
warrant	call for, permit
with reference to	about
your office	you

▲ **Table 4.1** continued

To use comparison and contrast as proof, compare or contrast what is well known to something that is unknown, then argue that what is true of the known is also true of the unknown. A good debate coach will recommend this sequence of events:

1. Develop the comparison or contrast.

2. Claim that the observations you have made are consistent (or inconsistent) with what the receiver already knows.

3. Claim that because the things compared are consistent (or inconsistent) in the ways that you have shown, they will also be consistent or inconsistent in other ways, too.

Comparison and contrast works best as proof when it doesn't leave anything to the imagination of the receiver. In short, don't assume that listeners will conclude what you want them to conclude. You must draw that conclusion for them.

To use comparison and contrast to build concreteness, you compare something that exists in the real world to the abstraction you want to strengthen and clarify. For example, the president of a major university declined the offer of a very large gift. A local broadcaster wanted to give the institution his AM radio station, including all the equipment, and the FCC broadcasting license. His idea was that the institution needed the station and that his gift would also enhance his application for a larger, clear-channel broadcasting license.

In declining the gift, the president said to a very disappointed committee of faculty and administrators, "This gift would be similar to someone giving you a thoroughbred racehorse. After he goes away, what are you going to do with the horse? You have to build a barn to house it. You have to hire someone to take care of it and to ride it. You have to maintain its health, and that involves contracting a veterinarian. You have to buy food, medicine, blankets, and saddles. You have to hire a trainer. You need a truck and a trailer, and you need someone to drive the truck. And after that, there'd be no guarantee that the horse would win any races."

Needless to say, it was a powerful use of comparison and contrast because it came from a man skilled in the appropriate uses of language.

Summary

The magic and power of language to create and maintain our world is often underestimated. Yet, we live in a world of words, not in a world of things. We defined "language" to include a body of words and a system of rules for their use that is agreed upon by a speech community. Then, language becomes the primary means by which people exchange messages.

The meanings of words and phrases reside in the users. When members of a speech community share a meaning, then that is called "denotation." When the word conjures affective associations inside the user, those associations are called "connotations."

We reviewed the Ogden and Richards *triangle of meaning* to illustrate the personal, mental process by which people associate words to their referents. That illustration lead directly to a discussion of how language controls our experiences of the world and of each other. We explained four phenomena involved in this process: abstraction, categorization, generalization, and timing. These four phenomena are at the heart of our inferences.

In addition, our inferences are molded by certain problems that are built into our language. These problems include signification (pointing to something), definition (marking its boundaries), polarization (two-valued thinking), reification (treating a symbol as if it were the thing it represents), paradox (inherently contradictory statements), and stereotyping (application of a fixed set of beliefs about a group to a single member of the group.)

Using language more effectively involves knowing how to compensate for the adverse effects of these problems. Look carefully at your own interactive style by thinking about the relationship between your language usage and your personal credibility and by choosing language wisely. Our suggestions include: expand your vocabulary, use simple language, use specific language, use action language, and use comparison and contrast. When you improve your language skills, you improve the most important feature of human communication.

Discussion Questions

1. Examine an editorial from a local or national newspaper. Look for interesting uses of simple words. Highlight four or five of these words, then write the definition that you believe the author had in mind. Compare your notes with your classmate's notes. How do you account for your findings?

2. Listen carefully as friends of both sexes talk about fashions, cars, or current affairs. Can you find any differences in how men and women use language in these contexts? What are the differences, and how do you account for them?

3. People sometimes repeat words out of habit to the point that others begin to notice the use of the words. Listen for such habitual use of words as you talk with a friend or loved-one. Make a list of such words and bring the list to class. What do you suppose caused the habit? How is the person using the word? Does it appear to mean different things under different circumstances?

References

[1]Michel Foucault, *The Archeology of Knowledge,* translated by A. M. Sheridan Smith (New York: Pantheon, 1972).

[2]For a thorough and well-documented discussion of these ideas see Gary Cronkhite, chapter 2, "Perception and Meaning," and Robert E. Sanders and Donald P. Cushman, chapter 3, "Rules, Constraints, and Strategies in Human

Communication," in Carroll C. Arnold and John Waite Bowers, (eds.), *Handbook of Rhetorical And Communication Theory* (Boston: Allyn and Bacon, Inc., 1984), pp. 51–270.

[3]This example was first described by Charles F. Hockett. *A Course in Modern Linguistics* (New York: The Macmillan Company, 1958), pp. 201–3.

[4]Charles K. Ogden and I. A. Richards, *The Meaning of Meaning,* 3d ed. (New York: Harcourt Brace Jovanovich, 1923).

[5]John C. Condon, Jr. *Semantics and Communication* (New York: Macmillan, 1985).

[6]S. I. Hayakawa, *Language in Thought and Action,* 3d ed. (New York: Harcourt Brace Jovanovich, 1972), p. 153.

[7]Charles Osgood, George Suci, and Percy Tannenbaum, *The Measurement of Meaning* (Urbana, IL: University of Illinois Press, 1957).

[8]Paul Watzlawick, *How Real Is Real: Confusion, Disinformation, Communication—An Anecdotal Introduction to Communications Theory* (New York: Vantage Books, 1977), pp. 18–19.

[9]Wendell Johnson, *People in Quandaries* (New York: Harper and Row Publishers, 1946).

[10]John O. Greene and Deanna Geddes, "Representation and Processing in the Self-System: an Action-Oriented Approach to Self and Self-Relevant Phenomena" *Communication Monographs* (December, 1988), p. 297.

Chapter 5

Nonverbal Messages

Objectives

When you finish reading this chapter you will be able to:

1. Identify and explain the major elements in nonverbal communication.

2. Understand the potential for miscommunication in sending and receiving messages.

3. Compare and contrast verbal and nonverbal message delivery.

4. List the six functions of nonverbal cues and provide examples of each.

5. Explain how nonverbal communication can add an attitudinal element to verbal communication.

Key Terms

accentuation

chronemics

contradiction

gestures

inflection

kinesics

paraverbal cues

personal space

pitch

posture

private space

proxemics

public space

regulation

repetition

substitution

supplementation/
  modification

tone (tonality)

vocal patterns

Introduction

When we think about communication, we think about the spoken word. We evaluate what people "say" and the force and flavor of how they say it. Our thoughts are usually about the words they use and their fluency of speech. But at the same time, we are also taking in information from nonlinguistic sources. Their mannerisms, their clothing, and their appearance are also important, as well as their tone of voice. In fact, their facial appearance and response may contribute more to our meaning of their message than all their words. These nonverbal elements are important matters in every communication event. Our appearance and behavior speak as loud or louder than all the words we may choose. As symbolic interactionists, we know how we "should be" and we attempt to present an image that is consistent with what we believe others think we should be.

We need to increase our awareness of nonverbal communication in every communication context. How people understand each other's talk depends, largely, on the nonverbal messages that surround the words.

This chapter examines the role and impact of nonverbal messages on others. It explores the influence of vocal and physical activity on audience reaction to messages. It also examines the effect that various interpretations may have on feelings and responses. Nonverbal communication involves many individual behaviors and perceptions. Hickson and Stacks say nonverbal communication is "that aspect of the communication process that deals with the transmission and reception of signs that are not part of natural language systems."[1] This definition does not include words that are part of the verbal communication system. Through an understanding of nonverbal behavior, we can better understand and evaluate the influence of that behavior upon receivers.

The Significance of the Nonverbal Act

For many years, researchers and scholars have told us that the bulk of information and some 93 percent of the impact of a message came from nonverbal features.[2] We communicate more than we say. Also, we know that some people can show emotion more effectively through nonverbal channels than through words.[3] To verify the truth of this claim, we need only to remember that deaf people communicate very accurately by "signing." We must pay attention to the nonverbal portion of our communication because it is the most powerful variable affecting our interpretation of the symbols that we use to interact with one another.

We may speak strongly, "I will *not* allow that person to ruin my evening," but do we appear and sound serious? Listeners use both eyes and ears. When we notice inconsistencies between the verbal and nonverbal messages, we believe the nonverbal. If we say that we are happy and act sad, people are more likely to believe that we are sad. When we communicate, the other parties are attending to both our nonverbal and verbal communication. In fact, one of the functions of nonverbal messages is to add an emotional element to our communication activities.

The newspapers are full of evidence that nonverbal messages have power. Remember when an artist in Chicago displayed the American flag on the floor and invited people to walk on it, or to express their reactions in a way they felt appropriate? This action created a furor. Many groups wanted to close the Art Institute. The story gained national attention because of a highly controversial nonverbal element of communication. If the artist had merely told his feelings about the American flag, he probably would have had less of a response than from placing the flag on the floor. His nonverbal behavior aroused deep feelings and had more force than many speeches that criticize the symbols of our society. There was an exchange of reaction to the flag's symbolism, but the shared meaning of the artist was not shared by most members of the population.

A Texas man was arrested and jailed in 1984 for burning the American flag in Dallas during the Republican National Convention. His symbolic, nonverbal act resulted in a jail term. In June 1989, the protestor's appeal that this action was protected by freedom of expression was upheld by the United States Supreme Court. Although this case may be distasteful to some people, it shows how significant and gripping nonverbal acts can be. In addition, it illustrates the ways that people can be stirred in their symbolic interaction with other people.

Relationship to the Verbal Process

Verbal and nonverbal acts often occur simultaneously. One complements the other. Paul may say, "I'm feeling very good about how I look today," and the tone of his voice, his clothing, and his general enthusiasm in speaking may provide a nonverbal confirmation of his words. At other times, the nonverbal message may be a substitute for the words. For example, in America, gesturing to someone with the middle finger extended carries a very specific meaning. Nothing else needs to be said; observers will get the message. Each day is filled with a combination of nonverbal and verbal communication. Our smiles, scowls, and amazed looks give others a clear hint of how we feel. Still they often want verbal confirmation of what they have seen. You may say, "I'm very interested in going to the Woody Allen movie," but your lethargic behavior and your monotone voice are nonverbal contradictions. The listener receives both the words and the nonverbal messages. It is difficult to believe you truly are interested in a movie, especially if you behave in such a lackadaisical manner. Your intentions are unclear because your verbal and nonverbal messages are contradictory.

Human communication is a complex behavior; it weaves together many elements. We have become so used to linking the verbal and nonverbal message systems together that we may not even associate the two on a conscious level. In verbal communication we have accepted rules that are often very formal. Those rules make our use of language more specific than our use of nonverbal messages. But even so, we can communicate nonverbally with reasonable accuracy. In a country like Japan where you may be unfamiliar with the language, it is still possible for you to get a hotel room, order a meal, show enjoyment, or seek directions nonverbally. Although nonverbal messages often are universal there is still enormous room for interpretation. Sometimes we make humorous mistakes. To illustrate, if you were in Japan you might point at your nose to indicate "I." Pointing at the nose in that culture may mean that there is a bad odor present. That is not what you meant, but it shows how confusion can result. However, most of the time we can perform the elemental parts of life using nonverbal messages, especially if the culture is our own.

If you want to be an effective communicator, you must be sensitive to the relationship between verbal and nonverbal modes of communication.

If you want to be an effective communicator, you must be sensitive to the relation between verbal and nonverbal modes of communication. Read the nonverbal messages people are sending. Listen to their actions and appearances. What they are *doing* means something, and you need to use that message to interpret their total meaning. Remember, meaning comes from shared messages and shared perceptions. If you remember the symbolic interactionist concept, then the role of nonverbal communication becomes even more significant.

The Functions of Nonverbal Messages

Nonverbal messages work with verbal messages to produce some kind of meaning. The question to ask is: How do the nonverbal messages work in relationship to speech? Given all the channels available for nonverbal messages, how can such a complex message potential be organized?

Nonverbal messages serve six major functions: repetition, contradiction, substitution, accentuation, supplementation/modification, and regulation.[4] Each of these functions contributes to what one person understands when another talks.

Repetition is defined as the process of reinforcing verbal messages through redundancy. For example, someone might ask, "How far to the next town?" You might respond, "Two miles," and at the same moment, you might hold up two fingers. Such redundancy repeats the verbal message through a different channel, thus helping others to understand what was said.

Contradiction is the opposite of repetition; it negates the verbal message. How do you "know" when a person is being sarcastic? It's when the tone of voice contradicts the words. Sometimes, however, we unintentionally contradict our words. Take the case of a small child who is trying to deny having broken a lamp. Even though the words sound honest, the face looks so guilty that we know we have the culprit.

Substitution is a function of inserting nonverbal messages for a verbal message. To illustrate, recently a student came to one of our offices to chat about her plans. She was thinking of graduate school, and wondered if her Graduate Record Examination scores had arrived. When we opened her file and found that her GRE scores were well above the requirement for admission, the woman smiled broadly, made a fist with a raised thumb, and gently shook her hand forward and backward. She did not have to say a word to express her happiness; she had conveyed it more strongly with the substituted gesture.

Accentuation is the result of nonverbal messages used to strengthen words. For example, some people shout for emphasis; others may gesture to emphasize a point. You may have noticed how some people tap the desktop with each word of an important message like: "I want you to do this today." We sometimes use nonverbal messages to accentuate our sentences.

Supplementation/modification result when nonverbal messages slightly change the words they accompany. To illustrate, you might have experienced a hug to supplement the sentence, "I love you." Or you may have noticed a smile when your friend said, "It's nice to see you." These nonverbal messages add to and modify the words as surely as tears add meaning to the sentence, "I'm sorry."

Regulation occurs when nonverbal messages help to control the flow of verbal messages. We continually use eye contact, touch, body position, vocal pitch, and so forth to regulate our talk in a conversation. For example, remember how your professors sometimes "called on" their students just by looking at them.

Thus, our nonverbal messages function in six ways. Sometimes the functions occur separately, and sometimes they occur in combinations. They occur through multiple channels, and often they occur at the same moment. Without them, we would have a very difficult time communicating. Despite this, however, our nonverbal messages may be the most fundamental cause of confusion and miscommunication.

Indicators of Feeling and Attitude

Nonverbal messages give us a great deal of information about the feelings and attitudes of other people. Those messages convey supplementary information. But the nonverbal channel is not as reliable or effective as the verbal channel because it requires more interpretation on the part of the listener. As listeners, we arrive at many conclusions that are based upon the furrows in a person's brow, the shaking of their head, the puzzled look on their face, and their grimace. We look at the way they move and stand. We also draw conclusions based on their gestures. These conclusions help us to understand the verbal messages better because they add information or emphasis.

Therefore, we rely on both verbal and nonverbal channels. Careful observers say they can infer a lot about the emotional state of a person by watching the person move and by observing their face. An old saying emphasizes how often we use our hands to express our feelings. "If you would cut off the hands of a Frenchman, he'd be unable to talk." The meaning is clear. The French use gestures and animation as such an important part of their communication that communication would fail if that element disappeared.

This is a good time to conduct a "reality check." Ask your roommate or a close friend how they think you feel today, based on your appearance and your mannerisms. If your shoulders sag and your eyes wander while others talk, your friend may say you appear bored or preoccupied. Indeed, the observer might identify correctly the general state you are feeling, but they might also be wrong. We often make judgments about people and ideas based on nonverbal cues. We interact with other people's nonverbal symbols. If we become more aware of the role of the nonverbal phase, we can improve our ability to manage our own nonverbal activity. As you will see, our sensitivity to nonverbal messages can enhance our ability to avoid communication errors and misunderstandings.

Elements in Nonverbal Communication

There are many ways to catalog the various nonverbal codes of behavior that have communicative potential. A simple organizational pattern includes three general categories: tonal cues, gross body cues, and discrete physical movements. In addition, three categories of significant, but not personal, messages are described. How we use space and how we use time have an enormous message potential. So do the artifacts with which we surround ourselves.

The human voice conveys not only spoken words, but also an enormously complex nonverbal message system. The nonverbal system, sometimes called **paraverbal cues,** conveys most of our message about how to understand what is said. The photo on p. 103 illustrates this complexity. If you spend a moment examining the illustration, you will see that the interpretations we place on the sentences that we hear are based on many potential combinations of vocal cues.

To simplify matters, focus your attention on only two elements: how pitch and pitch changes influence understanding, and how certain vocal patterns—pausing, phrasing, and so forth—contribute to the interpretation.

1.   Pitch and pitch change. **Pitch** refers to the "high" or "low" quality of the vocal sound. Pitch is one way of showing our feelings or the strength of our feelings. Often when the pitch is high, we are "raising" our voice and showing our strong feelings of excitement, fear, or happiness. When we speak lower than our optimum pitch (the level at which we do most of our talking), we are inferring our intensity or extreme seriousness. Our pitch changes reflect our feelings about the subject and even about the person to whom we are speaking. Remember how frantic some people sound when they feel anxious. We infer that they feel anxious because we hear the high pitch in their voice. When people are alarmed, they tend to speak loudly and in a high pitch. Stating strong emotional feelings (e.g., screaming) can rarely be done at a low pitch level. As an experiment, go to a secluded spot and attempt to scream at a low pitch. You will find it nearly impossible.

An important element of pitch is inflection. **Inflection** is a change in the way that we modulate our voice during speech.[5] For example, we realize someone is asking a question when a statement ends with rising inflection on the closing words. Much of the variety in our speech is the result of inflection in sound. Rising or falling inflections in sentences help to emphasize the idea or word that we hear. A voice without inflection is a flat voice. It holds little interest, and it suggests that all of the words are equally important.

Thus, pitch and inflection provide an additional dimension to the meaning of what we say. They do not compete with the language, but function as part of our message system to help clarify our meaning.

2. Vocal patterns. The tonal or **vocal pattern** that we use is revealing. A constantly flat pattern is a monotone. Monotonous talk becomes boring very quickly. We have learned to expect variation in tonal pattern as emphasis. In some cases, such as a radio announcer, we may even expect an exaggerated amount of variation. When people violate this expectation, we make certain assumptions about them. We may conclude that they are disinterested in what they are saying. We may believe that they are frightened by the experience of talking. We might feel that they are bored with us.

There are many different vocal patterns. Each one carries message potential that we do not intend to send. For example, you may hear a person speak in a "sing-song" pattern. This sing-song vocal pattern suggests lack of sincerity. Similarly, we sometimes interpret a pattern of vocalized pauses (ah, uh) or grunt-pauses to signal that the speaker is ill-prepared or uncertain of the subject matter. Of course, neither of these interpretations is necessarily correct.

Thus, variations in rate, pitch, force, and rhythm can communicate. So can pause patterns, the rhythms of speech, and the resonance of the speaker. How people articulate their words can make a difference, too. All of these features of vocal quality influence our interpretations of what is said.

So far, we have identified certain important paraverbal messages that influence communication events. If we heighten our awareness of these nonverbal features of communication, then we reduce the number of misunderstandings that occur because we misread them. This same argument is also true for a second category of nonverbal behaviors.

Kinesics

Kinesics are the "body language" elements of nonverbal communication. It involves such matters as gestures, eye behavior, facial expression, and walk. These body dimension categories can be examined in greater detail.

1. General physical movement. Movement can secure or detract from attention to any message, but it cannot accomplish both goals at the same time. For example, when we see a speaker pace back and forth in front of an audience, we often become more interested in the speaker's motion than we do in the speaker's message. The same is true in any context. If a body movement distracts from the idea, it is damaging. Some nervous speakers feel that they must constantly be on the move to "burn off" part of their excess energy. Physical movement can be effective, but only to the extent that it helps achieve a specific goal. Moving from one place to another is useful if it is used for a specific purpose, such as taking a few steps when making a transition from one major idea to the next. That provides visual evidence of the change of thoughts.

General physical activity can show the speaker's level of energy. If a speaker is active, but that action is not distracting, the audience is more interested. They are more likely to believe in both the speaker and the message.

2. Posture and gestures. American society places considerable emphasis on **posture** as an indication of feelings. We tell people to "stand tall" or "be erect" because that shows you are not a "sloppy, bored person."[5] Interestingly, people from the Orient consider American women bold and aggressive because of length of their stride and their upright posture.[6]

There are many cultural differences in posture, but we will concentrate on those of American society. When we listen to people, we believe they are more energetic and care more about their ideas if they stand erect. When we see a person slouched over a lectern or standing lazily with nearly all the weight of the body on one foot, we make negative interpretations. We say the person is not very interested in what they are discussing. Research confirms our suspicions. Ekman says that body positions are effective communicators of how intensely people feel.[7] This also applies to the feedback given by audience members. A listener who is interested tends to sit in a more alert posture.

The message is clear. If we want to appear concerned with our subject and convey that feeling of interest to our listeners, we should "stand straight and tall." People will perceive us as more confident, competent and sincere if we have good posture and if we do not have nervous habits.[8]

Gestures complement our words. They emphasize what we say. There are many types of gestures. The category system suggested by Ekman and Friesen works well to identify the kinds of gestures.[9] These consist of the following:

a. Illustrators. We use this type of gesture when we provide directions. Pointing to show a direction or moving a hand to indicate some trouble or uncertainty about an idea are examples of illustrators. Illustrators are also gestures that "draw" a picture of the object (e.g., a circle or an arrow in the air) to clarify the idea. Also, gestures that describe belong in this category.

Kinesics are the "body language" elements of nonverbal communication.

b. Regulators. A wave to indicate recognition, a head nod, and a handshake fit into this class. They are regulators because they provide guides that suggest when we should talk and when others should speak.

c. Emblems. Such gestures as finger pointing or forming a circle with the index and middle finger to indicate "okay" are signposts that could be translated into verbal language.

There is not an encyclopedia of gestures because they are too numerous to catalog. Although specific advice on how to gesture and what a gesture should contain, should be avoided, some people believe an effective gesture must contain three parts: the approach, the stroke, and the return. Gestures should be spontaneous and should help emphasize the statement of the speaker. Gestures should be natural and should not call attention to themselves. When you finish talking, people should not remember your gestures. If they remember the ideas and that gestures were present, then the gestures were effective. If they remember the gestures but cannot remember the ideas, then the gestures (and the message) were undoubtedly ineffective because the gestures became a distraction.

3. Discrete physical movements. Many of the nonverbal components in communication are slight, small physical movements that are easy to ignore. For the critical observer, however, they carry a significant message. We are most familiar with these movements in conversational settings. We make judgments about the feelings or intentions of others by interpreting a slightly furrowed brow, a squinting of an eye, or an avoidance of eye contact. These slight movements tell trained observers a great deal about the intentions and feelings of the speaker. The following section examines facial responses and slight body reactions as elements that we can use to more clearly understand and interpret meaning in communication.

4. Facial reactions. The eyes are one of the most reliable indicators of emotion. When people tell us they can "see it in your eyes," they are reasonably accurate. The dilation of the pupil and the rapid shifting of gaze tells us much about the feelings of a communicator. We conclude the person is very uneasy or is not being entirely honest. Because of this perception, it is a good idea for senders to make and to sustain eye contact with their listeners. When eye contact wanders, listeners feel that the speaker is not interested in them. That absence of eye contact can be due to nervousness or forgetfulness. Physicians in hospital emergency rooms are taught to watch the eye contact of incoming patients carefully. They learn that failure to make eye contact with others is one major component of serious psychological disorders. We would not suggest that people who do not make eye contact have a disorder. However, listeners will wonder about their interest in the subject and in the people to whom they are talking.

The mouth is another area that reveals much about a person's feelings. Pursed lips, a downturned mouth, or a constant smile send messages to listeners. Consider this fable:

> *A man sought help from a mystic about how best to influence other people. The mystic said, "I will give you a choice. You can either choose to have your mouth turned down for the rest of your life, or you can forever be smiling." The man considered the choice carefully and answered, "I will choose to have a smile on my face for the rest of my life." "Come back and see me in three years," said the mystic. "I want to hear how well you like your choice." Three years later the man returned and said to the mystic, "Please take this smile off my face. All my friends and business acquaintances are suspicious of me because I'm smiling all the time. If I looked like a grump they wouldn't believe I might have a trick up my sleeve."*

To smile only or to scowl only is not the answer to becoming an effective communicator. The mouth carries many significant messages about how you feel and think. Remember that your mouth is one of the most revealing indicators of your feeling and attitude.

5. Slight body responses. A slight shrug of the shoulders or a hesitating gesture are additional nonverbal activities that suggest particular mental states. We have heard others say, "I don't think you are interested. I guess it's the way you look; you seem too lethargic." They may be referring to our slight body responses. Audiences listen to much more than our words. Our entire body speaks. In fact, it may speak more loudly than our language.

People see our micro-movements and interpret them in various ways. The context in which those movements occur provides a large part of the meaning listeners may assign to the movement itself. Perhaps you shrug your shoulders slightly when you say, "I'm not sure if we can afford this plan of renovation for our older buildings." Listeners may be even more convinced by your actions that you may both doubt and not care if they are affordable. The physical action does not need to be large in order to affect your listeners. Remember, they observe and interpret even small movements. Audiences listen with both their ears and their eyes. Just as a "squeak" in your voice may have an impact, people may also interpret your physical movement, even when it is small or probably insignificant to you. Therefore, you need to consider all of your actions. Remember, message impact is a result of the total person speaking with voice and body.

Proxemics

Personal space is relative; we decide what amount of space is appropriate based upon the circumstances and the person.

Proxemics refers to our use of space and the way that we use space to govern the personal actions and behavior of others. Each of us needs "our space." We need a physical area where we are comfortable. Personal space is relative, and we decide what is appropriate based upon the circumstances and the person. The three dimensions of personal space are public, personal, and private.

Public space is approximately the distance beyond four or five feet. At that distance, people feel comfortable dealing with groups of others or with talking with strangers. Much of the time that we spend conversing with other students or dealing with salespeople occurs in a public setting. This is the distance most of us use when carrying on a public conversation.

Personal space is commonly referred to as "arms length" dealing. It is approximately a distance of three feet. For example, that's when you take a person into your confidence but you do not break into the intimate area that surrounds the individual. When we deal with people "personally," they feel psychologically and physically closer to us, and they feel more involved in the message. When people are more than three feet apart, the communication becomes less personal. That is why business people and others find that placing a chair for guests beside their desk—rather than directly across the desk—creates a more personal and intimate feeling. Both people can listen with their eyes and their ears. The space between them makes them feel that they can share more ideas.

Private space is a distance of less than three feet. When people communicate inside that distance, there is a perception of intimacy. For each of us, only certain people under certain conditions can come inside that space and deal with us without creating an uncomfortable feeling. Boyfriends, girlfriends, family members, and close personal acquaintances are among those people who can enter into our personal space. Such actions as whispering and speaking in confidence are part of the activity that occurs within this personal space. People who violate the space, which is often called the "three-foot limit," hurt their chances for communication. They also create a sense of uneasiness as they intrude nonverbally upon us. In certain Middle Eastern cultures, people want to "be close" to the other people. They converse inside the three-foot distance because it is the socially accepted cultural distance. In the United States, our private zone has been defined by our culture. If people violate our expectations about distance/space, communication is affected negatively. In the United States, the three-foot distance is the norm. Distance in communication affects how people perceive us and it suggests our possible intentions.

Space helps to define nonverbal relationships. We react to people, initiate communication, and engage in dialogue. Also, we develop feelings of security/insecurity, depending upon spatial relationships.

Chronemics

The way that each of us uses and structures time in our relations with others is called **chronemics.** Time is a powerful element of nonverbal communication. Many of us despise waiting for others. We attach a strong meaning to the tardiness of another person. If they are late, then we feel that they do not care about us or what we had planned. Suppose your spouse or friend says that they will meet you at the library at 7:00 P.M. But they do not arrive until 7:45 P.M. They explain that they just couldn't get there sooner. But you may feel victimized. You may ask, "Can't you ever be on time?" You may feel "second class," as if your time and your agreement to meet had no meaning to the other person. You considered the occasion and the time seriously and you arranged your schedule to be there as promised. However, the other party felt that punctuality was not important. They arranged their schedule to arrive near the agreed upon time but not punctually.

Time, as a definer, operates differently in various portions of the United States. People in metropolitan areas (e.g., New York, Chicago, Philadelphia, Los Angeles) are more restricted by time than people in the border states or in the South. City dwellers are very tied to the "clock" as an instrument that helps them to define their relationships. For example, in New York City if a tradesman tells you that he will work on your refrigerator in the early afternoon, he likely will appear or will at least notify you if he's going to be late. However, in Alabama or Missouri, the same tradesman would probably say that he will do the work that afternoon. But he may not appear for a day or two because "he just didn't get around to it because other things had interfered."

If you are a native New Yorker, you will find that the Alabama or Missouri time orientation is troubling. If you are a resident of Missouri or Alabama and go to New York, you are likely to feel that your life is run by the clock. You probably will not expect people to be so punctual. Therefore, there *is* a cultural phenomenon at work concerning our relationship with time.

We accept and expect timeliness as an essential element in some of our daily activities. The six o'clock news begins precisely at 6:00 P.M. Our favorite television program begins at 8:00 P.M.—not "about" 8:00 P.M. Classes

IT'S MORE FUN TO KNOW

Intrusion on Personal Space

American men and women react quicker to men intruding on their personal space than they do to women invading on their personal space. This is more true of Americans than of some other cultures. It was confirmed in interview studies with Turkish subjects.

See Ahmet Rustemli, "The Effects of Personal Space Invasion on Impressions and Decisions," The Journal of Psychology, 122 (2) (March 1988), pp. 113–118.

Comment . . .
These results suggest that American men should "keep their distance" more than American women.

in high school and college begin at specific times, although students and professors sometimes fail to observe the time restrictions. The classes also last for a specific time period (e.g., 40 minutes, 60 minutes, and 90 minutes). The participants expect them to end on time, since the time periods scheduled for classes in other departments is the same.

Punctuality can also express a power relationship between two people. For example, if there is an employee meeting at work, it is probably more acceptable for your boss to come in late than it is for you to come in late. Being late can also demonstrate social power as in the situation of being "fashionably" late to a party.

The power of chronemics is great. Waiting, rushing, and hesitating occur as a result of a time orientation, and our response to time delivers a strong message about us and other people. It suggests how we may feel about the individual or the mission. The time element is strongly receiver-oriented. The other person is negatively or positively affected by our actions. Perhaps we try to be on time and another person's late arrival may bother us. But think of the impact that it has on a "time oriented" other person. Remember the effect on the receiver. Just as words in a verbal message are evaluated from the receiver's perception, consider how others interpret timeliness or tardiness as part of your attitude. Lost or wasted time can be a powerful non-verbal message.

Environment

Our environment (i.e., surroundings) tell something about how we feel and how we will react to people and situations. Therefore, the environment is another powerful nonverbal message. The color or size of a room says something to you or about you. For example, one of your friends has decided to recarpet your living room according to your needs. Your friend, who owns the house, chose a color that was well suited for your lifestyle. A year later, he decided to sell his home and move to another city. When prospective buyers of the home saw the living room, they were immediately discouraged from purchasing the house. The room was carpeted with plush, expensive *electric blue* carpeting. It was a color that none of the prospective home buyers wanted in their home. Therefore, the sale price of the house was reduced to equal the expense of recarpeting the room that had been carefully carpeted only a year before. As your friend learned, colors send a strong message.

People prefer attractive surroundings and they evaluate other people based largely on their reactions to the immediate environment.[10] For example, people feel better about the surroundings and themselves when they are in a bright, sun-filled room. They respond to their environment. In fact, white reflects 80 percent of light, light buff 56 percent, pale blue 41 percent and dark green only 9 percent. Therefore, you probably would not choose dark green paint unless you wanted a room to appear smaller.

American business and industry has improved its work and selling environment by basing its rationale on this type of information. Grocery owners and department store managers play soft background music to create a positive mood for their clients. Shoppers stay in the store longer and spend more money when they are in a pleasant environment that makes them feel comfortable.

The arrangement of objects in an environment sends a message to the observer or listener. Suppose you enter a teacher's office and see a great clutter of papers on the desk and piles of books and folders strewn about the room. You probably wonder if that instructor is as disorganized in his thoughts about the subject as he is in maintaining order in his office. What does it say to you about the quality, organization, and nature of the communication of that person? Do you wonder if their communication also is as disorganized as their professional space?

In the discussion about personal, public, and private space, we observed the effect that distance had upon relationships. Similarly, the way we arrange space has a similar effect. The formal desk and chair versus a couch and coffee table as environments for conversation send different messages. The first suggests formality and power relationships. A couch and coffee table arrangement suggests that conversation and an open exchange of ideas is welcome and expected. How we arrange the areas where we hold conversations sends nonverbal messages to the participants about how open, frank, cautious, or unresponsive we might be. What does the arrangement of furniture in your living area suggest? Would a stranger feel like talking freely? Have you unknowingly built barriers to communication by the location of objects in your personal quarters?

Interpreting the Meaning of Nonverbal Messages

The potential for the misinterpretation of a nonverbal message is as great or greater than for the misinterpretation of a spoken message. Confusion can occur in a nonverbal message more easily because the nonverbal message has so many diverse elements. Interpreting a nonverbal message is even more varied than interpreting the meaning of words. When a sentence is spoken, we decode the words and interpret them in terms of our own reality. Our shared symbols affect us as symbolic interactionists.

When there is nonverbal communication, there is no "dictionary" of meaning for interpreting nonverbal cues such as vocal intonation, the light streaming through the window, the rumpled shirt of the speaker, or the bell ringing in the distance. Language is subjective. But nonverbal messages have even more individualized interpretation.

When you hear a person say, "I don't care if you pay attention to my wishes or not," the language may seem clear and virtually self-explanatory. There is only a small area for interpretation in the words themselves. But the vocal intonation, the physical stance, and the facial movements also have meaning. The location where the statement is made, the time of day, the distance between you and the speaker, and many other nonverbal elements work together to influence the statement. However, nonverbal communication is more complex, so it is more difficult to interpret accurately. The exchange of symbols can cause problems, and our misunderstandings indicate that symbolic interaction in nonverbal communication is very complex and therefore the possibility of many interpretations exists.

This confusion over meaning requires us to spend time in order to resolve the inconsistencies or misunderstandings. However, in speech if our tone suggests uncertainty, we may repeat a statement in different words, so that the tone accurately reflects our intentions. Our gestures may also suggest that we are more certain than we intended. Therefore, we can modify our gestures slightly as we rephrase or restate our idea. Much of this activity is like attempting to "unring a bell." Once the nonverbal action occurs, you cannot remove it from the receiver's mind. Attempts at clarification are useful, but they are often unsuccessful.

Conflicts between verbal and nonverbal messages sometimes are amusing. The fisherman who says, "I just caught a small bass" and extends his arms as far as they can go is illustrating a simple application of this notion. When you say in a very flat, unenthusiastic tone, "I'm just dying to see the latest Crocodile Dundee movie," the listener may conclude that you are only dying and not at all interested in seeing the film. This is a case where the nonverbal message (**tonality**) takes precedence over the spoken word. In these cases, a conversation often occurs over what the person truly means when they say they are "dying" to see the movie. Is it merely a statement to pacify the other person? Are they tired and not interested in doing anything? Are they trying to mask their true feeling that they do not want to see the movie, but do not want to prevent enjoyment by the other person?

These conflicts between the verbal and nonverbal are commonplace. Much of our communication time is spent resolving the differences between two messages. The old saying, "What you do speaks much more loudly than what you say" applies. The effective communicator tries to be consistent between what they say and the way they say it. The nonverbal element must complement the verbal message. When it does, there is successful communication. When it does not, unsuccessful communication occurs. The communication process means that the symbol systems must be complementary.

Summary

Nonverbal communication may convey our meaning even more effectively than verbal communication. The messages we send through physical, tonal, time, and space cues should be consistent with the meaning of our words. Effective speakers prepare messages that have the elements of gesture, posture, and voice control, as well as the ideas and the words that also convey ideas. The effective speaker understands that the nonverbal elements must be planned and must contribute to the goal of the communication event. Ineffective, contradictory, or distracting nonverbal activity seriously damages any speaker's effectiveness. Understanding and using the components of nonverbal communication is essential in communication preparation and delivery.

Discussion Questions

1. How important is proxemics in your world? Provide an example and explain why it is important.
2. Choose an example from a recent situation when vocal inflection provided you with important information. Why did inflection give you an indication?
3. What effect does posture have on your perception of friends? How does it apply to strangers? If there is a difference, why does it exist?

References

[1]Mark Hickson and Don Stacks, *NVC: Nonverbal Communication Studies and Applications* (Dubuque, IA: Wm. C. Brown Publishers, 1989), p. 5.

[2]J. R. Davitz, *The Communication of Emotional Meaning* (New York: McGraw-Hill, 1964), p. 201.

[3]A. Mehrabian, "Communication without Words," *Psychology Today* 2 (1968), pp. 51–52.

[4]Mark Hickson and Don Stacks, *NVC: Nonverbal Communication Studies and Applications* (Dubuque, IA: Wm. C. Brown Publishers, 1989).

[5]Jon Eisenson, *The Improvement of Voice and Diction* 2d ed. (New York: The Macmillan Co., 1965), p. 110.

[6]Burgoon, Judee K., Thomas Saine, *The Unspoken Dialogue.* Copyright © 1978 by Houghton Mifflin Company. Used with permission, p. 123.

[7]Paul Ekman, "Communication Through Nonverbal Behavior: A Source of Information About an Interpersonal Relationship." *Affect, Cognition and Personality,* ed. S. S. Tomkins and C. Izard (New York: Springer Publishing, 1965).

[8]Burgoon and Saine, p. 182.

[9]P. Ekman and W.V. Friesen, "The Repertoire of Nonverbal Behavior: Categories, Origins, Usage, and Codings," *Semiotica* 1 (1969), pp. 49–98.

[10]N. L. Mintz, "Effects of Esthetic Surroundings: II. Prolonged and Repeated Experience in a 'Beautiful' and 'Ugly' Room," *Journal of Psychology* 41 (1956), pp. 459–66.

Part II

Interpersonal Communication Settings

You have seen how the communication process operates, the way models explain much of our interaction, and the ways ideas are transferred between people. Now that you understand that meaning exists only *within* people because of their use and reaction to language, we want to discuss some of the contexts in which communication operates.

The interpersonal setting is the most common communication context. It involves one person talking to another. It is you speaking with your best friend; it is your neighbor talking to the meter reader; or it is the cook discussing problems with the owner of the restaurant. Interpersonal communications are the fabric of everyday life; they are the way that we relate to other people in the world. Through our interpersonal messages, we develop specific kinds of relationships with others. We like some people and dislike others, and we relate in different ways to people based upon how we perceive them and their attitudes. For the most part, our interpersonal relations occur through our use of language–through symbolic interaction. Although we may use a common language, we may not have common understandings or reactions to language. It is the uncertainty of reaction–the unpredictability of behavior–that makes verbal interaction with other people such a fascinating and challenging experience. Because this interaction is based primarily on the messages that we send to each other, we need to understand the principles that provide the basis for effective interpersonal roles and events. These concepts are introduced in this section. The processes and methods for improving your interpersonal communication activities are explained.

One category of the one-to-one relationship is the interview. In some ways, it has the form of an extended conversation. The aim of the interview and its formal structure help to distinguish it from conversation. As you will see, there are several different types of interviews and interviewing technique. The major emphasis will be placed on the information-securing interview, which emphasizes securing ideas and developing follow-up questions from the information already acquired.

Human communication is a powerful tool for changing the minds and actions of others. In order to relate effectively in group and interpersonal settings, you must understand the process of communication and the dynamics of people relating to people.

Chapter 6

The Interpersonal Event

Outline

When you finish reading this chapter you will be able to:

1. Specify the criteria that define an interpersonal communication event and separate it from other communication events.

2. Explain how interpersonal communication events exist in and consist of the exchange of messages.

3. Explain that the messages in an interpersonal communication event are about both tasks and relationships, and specify what the content of each of those dimensions includes.

4. Describe a hierarchy of rules that control interpersonal communication events, and explain the argument that interpersonal communication events cannot be understood without those rules.

5. Name, define, and explain six features that characterize effective interpersonal communication events.

6. Draw the Johari Window and explain how its panes describe self-disclosure.

Objectives

cultural pattern   group   rule
dyad   honesty   self-disclosure
empathy   life script   speech acts
episode   master contract   supportive
equality   positiveness

Key Terms

The number of people present in the event and their physical proximity affect the message exchange in many ways. The kind and the amount of feedback are affected. The formality of the event is affected. The ability of the parties to adapt to each other is affected. The role relationships are affected. And the completeness of the communication event is affected.

So long as parties in a communication can give and get feedback and can adapt to each other in that event, then that event may be called "interpersonal."

Exchange of Messages

This text takes a symbolic interactionist approach to the study of communication. That theoretical framework assumes three things: that the self evolves through message exchange, that communication occurs when people create and share symbols, and that this communication is only possible because people assign and take roles. We communicate with each other, and we exchange messages. Thus, do we create our relationships. Thus, we learn who we are in those relationships. This argument is absolutely essential to understanding the interpersonal communication event. (Review chapters 1 and 2, if necessary.)

Task and Relationship Issues

Table 6.1 shows that there are two dimensions in every communication event. Chapter 1, as you recall, argued that every interpersonal communication event includes both dimensions; that we send and receive messages about both of these dimensions, and that skill in sending and receiving those messages is critical to interpersonal effectiveness.

To review the basic idea, every time someone communicates with someone else, the exchanged messages carry both content information and information about how the sender understands or defines the relationship between himself and the other. Thus, for example, if your cousin says, "It's raining outside," you know instantly how to verify the "truth" of the claim. You can look through the window and see for yourself. That verification focuses attention on the content dimension of the event.

However, with this statement your cousin is also sending you signals about how he understands the relationship between you and him. In order for you to interpret the relationship messages, you must impose information from inside yourself upon it.

For example, in one context if the two of you had planned to take a long walk in the woods, the statement might "mean" something as complex

▲ Table 6.1

Two Dimensions in Every Communication Event

The Task Dimension	The Relationship Dimension

Focus on objects, phenomena and events outside of the relationship	Always in the present
	Always personal
	Observations
	Inferences
	    Feelings
	    Wants
	    Intentions
	    Openness
	    Images
	Check-out

Example: talk about the corporate profits for this quarter	

as: "I am feeling disappointed. I was counting on taking a long walk this afternoon. I like you. I feel equal to you and therefore comfortable in your company. I want you to know how I feel." But you would not be able to draw these important pieces of information from the sentence unless you knew how to interpret the talk in that context.

In another context, the same statement, "It's raining outside," might mean, "At last. There is still a chance the crop will be saved." In still another context, the sentence might "mean" something like: "I am feeling relieved. You were planning to involve me in an activity in which I didn't want to participate, but I didn't want to say that, and now I don't have to participate because the event will be canceled."

So, an interpersonal communication event includes messages about both the task dimension and the relationship dimension of communication. In order to understand the relationship dimension messages, it is essential that we understand the context in which the messages are sent. The problem is made even more complex by the fact that most of our relationship messages are sent through nonverbal channels. The tone of our voice, our phrasing, our vocal variety, and our bodily and facial cues that surround our utterances are all part of that context.

Even so, people are able to function. Moreover, most of the time we engage in interpersonal communication events without any difficulty. We are able to do this because we "know" some rules that inform our interpretations. Without such rules, we would not be able to coordinate our exchanges with other people. Without such rules, we would not be able to manage our relationships.[1]

We must be able to draw inferences about other people from the nonverbal messages they send.

Rules Control Communication Events

We believe that the ways people act depend upon their culture and their situation. The culture and the situation constrain the actions (i.e., organize them) through rules that people have evolved over time. A **rule** is a belief about what behaviors may or may not be performed in a given situation in order to achieve a particular goal.

Some rules concern meaning and some rules concern action. The rules that concern meaning are called "constitutive rules." They tell us how to understand what is said, and they control, in large measure, the things we say.

The rules that concern action are called "regulative rules." They tell us what we should and should not do. Indeed, people often speak about some of these rules if you listen carefully.

Sentences that depend on the words *should* and ought point to regulative rules. For example, you might hear someone say "You should read the assignment before you come to class on the day the assignment will be covered." Notice how that statement informs you of what you *should* do.

We know many such rules, and we can choose to follow them or to violate them. In any situation, we are confronted with a large number of rules. We choose which rules to follow and which rules to ignore.

We attach at least seven different "levels" of meaning to the messages that we exchange. So we have seven different levels of rules. These levels of rules are arranged in a "hierarchy of abstraction." Thus, each level moving up the hierarchy includes, and builds upon, the information from the more basic level below it. Each level in this hierarchy implies certain rules that influence and inform how, and how well, we understand each other. Figure 6.2 illustrates the hierarchy.

At the first level, communication occurs as data to be perceived. We live in a world of raw data. Imagine sitting in front of a major classroom building on campus between class periods. Try to be aware of the sights and sounds without actually focusing on anything specific. The stimuli in such an event are uninterpreted sight and sound data. Each bit of stimulus material is as important as any other, and none of them have any meaning. They exist merely as data—as vibrations in the air or as light waves.

Clearly, the way those sounds are formed and the nature of those visual stimuli are important parts of an interpersonal communication event. They attract attention to themselves, or they don't. They form units of speech, or they don't. They carry information about themselves that can be interpreted to mean certain things. Still, at this basic level the sensory data are only uninterpreted bits and pieces.

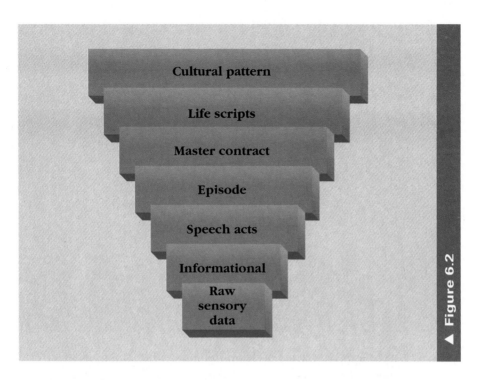

Cultural pattern

Life scripts

Master contract

Episode

Speech acts

Informational

Raw
sensory
data

At the second level, meaning occurs for the first time. The raw data from level one are interpreted and are converted into **information.**[2] Now you are focusing on facial expressions and catching bits of conversation from the people. This is the content level. A statement such as "It's raining outside" carries content, but it doesn't say anything about the speaker's attitudes or intentions. To understand the statement we need something more than content alone.

At level three, we learn of the speaker's intentions because speech acts are occurring. **Speech acts** are units of talk that convey intention. A statement such as "It's raining" may accomplish several different things. It may carry information to describe the weather, it may work to change the subject of a conversation, or it may express the relief of the speaker who is worried about his crops. It can comfort the listener. Thus, to understand the statement fully we must understand the speech acts that are occurring. At level three, the statement becomes something done by the speaker to the listener, and thus takes on an added level of meaning.[3]

At level four, we gather meaning from the kind of event—episode— that is occurring. An **episode** is a sequence or set of messages that have a beginning and an end, and it is understood as a unit. For example, we know when we are having a fight, having lunch, or having a meeting.

The master contract tells us who we are in relationship to each other.

Notice how the nature of the episode gives form to a statement like "It's raining outside." Suppose two separate episodes. In the first episode, your friend finds you sitting outside soaked with water for no apparent reason. In the second episode, you and your sweetheart are jumping for joy because now you don't have to go to that awful picnic to "meet the family."

You might understand the statement in the first episode as a question of why you are outside. In the second episode, you might understand the statement as a happy exclamation. Clearly, we must be able to identify the episode in order to understand each other. But even this is not enough.

At meaning level five, we begin to apply what are called master contracts. A **master contract** is an expectation that is composed from patterns of episodes of the kinds of communication events that should occur in a particular relationship. The master contract tells us who we are in relationship to each other.

For example, we expect professors to behave in certain ways. They organize and deliver lectures, write tests, offer academic advice, and so forth. We also expect professors to refrain from behaving in other ways. We don't expect them to ask students for dates. We don't expect them to show up at Friday night fraternity parties unless they have been specifically invited.

Similarly, your friend's master contract did not have an expectation of finding you sitting in the rain. This "abnormal" activity led to questions of what was wrong. All people have master contracts that inform them of who they are, what to expect, and how to behave when they are together.

At meaning level six, life scripts, your sense of yourself in the world, inform your communication events.[4] A **life script** is a set of assumptions, expectations, and rules for our lives that are established for us by our parents and other people with whom we interact. Scripts have cultural characteristics, (e.g., the American dream, black is beautiful, religious characteristics [protestant work ethic, Catholics don't use artificial birth control]), familial characteristics (Jones don't lie, Kennedys go into politics, the Smiths are a Navy family), and sexual characteristics (men are good journalists, women are good at business).

Notice how the life script is part of your sense of self. If you experience yourself as a "serious student," you are likely to form different master contracts and engage in different episodes from the person who experiences themself as a "party animal." Thus, life scripts are a very important part of the meanings that you can derive.

Finally, at meaning level seven, cultural patterns are added into the mix of things that influence our interpretations of communication events. A **cultural pattern** is a broad image of the world order and a human being's relationship to that order.[5] These cultural patterns provide a cultural framework that make the lower levels of meaning legitimate. A cultural pattern consists of such things as mythology and ideology that shape and reinforce our ways of acting in the world.

To illustrate, it is part of the American cultural pattern to value rugged individualism and personal freedom. This important cultural value forms the controversy over the 1989 Supreme Court decision to allow that a person had the right under the First Amendment to burn the American flag as a symbolic act. President George Bush's consequent initiative to win a constitutional amendment was also based on that cultural value, but from a different perspective. His view was that the flag symbolized the very freedom that the Supreme Court was protecting and that the flag was the one symbol that should not be desecrated.

In summary, we coordinate our interpersonal communication by relying upon an intricate and complex set of rules. As fluent speakers, and as part of the culture, we know these rules and we use them to inform our interpersonal communication events. The logic of the regulative rules that we apply in a conversation coordinate how we understand it. The rules also compel us to behave in certain ways in order to achieve our goals. They grow out of and give rise to our continuing exchange of symbols.

Thus far, an interpersonal communication event includes at least two people who can give immediate feedback, and two people who have the ability to adapt to each other. Their interpersonal event exists and consists of the exchange of messages (i.e., messages about their tasks and topics, and messages about their relationship).

Interpersonal Exchange Model

Chapter 1 introduced and described several models of communication, including the interpersonal exchange model that is presented in figure 6.3. The models were useful as you began your study of human communication because they provided an overview of the complex process of interpersonal communication. The Interpersonal Exchange Model may seem even more meaningful to you now that you understand the subtle complexity of the various parts.

Again, follow through the model as Person *A*. You come into contact with someone else, and that person waves and says "Hello" to you. You pick up on the person's verbal and nonverbal signals, and you check those signals against the hierarchy of rules that you have for relating to that person in that context. Your assessment of those rules informs what you can perceive, what you know about your relationship with that person, and what to expect from and how to behave in response to that person. On the basis of this assessment, you weigh the risks of your exchange, and then predict whether you can trust that person. That prediction results in another review of the complex set of rules that pertain to the moment and the context. You review the rules; then you select which ones to use as you formulate your messages.

After choosing your rules, you behave. Your behavior becomes the raw sensory data upon which they will act as they go through the same process as you. Then, you coordinate the moment with them. You evolve your behavior out of the logical force of rules that control the moment. You assign role expectations, and then you establish a contract to behave in certain ways with them in that context. Therefore, you create the relationship as you act.

Remember that people interpret a communication event. Their roles (i.e., roles are behavior patterns) in that event both inform and are informed by the message exchange. Your choices of behavior in that moment—the things you say and do—make the difference between being satisfied and dissatisfied with the interpersonal communication event.

The choices you make are up to you. They are your responsibility. However, a question arises: Are there any guidelines to suggest effective and satisfying ways to communicate? Fortunately, there are.

Six Behaviors for Effective Communication

Carl Rogers first articulated the idea that effective interpersonal communication can be characterized by certain, well-identified features.[6] The figure is not from Rogers, however. Since he published *On Becoming a Person* in 1961, a large body of literature has evolved that verifies and supports Carl

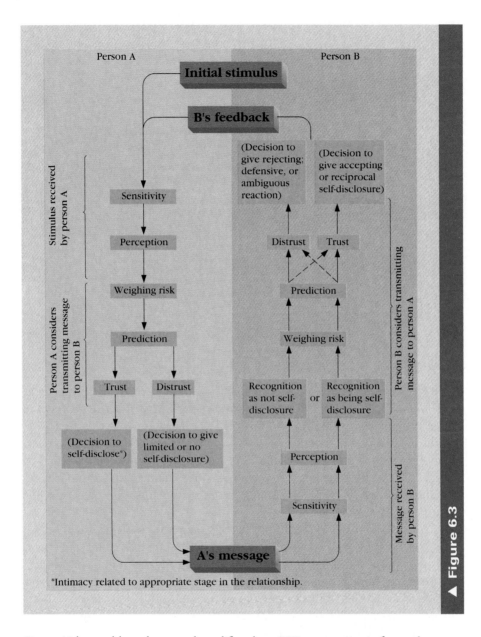

▲ Figure 6.3

Rogers' ideas, adds to them, and modifies them.[7] We are uncertain from where this information originated. But the source is not so important as its content. The six characteristics in figure 6.4—honesty, openness, empathy, positiveness, supportiveness, and equality—constitute a code of interpersonal behavior that you can adopt and follow if you wish. The benefit of adopting it is having greatly improved, more satisfying relationships.

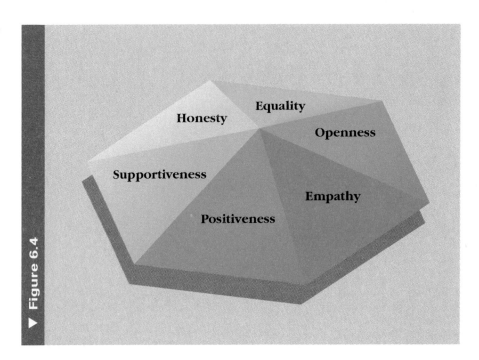

Honesty

Honesty, the quality of being honest, when applied to an interpersonal communication event, implies freedom from deceit or fraud. The event is characterized by truthfulness, sincerity, and frankness. To be honest is to behave in a way that is genuine. We can achieve the goal of honesty in communication events if we understand that it, as all the other characteristics of effective interpersonal communication, includes both attitude and behavior. Both the attitude, or pre-disposition to behave honestly, and the behavior are entirely a matter of choice.

But honesty may sometimes require enormous wisdom and courage. It is difficult to open yourself to others under the best of circumstances. In important relationships that must rest on the foundation of honesty, we may sometimes find that telling the truth is nearly impossible. We simply don't talk easily about feelings, wants, or our intentions. We don't focus well on our images of each other, and we certainly don't talk easily about them, especially when they are negative.

Do you always tell your loved ones when you are feeling hurt by their actions? Do you always make it clear when you think someone you love has hurt you? Do you express yourself truly and openly every time, even when doing so might risk hurting the other person's ego? Do you always say exactly what you want? Do you always confront betrayal? Do you always report your images of them to the people who are important in your life? We expect not.

Self-disclosure is essential to interpersonal growth and intimacy.

Partly, we're not fully honest with each other because people in our society do not have an attitude of being honest. More likely a lack of candor and frankness results because people do not have the communication skills that they need to be other than honest. In the next chapter, we will develop a system for talking about relationships.

Openness

Self-disclosure is defined as revealing one's thinking, feelings, and beliefs to another. There is a good deal of literature to support the idea that self-disclosure is essential to interpersonal growth and intimacy and that self-disclosure and trust are reciprocal. Hence, trust is a necessary precondition to self-disclosure, and self-disclosure is a necessary precondition to trust. Indeed, of all the features of effective interpersonal communication, self-disclosure may be the most widely researched.[8]

Despite all this research, researchers do not agree on how and what to disclose, or how much and what kind of self-disclosures are most conducive to effective interpersonal communication. For example, some scholars argue that self-disclosures should be positive, while others think the matter depends upon an array of variables. Some scholars argue that the greater the self-disclosure, the greater the intimacy in the relationship, while others aren't so sure.

IT'S MORE FUN TO KNOW

Interpersonal Communication and Personal Influence

"In lower-level election races, at least, where the visibility of the candidates and the coverage given by the mass media are low, interpersonal communication can play an important role in an election.

See Lynda Lee Kaid, "The Neglected Candidate: Interpersonal Communication in Political Campaigns, *Western Journal of Speech Communication*, 41:4 (Fall 1977), p. 252.

Comments . . .

Where there is a good opportunity to talk to people directly, and where personal influence is considered important, interpersonal communication is the best tool for gaining support. In local elections (or community campaigns), personal talk and contact has a strong influence.

The key to success is *appropriate* self-disclosure. Successful interpersonal communication is characterized by the right amount and the right kind of self-disclosure at the right time.

For example, we know that a relationship is growing when another person becomes increasingly able to predict our behavior, our wants, and our needs. Suppose the telephone rings, and a friend has called to invite Ellen and her husband to dinner on short notice. Knowing that John would rather relax at home after a hard day, and remembering his description as he left home that morning, Ellen might decline the invitation without asking John about it first.

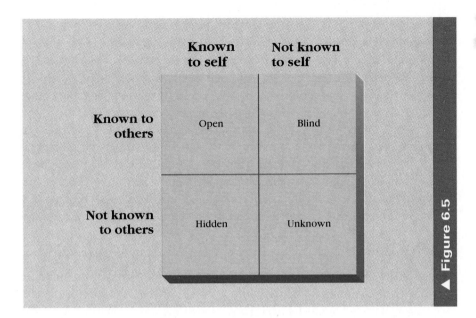

▲ Figure 6.5

Such accurate prediction of others can only occur if the people in a relationship accurately and honestly communicate their needs, wants, preferences, and expectations to each other. The more we know about how another person views themself, the better we are able to make such predictions.

Yet, there are some things that people should not disclose because to disclose them would be imprudent. For example, partners in a second marriage probably should not disclose very much about the intimate details of their first marriages. To do so would probably hurt other people.

Two psychologists, Joseph Luft and Harrington Ingham, have developed a well-known model, called the *Johari Window,* to help describe the importance of self-disclosure in a relationship.[9] It is presented as figure 6.5. A metaphor is used to present ourselves "through a window."

Information about you that is known to you and to other people resides in the "open self." For example, both you and your friend would probably know if you are a member of a social fraternity. That information is in your "open self."

Information that is known to you, but that you do not reveal about yourself is in the "hidden self." Your secret fears or your favorite success fantasy would be examples of such "hidden self" information.

When other people know things about you that you do not know about yourself, that information is in the "blind self." To illustrate, you may be unaware of the high regard others in your organization have for your leadership ability as reflected in your work in groups. Similarly, you may not realize that others have begun to count on you for certain kinds of expertise.

Finally, Luft and Ingham state that there must also be an "unknown self," that is, an area of information about ourselves that neither we nor others know. An example might be an undiscovered talent or a phobia.

In general, the more you know about someone, the fewer false assumptions you are likely to make about that person. On the other hand, it is also possible to be too open. The skill of self-disclosure is the ability to discover what degree of openness is appropriate in a given relationship at a given time. Chapter 8 will describe a method for talking about relationships that will help you to identify and manage an appropriate degree of openness.

Empathy

Empathy refers to supportive behavior that is characterized by identification with the experiences, feelings, and problems of others, and with the affirmation of the other's self-worth. Thus, empathy is a reaction to someone that reflects recognition and identity with a similar emotional state. When empathic people talk with each other, they make an effort to experience each other's point of view, and they look for opportunities to confirm each other. Empathy is so important to effective interpersonal communication that at least one scholar wants to equate empathy and communication competence, arguing that the behaviors and skills involved in both concepts are the same.[10]

There is general agreement that at least three separate dimensions to empathy exist.[11] One dimension of empathy is *perspective taking*—the ability to take on or adopt the view of another person. A second dimension of empathy is *emotional contagion*—experiencing an emotional response like the other person's, as a result of observing or anticipating the other person's emotion. A third dimension is *empathic concern* for the other person—or caring what happens to them.

When empathic people talk with each other, sentences are spoken that imply each of these dimensions. For example, "You've said you felt awful when you didn't get that job you wanted. I think I can understand the feeling. At least, I know how I felt when that happened to me." Or you might hear someone say, "I have had some frustration myself, so I can understand how you might be feeling," or "I think I can see your point of view, but I want to be sure." Such sentences confirm that the other person's experiences are valid, and they send the message, "I care about your point of view."

Thus, empathy is both attitude and skill. The attitude is genuine caring about the other person. The skill is in letting the other person know that you care, by both your verbal and nonverbal messages.

Gerald Miller and Mark Steinberg argued that empathy must flow from your sensitivity to the other person and that it is part of a transactional process.[12] That is, we receive information from others about their experiences. We read these messages accurately, decide how to respond, and then respond. This transactional process is very difficult because we can't always interpret the other person's nonverbal messages accurately. The next chapter describes how the skill in this case is learning to bring observations and inferences up to the level of talk. It is an ability to state what you are observing and inferring, and then to give and seek feedback often.

Empathy implies other-directedness and careful listening. To be empathic, you have to direct your energies away from yourself and toward other people. You have to focus upon them. You have to listen actively, as described in chapter 3, to what they have to say, and you have to learn how to talk about your relationships with them. The next chapter will describe a system for talking about your relationships.

Positiveness

As a characteristic feature of effective interpersonal communication, **positiveness** refers to behavior that is sure and constructive, rather than to behavior that is skeptical and doubtful. Positiveness emphasizes the hopeful side of things by looking to the good in people and events. Positiveness affirms and builds; it does not attack or tear down.

Positiveness is both attitude and skill. The attitude is that other people are basically OK, just the way they are. The skill is in learning to reflect the attitude with verbal and nonverbal messages.

Perhaps you have known someone whose behavior tends to be negative. You may have heard that person disconfirm others, find the worst possible view of a situation, or find fault with the organization or the people in the organization. How did you like being around that person?

We knew a man whose orientation was basically negative. As we observed his behavior over a period of time, we came to understand the destructive nature of that negative orientation. Let's call him Frank.

Frank entered our organization as assistant professor just out of graduate school; he'd received his Ph.D. with honors from one of the finest educational institutions in the United States. He had already published three or four essays in national, refereed journals by the time he had completed his degree. Everyone thought Frank would be one of the brightest young professors in America, and we were looking forward to having him in the department.

Soon, however, Frank began to find fault. Sometimes, of course, there was reason—people make mistakes. But Frank's fault-finding soon seemed intolerant. He found fault with the library staff. He didn't like the dean. He found fault with the chairman of the department. He found fault with his colleagues.

If you'd ask Frank, "How are you," he would say something like: "I'm lousy," or "I'm really mad right now," or "I'm disgusted with. . . ." If you didn't ask Frank how he was feeling, he might tell you anyway.

As time went on, Frank's research continued to be excellent, but students started to report that he was being unfair in his criticisms of them. They reported, as well, that he would often, by name, find fault with his colleagues in his lectures. Of course, people were offended. Faculty began to avoid working with Frank; students began to find ways to avoid taking his classes. These events became part of a massively damaging self-fulfilling prophecy. Frank became more and more sullen and angry as these things occurred. The department was on the brink of a very damaging split when the members realized that the source of the trouble was Frank's negativism.

Frank knew that he was a knowledgeable and productive scholar and a good teacher. His colleagues knew these things, too. Yet, when it came time to make the decision to award tenure to Frank, not one tenured member of the faculty voted in favor of him. Eventually, Frank had to leave the university.

Learning to be positive also implies learning how to ask for what you want in a positive manner. It implies learning how to be nurturing. It implies learning how to make constructive suggestions instead of destructive criticisms. Thus, positiveness is both an attitude and a skill.

Supportiveness

In the context of interpersonal communication events, **supportive** refers to behavior characterized by description (rather than evaluation), problem orientation (rather than control), spontaneity (instead of strategy), empathy (as opposed to neutrality), equality (as opposed to superiority), and provisionalism (rather than certainty). Supportiveness aims to sustain a person, to back him up, and to reinforce him. Supportiveness is behavior that maintains a relationship rather than damages it.

Supportiveness is both attitude and skill. It is an attitude in the sense that you think in other-directed and supportive ways. It is skill because the behavioral choices do not seem to come naturally. We have to develop the habit of supportiveness. We have to evolve habitual ways of behaving that are not competitive and that assume other people are okay, just as we find them.

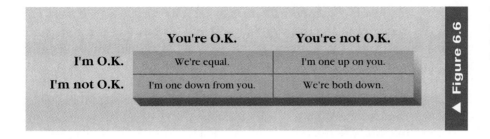

Figure 6.6

The central themes of transactional analysis

	You're O.K.	You're not O.K.
I'm O.K.	We're equal.	I'm one up on you.
I'm not O.K.	I'm one down from you.	We're both down.

Equality

In the context of interpersonal communication, **equality** refers to showing respect for another person and minimizing differences in ability, status, power, and intellectual ability. It is based on the idea that people are equally meritorious in their essential humanity. You may be bigger or smaller, older or younger, richer or poorer, but these things do not make you more or less human. You have equal humanity, and you are entitled as a right of birth to your dignity as a human being.

As a characteristic of effective interpersonal communication, equality is both attitude and skill. How you think about yourself and others is a matter of habit and of choice. So is how you treat other people.

About twenty years ago, Thomas Harris wrote a now-famous book with the catchy title, *I'm OK—You're OK* that centered directly on this idea of interpersonal equality.[13] In his book he presented a model that resembles the Johari Window. It is displayed in figure 6.6.

The basic idea is that we develop certain orientations or psychological positions toward life and the people in our lives and that these orientations determine the kind of behaviors we are likely to exhibit. For example, if you experience yourself, typically, in the first quadrant, the I'm OK—You're OK position, then you will find yourself feeling and acting confident. You are likely to be constructive in your conversations with others by making suggestions that help and nurture.

People whose life orientations are basically in the second quadrant, the I'm OK—You're Not OK psychological position, tend to act superior and to be arrogant. There is no sense of equality in this quadrant. In contrast, people who tend toward the third quadrant, the I'm Not OK—You're OK psychological position, experience themselves as inferior. They get depressed easily, and their behaviors may be dependent. They certainly do not think of themselves as equal, and they do not grant others that status.

People who experience themselves in the fourth quadrant, the I'm Not OK—You're Not OK psychological position, tend to feel that things are hopeless; that they, too, are without hope, and that this futility is a constant in their lives.

Interpersonal communication that is characterized by equality falls into the first quadrant. To borrow the language from transactional analysis theory, equal participants would each assume their own OK-ness, and also their partner's OK-ness. You can develop the habit of behaving in confident and constructive ways. You can learn the habit of treating people as equal. The attitude will then follow as a result of the behavior, and you will come to see others as equal.

Summary

This chapter has provided a broad description of an interpersonal communication event. Such events include at least two people interacting in some context. The event exists in and consists of the exchange of messages, and the messages are about both tasks and relationships. Interpersonal communication events are controlled by a complex set of rules that exist in a hierarchy. Without those rules, we would not be able to coordinate our meanings with each other.

An interpersonal exchange model of interpersonal communication was described and that model—understood in the context of controlling rules—suggests six kinds of behavior that characterize effective interpersonal communication. These characteristic features are honesty, openness, empathy, positiveness, supportiveness, and equality. Such features constitute a code of interpersonal behavior that anyone can choose to adopt.

Discussion Questions

1. Step 1. Working in a group of about six members, write down those features of a relationship that make it *healthy.* After about ten minutes of brainstorming with your group members and with someone making notes, then:
Step 2. Rank the top ten items in order according to how important your group members feel these characteristics are to a healthy relationship.
Step 3. Place your list on the chalkboard for comparison and contrast with other group lists. Working as a class, discuss these questions:

▲ Do you find any significant similarities or striking differences among the several group-produced lists? How do you account for these?
▲ What implications for your personal choices in behavior do you find in the lists of characteristics?

2. Look up the definitions for each of these terms; then in a discussion with three or four of your classmates, try to identify the impact on a conversation with a friend if each of these features of effective interpersonal communication were missing:

- ▲ openness
- ▲ empathy
- ▲ honest
- ▲ positiveness
- ▲ supportiveness
- ▲ equality

References

[1]This idea is called "Coordinated Management of Meaning." It is one of the several "rules theories" that underpin the present discussion. See W. Barnett Pearce and Vernon Cronen, *Communication, Action, and Meaning* (New York: Praeger Publishers, 1980). Vernon Cronen, W. Barnett Pearce, and Linda Harris, "The Coordinated Management of Meaning," in Frank E. X. Dance (ed.), *Comparative Human Communication Theory* (New York: Harper and Row, 1982). W. Barnett Pearce, "The Coordinated Management of Meaning: A Rules Based Theory of Interpersonal Communication," in Gerald R. Miller (ed.), *Explorations in Interpersonal Communication* (Beverly Hills, CA: Sage Publications, 1976), pp. 17–36.

[2]This notion of information—interpreted data—is different from the one used by information theorists. Their notion is that the information exists in the stimuli, themselves. In that theory, the greater the information, the larger the number of alternatives, and the less the certainty. So information is much like news. Information theorists argue that interpretation reduces the uncertainty and, thus, the amount of information in a situation. Eliminate all of the uncertainty and there would be no news left in a situation.

[3]John R. Searle, *Speech Acts: An Essay in the Philosophy of Language* (Cambridge: Cambridge University Press, 1969).

[4]This is Eric Berne's idea, first articulated in print in 1958, and part of what became the "Transactional Analysis Movement." The classic works are: Eric Berne, "Transactional Analysis: A New and Effective Method of Group Therapy," *American Journal of Psychotherapy* 12 (1958), pp. 735–43. Eric Berne, *Games People Play* (New York: Grove Press, 1964). Tom Harris, *I'm OK—You're OK* (New York: Harper and Row, 1969).

[5]Vernon E. Cronen and W. Barnett Pearce, "Logical Force in Interpersonal Communication: A New Concept of the 'Necessity' in Social Behaviors," *Communication* 6 (1981), p. 21.

[6]Carl B. Rogers, "The Characteristics of a Helping Relationship," *On Becoming a Person* (Boston: Houghton Mifflin Company, 1961), pp. 39–58. See, also, *Personnel Guidance Journal* 37:1 (September, 1958), pp. 6–15.

[7]For a recent and exceptionally fine example, see Donald P. Cushman and Dudley D. Cahn, Jr., "Interpersonal Communication and the Reassessment of Relationships," *Communication in Interpersonal Relationships* (Albany: State University of New York Press, 1985), pp. 87–100.

[8]For an excellent, brief review of this literature, see Howard Giles and Richard L. Street, Jr., "Communicator Characteristics and Behavior" in Mark L. Knapp and Gerald R. Miller (eds.), *Handbook of Interpersonal Communication* (Beverly Hills, CA: Sage Publications, 1985), pp. 205–62.

[9]The Johari Window was created by Joseph Luft and Harry Ingham during a summer laboratory in group development at UCLA in 1955. Their idea was later published by Luft in his book, *Group Processes: An Introduction to Group Dynamics* (Palo Alto, CA: Mayfield Publishing Company). See the second edition, 1970, pp. 11–20.

[10]Mark V. Redmond, "The Relationship Between Perceived Communication Competence and Perceived Empathy," *Communication Monographs* 52:4 (December, 1985), pp. 377–82.

[11]James B. Stiff, James Price Dillard, Lilnabeth Somera, Hyun Kim, and Carra Sleight, "Empathy, Communication, and Prosocial Behavior," *Communication Monographs* 55:2 (June, 1988), pp. 198–213.

[12]Gerald R. Miller and Mark Steinberg, *Between People: A New Analysis of Interpersonal Communication* (Chicago: Science Research Associates, 1975), pp. 174–76.

[13]Thomas Harris, *I'm OK—You're OK* (New York: Harper and Row, 1969).

Chapter 7

The Interpersonal Relationship

Introduction
Task and Relationship

Principle of Absolute Present

Principle of Personalizing

Observations and Inferences
Fact-Inference Confusion

Observations

Inferences
- ▲ feelings
- ▲ wants and expectations
- ▲ intentions
- ▲ openness
- ▲ images

Feedback
How to Give Feedback
- ▲ stay in the present tense
- ▲ personalize your talk
- ▲ talk about your feelings
- ▲ talk about your wants and expectations
- ▲ talk about your intentions, your openness, and the images that you have

How to Get Feedback from Others
- ▲ ask in present tense
- ▲ be supportive

Summary

Outline

When you finish reading this chapter you should be able to:

1. Compare and contrast the task dimension and the relationship dimension of communication.

2. Name and explain the component parts of the relationship dimension of communication.

3. Explain the principle of the absolute present.

4. Explain the principle of personalizing.

5. Describe the problem of fact-inference confusion.

6. Specify how to give and how to get feedback.

Objectives

---

absolute present	fact-inference confusion	observations
agenda for talking about relationships	feedback	openness
	feelings	personalizing
complementary	image	symmetry
emotions	inferences	want
expectation	intention	

Key Terms

Introduction

Chapter 6 described, in general terms, what is involved in an interpersonal event. Effective interpersonal communication is characterized by openness, positiveness, honesty, supportiveness, and equality. These characteristic features grow from the interpersonal sensitivity exhibited by people in relationships. That sensitivity is the basis for interpersonal accommodation, for trust, and for self-disclosure.

This chapter will focus on the relationships. The goal is to suggest the means by which partners in a relationship can manage their relationships more effectively. To accomplish this goal, the chapter is designed around a particular strategy. First, it will review the two dimensions that exist in every communication event and will identify the component parts of all relationships. Second, it will discuss the idea that those relationships can exist only in the present tense and that they are a function of the individual's own nervous system. Finally, it will develop an **agenda for talking about relationships** that will guide you when you want or need to talk about your relationship with another person. In particular, it will discuss in detail the skills you will need if an important relationship is at risk. The major features of that agenda are observations, inferences, and feedback.

This chapter's fundamental argument is that you can do a lot to improve the quality of your life if you take the trouble to learn how to manage your relationships more effectively.

Task and Relationship

When we talk with each other, we usually select words that refer to topics and to tasks. For example, you might say, "Mary, please pass the salt." The task is clear. You want Mary to pick up the container of white crystals and hand it to you. All of this is in the task dimension. Every communication event includes both a task dimension and a relationship dimension. (See table 6.1.)

Notice that the sentence, "Mary, please pass the salt," also suggests how the speaker understands the relationship. The speaker and Mary are equals. If Mary were in a superior (one-up) position in the speaker's mind, then the sentence would have been a request, something like: "Mary, when it is convenient, would you be willing to pass the salt?" If Mary were in a subordinate position (one-down), then the sentence would have been a command, something like: "Pass the salt, Mary."

The matter of defining the relationship is typically achieved without direct talk about the relationship. We imply by tone of voice, by the choice of words, or by some combination of verbal and nonverbal cues what we understand the nature of our relationships to be.[1]

When power is balanced in the relationship dimension, it is called **symmetry.** If the power is not balanced; that is, if the speaker implies that someone is one-up or one-down, then the relationship is termed **complementary.**[2]

This matter of symmetry and complementary can be enormously important to the success of an interpersonal communication event. If you are like most people, when someone "puts you down" you are likely to be offended. Perhaps you respond to the put-down with defensiveness. Perhaps you attack, or want to attack, the person who put you down. And, of course, if you do decide to indulge yourself in that attack, the other person is likely to defend themself.

The model in table 6.1 rests upon two fundamental assumptions. The first assumption is that we cannot escape the present tense. This idea is called "the principle of the absolute present." The second assumption is that each person is responsible for the feelings, wants, interpretations, and so forth that they impose or project into the communication event. Let's discuss these ideas one by one.

Principle of Absolute Present

We live in the present tense. We live right now. You are alive right now, as you are reading this line. All of your experience is occurring now. You can't escape the present.

You can remember the past, of course, but that reminiscence is now a present tense activity. What you remember is stored, in the present, in your mind/brain, and you access it in the present.[3] You can also anticipate your future. For example, you can imagine how it will feel and what it will be like to go to bed tomorrow night. You can get an image in your mind of your bedroom and of yourself reaching over to turn off the light, and then snuggling down under the covers, sinking happily into the mattress as you relax. You can imagine all of that, but notice that the imagination is a present tense activity.

You can also imagine interactions that have yet to occur. For example, you might imagine a conversation with your roommate as a way to rehearse what you want to say. That anticipation can be enormously important to your success in the event, or it might be dysfunctional. However, the point is that people do it in the present tense. Notice that such imagined interactions are dominated by one's self and that they occur primarily about relationship issues.[4]

This idea of the **absolute present** is a liberating idea; for once you accept it, you understand that all of your relationships are in the present, too. Everything in your relationship with your mother, including all of your remembrances and all of your imagined futures with her, are locked into the

We can think about the past and the future, but we cannot escape the present. This woman's relationships are stored inside her in the present tense.

present tense. What has passed between you and your mother (or anyone else in your life) has vanished, except for a stored memory somewhere in your mind. You are in charge of that memory. You give it shape and detail and focus and point of view. You are creating that recollection out of your own storage banks, always in the present.

Now combine this idea with another. Your memory of the past is probably not accurate. You have forgotten many of the details. You have distorted other details. And finally, you have interpreted all of the details in your own peculiar way. Thus, your recollection is not of what actually happened. It is your image, stored in the present, of what happened. And your recollection is never going to be like your mother's recollection of the same event.

The main idea is that we live in the present, and so all of our experience is in the present, including our relationships with other people. We can think about the past (not very accurately) and we can think about the future (pure guesswork), but we cannot escape the present.

Principle of Personalizing

A second valuable idea flows directly from this one. This idea is called **personalizing.** The point, the second basic assumption of the chapter, is that we are personally responsible for all of our relationship experiences. The idea of personalizing requires some explanation.

Basically, because we construct interpretations of each other, we're responsible for those interpretations, and we can change them.

▲ Figure 7.1

If you experienced this person as attractive, where does the responsibility for that experience lie? Is it an attribute of the person or a judgment you yourself made?

We can illustrate this idea in a couple of ways. For example, suppose your friend, Sharon, and you meet the man in figure 7.1 one afternoon. Sharon says to him, "You're beautiful." As you think about Sharon's statement, you come to understand the idea of personalizing. Sharon sees the man. Then she compares her experience of the man to a set of standards in her mind. The comparison yields a personal judgment, one of her own doing. She is personally responsible for the judgment.

Now, if Sharon were going to express this judgment accurately, she would not say, "You're beautiful." Rather, she would choose words to make clear that she knows she's judging the man. She would then say something like, "I experience you as beautiful," or "You seem beautiful to me."

Beautiful is a judgment. It is a construction that comes out of Sharon's nervous system. Other things, besides judgments, are functions of a person's nervous system. For example, your feelings flow from your nervous system. To give you a second example of personalizing, suppose you hear Sharon say something like this to the man:

"You make me want to dance. You make me smile. You make me happy."

Clearly, Sharon, and not the man, is responsible for her feelings and her wants. Because they are a function of her nervous system, they are not the man's responsibility. So, if she were going to personalize those sentences correctly, she would make it clear that she, and not he, is responsible for what's going on inside herself.

She would say	She would not say
When I'm with you, *I* feel happy. *I smile* when I'm with you, and *I want* to dance.	*You make* me happy. *You make* me smile. *You make* me want to dance.

If you learn these two ideas, the principle of the absolute present and the principle of personalizing, and if you internalize them and make them a part of your interactive style, then you will eliminate most of the problems that occur in your relationships with other people.

Observations and Inferences

Relationships exist in the present and they are always inside the individual parties in the relationship. Knowing that, it makes sense to identify all of the component parts of a relationship. Table 6.1 lists all of those component parts.

Remember from chapter 2 that you take information inside yourself and then interpret that information. The information is about yourself, and it is about the world outside yourself. That idea of personal perception becomes the foundation for learning to identify and to talk about your relationships when you want to do so. A relationship exists in the present tense as a function of what you observe and of what you make of the information you observe.

Fact-Inference Confusion

It seems to be very difficult for some people to separate what they are observing from what they are guessing. Such a simple sentence as "Billy, you look happy this morning" illustrates the problem of **fact-inference con-**

fusion that so often gets in the way of effective communication. If someone says to you, "You look happy this morning," you know that the person has observed something about you, and then has drawn an inference about your emotional state.

It is not possible to look at a person and see the current affective state. Rather, we see facial expression, bodily tension, posture, gesture, and other nonverbal cues. We listen to the sound of a person's voice or to the tone and their delivery. Thus, we observe information, take it inside ourselves, and then we interpret it.

What does "happy" look like? You cannot see it; it has no "look" at all. When a statement like "Billy, you look happy this morning" is made, the speaker is guessing. The entire statement, including the inference, is a function of the speaker's nervous system.

Observations

The first important element to consider is the matter of observations. From the point of view of our interpersonal communication model, **observations** result from noticing the behavior of other people. Observation is a process of taking in information about another person. The mechanisms by which we take information inside ourselves are our five senses: sight, touch, taste, smell, and hearing.

Look at this detail from figure 7.1. What can you observe? The man is smiling. He has brown hair and brown eyes. If you were standing next to him, you could estimate his height (i.e., you can't tell this from the photograph) and his weight. You can observe the surroundings in which the photograph was made. If you were actually at the scene where this photograph was taken, you could touch the man. You could smell his aftershave and hear his chuckle as he observes you observing him. All of these things are examples of what you could actually observe.

Inferences

You have to guess about this man's emotional state; you can't observe it. You can't get inside his skin. Even if you could, you would not find his emotion. In addition, you can't observe a person's wants and expectations. You can't look at the man and see his intentions; you have to guess about them. In short, you have to draw **inferences.**

Table 6.1 shows five component parts of a relationship that you must infer: (1) feelings, (2) wants and expectations, (3) intentions, (4) openness, and (5) images. These are arranged in the order of importance for talking about your relationships.

Feelings

Feelings and emotions are not quite the same thing. **Feelings** are physical, bodily experiences. **Emotions** exist in words that we use to talk to ourselves and to each other about our feelings. Feelings occur in the present tense. When we feel, we experience some kind of electrochemical sensation in our bodies. Thus, we can perceive through touch. We can feel. We can also become aware of our body parts and can monitor our personal, physical well-being.

We also use the word, *feelings,* to refer to our affective states. We feel "glad" or "mad" or "sad." In the context of this model of relationships, we will use the term "feelings" to discuss both our physical states and our affective states.

Notice that feelings are present in every one of our relationships. It feels good to be with someone whom we love. It hurts to be betrayed. It is exciting to be the center of attention, and it is maddening to discover that someone else has taken advantage of us. As you will see, our feelings are critical to successful relationship communication.[5]

Wants and Expectations

The second component of a relationship that must be inferred is called wants and expectations. A **want** is something that we wish or desire or some deficiency that we experience. In relationships, our wants are typically tied to our experience of the other person. Thus, for example, we can want someone we care about to reinforce our attitudes. We can want others to act, to feel, or to believe in certain ways.

Expectations are very much like wants. An **expectation** is the anticipation of some occurrence. It is a prediction or an assumption. To illustrate, if you tell someone that you will pick them up at 7:30, they will expect you to arrive at or around 7:30. They predict that you will do that. They both assume and anticipate that occurrence.

Wants and expectations are a part of every relationship. Suppose you agree to pick someone up at 7:30, and then simply neglect to do so. Their want or expectation will then yield a feeling state.

Intentions

Intentions are also part of every relationship. **Intention** is defined as the will or determination to achieve some end. For example, a good teacher intends for students to learn. The professor wants to bring about a change in the students. The change can be behavioral; it can be mental; it can be emotional. Regardless of the kind, change is the goal of the instruction. The professor intends to bring about a change, so the intention is part of the relationship.

Intentions are very close to what a person is willing to do to get what is wanted. Thus, a professor may be willing to prepare carefully, to explain thoroughly and repeatedly, to illustrate and give many relevant examples, and to meet with students in private in order to bring about the learning goal.

Openness

Openness is willingness to receive and consider ideas from another individual. Thus, openness is always part of a relationship to some varying degree. Notice that openness is almost always changing. For example, sometimes you are more open to your friend's complaining than you are at other times. Similarly, there are times when you would rather be alone and times when you would rather be with other people. Openness is a constantly changing thing.

At any given moment, you and the other person might be "in phase" or "out of phase." That is, you might be far more open to them than they are to you. You might be less open to them than they are to you. Or, you might both find that you are both wide open. Think about the best social event that you've had recently. The social event was happy for you because you were "in phase" with others.

Have you ever been bored at a party, while other people seemed to be happy? This possibility can be avoided. For example, Dan found a way never to be bored at a party. When he and his wife arrive, Dan tests his own feelings toward the people at the party. If they are positive, then Dan joins in. But if they are negative, for whatever reason, then Dan challenges himself with a game. He makes a point of learning the names of as many people as he can.

One day while they were driving home from a large social function, Dan's wife said to him, "You hated it. I know you hated the party."

"Why do you say that?" Dan asked.

"Because you knew everyone's name," his wife answered. She had learned one of Dan's private ways of managing his boredom.

Images

The final component of every relationship is the set of images each party carries in the relationship.[6] An **image** is a mental representation, idea, or form; a description or conception of something. You have images of everyone you know, and you have images of what they think of you. To illustrate, get a picture in your mind of your mother or father, or someone else close to you. Now, respond to the following questions:

1. Name someone close to you.

2. About how tall is he or she?

3. What color is the person's hair?

4. Can you see the person's general body shape in your mind?

5. On a scale of one to ten, where ten is greatest, how much would you say the person likes you?

6. On the same scale, how would the other person answer that last question about your liking him or her?

You were able to answer those questions because you have images in your mind about the other person and what the other person thinks of you. In addition, you have images in your mind about who you are and how you are supposed to behave in a large range of events.

You will recall from chapter 2 that your images of yourself and of the situations in your life are a function of how you and "significant others" have interacted. They're the result of countless message exchanges. You can do a lot to change those images and to change your self-concept.

The point to remember is that your images are the creation of your own mind. No one decided to put an image into your mind. You created it. Whether beautiful or ugly and whether functional or dysfunctional, you have created your own images, and you can change them if you choose.

We all have images. When we talk with each other, we continually adapt ourselves to our images. To illustrate, suppose you determine to ask your friend, Fred, to go fishing with you. Consider some of the images involved in that simple invitation:

1. Going fishing.

2. The third rapids on the Taylor River.

3. Yourself wading in Taylor River with a fly-rod in your hands.

4. Fred, knee deep in the white water about 75 yards off, casting into a small back-roller under that rock.

5. Fred smiling as you imagine asking him to go fishing.

6. Yourself, in the present, in relationship to Fred. (You're his friend, aren't you? You like him and enjoy his company, don't you?)

7. Your image of Fred's image of you. (He's your friend, too, and you know that he likes you.)

8. Your image of Fred's image of fishing.

9. Your image of Fred's image of fishing with you.

Reflecting on all of these images points out how much of your own mental activity is involved in extending a simple invitation.

Most of the time, our images are sufficiently accurate so that we get along very nicely. Although they are never completely correct, they're close enough. Unless, of course, the errors in our images cause us problems.

Since you create your own images, and since those images are never completely correct, it is worthwhile to remember that you can change them with more accurate information. That's a valuable idea.

In the invitation to go fishing, suppose Fred says, "No, thanks. I can't," and gives you no further explanation. If your image of yourself is somewhat negative, for example, if you have a low self-concept, you might decide that Fred didn't want to go fishing with *you*. You would, on the basis of your image of yourself, develop a modified image of Fred's image of you. But you wouldn't *have* to do that. With a strong self-concept, you would be likely to attribute Fred's, "No, thanks, I can't" to conditions beyond Fred's control. If you do this, you are much less likely to experience conflict or to engage in conflict behavior with Fred. Clearly, your images you have, and the images that the other person has, are part of every relationship.

Now look at table 6.1 again. Notice that feelings, wants, (etc.) are indented in the model, but that observations, inferences, and feedback are not.

The component parts that are indented are going on inside your mind. They are real, of course, but they are also a function of your own creativity—your own nervous system. In interpersonal communication events, you need to give and get feedback. The right-hand column of table 6.1 constitutes a complete agenda that will help you to do that.

Feedback

The term **feedback** refers to messages sent from a receiver to a source. The purpose of these messages is to correct or control error. Feedback can take the form of talk, of verbalized cues, and of nonverbal cues. To give feedback is to send messages. To get feedback is to seek messages from someone else. These messages can be intentional or accidental. For example, if you ask someone to tell you how they feel about your idea, you are asking them for feedback. If you ask someone to respond to your request, you are, again asking for feedback. However, you may also notice an unintended message that the other person did not intend to send to you. The pause before a person declines your invitation may be an unintentional message. In any event, if you *decide* that it is a message, then it serves as one.

The model in table 6.1 clearly shows that feedback is an essential component of all relationships. You can observe your friend's behavior and *infer* how you are feeling or what they want. But you can't read their mind. You can't get inside their skin to look around; and even if you could, you would

IT'S MORE FUN TO KNOW

Clues to Deception

If you are trying to determine whether or not someone is misleading or deceiving you, watch their feet and legs. Those are the most effective channels to use when you look for deception in nonverbal messages.

See Paul Ekman and W. V. Friesen, "Nonverbal Leakage and Clues to Deception," Psychiatry, 32 (1969), p. 88–106.

Comment . . .

We often are told that the face is one of the best cues of feeling. You also should watch leg movement and position, as well as placement of the feet, for clues of deception. Excess movement is among those clues.

---

not find anything that looks like a feeling. Therefore, in order for you to know with confidence about how they're feeling, they have to tell you. They can volunteer that information, or you can ask for it.

But, we often don't ask for feedback very well. Instead, most of us (most of the time) pretend that we can read each other's minds.[7] We project our guesses onto each other without verifying if our guesses are accurate. As you consider the following examples of such mind reading behavior, you will see how important clear and immediate feedback can be to a relationship.

What is said	Explanation
1. "You are beautiful."	The judgment "beautiful" is a function of the speaker's thinking, not an attribute of the person being described.
2. "You're a jerk."	Again, a judgment arising in and projected by the speaker.
3. "You look angry. What is the problem?"	How does anger look? This is a projection, too. It reads the person's mind and assumes both an emotion and a problem.

4. "What's wrong with me?"

The question projects two things onto the receiver: (1) that something is wrong with the speaker, and (2) that the listener knows what it is. Notice that the "wrongness" is in the mind of the speaker.

5. "It's not fair to slough off your share of work."

Speaker assumes special knowledge of the listener's attitudes, accuses the listener of "sloughing off," pretends to know the listener's appropriate share, and how much of that work the listener has done or will do.

Remember that in each of these five examples, the speaker is actually *saying* something. What if the speaker thinks statement five, but does not say it? Instead the speaker squints, juts his jaw forward with a frown, audibly forces air through his nose, and then turns on his heel and stalks away without saying a word. How could the receiver know what is going on inside the sender? And how could the sender reasonably expect the receiver to know?

Yet, we often assume not only that we can read the other person's mind, but also that they can read ours. Does this scenario serve as an example for you? "If he really loved me then, he'd know what I feel," says one young woman through her tears. "Yes," says her friend as she attempts to comfort her, "and he'd have enough sense to respect your feelings, too." Clearly, both of these women are assuming that the man can read his friend's mind. She even claims that such ability is a condition of their relationship, and that she can measure his affection for her against his ability to read her mind.

What's needed in all of these cases is feedback. Thus, feedback skills become essential to successful relationships. Chapter 3, on listening, covers a lot of information pertinent to giving and getting feedback.

How to Give Feedback

The following five pieces of advice about giving feedback seem especially appropriate:

1. Stay in the present tense.

2. Personalize your talk.

   ▲ Talk about your feelings.
   ▲ Talk about your wants and expectations.
   ▲ Talk about your intentions, your openness, and your images.

Stay in the Present Tense

First, when you feedback, stay in the present tense. Use language that reminds yourself and the other person that you are trying to be involved right now. This advice makes good sense regardless of whether you are talking about topics or about your relationship with the other person. However, it is easier to apply the principle when you are talking about topics than to apply it when you are talking about relationships. Remember, your recollection of the past is faulty. Make it clear that you are open to clarification.

To illustrate, consider the following sample statements.

QUESTION: "What did you do last Wednesday night?"

PAST TENSE, TOPIC DIMENSION: "I went to the movies with Jim and Suellen, and then we went for pizza."

BETTER: "As I recall, I went to the movies with Jim and Suellen. I remember that we went for pizza after the movie."

Notice that the qualifications (i.e., I recall, I remember) are in the present tense. They acknowledge that your memory may be faulty, so they make the sentences tentative rather than certain. Since this question and answer seem innocuous, you may be wondering where the problem exists. Not all questions and answers are as free from emotional loading. The following is a more problematic example.

QUESTION: "What was your hang-up last night that made you so mad?"

PAST TENSE, RELATIONSHIP DIMENSION: "I was mad because you ignored me most of the night."

BETTER: "I think you ignored me last night, and I'm still angry about it."

In this case, the real issue is a present tense feeling of anger. The second sample is better because it acknowledges the speaker's question, brings the issue into the present tense, and brings the feeling up to the level of talk. The speaker discloses her current thinking and feelings to the other party.

Personalize Your Talk

Learn to talk about yourself, not about the other person. This idea has been called "personalizing" your talk. Make it clear that you are owning responsibility for your own feelings and beliefs. Be clear that you own your own wants and your perceptions.

For example, rather than "You make me angry," or "You're wrong," you could say, "I am angry because . . .," and "That doesn't seem right to me."

Notice that the speaker who said, "I think you ignored me last night, and I'm still angry about it," talked about herself. She personalized her statement. She claimed responsibility for her own feeling, and she did not attempt to blame the listener for it.

Now compare the following alternative statements. They are deliberately loaded so that you can see how valuable the skill of personalizing can be in reducing defensiveness.

NOT PERSONALIZED: "You made me so mad last night when you ignored me all night."

Here the speaker blames the listener for her angry feeling and states as a fact (rather than as a perception) that the listener ignored her *all* night.

BETTER: "I think you ignored me last night, and I'm still angry about it."

The speaker allows for the possibility that her perceptions about the circumstance might be faulty, and she owns up to her own responsibility for her feelings of anger. She's talking about herself.

The following examples represent sentences that compare and contrast personalized sentences and sentences that are not personalized. If you study them, you will see how easy it is to learn to talk about yourself instead of about the other person, and, you will greatly improve your interpersonal communication. Certainly, such clear and accurate feedback will be less threatening to the other person and will be far more self-disclosing than the alternatives.

Not personalized	Personalized
You're beautiful.	You seem beautiful to me.
You're ugly.	I don't like the way you look.
You're right.	I agree with you.
You make me angry.	When you do _____ , I feel angry.
You're crazy.	I can't make sense of that behavior.
It's important that we . . .	I think it's important that we . . .
Don't you think . . .	I think . . . and I'd like you to agree with me.

If you can learn to stay in the present when it is helpful to do so (i.e., it is helpful most of the time), and if you can learn to talk about yourself instead of talking about the other person, then you will progress toward more effective relationship management.

Talk about Your Feelings

Feelings and wants must be shared. In *The Secret of Staying in Love,* John Powell argues that people need to tell each other what they feel and what they want. He says:

> *There must be an emotional clearance (dialog) between two involved partners . . . before they can safely enter into a deliberation about plans, choices, values. The assumption behind this [argument] is that the breakdown in human love and communication is* always *due to* emotional *problems.*[8]

According to Powell, a clear sharing of feelings and emotions must exist before any meaningful discussion about the important things, such as plans, choices, and values, can occur. But very few people find such talk easy or comfortable to do.

For one thing, people can't fully express what they are experiencing. Human language is not that accurate. Our words are only part of our experience. There is also an "unspeakable level" of experience—something that comes before thought or expression of the thought.[9]

For another thing, our society punishes clear talk about feelings. It especially punishes clear talk about unpleasant or negative feelings. How many times have you heard "If you can't say anything nice, don't say anything at all"? Our society teaches us, wrongly, that some emotions are bad and others are good. This teaching discourages clear talk about the feelings that are supposed to be "bad."

Still, we must try to express ourselves, so that others can know us and so that they can know themselves in us. Your affection for a loved one, for example, is part of you. But it is also part of the other person, as well. Other people in your life must know what you think and how you feel in order to confirm their own self-concepts and their own ideas about the relationship with you.

If you listen carefully, you can often hear people teaching others how to identify, and bury, the so-called "bad" feelings. "Don't you say that to me!" says a mother when her small child, who is frustrated about having to leave his game, says "No, I won't go home!" "Stop that this minute!" says a father who breaks up a squabble between his two small children.

"You have no right to feel that way," says a brother to a sister. But, of course, the sister has every right to feel anything she feels. The brother is punishing her statement by judging it.

"Don't worry, everything will be all right," says the well-intended and sympathetic adult in response to her friend's statement that she's worried. This adult is actually saying, "I don't want to hear you express your worry any more."

"Why do you feel that way?" asks a teacher. Her pupil has just said, "I hate you." You see, she was trying to be understanding, but what she actually did was deny the feeling statement by analyzing it.

"I know how you feel," says Wilma. "Just the other day a situation happened to me. It happened like this. . . ." With that sentence, Wilma takes the talk and the focus away from the other person and turns it instead upon herself. That way, she doesn't have to listen to the other person's feeling statements.

Therefore, our society teaches us that some feelings are good and that other feelings are bad. In addition, our society teaches us to suppress undesirable emotions, and that some emotions conflict with basic values.

To illustrate, consider the rules in your own family about demonstrating your feeling. Were you allowed or encouraged to express all of your emotions? Or were there rules about certain expressions?

One student related an experience when she "sassed" her mother. She and her mother were arguing about something while preparing the family breakfast. The daughter was angry because she could not go to her friend's house that morning. Instead, she had to stay home and do her "Saturday chores." Her mother happened to be buttering a slice of toast when her young daughter said, "Mother, you're mean and awful, and I hate you."

"Mother never even slowed down," the daughter stated. "She took that slice of buttered toast and turned it, buttered-side-down on my head and said, 'Don't you ever talk to me in that tone of voice again.' "

The mother gave her daughter a clear message that some expressions of feelings were not acceptable because they conflicted with a value system.

Therefore, we need to learn to talk about our feelings; however, because of our limited training, most of us do not have the necessary skills. Fortunately, the skills are simple and can be easily learned. Sometimes, however, they are difficult to practice. You can easily learn the following three skills and they will help you in talking about your feelings.

1. Talk about yourself, not about the other person.

2. Stay in the present tense.

3. Learn more words to describe your feelings.

We have already discussed the first two of these skills. They are the skill of personalizing, and remembering that relationships and feelings are always in the present. What you feel—you feel right now.

The third skill may be more difficult to learn. Although you know how to read and how to understand approximately 25,000 to 30,000 words, you

Primary Affective States

Primary Emotion	Strong	Mild	Weak
HAPPY	Delighted	Amused	Calm
	Elated	Cheerful	Contained
	Excited	Eager	Glad
	Great	Proud	Good
	Overjoyed	Up	Satisfied
	Turned on		
SAD	Drained	Down	Ashamed
	Hopeless	Discouraged	Bad
	Lonely	Distressed	Hurt
	Miserable	Helpless	Lost
	Sorrowful	Upset	Sorry
ANGRY	Bitter	Aggravated	Bugged
	Disgusted	Agitated	Disappointed
	Enraged	Annoyed	Dismayed
	Furious	Peeved	Put out
	Seething	Resentful	Uptight
AFRAID	Afraid	Apprehensive	Nervous
	Alarmed	Insecure	Tense
	Fearful	Uneasy	Light
	Panicky	Worried	Timid
	Petrified		Unsure
	Terrified		
CONFUSED	Bewildered	Blocked	Bothered
	Conflicted	Disorganized	Puzzled
	Pulled apart	Disturbed	Uncertain
	Torn	Frustrated	Uncomfortable
	Trapped	Mixed up	Undecided
	Troubled		

▼ Table 7.1

probably don't use more than about 6,000 or 7,000 of those words regularly. Moreover, you probably don't have many words to talk about your emotional states. But you can learn to enrich your feelings vocabulary, and you should. The more words you can use to talk about your feelings, the richer your emotional range. For example, if you can use more words in order to talk about your feelings associated with anger, then you'll experience less anger.

Table 7.1 suggests a way for you to learn more feeling words. In the left-hand column, there are five primary emotional states. Along the top, there

Feeling Words from International Marriage Encounter

Happy	Sad	Affectionate	Afraid
Festive	Sorrowful	Close	Fearful
Relaxed	Unhappy	Loving	Frightened
Calm	Depressed	Sexy	Timid
Complacent	Melancholy	Tender	Wishy-washy
Satisfied	Gloomy	Passionate	Shaky
Serene	Somber	Aggressive	Apprehensive
Comfortable	Dismal	Appealing	Fidgety
Peaceful	Heavyhearted	Warm	Terrified
Joyous	Quiet		
Ecstatic	Mournful		
Enthusiastic	Dreadful		
Inspired	Dreary		
Glad	Flat		
Pleased	Blah		
Grateful	Dull		
Cheerful	In the dumps		
Excited	Sullen		
Cheery	Moody		
Lighthearted	Sulky		
Buoyant	Out of sorts		
Carefree	Low		
Optimistic	Discontented		

▲ Table 7.2

are the categories "strongly felt," "mildly felt," and "weakly felt." The table implies that it is possible to experience the primary emotions strongly, moderately, or hardly at all. What words would you put into each of the categories in table 7.1?

Find five or six words from the list in table 7.2 for each of these categories, place them in the correct category, and then memorize them.

You can use your image of table 7.1 to help you when you wish to talk about your feelings.

You already know everything that you need to know in order to ask clearly for what you want. To verify this, suppose that your professor says to you, "There will be a major term-paper requirement for this course." You know what questions must be asked. "Does it have to be typed?" "How many pages long?" "Does it require footnotes?" If so, "how many?" "When is it due?"

How to Express What You Want

Attitude	Observable Behavior
To love	Call me on the phone . . .
To improve	Get to work . . .
To be professional	Research and write for publication . . .
To help, or participate	Offer to sit with the kids . . .

*After Gerald L. Wilson, Alan M. Hantz, and Michael S. Hanna, *Interpersonal Growth Through Communication,* 2d ed. Copyright © 1989 Wm. C. Brown Publishers, Dubuque, Iowa. All Rights Reserved. Reprinted by permission.

▶ Table 7.3

Notice that these questions imply the skills needed in order to make a request clear and specific. (1) Ask for something that can be observed. (Does it have to be typed? Does it require footnotes?) (2) Ask for a measurable amount. (How many pages? How many footnotes?) (3) Specify a time frame. (When is it due?) Confirm and reinforce the feedback and the decision to give the feedback.

Talk about Your Wants and Expectations

As you will recall, a relationship includes not only feelings, but also wants and expectations. In fact, feelings and wants are so intimately related that they can rarely be isolated from each other. We usually feel one of the primary emotions (glad, sad, mad, afraid, ashamed, confused) when our wants and expectations are involved. For example, we feel glad when we get what we want. We feel sad when we lose something that we want. We feel betrayed when we expected something but didn't get it. Sometimes, that sense of betrayal becomes anger.

Wants and expectations flow directly from the roles that we assign to each other and from the roles that we take. You know what to expect from your professor because you have assigned the role of professor to that person. (Remember, a role is a set of behaviors.) You know how to act in relationship to the professor because of the role you have taken in that relationship. If you have taken the role of student, you act "like a student." If you have taken the role of friend, you act "like a friend."

Measurable Amount	Time Frame
at least once	every day.
on time . . .	every day.
two or three essays in professional journals . . .	each year.
a few times . . .	every week.

▲ Table 7.3 continued

If you talk about what you want and expect, you clarify what *behavior* you would like the other person to perform. You already know the skills involved in learning to ask for what you want: ask for an observable behavior, specify a measurable amount, and identify the time frame within which you would like the behavior performed. Table 7.3 provides some examples of how to do this.

In order to give feedback, it is important to talk about what you are feeling and what you want. You may also need to help the other person in order for them to give you feedback about these things when they seem important to you. Remember, you cannot read the other person's mind. You have to ask for the information you need. So ask questions like these:

"I can tell you are feeling something, but I'm not sure what it is. Will you tell me?"
"You have said you are angry, and I'm sorry about that, but I don't know what you want. What would you like me to do?"
"What are you feeling about me right now?"
"What do you expect me to do?" "When would you like that done?"

Talk about Your Intentions, Your Openness, and the Images That You Have

Relationships always include intentions, openness, and images. Thus, these attributes and indicators may become as important when giving and getting feedback as feelings and wants. In talks about relationships, include sentences like these:

INTENTION: "How far are you willing to go with this?"

INTENTION: "I'm not going to take any papers that are not handed in by 4:00 P.M. on Friday."

INTENTION: "I'm unwilling to go that far. Instead . . ."

OPENNESS: "Right now I don't want to talk about this."

OPENNESS: "I'm feeling overwhelmed just now. Can we talk about this tomorrow?"

IMAGES: "I think you're playing a game with me."

IMAGES: "Are you really as upset as you seem?"

Notice how this last sentence implies the next suggestion. At the same moment that it displays the speaker's image, it also asks for verification from the other person.

How to Get Feedback from Others

You can't read another person's mind any more than the other person can read your mind. Thus, it is essential that you learn to ask and secure feedback from other people. But you should never ask for feedback that you don't really want.

The best way to secure feedback from others is to create a communication climate in which trust and self-disclosure can occur.

Ask in Present Tense

Recall the principle of the absolute present. It states that all relationships exist in the present tense. Since it is impossible to return or to alter the past, it seems wise to ask for feedback in the present tense. By doing so, you build trust in relationships; individuals do not have to rely upon their memory, nor do they have to experience any negative feelings or defensiveness.

> *First, inquire about other people's feelings and wants, but do not assume that you know their wants or feelings.*

The idea is to ask questions. You can't read other people's minds, so you must rely upon them to tell you what is going on inside. Fill your relationship talk with questions like these: "Are you angry?" "I can't tell what you are feeling." "What's going on in there? What are you feeling?" "I can tell you are frustrated, but I don't know what you want from me." "Can you tell me what would make you happy?" "What can I do to make a difference?"

> *Second, state what you observe and report the inferences that you draw. Ask for verification of those inferences.*

The best way to secure feedback is to create a climate in which trust and self-disclosure can occur.

Sometimes feedback needs to be provided about the most fundamental parts of a message system. People shrug, frown, smile, lean, blink, clear their throats, and clench their jaws. These mannerisms may mean something, or they may not. We guess about people's reactions based on such behavior. However, because we cannot know for sure what these mannerisms "mean," it's a good idea to ask whether your guesses are correct. Ask questions such as: "I can see the frown, but I'm puzzled about what it means." "Does that shrug mean that you are indifferent?" "Where did that chuckle come from? Are you amused? Or is it something else?"

Learn to ask whether your guesses are correct. The more questions you ask, the more you give the other people an opportunity to correct and control the errors that sometimes cause trouble between people.

Be Supportive

A theorist named Jack Gibb developed one of the most well-anthologized essays in the entire field of communication over thirty years ago.[10] It is as useful and relevant today as it was when it appeared in 1961. Gibb described the kinds of behavior that he observed while listening to groups who were engaged in defensive communication. He wanted to know what caused people to feel defensive, and he attempted to describe the behavioral opposites; that is, communication behaviors that were essentially supportive. Table 7.4 summarizes his essay.

Defensive and Supportive Behaviors

▼ Table 7.4

Behavior That Makes People Defensive	Behavior That Reduces Defensiveness
EVALUATION	DESCRIPTION
Judgments or assessments of another that imply "You're not OK."	Statements that confirm the other as OK, and that treat the other with respect.
CONTROL	PROBLEM ORIENTATION
Behaviors that attempt to manipulate others—or impose a point of view.	Behavior that makes clear your desire to cooperate in defining/ solving a problem.
STRATEGY	SPONTANEITY
To pre-plan a goal then talk the other into believing it was his or her idea.	Straightforward, candid expression of one's own attitudes, beliefs and feelings.
NEUTRALITY	EMPATHY
Behavior that treats another person as a thing, capable only of functions, not choices.	Behaviors that attempt to identify with another's thinking and feeling, and confirm his values & beliefs.
SUPERIORITY	EQUALITY
Behaviors that express or imply a "one-up" position.	"I'm OK—you're OK" behavior.
CERTAINTY	PROVISIONALISM
Behavior that shows rigid commitment to an idea or position. "I am right—you are wrong."	Shows of willingness to be tentative, to cooperate, and to develop a Win-Win definition of a situation.

There is a tendency toward using behaviors that make people defensive. More people in our society use these behaviors than don't. However, behavior is always a matter of choice, although you may have to learn a new pattern of behaviors to replace the old habitual ones.

You can learn new ways to communicate if you concentrate and choose to describe behaviors rather than to judge them. You can choose to cooperate rather than to compete, manipulate, or "sneak up" on others. You can treat others with respect, rather than treat them like things, or as though they were, somehow, beneath you. In addition, you can choose to be tentative when you draw inferences and conclusions, rather than determine that you're absolutely correct every time.

Summary

This chapter has described interpersonal relationships as occurring inside oneself, and always in the present tense. The argument has been that, when human relationships are at risk, a person who can talk wisely about the component parts of a relationship can improve the quality of that relationship. The component parts are observations, inferences, and feedback.

We observe behavior through our sensory mechanisms, which draw these observations into our minds. In turn, we infer what those observations mean. If we're wise, we give and get feedback often, knowing that there is no other way for us to correct and control for our errors as we attempt to manage our relationships.

The key concerns in the relationship are listed as an agenda for talking about our relationships. Arranged in order according to the amount of trouble they cause us, those concerns are our feelings, our wants and expectations, our intentions, our openness to each other and to each other's ideas, and to the images we hold.

Getting and giving feedback involves certain skills implied by this model of relationship management. When you want to give someone feedback, stay in the present tense and talk about yourself rather than about the other person. Talk about feelings, wants and expectations, intentions, openness, and images.

To draw feedback from someone else, inquire about feelings and wants but do not assume that you know the person's feelings and wants. You should state your observations and report your inferences. Ask for verification of your inferences. These things create a climate for self-disclosure.

It is easy to describe these things, but it is more difficult to incorporate them into your behavior patterns. The aim of this chapter has been to heighten your awareness and understanding. It will be up to you to put new and more positive communication skills into practice.

Discussion Questions

1.   Ask two members to role-play one of the following situations as fully as they can for two or three minutes. Make quick notes as you observe evidence of communication in the task dimension and communication in the relationship dimension. Then working as a class, discuss these questions:

   a. Under what conditions do people move into the relationship dimension? Do you find any significant pattern involved? Do you think the role players were ever using the nonverbal messages instead of the verbal messages?

b. Do the role playing situations suggest any advice you might give to people in a real situation?

The situations:

The partners share living quarters. One is super tidy; the other is super sloppy. Tidy partner decides to confront sloppy partner about the mess.

The partners are a new employee and an experienced supervisor who has been on the job for more than ten years. The supervisor is having a very bad day when the new employee makes an apparently simple mistake. Supervisor reprimands the new employee.

Using the same employee/supervisor relationship, let the new employee approach the supervisor with an idea for improving the way that things are done.

2. Working with a partner and while taking turns, try to imagine how you might express each of the following emotions nonverbally:

▲ mild joy
▲ strong surprise
▲ strong anger
▲ moderate sadness
▲ moderate fear
▲ strong fear
▲ mild anger
▲ strong embarrassment
▲ moderate shame
▲ great happiness
▲ strong affection

Do you think it is possible to mask such nonverbal expressions of feeling when you are truly experiencing them? Do you think other people are good at identifying your feelings? Are you good at identifying theirs?

References

[1]Mark L. Knapp, "Chapter 6: Dyadic Relationship Development" in John M. Wiemann and Randall P. Harrison (eds.), *Nonverbal Interaction* (Beverly Hills, CA: Sage Publications, 1983), pp. 179–207.

[2]Frank E. Millar and L. Edna Rogers, "A Relational Approach to Interpersonal Communication," in Gerald Miller (ed.), *Interpersonal Communication* (Beverly Hills, CA: Sage Publications, 1976), pp. 87–203; Paul Watzlawick, Janet H. Beavin, and Don D. Jackson, *Pragmatics of Human Communication: A Study of Interactional Patterns, Pathologies, and Paradoxes* (New York: W.W. Norton and Company, Inc., 1967), pp. 67–69.

[3]John A. McGeoch and Arthur L. Irion, "Chapter X: Retention and Forgetting," in *The Psychology of Human Learning*, (New York: David McKay Company, Inc., 1952), pp. 355–467; Stephen B. Klein, "Chapter 8: Memory Storage," and "Chapter 9: Memory Retrieval," in *Learning: Principles and Applications* (New York: McGraw-Hill Book Company, 1987), pp. 354–451.

⁴John O. Green and Deanna Geddes, "Representation and Processing in the Self-System: An Action-Oriented Approach to Self and Self-Relevant Phenomena," pp. 287–314, and Hal Whitteman, "Interpersonal Problem Solving: Problem Conceptualization and Communication Use," in *Communication Monographs* 55:4 (December 1988) pp. 336–59; Renee Edwards, James M. Honeycutt, and Kenneth S. Zagacki, "Imagined Interaction as an Element of Social Cognition," in *Western Journal of Communication* 52:1 (Winter, 1988), pp. 23–45.

⁵Willard Gaylin, M.D., *Feelings Are Good for You* (New York: Ballantine Books, 1979).

⁶Kenneth L. Boulding, *The Image* (Ann Arbor: University of Michigan Press, 1956).

⁷Jeffrey Schrank, "Nonverbal Communication: Seeing Through Deception in Communication," in *Deception Detection* (Boston: Beacon Press, 1975), pp. 36–62.

⁸John Powell, *The Secret of Staying in Love* (Niles, IL: Argus Communications, 1974), p. 73.

⁹Alfred Korzybski, *Science and Sanity: An Introduction to Non-Aristotelian Systems and General Semantics* (Lancaster, PA: Science Press Printing Co., 1933); S. I. Hayakawa, *Language in Thought and Action*, 2d ed. (New York: Harcourt, Brace & World Co., 1964); John C. Condon, Jr., *Semantics and Communication* (New York: The Macmillan Company, 1966).

¹⁰J. R. Gibb, "Defensive Communication," *The Journal of Communication* 11:3 (September 1961), pp. 142–45.

Chapter 8

Interviews

Outline

When you finish reading this chapter you should be able to:

1. Name and describe six types of interviews: (1) employment, (2) performance appraisal, (3) information, (4) persuasive, (5) grievance, and (6) exit.

2. Specify and describe the three phases constituting the organization of all interviews: (1) opening phase, (2) question-answer phase, and (3) closing phase.

3. Explain the recommended strategies for each of the phases of an interview.

4. Name and explain the kinds of questions that commonly occur in interviews, and provide examples of each kind.

5. Describe how to prepare for and participate in a job-search interview in the role of job-seeker.

Objectives

action plan

closed questions

closed-to-open pattern

closing phase

direct questions

employment interview

exit interview

good-by pleasantries

greetings segment

grievance interview

indirect questions

information interview

interview

motivation segment

open questions

open-to-closed sequence

orientation segment

performance appraisal interview

persuasive interview

problem-solving questions

question-answer phase

summary

Key Terms

Introduction

Students are often surprised to learn that interviews are among the most common planned form of communication that will happen in their lives. Instead, they tend to believe that interviews are relatively rare. "Once I have a job, I won't do much interviewing," said one person. "I expect I'm going to stay with one company," said another. "My dad and both my uncles did, and it's kind of a family tradition. So I won't need interviewing skills much."

This chapter describes the interview as a common, planned form of interpersonal communication and suggests the analytical and performance skills that you are most likely to need. It describes a broad range of common interview events, and then it applies the relevant skills to the job placement interview.

Let's begin with a definition. An **interview** is a face-to-face interpersonal event in which at least one person has planned to achieve a specific goal. This definition emphasizes that an interview is a special event. Interviews have a specific purpose. Interviews usually are planned, and interviews tend to be structured.

Types of Interviews

Interviews occur so often and are used to achieve so many goals that it is almost impossible to name them all. However, it is possible to catalog and to describe six of the more common interview types. Notice that they all share certain common features, but that they also have special features.

1. The **employment interview** is sometimes called the job-search interview and the selection interview. It is an interview in which the participants exchange information in order to make an employment decision. This type of interview occurs every time a recruiter visits a campus to search for new employees. This type of interview will be described in detail later in the chapter.

2. The **performance appraisal interview** is sometimes called a counseling interview, and it is a work-related interview in which the supervisor gives the employee feedback about his or her job performance, and consults with the employee to establish goals to be met by the employee. Performance appraisal interviews are also used to encourage and reward employees, to discover and solve communication problems with employees, and to motivate employees.

3. The **information interview** can work two ways. In one way, the information *seeker* organizes the interview. In the other way, the information *giver* organizes the interview. Examples of information interviews occur almost everywhere in our society. For example, you may answer the telephone one evening and discover that you are involved in a survey. Or, you may go to your doctor with a complaint. He or she interviews you to determine what treatment, if any, is appropriate. You may also be asked to participate in an orientation interview in which someone seeks to impart knowledge about the organization or its rules to you.

Journalists conduct information interviews to prepare for the stories they write. Police conduct interviews in the process of investigating crimes.

4. A **persuasive interview** occurs whenever one person seeks to change the thinking or behavior of another person. The most common persuasive interview is the sales event in which a sales representative explains the features and benefits of a product or service in order to persuade the listener to make a purchase decision.

5. A **grievance interview** sometimes occurs in organizations. Such interviews are initiated by employees in order to focus upon a matter of employee discontent. In the academic community, students sometimes request grievance interviews to complain about how they were treated in a classroom or to challenge their course grades.

6. An **exit interview** is designed and conducted by managers when valued employees decide to leave their companies. The goal of an exit interview is to discover the reasons for the employee's decision to leave and to identify any changes that must be made in the administrative structure or procedures, or in the communication climate of the organization.

Some organizations include job placement assistance and counseling in exit interviews. They use the opportunity of an exit interview to try to cement goodwill for the organization.

Because exit interviews are about conditions in the organization, some employees are reluctant to participate in them. They may be suspicious that anything they say during the interview, especially negative criticism of the organization or members of the organization, may adversely affect any recommendations that the organization might give. Thus, exit interviews require exceptional skill on the part of the managers who conduct them.

Organization of All Interviews

Regardless of the purpose of an interview, the general format is essentially the same. Some party identifies a goal, then organizes his or her thinking in order to achieve that goal. Like almost all communication events, an interview includes an *opening phase,* a body (*question-answer phase*) that, in the case of an interview, consists of questions and answers, and a *closing phase.* Each phase makes an important contribution to the success of an interview, and each phase requires certain identifiable skills.

Opening Phase

The opening of an interview serves the same function as the opening paragraph in an essay or the opening remarks of a speech. The idea is to get the attention of the respondent, to put the respondent at ease, and then to prepare the respondent for what is to come. To accomplish these goals, interviewers usually begin with greetings, follow up with an orientation, and then move into motivation. Each of these techniques requires further description.

During the opening phase of every interview, the interviewer has the same goals: to get the attention of the respondent, to put the respondent at ease, and to prepare the respondent for what is coming.

The **greetings** that occur at the beginning of an interview are very important to both parties. The goal is to establish rapport. Participants exchange names and niceties in an effort to put each other at ease and to encourage a receptiveness and a willingness to talk.

The first few minutes of the first encounter are very important. Indeed, Leonard and Natalie Zunin argued successfully that the rapport established during the first four minutes of contact is so crucial that it will determine whether strangers will remain strangers or become acquaintances, business associates, friends, lovers, or lifetime mates.[1]

Remember that an impression is something that the other person forms of you based upon the world of words that has evolved inside his or her head. Your actions, your choices of language, your dress, posture, and so forth must seem consistent with the other person's image of what is appropriate and desirable. Knowing this gives you something with which to manage those precious first four minutes. Three good strategies follow for making the most out of the greetings.

1. Look for evidence of the other person's self-identification. Look and listen for names, ethnic occupations, age and gender cues, social and marital status, and other pieces of information that people use to help to define themselves. Remember that people are more interested in themselves than in anyone else; thus, they usually enjoy talking about themselves.

With this in mind, you may want to ask questions that will express an interest in the other person as an individual. It can also help if you make positive comments about their responses. However, in certain interview situations (i.e., employment interviews), it may be illegal to ask questions regarding ethnic background, marital/family status, religion, or other personal features because of equal employment opportunity regulations. While most of us enjoy making "small talk" on such personal topics, they are best avoided in the employment interview.

> "Hello, I'm Bill Muir. What's your name?"
> "Ellen Larson."
> "Larson. That's Swedish, isn't it?"
> "Yes. My grandparents are from the old country."
> "Where did your people settle?"
> "Minnesota. Can't you tell by my accent?"
> "To be honest, I can't hear an accent. Are you from Minnesota, then?"
> "Well, I was raised there, but now I live near Chicago."

2. Look for attitudes and judgments and feelings.

> "Hello. Did you have a pleasant holiday?"
> "I surely did! I got away from the stress and pressure of work for six days. It was wonderful."
> "I've always found that people are more pleasant at this time of year; more relaxed. . . ."
> "Yeah, me too. . . ."

3. Look for ways to say, "I like you. You're special."
This involves the art of making an honest compliment. If you are not sincere in making a compliment, don't make it. However, if you are sincere, making a compliment is very hard to resist. It's also hard to resist liking the person who made it.

> **AFTER THE PRELIMINARIES:** "I was noticing that beautiful pin you are wearing."
> "Thank you. It was my mother's wedding present from my aunt."
> "It seems just right for the outfit you are wearing. It sets it off."
> "I'm pleased that you noticed it."
> "Well, I have always been interested in jewelry. Took a course in lapidary at college, and. . . ."

The **orientation** segment of the opening is designed to absorb uncertainty. The idea is to put the respondent at ease by providing a brief overview of what is to come. This segment also serves to establish the *interviewer's* responsibility for the interview. It is the interviewer's segment. The interviewer sets the agenda.

Notice that responsibility for an interview has little to do with authority or power. Rather, it has to do with the purpose of the interview, and who has initiated it. Thus, in an employment interview, the employer sets the agenda. In a sales interview, the sales representative sets the agenda. In a journalistic interview, the journalist sets the agenda. In a research interview, the researcher sets the agenda. Four things help to orient an interview for maximum success.

1. Be sure each person knows the other person's name. Too often in our society, people do not listen and "get" each other's names. But names are very important to the success of the interview. If you don't have a business card, get one printed that carries your name, your current address, and your telephone number. Carry your cards with you into the interview. Exchange cards as part of the interview. Call the other person's name out as a way of fixing it in your mind. Be sure that you tell the other person your name.

"Hello. My name is Martha Whitford. You're Mrs. Jackson?"

2. State the reason or purpose of the interview. Your goal is to focus the talk and to take away the other person's uncertainty about what is going to happen. For example, suppose your employer called you on the phone:

"I'd like you to step into my office," the employer says. You go there. "Let's talk for a while about your hopes and dreams," says the employer. "Tell me about the future you imagine for yourself."

If you did not know what the employer was looking for, you might be anxious. Are you about to be promoted? Are you about to be fired? Are you about to be reprimanded? A wise interviewer states the reason or purpose of the interview for the persons being interviewed. So, an employer would be wise to say something like:

"We're expanding our operation, and we're looking for people to fill leadership positions in our expansion office. I wanted to talk with you about your own interest in such a role, and about your ideas."

3. If it is to be an information-gathering interview, be *clear* about the information you need and about what you plan to do with it. One employer, who delighted in taking his employees by surprise, called his employee to ask: "Can you come to my office now?" without saying what it concerned. His employee, of course, went to the office ill-prepared or second-guessing the employer. The employer would have been more likely to secure the needed information if he or she had specified the nature of the interview.

The previous case of a business expansion provides an example of how to specify an interview. The employer might say:

"I'd especially like to know if you would be interested in serving as office manager out there. I know that's not quite in the line you're doing now, but I think your skills and talents might be a good fit with our needs in the new office."

Sometimes managers must ask questions that require confidentiality because of the sensitive nature of the information. For example, an employer may want to ask one person about the leadership talents of another person. In that case, the confidential nature of the interview becomes part of telling the interviewee what information is needed and how it will be used.

Therefore, the employer might say something like:

"I'm trying to identify likely candidates from inside our operation for promotion into leadership positions in our new office. I'd like to ask you some questions about two or three of the people in your department. Of course, this information is sensitive, so I promise to keep our conversation confidential."

4. Set the approximate length of the interview. People who get things done are busy people. Their time is always limited and always valuable. So they protect it. You can facilitate an interview by setting the approximate length of time that it will take. Say something like:

"I'd like to ask you some questions about an idea I have just hatched. Could I take ten minutes of your time?" Extend this common courtesy in both directions. Your boss is entitled to know how much time you want, and so are your peers in the hierarchy and employees.

People who have an idea of the time limits tend to be more relaxed than people who do not. However, notice that your estimate of the time needed may take on the significance of a contract in the other person's mind. Therefore, when you estimate the time limits, keep them. If you tell someone you need only five minutes, take only five minutes. If you need fifteen minutes, tell them that from the outset.

The **motivation segment** of the opening attempts to secure the co-operation of the respondent. Not everyone is as involved and interested in your ideas as you. The other person must see a reason to participate with you.

Chapter 15 describes persuasion strategies based on Maslow's *Hierarchy of Needs* and on Vance Packard's *Hidden Persuaders.* One or a combination of the following motives can be the respondent's reason to participate.

Security *Power*	"I thought you would want to participate in the decision making on this issue."
Worth *Ego gratification*	"Your name came to mind when I was thinking about the really talented potential leaders already working here."
Creative outlets *Love objects*	"I thought your ideas would be especially helpful right from the start. I know that idea was your baby first."
Immortality	"Your ideas can have a lasting influence on the directions we'll take in the future."

Question-Answer Phase

The second major section of every interview, regardless of its type or purpose, is called the **question-answer phase.** If an interview flows smoothly, and if it accomplishes its goals for both participants, you can be sure that both participants have prepared carefully. During this phase, questions and answers are exchanged.

Both participants share responsibility for the success of the question-answer phase. The *interviewer* has the responsibility to control the focus of the conversation, to probe for important information, and to listen carefully. The *respondent* has the responsibility to give clear, detailed answers and to address his or her own agenda for the interview. Preparation—especially the preparation of appropriate questions—is the hallmark of success.

Kinds of Questions

A question is always an inquiry. By themselves, questions do not carry much information, except information about the direction and thinking of the questioner. Although the point is sometimes overlooked, questions *always* seek information. Therefore, in order for you to identify the right questions to ask, you have to know what information you want to discover. The types of questions will influence the kind and quality of information that you elicit from the other person.

Most people have experience with question types, although they may not know it. For instance, every time someone takes a test, they are responding to various question types.

Characteristics of Open and Closed Questions

		Open	Closed
1.	Potential detail (breadth and depth) of response	High	Low
2.	Opportunity for interviewee to volunteer information	High	Low
3.	Interviewer's control over questions and response	Low	High
4.	Interviewer skill required	High	Low
5.	Degree of precision in specific responses	Low	High
6.	Reproducibility and reliability of data from interview to interview	Low	High
7.	Economical use of time	Low	High

▲ Table 8.1

Source: Ronald B. Adler, *Communicating at Work: Principles and Practices for Business and the Professions,* Second Edition (New York: Random House, 1986).

Open questions invite a broad interpretation and response. For example, real estate agents try to find out what their buyers want by conducting a qualifying interview before actually going out to look at homes. "What kinds of things must you absolutely have in your home?" is an open question because it allows the buyers to respond in their own words and in as much detail as they want.

Closed questions limit and focus the respondent. "Do you prefer a two-story home or a rambler" is a closed question because it gives the respondent very specific options. Sometimes closed questions work very well to push for a decision that can then be explored with open questions.

These two kinds of questions are both necessary to successful interviewing. One is not always better than the other. Table 8.1 compares and contrasts open and closed questions.

Some questions are **direct questions.** They ask for specific information, and they are both efficient and effective. Again, you have had experience with lots of examples of direct questions on tests. For example, suppose you came across the following test item, which is an example of a direct question. "In the spaces provided below, name the three phases of every interview."

Questions such as these are essential if you want to find out specific information. For example, the question, "Would you be willing to move to a new part of the country?" may be the only way to discover that piece of

vital information. But direct questioning may not always get you the information you seek.

For example, suppose your professor wanted to discover if you understood the difference between open and closed questions. A direct question would be:

"Do you understand the difference between open and closed questions?"

Because this question does make you actually prove that you understand the difference correctly, it would not be useful to the professor for this purpose. An indirect question would work better. An **indirect question** provides focus and guidelines, and it asks the respondent to create an answer that fits within those guidelines. For example, the professor would ask for an essay with a test item something like this:

"Compare and contrast open questions and closed questions. Include in your response both the characteristic features of each, and the conditions under which each type of question is most appropriate."

Sometimes the interviewer holds more power than the respondent. Performance appraisal interviews provide an example, as well as many job-search interviews. In these cases the respondent may not know how to answer or be willing to answer a direct question. For example, during a performance appraisal interview, the employer may want to secure feedback from the employee about the worker's perceptions of the boss' leadership. A direct question might be threatening:

"Tell me. Do you like my leadership style?"

What sensible employee would want to answer that direct question? If the supervisor is truly interested in securing feedback from the employee, an indirect question would work better:

"I'm looking for your insight, here. You're a lot closer to the actual functioning of our department than I am. If you were the boss, would you make any changes in how we're doing things? Do you have any suggestions?"

Problem-solving questions are sometimes called "hypothetical questions" and they ask the respondent to describe how he or she would solve a problem. They are characterized by words like *if,* and *suppose.*

"If you were supervisor, and a quarrel broke out between two of your people, what would you do?"

Problem-solving questions are useful when you want to understand a person's attitudes and beliefs, and when you want to discover how the person would likely act in a particular situation. Of course, there is no guarantee that the answers you get from such questions are truthful. A respondent might decide to tell you what he or she thinks you want to hear. Still, in the context of a carefully planned interview, you should be able to draw some approximate inferences about the quality of a respondent's thought.

In summary, the question-answer phase of an interview consists of the exchange of carefully planned questions and responses. This phase is the heart of every interview. Thus, each participant must think carefully about the questions to be asked, and also about how to organize those questions.

Organization of Questions

How you sequence questions in an interview may govern your success in discovering the necessary information. Two basic organizational patterns can be applied to any interview. Each pattern is useful in some situations and limited in others.

The **open-to-closed** sequence is sometimes called the "funnel sequence" because it begins with broad questions, then moves to more specific closed questions. This pattern is especially useful when an interviewer is unsure of the exact information they are seeking, or when the interviewer is sure that the respondent has needed expert knowledge. For example, in an exit interview, the employer will probably use the open-to-closed sequence. Similarly, in a performance appraisal interview, the supervisor may use this pattern.

MANAGER: "Suppose you were head of your department. Can you tell me about any changes you might make that would help the department do its job better?"

EMPLOYEE: "Well, I know there's been some trouble about sharing the laser printer, but I'm not sure what to do about it."

MANAGER: "What do you think causes the problem?"

EMPLOYEE: "There are just too many computers hooked up to it. And, of course, the switch box that controls who uses the printer won't hold a file for printing from one computer while it's printing a file from another."

MANAGER: "Do you think we need to do something about this? And do you have any ideas?"

EMPLOYEE: "I don't know if we can afford it, but it sure would help if we had an electronic queue-box. Also, in the future, when Jim and Cornella begin to use computers, we're going to have to have another printer or two."

The **closed-to-open pattern** is sometimes called the "inverted funnel" because it moves from very specific questions to more open, general questions. This pattern is helpful when the respondent might be intimidated or threatened. Closed questions are easier to answer than open questions. Therefore, a reluctant interviewee is more willing to answer them. In addition, the answers to closed questions may suggest appropriate follow-up questions. The follow-up questions, of course, are more likely to be open questions.

RECRUITER: "Would you be willing to relocate to another part of the country?"

RESPONDENT: "Well . . . (pause) That would depend."

RECRUITER: "What would it depend on?"

RESPONDENT: "I have family here. And my wife won't graduate for another year, and her education is very important."

RECRUITER: "Can you think of a way that we could solve that problem for you?"

The point is that an interview succeeds or fails on the strength of its planning. Of course, both interview participants must plan. However, the interviewer has the primary responsibility for planning the question-answer phase. If you are the interviewer, plan both the questions and the sequence of those questions very carefully.

The closing phase of a situation must include a summary, where appropriate, and an action plan.

Closing Phase

An interview should never end abruptly after the last question has been asked and answered. There is still much to do. So, just as other communication events have introductions, discussions and conclusions, so does an interview. There are three functions every interview **closing phase** should perform: (1) to summarize the key ideas and agreements, (2) to establish action plans growing out of the interview, and (3) to leave the participants with positive feelings about the interview experience.

The **summary** is a review and a clarification of the agreements and of the key ideas generated in the question-answer phase. Either person can provide a summary, but usually the interviewer takes the initiative to do so. The summary does not have to be lengthy, but it must be specific and accurate and it should include an **action plan,** if appropriate. For example, a summary of agreements might sound like:

> *"Well, it's just that simple. We've agreed that you will study the need for a new printer and that you'll report back to me by next Wednesday. For my part, I will look into sources and prices. I'll bring that information to Wednesday's meeting so we'll be able to make an informed decision on this matter."*

A summary of the key ideas introduced and discussed is also important to the success of an interview. An example of a summary might sound like this:

> *"Well, let's review. We have agreed in principle that two-way communication must open up in this department, and that each of us can do some things to make that happen. We've also agreed that I will keep a regular "office hour" twice each week so that our people can be confident that they can get a hearing for their ideas."*

It is essential to clarify for each party how agreements arrived at during the interview will be acted upon. A sales representative might say something like:

"I'll put a catalog with a special price list into the mail to you this afternoon. Then, on Wednesday of next week I'll phone you to assure that you got it, and what you've decided to do."

A manager might include this statement in the closing phase of a performance appraisal interview.

"So you're going to hand me a list of performance objectives for the next quarter on Monday? I'll look it over, then drop by your office on Wednesday. That way, we should be all set by the time we leave here Wednesday evening."

Good-by pleasantries are as important to an interview as they are to the end of an evening's entertainment. The purpose is to leave a positive impression; that is, to finish on an up-beat. Such pleasant good-bys do not need to be lengthy, but they need to be sincere. If these conditions exist, then they're easy to do.

For example, you can express your thanks for the other person's co-operation or help. Look at some of the following examples:

"I really appreciate your bringing this to my attention, Virginia. You have been truly helpful."
"I know this wasn't easy for you. Thank you for your interest."

You can show your concern for the other person and for his or her ideas as a way to say good-by.

"If I can help you succeed on this project, please let me know."
"It's a big job, Sam. And it can get as big as you let it. I hope you won't consume all of your energies on it."
"I'll be thinking of you next week. Let me know how it comes out."

A last good-by pleasantry might be to mention some specific point in your future relationship with the other person. You know how:

"See you next Monday."
"I'll be in touch with you by phone this afternoon."
"I'll be waiting for your call."

In summary, the closing phase of an interview serves to focus the thinking and feelings of the participants on what has been accomplished. It summarizes key ideas and agreements, sets the action plan, and ends the interview on a positive note. Table 8.2 presents an interview planning checklist.

Interview Planning Checklist

_____ *1.* Set objectives.
_____ *2.* Analyze the other person.
_____ *3.* Prepare the topics.
_____ *4.* Plan questions to be asked.
_____ *5.* Structure the interview situation.
_____ *6.* Choose and plan the setting.

Notice that you may apply the interview planning checklist to every interview event.

Job-Search Interview

Students express more interest in job-search interviewing than in any other kind. Some experience anxiety when they think about the job-search process. Others are more comfortable with the idea of being evaluated by a recruiter. Because the job-search interview is so important to college students, we wish to focus attention on this particular kind of interview.[2]

An important point concerns the balance of power in a job-search interview. Both parties in the job-search interview have power. It is reciprocal.

However, not everyone believes this claim. Some students believe that the recruiter is doing them a favor by meeting with them. Other students take the position that they are doing the recruiter a favor by participating. Both of these positions are *wrong*.

The purpose of a job-search interview is to find a match between the candidate for a position and the company that needs help. Each party in the job-search interview has something to offer and something to gain. The employer, represented by the recruiter, has a job to offer. The respondent has talents, skills, training, drive, and so forth to offer. The problem is to find a match.

This section emphasizes what the job seeker can do to get ready for a job-search interview. But it does not ignore the recruiter. Your life and career may provide you with an opportunity to play both parts. Therefore, what are the responsibilities of the job seeker?

Responsibilities of the Job Seeker

Looking for an employment position requires knowing yourself, knowing your business, and knowing the organizations with whom you will interview.

IT'S MORE FUN TO KNOW

Apprehension and Interaction Distance

People who are highly apprehensive about communicating have a closer interaction distance than nonapprehensive people.

See J. Cardot and C. Dodd, ''Communication Apprehension as a Predictor of Proxemic Establishment,'' paper presented at the Speech Communication Association Convention, San Antonio, TX, (November 1979).

Comment . . .

If you are a person who is anxious about communication, you are more likely to want to communicate at close distances. These results suggest that apprehensive people want a more private atmosphere for their communication.

Based on that information, the job seeker prepares a resume and cover letter, and plans for and practices the role of job seeker. Each of these activities can be examined.

Know Yourself

Many college students have difficulty imagining what a particular job involves. They know that they're interested in a certain career area, but they can't imagine themselves actually working in that area. Hence, they come ill-equipped to a job-search interview.

Therefore, how do you find out what the work-a-day world is like in your chosen area? When this ignorance of the work world is expressed in interviews with recruiters, a common complaint is that the applicants have no real-world experience.

To alleviate this perception, ask one or two professionals already working in the area about a typical day. Two benefits are gained from this activity. First, you will gain more information about the work in that area. And second, that information will help you to determine if you really do want to pursue that career.

Take the real situation of someone who started out to become a commercial artist. The individual completed the major in commercial art, took a position as a working artist, and discovered that the creative life of a commercial artist was not right for her. A commercial artist works alone, but she is a social person who thrives on interaction. The creative life of the commercial artist requires solitude. Therefore, for a social person, that lifestyle can be isolating and unpleasant. An information-seeking interview with two or three commercial artists might have saved this person from several years of unhappiness and disappointment.

Here are some questions that you might ask in an information-gathering interview that focuses on a career.

1. Will you describe a typical work day?

2. What skills do you find most valuable on your job?

3. What courses did you take that were most helpful to you?

4. What are the most difficult problems you face?

5. What are the most rewarding parts of your job?

6. What are some of the job titles for people with your training?

7. How far and how fast can people in your job advance?

8. What would be a reasonable career goal for a new person to set for a five-year goal? A ten-year goal?

9. What professional organizations would a person in your job want to join, and why?

10. What is a realistic salary figure for an entry-level employee in this line of work? What can a good employee expect to be earning in five years? Ten years?

Part of finding out whether you are matched for a particular job is finding out the answers to such questions.

Another part of knowing yourself is coming to understand which of your personal characteristics might be valuable to an organization. Table 8.3 will help you to identify personal preferences that may bear directly on the job for which you are applying. Table 8.4 will help you inventory your personal traits.

Preferences in Job Characterization

Factors	Importance		
	not important	*average importance*	*very important*
1. Challenge	☐	☐	☐
2. Responsibility	☐	☐	☐
3. Stability of company	☐	☐	☐
4. Security of job within company	☐		☐
5. Size of company	☐	☐	☐
6. Training program	☐	☐	☐
7. Initial job duties	☐	☐	☐
8. Advancement opportunities	☐	☐	☐
9. Amount of contact with coworkers	☐	☐	☐
10. Amount of contact with the public	☐	☐	☐
11. Starting salary	☐	☐	☐
12. Financial rewards "down the road"	☐	☐	☐
13. Degree of independence	☐	☐	☐
14. Opportunity to show initiative	☐	☐	☐
15. Degree of employee involvement in decision making	☐	☐	☐
16. Opportunity to be creative	☐	☐	☐
17. Type of industry	☐	☐	☐
18. Company's reputation in the industry	☐	☐	☐

▼ Table 8.3

You need to consider your working background. If you have held a job—any job—successfully, then you are in a better position to be hired than a person who has never held a job. List every job you have held. List the names of your supervisors. Would your supervisors recommend you as a good employee? Why or why not?

Factors	Importance		
	not important	*average importance*	*very important*
19. Prestige of job within the company	☐	☐	☐
20. Degree of results seen from job	☐	☐	☐
21. Variety of duties	☐	☐	☐
22. What the boss is like	☐	☐	☐
23. What the coworkers are like	☐	☐	☐
24. Suburban or metropolitan community	☐	☐	☐
25. Hours	☐	☐	☐
26. Benefits	☐	☐	☐
27. Commuting distance involved	☐	☐	☐
28. Amount of overnight travel involved	☐	☐	☐
29. Number of moves from one city to another involved	☐	☐	☐
30. Facilities of office or plant	☐	☐	☐
31. Spouse's desires	☐	☐	☐
32. Others (list)	☐	☐	☐

Source: From Lois Einhorn, *Interviewing . . . A Job in Itself*, p. 3. Used by permission of the Career Center at Indiana University.

▲ **Table 8.3** continued

What working skills did you acquire on each of your jobs? Do you see a relationship between these skills and your self-traits analysis? Have you financed all or part of your education? Have you held any offices in civic or student organizations? Have you been elected to any student government

Inventory of Personal Traits

Trait	Rating				
	Poor		Average		Excellent
	1	2	3	4	5
1. Dependable	☐	☐	☐	☐	☐
2. Honest	☐	☐	☐	☐	☐
3. Motivated	☐	☐	☐	☐	☐
4. Assertive	☐	☐	☐	☐	☐
5. Outgoing	☐	☐	☐	☐	☐
6. Persistent	☐	☐	☐	☐	☐
7. Conscientious	☐	☐	☐	☐	☐
8. Ambitious	☐	☐	☐	☐	☐
9. Punctual	☐	☐	☐	☐	☐
10. Creative	☐	☐	☐	☐	☐
11. Intelligent	☐	☐	☐	☐	☐
12. Mature	☐	☐	☐	☐	☐
13. Emotionally stable	☐	☐	☐	☐	☐
14. Enthusiastic	☐	☐	☐	☐	☐
15. Flexible	☐	☐	☐	☐	☐
16. Realistic	☐	☐	☐	☐	☐
17. Responsible	☐	☐	☐	☐	☐
18. Serious	☐	☐	☐	☐	☐
19. Pleasant	☐	☐	☐	☐	☐
20. Sincere	☐	☐	☐	☐	☐
21. Analytical	☐	☐	☐	☐	☐
22. Organized	☐	☐	☐	☐	☐
23. Having a good appearance	☐	☐	☐	☐	☐
24. Able to get along with coworkers	☐	☐	☐	☐	☐
25. Able to get along with supervisors	☐	☐	☐	☐	☐
26. Having oral communication skills	☐	☐	☐	☐	☐
27. Having written communication skills	☐	☐	☐	☐	☐
28. Having good references	☐	☐	☐	☐	☐
29. Having good school attendance	☐	☐	☐	☐	☐

▼ Table 8.4

Trait	Rating				
	Poor		*Average*		*Excellent*
	1	2	3	4	5
30. Having good job attendance	☐	☐	☐	☐	☐
31. Willing to work long hours	☐	☐	☐	☐	☐
32. Willing to work evenings and weekends	☐	☐	☐	☐	☐
33. Willing to relocate	☐	☐	☐	☐	☐
34. Willing to travel	☐	☐	☐	☐	☐
35. Willing to commute a long distance	☐	☐	☐	☐	☐
36. Willing to start at the bottom and advance according to own merit	☐	☐	☐	☐	☐
37. Able to accept criticism	☐	☐	☐	☐	☐
38. Able to motivate others	☐	☐	☐	☐	☐
39. Able to follow through on something until it is done	☐	☐	☐	☐	☐
40. Able to make good use of time	☐	☐	☐	☐	☐
41. Goal- (or achievement-) oriented	☐	☐	☐	☐	☐
42. Healthy	☐	☐	☐	☐	☐
43. Able to take initiative	☐	☐	☐	☐	☐
44. Able to follow directions	☐	☐	☐	☐	☐
45. Detail-oriented	☐	☐	☐	☐	☐
46. Able to learn quickly	☐	☐	☐	☐	☐
47. Willing to work hard	☐	☐	☐	☐	☐
48. Having moral standards	☐	☐	☐	☐	☐
49. Poised	☐	☐	☐	☐	☐
50. Having growth potential	☐	☐	☐	☐	☐
51. Others	☐	☐	☐	☐	☐

Source: Adapted from Lois Einhorn, *Interviewing . . . A Job in Itself,* pp. 4–5. Used by permission of the Career Center of Indiana University.

▲ **Table 8.4** continued

Table 8.5 ▸

Questions from Public Sources of Information

1. What are the locations of the organization's plants, offices, and branches?
2. What is the age of the company?
3. What are the highlights of the company's history?
4. What services and/or products does the company offer?
5. What are the company's yearly sales? Growth potential? Rank within its industry?
6. Who are the competitors in the industry?

committees? Have you served at any time as a volunteer? Have you provided leadership or held leadership positions in any student organizations?

Every one of these questions that yields a "yes" points to an individual who has acquired valuable, marketable, and employable skills.

Know the Organization

You will be ahead of many other employment candidates if you are willing to put in the time to research the recruiter's company. To know the organization is to say to the recruiter, "I care." Acquire two kinds of information: information that is available publicly, and information that only insiders usually know.

Your school library holds many public sources of information about a company. In the reference section, you will find Thomas' *Register of American Manufacturers;* Standard and Poors' *Industrial Index and Register;* Moody's *Industrial Manual;* and three Dun and Bradstreet publications: *Middle Market Directory, Million Dollar Directory,* and *Reference Book.* Don't overlook Fortune's *Plant and Product Directory.*

In addition, local companies are usually listed with the chamber of commerce. The company's *Annual Report* is usually on file there, and always available for the price of a phone call or a visit to the company.

Table 8.5 lists some of the kinds of information you will want to know about a company *before* you go into an interview with its recruiter.

There is nothing wrong with taking a direct approach in researching a company, and you have much to gain from it. A phone call to the personnel department of the company can be very informative. In addition, if word that you called gets to the recruiter (as it probably will) that is likely to be impressive. Alumni, friends, stockbrokers, and current employees of the company can all tell you things about the company. Ask around. Table 8.6 lists some questions you might wish to ask these people.

Questions to Ask Sources of Private Information

1. In your opinion, what is the public image of the organization?
2. Is there a high personnel turnover? If so, why?
3. What educational and training programs does the company offer?
4. Will the organization help employees return to college for advanced study?
5. What is a realistic starting salary for an entry-level person in my professional area?
6. What kind of benefits does the company offer?
7. What is the company policy on transferring people to other locations?
8. What is the general work climate?
9. Do subordinates participate in decision making?
10. What are the most serious problems faced by people in your part of the organization?

▲ Table 8.6

Study the company's literature and recruitment materials for evidence of the organization's culture. Get a copy of the organization's annual report. What kinds of business does the company do, and how? For example, does the business rely heavily on direct sales to customers? Do the primary values of the organization appear to center on the customer's needs? If so, to be successful will require persistence, and a focus for the recruiter will be to look for evidence of your own persistence.

Do the brochures and other materials suggest an organization that is formal? Friendly and chatty? Can you find stories about the organization's heroes? If so, what characteristics seem to be emphasized in those stories?

Can you find any corporate themes in the organization's literature? For example, does the organization brag about its quality? Does it focus on service? Does it brag about its leadership or its high technology? These themes provide you with insight about what's important to the recruiter.

For example, suppose you realize from the company literature that it is quality conscious. The word *quality* appears often. People talk about quality. To illustrate, the slogan, "Quality Improvement Process," has been the guiding theme for the International Paper Company since about 1983. If you discover the quality theme, then you know that the recruiter is going to be looking for evidence that you do quality work, that you value quality, and that you have a positive attitude about doing what is necessary to assure quality work and a quality product.

After you have studied your own strengths and weaknesses and know the organization with which you will interview, you are ready to develop your resume and your cover letter.

Checklist for Cover Letters

1. Is this letter an original? Typed on bond paper? Error free?
2. Is this letter addressed to a real person? Are all names and titles correct, and correctly spelled?
3. Does the letter follow a standard business format? Does it look well placed on the page?
4. Does the bond paper match the envelope? Is the paper white or off-white? Is the paper of good quality?

Prepare Your Resume and Cover Letter

The purpose of a resume and cover letter is to secure an interview. The resume provides a brief and attractive summary of your training and experience. The cover letter provides an opportunity for you to show that you can write and that you can adapt to the dictates of a particular situation. Therefore, the package must be designed to persuade the interviewer that he or she wants to meet with you. Thus, spend enough time to assure that your letter and resume are as perfect as possible.

There are many books and reference materials available that can help you to develop the appropriate job-search materials. Visit your campus placement or personnel office and ask for help. Every college or university library owns a section of reference works, brochures, and pamphlets designed to assist you in the job search. The local book store, or your college or university bookstore, will have current materials for sale. The materials are inexpensive and well worth the price.

Table 8.7 provides a checklist that will guide you in preparing the cover letter. Table 8.8 provides a checklist to guide you in preparing your resume, and figures 8.1 and 8.2 provide a sample cover letter and sample resume.

Plan and Practice the Role of Job Seeker

Finally, you are ready to practice the actual job-search interview. The best way to do this is to anticipate and answer as many typical interview questions as possible. This practice helps you to focus your own attitudes and opinions and helps you to think through the answers, thereby finding the most suitable answers. Table 8.9 lists sixty typical interview questions that you will surely want to review before you go into a job-search interview.

Checklist for Resumes

▲ Table 8.8

1. Is the resume an original? Typed on bond paper? Error free?
2. Is all the following information clearly identified and easy to find?
   - Your name
   - Your address
   - Your telephone number(s)
   - Your career objectives or goals
   - Your educational background (i.e., degrees, with location and dates of completion)
     - Educational major
     - Educational minor
     - Special training, with dates of completion
   - Your work-related experience
   - Honors you have received
   - Your activities and interests
3. Does the resume conform to these standards?
   - Paper size—8 1/2″ × 11″
   - Maximum length—2 pages
   - Pleasing appearance on the page
   - Error free

Keep in mind that the recruiter needs information about you in order to find a match between you and a job, and that you need information about the company in order to see if your training, experience, and inclinations provide that match. Moreover, the recruiter will expect you to ask questions.

Do *not* ask questions that a little research will answer. These include such factual information as what the company does and where it's located. Also do not ask questions about money and fringe benefits. These topics are important, but they should not be your first priority. Moreover, many recruiters consider that such questions imply that the candidate has the wrong priorities. The company has a salary range in mind for the position, and it will tell you that salary range in plenty of time. The company also has a fringe-benefits package, and it will tell you about that in plenty of time.

Depend upon the fact that a reputable organization must pay "market wage," and it must carry an appropriate fringe-benefits package in order to attract and keep employees. You should already know the going rate for someone with your talents, skills, and experience before you enter the interview.

6323 Las Cosas Ct.
Mobile, AL 36609
February 26, 19XX

Ms. Laura N. Hall
Personnel Manager
ComSouth Corporation
799 Corrington Street
Kansas City, MO 64009

Dear Ms. Hall:

The purpose of this letter is to apply for the entry level position in public relations
that you advertised in the February 25, 19XX, edition of the *Mobile Press
Register*. I believe I am well trained for such a position.

Currently I am a senior at University of South Alabama, with a double major, the
first in public relations, the second in marketing. I will graduate in June, 19XX,
with a 3.85 grade-point average. For the past three years I have worked as public
relations intern at McDonald Communications, Inc. where I have assisted in
planning and implementing three successful corporate and political public relations
campaigns. I have also served as Vice President and, currently, as President of
the Public Relations Society of Alabama, USA Student Chapter.

I will be in Kansas City during our spring recess, from March 15 through March 22,
19XX. Would it be possible for us to meet during that week? If I have not heard
from you by March 12, I will phone you to see about setting up an appointment.

May I say, again, that I am very interested in the position you advertised?

Sincerely,

Andrew Jackson

Andrew Jackson

enclosure

APPLICANT'S NAME

ADDRESSES: *Home*   *College*
              0000 Hillcrest Road   Smith Residence Center
              Mobile, AL 36609   University of South Alabama
              205-000-0000   205-000-0000

OBJECTIVES: My immediate objective is to obtain a position in business in the
              field of public relations. My long-range goal is public relations
              management.

EDUCATION: B.A., University of South Alabama, expected May 1988.
              Major area: Organizational communication and public relations.
              Minor area: Marketing

GPA: Overall: 3.2; Major area: 3.5; Minor area: 3.3 (4.0 scale)

EXPERIENCE: *Information clerk, Smith Residence Center.*
  1986-87   Responsible for answering phone and giving information.

  1985-87   *Editorial staff, Vanguard*, student weekly newspaper.
              Researched and wrote news stories and editorials, assisted in
              layout and design.

  Summer   *Part-time assistant, public relations, Illinois Bell Telephone
  1984   Company*, DeKalb. Helped to design brochures; wrote a
              speech for use in the high school; edited in-house newspaper.

  1983-84   *Part-time salesperson, Hall's Shoe Store*, Mobile.
              Sold men's and women's shoes, took departmental inventory.

  Summer   *Lifeguard, municipal swimming pool*, Mobile.
  1983   Taught swimming and enforced water safety programs.

HONORS: Dean's list for junior and senior years.
              Outstanding Student in Communication Arts, 1986-87.

ACTIVITIES: Member, Public Relations Council of Alabama,
              Student Chapter, 1984-88, and vice-president 1985-88.

PERSONAL: Single. Born: 6/25/65. Weight: 155 lbs.
              Height: 5'9". Health: Excellent.

REFERENCES   Furnished upon request.

Typical Interview Questions

1. What are your long-range and short-range goals and objectives? When and why did you establish these goals? How are you preparing yourself to achieve them?
2. What specific goals, other than those related to your occupation, have you established for yourself for the next ten years?
3. What do you see yourself doing five years from now?
4. What do you really want to do in life?
5. What are your long-range career objectives?
6. How do you plan to achieve your career goals?
7. What are the most important rewards you expect in your business career?
8. What do you expect to be earning in five years?
9. Why did you choose the career for which you are preparing?
10. Which is more important to you, the money or the type of job?
11. What do you consider to be your greatest strengths and weaknesses?
12. How would you describe yourself?
13. How do you think a friend or professor who knows you well would describe you?
14. What motivates you to put forth your greatest effort?
15. How has your college experience prepared you for a business career?
16. Why should I hire you?
17. What qualifications do you have that make you think that you will be successful in business?
18. How do you determine or evaluate success?
19. What do you think it takes to be successful in a company like ours?
20. In what ways do you think you can make a contribution to our company?
21. What qualities should a successful manager possess?
22. Describe the relationship that should exist between a supervisor and those reporting to him or her.
23. What two or three accomplishments have given you the most satisfaction? Why?
24. Describe your most rewarding college experience.
25. If you were hiring a graduate for this position, what qualities would you look for?
26. Why did you select your college or university?
27. What led you to choose your field or major study?
28. What college subjects did you like best? Why?
29. What college subjects did you like least? Why?
30. If you could do so, how would you plan your academic study differently? Why?

▼ Table 8.9

31. What changes would you make in your college or university? Why?
32. Do you have plans for continued study? An advanced degree?
33. Do you think that your grades are a good indication of your academic achievement?
34. What have you learned from participation in extracurricular activities?
35. In what kind of work environment are you most comfortable?
36. How do you work under pressure?
37. In what part-time or summer jobs have you been most interested?
38. How would you describe the ideal job for you following graduation?
39. Why did you decide to seek a position with this company?
40. What do you know about our company?
41. What two or three things are most important to you in your job?
42. Are you seeking employment in a company of a certain size? Why?
43. What criteria are you using to evaluate the company for which you hope to work?
44. Do you have a geographical preference? Why?
45. Will you relocate? Does relocation bother you?
46. Are you willing to travel?
47. Are you willing to spend at least six months as a trainee?
48. Why do you think you might like to live in the community in which our company is located?
49. What major problem have you encountered and how did you deal with it?
50. What have you learned from your mistakes?
    We think it would be helpful to you to add these additional, somewhat difficult questions to the list.
51. Did you do the best job you could in school? If not, why?
52. What kind of boss do you prefer? Why?
53. Describe a typical day of work at the XYZ Company for which you worked.
54. What are some of the important lessons you have learned from jobs you have held?
55. What types of books do you read? What was the last one you read?
56. What kinds of things cause you to lose your temper?
57. Are you a leader? Give an example.
58. Are you a creative person? Give an example of your creativity.
59. Are you analytical? Give an example.
60. What are the most important books in your field?

Source: From *The Endicott Report*, published by the Placement center, Northwestern University, Evanston, Illinois 60201. Used by permission.

▲ **Table 8.9** continued

Summary

This chapter describes six types of face-to-face, planned communication events commonly called the interview. All of the types of interviews are organized in approximately the same way. Each has an opening phase that includes greetings, orientation, and motivation. Each has a question-answer phase, and each has a closing phase that includes a summary and good-by pleasantries.

Open questions invite a broad response. Closed questions seek very limited and focused responses. Questions can be asked directly, in order to get at specific information. Questions can also raise hypothetical situations to encourage respondents to disclose something about themselves.

How questions are organized can be very important. Open-to-closed questions (the funnel sequence) encourage respondents to provide expert information and allow the interviewer to take advantage of the opportunities for information gathering that present themselves in an interview. The closed-to-open pattern (the inverted funnel sequence) encourages a timid respondent because the questions are easier to answer.

The job-search interview captures the attention of most students. A job seeker's responsibilities include knowing himself, learning about the organization, preparing a resume and cover letter, and planning and practicing for the role of job-seeker.

Throughout the chapter, numerous examples of questions, resumes, and cover letters, and a wide variety of tables have been provided to help you in the planning stages of interviews.

Discussion Questions

1. Interview two or three individuals who hold management positions in their companies. Determine from these interviews how each manager evaluates his or her company's performance appraisal practices. What are the strong points and what are the weak points of those practices? Bring your notes to class for comparison and contrast.

2. Perform a self-analysis, jot down a profile of your findings, and then get feedback from your boss and a few trusted friends. Do these people agree with your self-analysis? Does this self-study cause any surprises? Come to class prepared to discuss these questions.

3. Go to the career planning and placement office of your college or university and secure as much information on preparing a resume as you can. Using that information and the suggestions in this chapter, develop a resume for yourself. Bring several copies to class so that your classmates can provide you with feedback and suggestions.

References

[1]Leonard Zunin and Natalie Zunin, *Contact the First Four Minutes: An Intimate Guide to First Encounters* (New York: Ballantine Books, 1972). See, Cheryl Hamilton and Cordell Parker, *Communicating for Results: A Guide for Business and the Professions* (Belmont, CA: Wadsworth Publishing Company), 1987, pp. 183–84.

[2]Martin John Yate, *Knock 'Em Dead* (Boston: Bob Adams, 1987).

Part III

Analysis and Larger Communication Contexts

We have explored several facets of the communication process. Each has unique characteristics, but there is a commonality among all of the elements: each integrates some feature of another element in its impact on communication and verbal behavior.

The features of the communication process appear in all of the other sections. Nonverbal communication, verbal communication, listening, the interpersonal relationship, and the other chapters each share a substantial portion of their impact with the materials that precede and follow them.

This is especially true of this section of the book. Any communication event involves the critical analysis of ideas and concerns the character of group communication experiences. As you examine the settings for the communication experience, you also need to understand how communication operates in organizations. Therefore, this section identifies the characteristics of organizational communication and discusses how one-to-one communication has different characteristics from communication within the organization.

The organization is a communication-processing entity; the bases of communication have general application in organizational behavior. Additionally, some specific suggestions improve organizational sending, receiving, and processing of messages. Organizational communication is a specialized field of study for communication researchers and theorists. Chapter 9 introduces you to the basic concepts in this unit and relate those concepts to communication elements in other contexts.

to discover what issues exist, what alternatives exist, and what evaluative criteria exist that may be applied. Value is placed on withholding any judgments until all the views and alternatives have been stated and examined. A popular term applied to this approach is "suspension of judgment." This kind of critical thinking is rigorously applied in some business problem-solving groups. To a lesser extent, this is the method of critical thinking that occurs when people are deciding on how to spend their evening. "Shall we go to a movie?" "What movie?" "What else is there to do?" What time should we meet?" "Shall we eat first?" "Maybe we should eat after the show." "What are you hungry for?"

A third approach to critical thinking seems almost persuasive. In this approach, people present ideas and evidence as a means of influence. They may hold a position on some controversial issue such as capital punishment, mercy killing, or governmental involvement in the abortion decision. Then, they present evidence and arguments aimed at supporting that point of view. The thinking process revolves around identifying what arguments and evidence best support some claim or conclusion. This approach has been called the "rhetorical" approach.

This chapter examines all three of these approaches. The goal is to provide a background in the critical methods that will be applied in all the contexts where reflection on arguments and ideas is necessary.

Again, critical thinking is not a cold and calculating approach to life. Instead, it is an approach that enhances the quality of life by reducing the frequency of error. It involves identifying the thought(s) to be considered and calmly applying reasonable standards in order to determine their value or use.

Creative and critical thinking are entirely different processes. **Creative thinking** involves developing new ideas or solutions, or recombining things already known into something different. *Critical thinking* applies judgment processes to already existing ideas. Critical thinking can be as simple as deciding on whether to go to the baseball game; on whether a rock concert will be too expensive; or on whether to trade in your old car. However, critical thinking does involve a modest amount of mental discipline, which includes some of the following.

The Reflective Thinking Process

Reflective thinking involves identifying an idea or problem, applying standards to evaluate its worth, and arriving at a judgment about keeping or rejecting the conclusion. For example, consider the problem of wanting a new item of clothing. You reach into your pocket to discover that you don't have enough money to buy it. How important is the purchase of that clothing to your welfare? Should you use your credit card? Will the item be on sale when you get paid next week?

There is debate about whether a single set of critical thinking procedures can be effective across varying problems.[1] Flesch discussed several of the advantages and problems of trying to apply a single method to problem-solution in *The Art of Clear Thinking*.[2] There is general agreement, however, that a system like the scientific method works for us in most situations. Applying objective procedures and standards often helps us to face problems.

What are the problems we need to face? In human discourse, the problems that most often need to be examined critically involve something called "claims." A **claim** is an expressed conclusion that is characterized by its rhetorical purpose. That is, a claim is a conclusion someone *wants* you to accept. It involves the use of language to create a perception of reality, value, or conclusion. The following are some common examples:

> *"I'm telling the truth."*
> *"Wilson was the last person to drive the car. He must know how the damage was done."*
> *"That was a great movie. You've got to see it."*
> *"Communication 75 is a great course."*
> *"The blue dress looks a lot better on you than the red one."*
> *"It's time to go home."*
> *"You'd better study for that examination. She's a really tough grader, and her exams are usually rough."*

Claims are usually—but not always—clearly stated. Some are implied. Either way, if you learn to listen carefully to claims you can usually discover the speaker's purpose and agenda.

Claims of Fact, Value, and Policy

There are three kinds of claims: claims of fact, claims of value, and claims of policy. Each one is a statement, which is either directly stated or implied.

A *claim of fact* is a statement about some past or present condition or relationship. It is characterized by forms of the verb "to be." A factual claim moves from something that is known or believed to be true, and it draws an inference about something that is controversial.

Sometimes factual claims are easy to identify because they are clearly stated:

> *"We can't go fishing today—the water is too rough."*
> *"Columbus discovered America."*
> *"Mary is older than Janice."*

Sometimes factual claims are difficult to identify because they are assumed, but not stated.

> *"We should eliminate capital punishment [. . . because capital punishment is not an effective deterrent to crime.]"*

*You ought to give up smoking, Carl [. . . because smoking is
dangerous to your health.]"*
*"There ought to be a law to control handguns and automatic
weapons [. . . because handguns and automatic weapons are
responsible for most violent crimes.]"*

Finally, some factual claims are troublesome because they assume the
past and the future can be easily verified:

"The United States will put a man on Mars by 1995."
*"We're going to have a serious shortage of scientists by the turn of the
century."*
"Shakespeare didn't write Shakespeare's plays."
"American involvement in Vietnam was illegal."

Clearly, what sounds like a fact (because of the sentence form in which
the claim is made) is not always a fact. Critical thinking will help the listener
to find the flaw in the reasoning behind a claim like "*How* do you know the
United States will be on Mars by 1995?" Critical thinking demands proof.

A *claim of value* is a conclusion about the value or worth of some idea
or object, or of some policy or practice. It is characterized by words such as
good or *bad,* or other judgmental words. Some examples are:

"Gun control would be beneficial to the American people."
*"Abortion is wrong. There is no standard against which it can be
made right. Abortion is murder."*
"Picasso's Guernica *is the greatest painting of the century."*
"The schools are the best place to provide sex education."

The key feature of a claim of value is that it expresses some funda-
mentally positive or negative attitude about its subject matter. It seeks to gain
acceptance of a value judgment.

A *claim of policy* calls for action. It asks for some change in policy or
behavior. It is characterized by the words *ought* and *should.* Some examples
are:

*"The federal government should ban the manufacture, importation,
or distribution of handguns and automatic weapons."*
"You ought to stop smoking, Margaret."
"Mother, you should buy a car you like, not just the cheapest one."

These three kinds of claims—fact, value, and policy—usually occur together in a complex and sometimes very subtle mixture. For example, in
order to make a wise decision about which car to buy, you might have to
consider all of these claims:

*"This car is going to be reliable (value) and inexpensive (value).
Not to mention that it's beautiful and has only 3,000 actual miles*

(fact). We know that this brand has the fewest repairs in its class (fact) and that it will continue to give trouble-free service (fact/ value) for another 90,000 miles. Besides, this car has been well maintained; we have the maintenance records (value/fact). So it boils down to this (fact): you like the car (fact), you can afford the car (fact), the car is solid (value), priced right (value) in your price range (fact). So what are you waiting for? (You ought to buy the car. [policy])

To work your way through such a jungle of claims, you must know how to think critically. Arguments are stated, but are they true? Each argument must be evaluated separately. The distinctions between fact, value, and policy are important, but it is vital to apply critical standards. Otherwise, people become mindless consumers of the claims of others and rely on the accuracy and honesty of the source alone to protect them from being misled.

Evaluation of New Ideas

We develop new ideas every day, usually, as a result of trying to solve problems in our lives. However, these new ideas do not just pop into our minds in some magically complete form. They must be shaped and tested. For example, you may say, "I have a great idea for a fund-raising campaign." That idea probably came into your mind because you were not completely satisfied with the present ways of fund-raising. Or you may have thought your fund-raising approach would be better than the one in place.

New ideas are not like the light bulb that appears in a comic strip. New ideas do not suddenly switch on. Rather, they are the result of years of experience and frustration, and they often represent an answer to a difficulty that has been experienced for a long time.

Most good ideas result from a period of worry, followed by a period of trial and error, and then followed by evaluation of the various trials and errors. If the idea seems "good" or "terrible," we accept or reject it, or we modify it through more worry and more trial and error.

Thus, for the present discussion the specific idea is not the area of focus. The interest is in the *procedures* by which ideas may be evaluated. The motivating questions are: Is there a problem? If so, what is the nature of the problem? What is the extent of the problem? How should we measure whether the idea is good or bad? What criteria should be applied to alternative solutions when trying to solve the problem? What can be done? What should we do? Let us examine each of these questions in order to better understand their applications in public communication. Whether in interpersonal communication or public speaking, these questions are the basis of reflective thinking.

New ideas result from years of experience and frustration.

Be certain you understand the problem.

Here are some common questions that apply to all problems:

1. Is the problem significant in this situation for this group of people?

2. Is the problem typical or is it somehow unique?

3. What are the major characteristics of the problem?

4. Is it possible to solve the problem characteristics?

Determine the criteria to apply.

Now, let's look at some standard criteria to use to evaluate solutions.

Determine your criteria. **Criteria** (i.e., standards) are the yardsticks used to measure whether ideas, positions, or proposals make sense and are worthwhile. They are useful and can also be applied to materials used for public presentation.

What are your goals? In evaluating ideas, decide on your objective and the process to reach the objective. Is the goal to find the idea that is the least expensive? For example, do you want to spend the least amount of money to put an addition onto your home? If the answer is "Yes," then that simplifies the process. If the objective is to identify the idea that is acceptable to the greatest number of people, then that is an entirely different end. In the case of an addition to your house, that means satisfying all of the members of your family while still spending the least possible amount of money on the house. Popularity—plus the least expense—may not work together.

Are you looking for a workable solution that has only a few major shortcomings? If the answer is yes, then do the cost and immediate use of that solution make a difference? Let us critically evaluate a solution to one of the major problems in our society—automobile deaths on the highways.

Be certain you understand the problem. What is the problem on our highways? How many people are killed each year and how many are maimed? Everyone agrees that we should stop killing so many people with automobiles. Could Detroit build a safer car and significantly reduce the danger of death in a collision? Probably. Are people concerned with this problem? It seems that they are only concerned when the problem involves someone they know or when the accident is especially gruesome.

In the automobile example, what is the extent of auto deaths? How many people are victims and how do they become victims? Are the characteristics of the problem clear to you? Is the problem involved with some other problem or does it involve only itself? Are highway accidents involved with speed, alcohol consumption, or other variables? Are most accidents the result of poor judgment?

If your way of stating the problem does not help you to reach a solution, try restating the problem another way. This restatement may help you to reach an answer. You could say, "Are our licensing requirements for drivers too lenient?" Or you might approach it by saying "Should the state highway patrol and local law officers rigidly enforce speed limits?" Those ways of stating the problem provide another perspective on the problem. They direct your attention to the broad issue and allow you to focus on alternatives.

Try to state the problem in concrete terms. You could say, "Our problem is that we have a large number of automobile-related highway deaths." But the problem could be stated more concretely. You could say, "Twenty thousand people died in auto accidents on the highways in this country during 1989. Many of them died needlessly." Or, "Two of my best friends were killed in car accidents last year. And they were only part of a larger slaughter!" That certainly is concrete and specific. In a public setting it will seize the attention of your listeners.

Once you can establish the existence of a problem by using believable evidence and sources, what requirements do the automakers and the consumer use to evaluate the design? The following include a few of the requirements:

1. How much would it increase the cost of a new car?

2. Would it be appealing to a large number of car buyers?

3. Could redesign be incorporated into an attractive existing design?

4. If improvement requires a new design, will it be cost attractive and will the design appeal to new car purchasers?

5. Would it hamper the operation of the car?

This is not an exhaustive list. These are only a few of the questions that carmakers would have to answer in order to design and to use such a system. They are *practical* questions. They relate to issues of *desirability and usability*, and they are the kind of questions that are asked each day. For example, when we make purchase decisions, these questions are part of our critical thinking process. Any merchant or manufacturer would ask these questions before bringing a product to market. This is part of the critical thinking process, and it is an essential part as you develop ideas for public communication.

The practical phase is tied into the solution and its evaluation. The process of critical thinking is simple. What is wrong? How large is the problem and how can the problem be described? What are the ways to solve it? What are the best solutions (for the affected people, organizations, or society)? Once you develop satisfactory answers to these questions, you are on your way to the application of the solution.

Nature and Tests of Reasoning

The mental process of manipulating ideas and trying to discover relationships among them is one of our most complex and highest level tasks. Every day we make judgments based on basic values and information. These decisions are the product of a set of values, associations, and perceptions that we bring to the reasoning process. We decide how rapidly to walk over ice. We choose our preference for music. We develop an image of the "ideal" partner. We apply standards as we evaluate proposals. Therefore, it is important that we examine the process, tests, and fallacies in reasoning so we can better evaluate our thinking and the conclusions of others.

The Reasoning Process

We know that reasoning involves the showing of relationships. **Reasoning** is the mental process in which people move from the evidence, through a set of claims, to acceptance or rejection of a conclusion. When we engage in this process, we do it either inductively or deductively.

The most important thing to remember about inductive and deductive reasoning is that the goal is to draw an inference about the likelihood that some statement is true. That is, the goal is an acceptance of a claim. However, it is also wise for a critical thinker to develop a little healthy skepticism.

Induction involves going from the specific case to the general conclusion. **Induction** may be defined as a pattern of reasoning that moves from evidence about certain members of a class or category to a conclusion about other or all members of the class or category. Suppose that a study of a large number of auto accidents reveals that in most of those automobile accidents the driver was a male, who was under nineteen years of age. Using inductive reasoning, we might conclude that young males are less safe drivers than young women drivers. This conclusion began with the specifics (i.e., the drivers, their age, their sex) and the occurrence (i.e., the type of accident).

Remember that the conclusion drawn in this case is not necessarily true. There may be factors other than the sex and age of the drivers and the seriousness of the accident. Furthermore, we probably would not investigate each of these accidents and see all of the conditions. Because inductive reasoning proceeds from the specific to a general conclusion, the conclusion may contain some inaccuracies because not all of the specific facts may generalize to every case.

The other primary approach is called deduction. Deductive reasoning proceeds from the general to the specific. **Deduction** is a pattern of reasoning that moves from a general statement about a class or category to a conclusion that the statement applies in a particular case.

IT'S MORE FUN TO KNOW

Making Communication Contact

"While extremely short ring times (of telephones) miss significant proportions of at-homes, only four rings are necessary to reach 97 percent. Thus, it appears that almost half of the research firms surveyed waste time by allowing the phone to ring more than four times."

See: Raymond J. Smead and James Wilcox, "Ring Policy in Telephone Surveys," *Public Opinion Quarterly*, 44:1, (Spring 1980), p. 116.

Comment . . .

If you want to use the telephone effectively as an instrument of communication, when you place a call the most efficient method is to allow the phone to ring four times. Waiting longer than four rings gets an answer only three percent of the time.

Deductive reasoning is used infrequently in everyday life. Instead, we tend to reason inductively. We examine a case, locate another and another, and then draw an inference. Deduction is more the province of philosophical analysis or arguments of points of law. For example, if we begin with a general statement that all high school teachers must be college graduates and we identified Mr. Kumquat as a high school teacher, then the conclusion is that Mr. Turbo Kumquat has completed a college degree. However, two cautions should be observed. Do these generalizations apply to all teachers? Are there exceptions? In this case, are *all* high school teachers college grads? If there is an exception, then the reasoning becomes invalid. We cannot reason validly when the general statement has exceptions. If all high school teachers are college grads and Kumquat is a high school teacher, then we know that he *has* completed college.

The procedures and conclusions of reasoning often are flawed. We do not always follow all of the steps of an argument or some of the elements may lack soundness. However, some tests may be applied to your own arguments and the arguments of others.

Argument by example is sometimes called "argument from a partial case." Argument by example is an inductive pattern of reasoning that claims that what is true of one case in the class or category is also true of some other case in the same class or category.

Argument by generalization is an inductive pattern of reasoning that claims that what is true of certain members of a class or category is also true of other members of the category, or of the category as a whole.

Compare the arguments below. Both are inductive. The one on the left is an argument by example because it focuses on one case in the class and it argues that the claim is true about a second case in the class. The argument on the right is argument by generalization because it takes a much broader view.

Argument by example

The waste-water treatment method used at the *XYX* chemical plant works. It will also work at the *ABC* plant.

Argument by generalization

The smoke-control plan was effective in Kansas City, in Charleston, and in Jackson. It will also work well in Memphis, St. Louis, or in any other city in America.

Tests of Argument by Example

1.   Is the example *relevant?*

2.   Is the example *typical?*

3.   Is the example *timely?*

4.   Are there *any* critical counter examples?

Tests of Argument by Generalization

1.   Are there *enough* examples to support this generalization?

2.   Are the examples *relevant* to the claim?

3.   Are the examples *representative* of the class about which the generalization is made?

4.   Are there *any* critical counter examples?

Argument from analogy reasons that because two things are known to be similar in some particular ways, that they will also resemble each other

in other ways. There are two kinds of argument from analogy: *literal analogy and figurative analogy*. In a literal analogy, the comparison is drawn between two members of the same class. The argument is that the two objects share many features; thus, all (or most) of the features of one are shared by the other. In a figurative analogy, the comparison is drawn between members of two different classes. The argument is that a relation or quality in one is similar to a relation or quality in the other (see examples).

This differentiation is important to critical thinking because the evaluative standards are so much different. If you put literal and figurative analogy side-by-side, then you will begin to see the differences.

Literal analogy

The first thing compared has features *A, B, C,* and *D.* The second thing has features *A, B,* and *C.* It will probably also have feature *D.*

Figurative analogy

The years of your life are like a walk through the woods. From time to time you come to a fork in the path, and you have to make a choice about which direction to go.

Tests of Argument by Literal Analogy

1. Are the compared objects in the *same class?*

2. Are the points of comparison *relevant?*

3. Are the points of comparison *significant?*

4. Are the points of comparison *sufficient?*

5. Are any points of difference *critical?*

Tests of Argument by Figurative Analogy

A *figurative analogy* can never be supported in a logical or probable way. A figurative analogy can never be "true" or "false" or "probable." However, it still can be a highly effective form of argument, and the figurative analogy can still be tested. The tests, however, turn out to be questions of the rhetorical effectiveness of the argument by figurative analogy.

1. Does the analogy *elicit* the desired response?

2. Are there *damaging* points of comparison?

Argument from sign is a pattern of reasoning that asserts the presence of some feature, artifact, characteristic, or condition that is evidence of the presence of a related feature, artifact, characteristic, or condition. Figure 9.1 illustrates argument from sign. See figure 9.1.

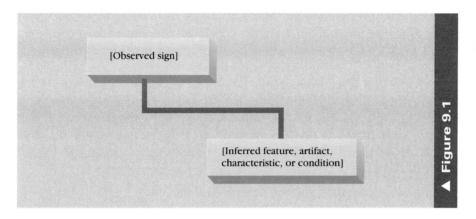

[Observed sign]

[Inferred feature, artifact, characteristic, or condition]

Tests of Argument from Sign

There are three tests of sign argument. It is easy to remember them as the Three *C's:* Constant, Cumulative, and Contrary.

1. Is the relationship between sign and inference *constant?*

2. Is the relationship between sign and inference *cumulative?*

3. Are any *contrary* signs present?

An **argument from cause** claims that one event, set of events, condition, or set of conditions brings about another event, set of events, condition, or set of conditions. There are two kinds of argument from cause. The first, and weakest, is based on the notion called "necessary condition." The argument is that a necessary condition must exist in order to cause the effect. The second, and stronger, form of causal argument rests on a notion called "sufficient condition." The argument is that the presence of a certain condition is *sufficient* to cause some effect.

To help separate the ideas of necessary conditions from sufficient conditions, think of baking a cake. It is *necessary* to have all the ingredients (milk, flour, eggs, etc.). But would this list be *sufficient?* Not unless you also have a mixing bowl, something with which to mix the ingredients, a container to hold the batter, and an oven that works.

Tests of Argument from Cause

1. Is the cause *capable* of producing the effect?

2. Is this the *only,* or *most important* cause?

3. Is the cause *necessary?*

4. Is the cause *sufficient?*

5. Could a different cause *offset* the effect?

Arguments are made from authority as often as they are made in any other way. Sometimes, the arguments from authority are very subtle and sometimes they are fairly transparent. An **argument from authority** says that statements by an expert or some knowledgeable person are sufficient grounds for accepting a claim.

Each one of the following claims is an argument from authority.

UNNAMED AUTHORITY: "European researchers have discovered a new formula for growing hair."

RELIGIOUS AUTHORITY: "The Bible clearly says 'Thou shalt not murder.' How, then, can you support legal abortion?"

MASS AUTHORITY: "Everyone agrees that the flag is our most precious symbol."

MASS AUTHORITY: "Budweiser—Largest selling beer in the world."

WELL-KNOWN AUTHORITY: "Great book! Be sure to read it!"—*Boston Globe.*

WELL-KNOWN AUTHORITY: "Jack Nicklaus is a 'Champion'. And he uses one. The American Express Card."

WELL-KNOWN AUTHORITY: "Master of possibilities, Andre Previn uses MasterCard."

Tests of Argument from Authority

1. Is the source *well qualified?*

2. Does the source have the *necessary* information?

3. Is the source *biased?*

4. Is the testimony *consistent* with other known information?

The Sources and Tests of Evidence

Evidence may be defined to include (1) directly observable facts and conditions, (2) beliefs and claims that are generally accepted as true, and (3) previously established conclusions. In human communication, notice that each of these categories of evidence is expressed as statements that may be used to gain acceptance because they are believed by the receiver.

There are two kinds of evidence, real evidence and personal evidence. *Real evidence* is always some kind of artifact. For example, the handgun at a murder scene is real evidence. The fingerprints on the gun that establish the argument, "John held the gun" are real evidence. The ballistic markings on the bullet that came from the gun are real evidence.

Caption (left margin): An argument from authority says that a statement from an expert is sufficient grounds to accept a claim.

Every other form of evidence is called *personal evidence* because it always comes (directly or indirectly) from people. "I think that John might have wanted to kill Mary" fits into this category. Remember that evidence is a statement. These statements are based on people's opinions or on documentary information, such as statistics generated from a data base or from a newspaper account of an event.

The most commonly used evidence fits into five categories.

Specific information consists of real numbers, real names, colors, and so forth that are used to build concrete images in receivers. These can be listeners in an interpersonal setting or in a public communication experience. *Statistics* are grouped facts. They provide a shorthand method for summarizing large numbers of examples. "Domestic automotive sales fell significantly from the similar period last year" illustrates this use. Statistics are different from ordinary numbers. *Testimony* is any direct quotation or paraphrase of what a person has said. *Definition and explanation* involves a formal statement of the meaning or significance of some word. Thus, definition and explanation bring a claim into focus and clarify the meaning and intent of the claim. *Illustration and example* are instances that serve as representative of a group of things and that show the nature or character of the group.

We present evidence when we say, "Three of my friends were treated rudely at that restaurant," or if we maintain "The people who supported the tax increase did not understand the real issue." If a speaker asserts, "Twenty prominent doctors said they used the ingredients contained in this medicine," we are using evidence. As public communicators and listeners, we should apply our standards to these statements. Do not accept them just because someone says that they indicate the truth of a position. Consider these tests of evidence discussed by the authors in another work.[3]

1. Is there enough *evidence* to establish the point? This is a difficult question to answer. Make a continuing series of judgments about how much evidence to present in order to establish your point. It is rare that enough evidence exists to establish a point with complete confidence. Instead, you may have to settle for high quality evidence that appears to carry weight with the audience.

2. Is the evidence *clear?* Sometimes people decide that a piece of evidence is relevant merely because they personally understand it. You cannot assume that your listeners will understand how a piece of evidence supports your ideas. Be careful to select evidence that clearly supports your point or can be made clear.

3. Is the evidence *consistent* with what is already known? People tend to believe new information if it seems consistent with what they

already know and believe. If the evidence makes sense based on their previous knowledge, then it adds weight to your argument. If the evidence is not consistent with what is already known, then you must be prepared to show that the new evidence is more believable than what your listeners already know.

4. Can the evidence be *verified?* In selecting evidence, be careful to ensure that your evidence agrees with other sources. Satisfy yourself about the validity of your evidence. Otherwise, some listeners may attempt to verify it, discover it is invalid, and decide that it is unbelievable. Similarly, you would make the same decision if you caught someone presenting unverifiable evidence.

5. Is the source of the evidence *competent?* Clearly, if a speaker uses testimony as evidence, the source must be qualified if the evidence is to be believed. When a celebrity endorses a product, does he or she actually know anything about that product? Remember that personal evidence can come from an expert, or it can (and more frequently does) come from a nonexpert.

6. Is the source of evidence *without bias* or *prejudice?* A person who has an ax to grind might honestly give unreliable evidence because he or she has a strong bias. A person who wants a certain outcome might try to influence that outcome with his or her testimony. The question of bias and prejudice is an important test of personal evidence.

7. Is the source of evidence *honest?* Can the source of the evidence be trusted to tell the truth? Does that person have a reputation for honesty and candor? Is the person believed to be a liar? Obviously, one of the tests of personal evidence is the honesty of the source of that evidence.

8. Is the evidence *relevant?* Sometimes a speaker uses a piece of evidence that isn't relevant to the argument, but has the appearance of relevance. For example, a student picked up a quotation from the president of the university to support a statement that a large classroom building would soon be built. When the president was later asked about the statement, the president admitted saying those words but they were about an addition to the hospital owned and operated by the university. Thus, the president's statement was not relevant to the student's argument. Also, think about the effect that statement had upon the credibility of the student.

9. Is the evidence mathematically and statistically *correct?* Sometimes evidence is inaccurate. Ask several questions about

Critical Thinking

A fallacy is an argument that is damaged because of inadequate evidence, invalid reasoning, or faulty expression. What is wrong with this picture?

statistical information that you plan to use as evidence. Are the statistics accurate? Have they been collected in a way that does not prejudice them? Have the statistics been interpreted correctly? Is the data presented in a way that is misleading?

Fallacies in Reasoning

A **fallacy** is an argument that is damaged, thus invalid, for one of three reasons: (1) inadequate evidence, (2) invalid reasoning, or (3) faulty expression. It is common to fall into the trap of one or more errors in reasoning. These errors are identified and explained so that you will be able to avoid them and to recognize them.

Ad Populum

Ad populum names a fallacy in which the advocate ignores the substance of an argument and claims that popular opinion justifies a claim.

A candidate for county auditor of Boone County used this argument in a political campaign. "I am a lifelong resident of Boone County and a graduate of Ashland High. I understand the values and traditions of people in this part of the state. Just like all of you, I am opposed to county zoning and the renumbering of rural routes." These appeals to the prejudices of longtime residents have no application to the office. Residence in the city/county has no effect on the ability of a person to audit the books and records of county government.

Two-Valued Thinking

Two-valued thinking, often called polarization, is a fallacy that claims some aspect of the world has only two values (e.g., good or bad, right or wrong). Most problems and situations have several answers or choices. Two-valued thinking suggests that the options are limited to one of two choices.

"On the issue of whether we should fire Charlie, you're either for me or against me. It's that simple!"

It is not that simple. A person does not have to be clearly in favor of or opposed to an entire action. In this case, perhaps you feel Charlie should be warned about his problem and told that he will be dismissed unless he changes his work habits. It is simpler to make it appear that there are only two choices. However, matters are infrequently either black or white; they are shades of gray.

"I've had it with the state legislature. About ten years ago, we had some people there who really did a good job. For the last five years, it's been a bunch of do-nothings down there!"

Now, we have a group of lawmakers who cannot do anything right. They are all bad. However, common sense tells us there is something good about every person and every group. It is incorrect to suggest that all of the legislators are no good. They may be a group of rascals, but they do have some merit. In fact, this person probably does not feel that they are totally useless, but only partially useless. Yet, the statement suggests that they are either all good or all bad legislators. This is a use of the two-valued orientation.

Begging the Question

Begging the question is a fallacy that rests on the assumption that the basic premise has been proved when it has not. The following statement is an example:

"Tuition at Sowash University should be free because that would serve the interests of the average person. The average person can't afford tuition at Sowash University."

Nowhere has it been established that the interests of the average people are helped by providing education. Certainly, we could argue and perhaps could prove that a more educated population promotes society, but that argument was not done here. Therefore, it is wrong to argue that we should provide free tuition when the outcome that it creates has not been proven. The conclusion needs to be proved before we can consider the principle stated.

"For a physician to be a member of a health maintenance organization (HMO) and have his personal income schedule regulated is wrong. The HMO sets the fees doctors can charge. Physicians should be free to establish their own fees."

The final sentence is merely a restatement of the first. This argument tries to prove through repetition of the initial sentence that first assertion. It assumes that proof has been given that physicians should not have their income regulated, yet that still remains to be proved.

Other examples of question begging are:

- ▲ "The soul lives forever because it cannot die."
- ▲ The national trade deficit must be reduced so that we can improve our trade imbalance.

Hasty Generalization

Hasty generalization is a fallacy that draws a conclusion about some class or category on the basis of too few examples, or on the basis of inadequate or atypical examples. The problem occurs in many situations.

> *"Everyone at school is going to the formal. I know because Mary and Fred will be there."*

If you change the names or the event, you may see your own reasoning on some issue when you were in high school. For some people, "everyone" involves the people who are important. This type of statement is used frequently to get the family car or to ask for financial relief.

> *"This is going to be a terrible day. Already I have overslept by an hour and missed my bus."*

There is much more to a day than the first hour after you are awakened, although that first sixty minutes may set a mood for the remainder of the day. Even with those events, some good news may possibly appear. You may see someone that you have missed, or a new job may suddenly occur. Good communication involves sound reasoning. Draw conclusions and make generalizations only when you have enough evidence that will justify that conclusion.

Ad Hominem

Ad hominem is attacking a person or an organization instead of an issue. It is a common way of dealing with a problem. Study the following example.

> *"We can't have Moe Zilch as an employee. He is vicious. Besides, he once was convicted of shoplifting."*

The fact that Moe once was convicted of shoplifting is one way to establish that he is a "bad" risk. However, perhaps he is vicious and then perhaps he is not. That he is vicious has not been proven. We know only that he has a previous conviction and that the speaker uses that information to raise serious questions about him.

Another example may make the issue clearer.

WITNESS PAUL: "My objection to the proposed legislation is that its sanctions deprive people of their jobs without informing them of the nature or source of the evidence against them. Under these conditions there is no proper chance to answer the charges."

SENATOR PETER: "You are a member of the American Civil Liberties Union, which defends Communists?"

WITNESS PAUL: "I do belong to that organization."

SENATOR PETER: "And you expect this committee to give weight to your testimony?"

Comment: There is no reason to suppose membership in the American Civil Liberties Union has any bearing on the individual's willingness or capacity to tell the truth. Senator Peter's technique is to discredit both Witness Paul and the American Civil Liberties Union with the brush 'defends Communists'. . .[4]

Non Sequitur

Non sequitur is a fallacious claim because it is irrelevant or unsupported by the arguments or evidence that pretend to support it. For example, "The best college graduates come from the Ivy League. Most of the career officers in the State Department in Washington, D.C. are graduates of those schools." Because most of the career officers graduated from the Ivy League proves nothing about the quality of the schools. We know only that many of the graduates find employment with the State Department.

False Authority

False authority is a fallacy in which the claimed authority is not truly qualified to render an opinion. It is an appeal to some source that is biased, unidentified, or unqualified to support a claim. The person is an authority. The problem is that the person's authority is in a different field.

> *"My friend, Paula, is a respected mechanical engineer, and she says the school tax levy makes no sense. We just don't need more money for the schools!"*

Paula may be a respected mechanical engineer but that does not qualify her in school finance or in taxation. If she were cited as the source for matters related to her field, that would be a different matter. On taxation she is outside her realm of expertise.

> *"You're an attorney who knows the businesses in this town. I'm getting ready to buy a new car. I understand you recommend a Whammo."*

Here is the same problem. If the prospective auto purchaser had asked the lawyer about the stability of businesses in the city, then the attorney would be a legitimate authority. But the attorney is not an expert on reliability or cost/benefit analysis of new cars. Therefore, the opinion is not worth much.

Appeal to Tradition

Appeal to tradition is a fallacy that claims we should continue to do something because it always has been done that way. For example, "We should stay on the quarter system because we have always been on the quarter system." For example, "You should join the Navy when you get out of high school. Men in our family have always joined the Navy when they graduate."

Summary

The process of critical thinking is vital to the development of ideas. Material for speeches must be tested vigorously against your goals. Consider the character of the problem and the solutions, and the practicality and desirability of the answers. This process of reasoning and evaluating involves both inductive and deductive thinking. As part of reasoning, a speaker should evaluate what types of reasoning (i.e., reasoning from example, analogy, or sign) were used and whether the conclusions were valid. Examine all of your reasoning carefully to avoid fallacies, such as errors in two-valued thinking, begging the question, hasty generalization, and ad hominem argument. Sound thinking is the base for effective communication. That base works best when all ideas are tested critically.

Discussion Questions

1. What are some fallacies that enter your thinking? How can you deal with them more effectively?

2. What recent television commercials or advertisements have used argument from authority? Why were they effective or ineffective?

3. Explain when deduction is more effective in the analysis of ideas than induction. Cite two or three specific examples.

4. Which is more effective in supporting an idea, a literal or a figurative analogy? Provide an example of each to show how they can be used.

References

[1]Raymond S. Nickerson, David N. Perkins, and Edward E. Smith, *The Teaching of Thinking* (Hillsdale, NJ: Lawrence Erlbaum Associates, 1985), p. 74.
[2]Rudolph Flesch, *The Art of Clear Thinking* (New York: Harper and Row, 1951).
[3]Michael S. Hanna and James W. Gibson, *Public Speaking for Personal Success,* 2d ed. (Dubuque, Ia: Wm. C. Brown Publishers, 1989), pp. 210–14. Reprinted with permission of the publisher.
[4]W. Ward Fearnside and William B. Holther, *Fallacy, the Counterfeit of Argument* (Englewood Cliffs, NJ: Prentice-Hall, Inc., 1959), p. 100.

Group Communication

Outline

When you finish reading this chapter you should be able to:

1. Identify and explain the characteristic features of decision-making groups.

2. Explain why people need groups.

3. Describe the ethical responsibilities when participating in group decision making.

4. Compare and contrast task leadership and social leadership, and describe the role behaviors in each one.

5. Describe how communication is a crucial element in participation activities.

6. Describe the four most common public formats for presenting a decision-making group's thinking, and where appropriate, contribute the kind of leadership necessary to present each of these formats.

Objectives

colloquium	meetings	risky shift
conflict phase	interpersonal conflict	role
decision-making group	leadership	small group
emergence phase	member satisfaction	special events meeting
forum	orientation phase	symposium
group	panel	tension
groupthink	problem-solving meetings	
information-sharing	reinforcement phase	

Key Terms

Introduction

It is often said that the business of business happens in groups. Certainly the organization's decision-making processes are heavily centered in groups. Throughout college, the world of work, and civic involvement, you will be surrounded by all types of decision-making groups. The purpose of this chapter is to describe the most important kinds of communication behavior required by decision-making groups. You will learn what you can do to become a more skillful and effective group member.

You will also come to understand the processes that drive effective decision-making groups. Ultimately, the goal is to increase your analytical and performance skills in the group context. If you want to be upwardly mobile in an organization, you must have these skills. It is in group contexts where individuals have the greatest number of opportunities to demonstrate their competencies to others in their organizations.

Decision-Making Groups

There are many different kinds of groups. Your family represents one type of social group. Your public speaking classroom experience might include an informal discussion group. This chapter focuses on a special kind of small group called a decision-making group. The terms **group, small group,** and **decision-making group** are nearly synonymous. They refer to any collection of three or more individuals who share some problem or some common goal. Their interactions and behaviors mutually influence the members of the group.[1] They communicate with each other face-to-face and are aware of each other's roles. The critical elements in this definition include (1) group size, (2) mutual influence, and (3) goal orientation.

Two individuals (a dyad) cannot be a group because they cannot create the unique environment necessary for group processes. They cannot join together to exert pressure on a third person. On the other hand, a group that grows to about eleven individuals has reached the outside limit of manageability for a decision-making group. Beyond this number, controversial issues tend to cause the formation of subgroups, often with opposing goals. This chapter is about groups of people ranging in size from three to about eleven members. Almost all decision-making groups fall into this range. In fact, most of those groups will only have about six members.

Our definition of a decision-making group makes it clear that the interactions of individual members have an impact on the group. The members listen and talk with each other. They attempt to change each other's thinking and feelings. They are, in short, dependent upon each other.

Every organization is an organization of groups. Groups are everywhere. You will find them at work, at home, at church, at school, at service organizations, and in many recreational contexts. Group activities occur because individuals need each other. Among other reasons, people need each other for decision making as they address problems of a variety of kinds.

Decisions, of course, can be made in at least two ways. For example, suppose your car stops running about halfway between a nearby town and your home. You are faced with making a series of decisions in a sequence of problems.

The first decision is what to do right now. You have to make that decision alone. You may decide to go to the Firestone store across the road and ask for help. If so, you turn much of the decision making over to another person.

Situations that require technical expertise typically have one preferred answer. Someone with the technical know-how can make the best decision without group processes. To illustrate, you would probably try to find "the best" cardiac surgeon available, and then turn over all the technical decisions about open-heart surgery to that person.

A larger number of decisions do not have a single technically correct or preferred answer. Under these circumstances, most people prefer to pool their resources, talk things over, suggest and reject alternatives, and try to achieve a consensus. (Consensus is when *all* the members of a group agree.) For example, groups of professors often teach separate sections of the same course, using the same textbook in each section. In doing so, they probably try to arrive at a consensus on the question, "What textbook should we use for this course?"

A decision-making group shares a problem or a common goal. Members feel a common need. They get together to help each other. If three to eleven individuals in a room do not experience a need to work together, they do not constitute a group by the definition applied for this chapter. You can put people into the same room, but you cannot turn them into a decision-making group unless the members have a common purpose. Individuals who do not need to work together have no need to listen to each other or to consider each other's ideas.

People need groups for at least two reasons. First, groups collectively provide more resources than individuals. For example, a group can usually gather more information, and process that information more completely, than an individual. A group can also approach information from a wider variety of viewpoints and probe the substance of each member's thoughts more completely because the group members can work off of each other. This symbolic interaction of group members is usually more efficient and productive than an individual acting alone. Some tasks are more easily accomplished by a group than by an individual. For example, a group of scouts may volunteer to pick up litter along a certain stretch of roadway. That kind of job is called an *additive*. Groups perform additive tasks better than individuals.

Second, decision-making groups tend to be better at controlling an error than individuals. Group members can double-check their work more readily and more accurately than individuals.

The quality of thought generated by a group will typically be superior to the quality of thought generated by an individual, since the group members can usually contribute far greater reserves of information. There will be some times when the best trained individual can make better decisions than a group—even if the group includes an expert. For instance, in an emergency situation, such as a fire, one individual is in control because decisions must be made quickly. You certainly would not want a group of firemen standing in your front yard and voting on where to start spraying water. Tasks that require quick decisions and tasks involving routine decisions are often performed better by an individual. However, tasks that are additive or decisions that result in policy are generally performed better by a group.

Kinds of Group Meetings

Decision-making groups hold at least three very common kinds of meetings: (1) information-sharing meetings, (2) problem-solving meetings, and (3) special events meetings. It is useful to know the differences among these three kinds of meetings because they require somewhat different skills of the participants.

The first kind of meetings, the **information-sharing meetings,** occur in families, learning groups, work groups, churches, business and service organizations, fraternities and sororities, and so forth. This kind of meeting occurs on a regular basis, and it is characterized by a predictable agenda format and a clear set of procedural traditions.

The regular Monday morning department meeting is an example. The weekly meeting of department heads is another example. Every meeting follows the same agenda: announcements, reports and discussions of unfinished or ongoing business, assignments for the week, and adjournment. These meetings allow the members to be informed of what is going on in their organizations, to have a say in those events, to get and give assistance, to clarify short-term and long-term goals, and to cement their working relationships with each other.

The second kind of meeting, **problem-solving meetings,** can occur on an *ad hoc* basis (i.e., one meeting only, or a limited number of meetings), and in ongoing groups. Problem-solving meetings focus upon a single concern and usually follow a loose agenda.

Problem-solving meetings are very common. They occur when people feel that they share some problem that they want to solve. For example, a group of students got together one afternoon after classes to have a cup of coffee and to enjoy each other. One of them casually mentioned that they felt a need for a student club or organization that would reinforce their interest in public relations. Other people at the table agreed—they had felt a need for such a club, too.

As they talked, they began to change into a problem-solving group. One student said, "We ought to get Professor Wright involved in this. He's some kind of an officer in the public relations council in town." Another student said, "Sure, and we ought to see that Jim Johnston and Hellen Mackey are involved, too. He used to work for a public relations firm before he came back to school, and she works for one now, on a part-time basis."

Soon this group agreed to meet again the following week and to include the three individuals they had identified. In short, they wanted to solve a shared problem.

A third kind of meeting, the **special events meeting,** happens less frequently. The annual conference of a professional association provides an example. A "sales meeting" hosted by one of the company's suppliers is such a meeting. A seminar about fund-raising for the United Way is another example. Special events meetings are similar to the information-sharing and problem-solving meetings because people share information, and they address problems to solve. However, special events meetings also require certain organizational and communication skills not demanded by the other kinds of meetings.

Thus, decision-making groups work within three separate but overlapping contexts that draw upon different performance and analytical skills. Notice that each of the contexts evolves out of the members' exchange of symbols. The symbolic interactionist perspective makes it clear that what happens in each context results when members communicate with each other as they try to create group understandings.

Randy Y. Hirokawa and Roger Pace studied the communication bases of effectiveness and ineffectiveness in decision-making groups.[2] They concluded that at least four separate communication-related characteristics set these groups apart. These groups include the manner in which groups examine the members' opinions, how they go about evaluating alternative choices, how people exert influence, and the nature of the premises that underlie the groups' decisions.

How an individual experiences himself, how he perceives others, and how well the individuals establish and maintain group identity and group imagery are all based upon symbolic interaction. For example, a person whose self-concept includes the image of self as having leadership ability is more likely to volunteer leadership to a group than someone who does not have leadership ability as part of his self-concept. The self-concept of being a leader is created and supported by symbolic interaction when someone else has expressed approval through praise or through agreeing to follow the leadership.

Similarly, the whole character of a group's problem solving is affected as the members use language. Members of one group, for example, might do a lot of talking about "beating the system," or "confronting the establishment." Members of another group might talk about "working within the system" to establish its goals. You can see that two very different kinds of group events will result from these kinds of talk.

Finally, group values and group culture evolve out of the talk. Thus, if members refer to their goals as unimportant or insignificant ("Here we are again, another worthless committee." or "Let's get this silliness over.") they not only define the goals, but they also set up an expectation about how the members will work to pursue the goals. The talk of the members identifies what goals are important, what their attitudes ought to be about certain issues, and the basic perception of what their work as group members can contribute. The talk organizes the group's tasks, sets up the individual differences in member status and power, and renders the group climate either productive or unproductive.

Participating in Groups

The advantages of group decision making cannot have an effect unless individual members make certain commitments to the group. Every member of every group assumes four responsibilities by joining the group. Every time they agree to engage in decision making with other people, they agree to give up some of their individual sovereignty so that the group process can work. They assume an obligation to make decisions by certain ethical standards.

Do Your Best

You have something to offer a group. You have knowledge. You are sensitive and analytical. You think. You feel. You believe. You cannot change your strengths and weaknesses, and you do not need to. You are okay just the way you are, and you can contribute to a group. Give your group the best that you have. Do not hold back.

Every group member has a responsibility to do his or her best and to behave responsibly and rationally.

Sometimes individual group members do hold back. For example, people sometimes decline to take a leadership role because they think someone else might want to do it or because they resent a perceived manipulation by others. If you agree to involve yourself in a decision-making group, commit yourself to help that group to make the best decisions possible. If you give less, you violate a standard of excellence that is widely valued in our society.

Behave Rationally

Keep an open mind, listen to evidence and arguments, and withhold personal decisions until the evidence and the arguments have been presented. Behaving rationally means putting the interests of the group ahead of your own personal interests.

We have all known individuals who were unable to put aside their personal convictions in order to listen to another group member's position. These impatient people bring to the decision-making group their own private truths and their private agendas. For example, a person once served on a committee appointed by the mayor to make recommendations about how the mayor's office could improve two-way communication between the mayor and the community. A member of that group had a personal interest. The person tried to get the group to advocate the support for the improvement of the city-owned art museum. The person's idea was that the museum provided the best "out-reach" opportunity for the mayor. Unfortunately, the person did not want to talk or listen to any other ideas. A private agenda such as this interferes with a group's ability to choose the *best* alterative from a field of possibilities.

Rational behavior implies critical thinking, such as described in the last chapter. Do not behave irrationally. Your responsibilities to the group require that you listen carefully with an open mind, that you consider all the information, and that you work to evolve the most sensible group decisions.

Rational behavior may sometimes require great personal courage. It may mean setting aside personal animosity. It may mean agreeing to work constructively and positively with someone you do not like. It may require you to face and deal with rejection of your ideas. Even so, rational behavior is absolutely necessary. If the members of the group are not rational and do not cooperate, then the group cannot be productive. You take on an ethical responsibility to rational behavior every time you agree to work in a decision-making group.

Play Fair

Group decision making is a cooperative activity. It is not a competitive event at which you champion your viewpoint. This means that group members have the responsibility to seek and to present all of the ideas and evidence, whether or not the information seems contradictory. Every member of the group has a right to expect you to play fair, just as you have a right to expect every other member to play fair. Do not engage in debate in a group decision-making meeting. As a matter of ethical responsibility, you are constrained from competing with other group members.

Listen and Participate

When you have prepared carefully and have something important to say, you want other people to listen to you. You have a right to expect them to take you seriously, to listen to you carefully, to ask you questions, to give you feedback, and to evaluate your ideas with an open mind. If they did less than that, they would be mistreating you.

Similarly, you have the same ethical obligations to other group members. You have a responsibility to listen carefully and to participate fully with them, and they have a right to expect it. Listen to what they say and to what they do not say. Ask them questions, keep an open mind, and express your feelings and thoughts about their ideas. It is unfair to your colleagues and may damage the group's productivity to do less.

In summary, participating in a group means that you have an obligation to do your best, to behave rationally, to play fairly, to listen carefully, and to participate fully. These things are a matter of choice; it is up to you to set high standards for yourself and act accordingly. In a larger sense, these obligations are a matter of ethical responsibility.

Leadership in Decision Making

Decision-making groups cannot function without effective leadership. Decision-making groups need leadership to identify and to understand problems and solutions. When the members of a group engage in talk about controversial issues, they often get sidetracked. Sometimes group members do not know what to do next, so they need the guidance of one of the members. When an individual member places personal goals before the goals of the group, leadership is needed. The kind of leadership that addresses these situations is called *task dimension leadership.*

Group communication also has a relationship dimension. A group must be cohesive to be productive. The members must feel like a unit; they must want to cooperate to accomplish their common goal. Maintaining that sense of groupness is a relationship problem that also calls for leadership.

Remember, leadership is not the exclusive right of an appointed authority. Moreover, it is not something that can be conferred upon an individual. **Leadership** is an individual's ability to assess a communication situation and to provide the ideas and information that the group needs. Because this is true, *every* member of every decision-making group can and should contribute leadership.

You can make a contribution in leadership even if you are not designated as the chairperson. Indeed, your personal and professional success, your upward mobility in your organization, and your credibility in the eyes of your colleagues will be enhanced if you learn to provide the leadership that a group needs.

Characteristics of Effective Leaders

Gerald L. Wilson and Michael S. Hanna described the characteristics of an effective group leader.[3] Effective group leaders are well informed and able to adapt their leadership styles to meet the needs of the group; they are flexible. They usually adopt a democratic style of leadership. A democratic style of leadership is one that takes into account the interests and expertise of other group members and that values group processes over individual processes. Effective group leaders monitor and guide the group's activities with careful planning. Effective leaders provide direction and structure to the group's activities through skillful communication, and they are sensitive to the social tensions of a group.

Effective group leaders seem to know when to focus attention on task concerns, when to focus attention on relationship issues, and when to focus attention on procedures.

Understanding Group Leadership

Why do effective group leaders seem able to contribute the right kind of leadership when it is needed? How do effective leaders operate? How might you behave during a meeting to increase your leadership contribution? These questions have been asked by people for many generations. Some of the best answers appear in an essay developed by Kenneth D. Benne and Paul Sheats.[4] These scholars studied the role behaviors that are characteristic of successful decision-making groups and divided their findings into three categories. The categories include matters of (1) task and goal achievement, (2) group maintenance and identity, and (3) counterproductive behavior. A discussion of each of these three categories of role behaviors follows. These categories can help you to decide how to behave when you are in a group meeting. Remember, these behaviors do not occur by chance; you choose whether or not to perform them.

Task Leadership

Since **role** is a collection of behaviors, Benne and Sheats listed those behaviors that help groups achieve their goals. Look at table 10.1. Notice that not one of the group task roles listed requires that you be designated as a group leader. Each of the behaviors can be contributed by any willing member, and all of the behaviors are necessary to the functioning of an effective decision-making group.[5]

Social Leadership

Decision-making groups also require behaviors that build the cohesiveness of the group and strengthen and maintain relationships among group members. These behaviors, listed by Benne and Sheats, appear in table 10.2.

Again, notice that none of these behaviors requires that you be an appointed leader. You can and should contribute to the relationship dimension of group communication. Every decision-making group needs these contributions, and every group values the people who contribute them. Thus, the group context provides you an opportunity to make important contributions to others and at the same time to show that you are a competent person and a valuable asset to the group.

Counterproductive Behavior

Benne and Sheats identified and listed a third category of behaviors: self-centered roles that diminish the performer's effectiveness and damage the group's productivity. These self-centered roles are listed in table 10.3. Know and avoid them.

Problems in Group Communication

Sometimes problem-solving groups run into problems that the members don't know how to handle. One of the most common problems is that individual members become dissatisfied. When this happens, the cohesiveness of the group can break down and interpersonal conflict can result. At the other extreme, a group can become too cohesive for its own good. Too much cohesiveness can produce a phenomenon called "group think." Each of these problem areas can be managed if responsible group members know what to do.

Membership Satisfaction

As early as 1964, Heslin and Dunphy were concerned about the relationship between group member satisfaction and cohesiveness.[6] They reported their belief, based on research, that **member satisfaction** depends upon three factors: (1) perceived progress toward the group goals, (2) perceived freedom to participate, and (3) status consensus. These three conditions all result from how the group members interact.

The members perceive that they are making progress most easily when they are actually making visible progress. However, progress is not so important as the perception of progress. The members must believe that they are making progress. They must be able to perceive it. That perception depends on the talk that goes on in the group. Thus, you can make an important contribution to the cohesiveness of a group by frequently pointing to its progress. It is as simple a thing as saying, "Look at how much we have accomplished" and then summarizing the accomplishments of the group.

Group members perceive that they are free to participate when the communication climate in the group is accepting and supportive. Freedom to participate results when members feel respected for their view and for their personal worth as human beings. They make these judgments on the basis of the talk in the group. When members disclose themselves, empathize with each other, and are honest with each other about themselves and their information, they are creating a climate in which the other members feel free to participate.

Every group member is responsible for the communication climate in a group. You can choose to be supportive of others. You can choose to interact with the other members on an equal basis. You can choose to take a problem orientation approach instead of a "know-it-all" approach. You can resist making judgments about other people or their ideas. You don't have to put yourself one-up and the other person one-down. You can intervene if some other group member chooses to disrupt the communication climate.

The third condition necessary to member satisfaction is status consensus. Status consensus is the group's agreement that for that time and place their roles and their relative status are correct. Some members want to lead. Others do not want positions of leadership. Still others are quite willing to exercise unofficial leadership as long as they are not singled out. A problem

Group Task Roles

Roles	Typical Behaviors	Examples
1. Initiator-contributor	Contributes ideas and suggestions; proposes solutions and decisions; proposes new ideas or states old ones in a novel fashion.	"How about taking a different approach to this chore? Suppose we . . ."
2. Information seeker	Asks for clarification of comments in terms of their factual adequacy; asks for information or facts relevant to the problem; suggests information is needed before making decisions.	"Wait a minute. What does that mean?" "Does anyone have any data to support this idea?"
3. Information giver	Offers facts or generalizations that may relate to personal experiences and that are pertinent to the group task.	"I asked Doctor Jones, a specialist in this kind of thing. He said . . ." "An essay in *The New Yorker* reported . . ."
4. Opinion seeker	Asks for clarification of opinions stated by other members of the group and asks how people in the group feel.	"Does anyone else have an idea on this?" "Can someone clear up what that means?"
5. Opinion giver	States beliefs or opinions having to do with suggestions made; indicates what the group's attitude should be.	"I think we ought to go with the second plan. It fits the conditions we face in the Concord plant best . . ."
6. Elaborator-clarifier	Elaborates ideas and other contributions; offers rationales for suggestions; tries to deduce how an idea or suggestion would work if adopted by the group.	"Do you mean he actually said he was guilty? I thought it was merely implied."
7. Diagnostician	Indicates what the problems are.	"But you're missing the main thing, I think. The problem is that we can't afford . . ."

8.	Coordinator	Clarifies the relationships among information, opinions, and ideas, or suggests an integration of the information, opinions, and ideas of subgroups.	"John's opinion squares pretty well with the research Mary reported. Why don't we take that idea and see if . . ."
9.	Orienter-summarizer	Summarizes what has taken place; points out departures from agreed-upon goals; tries to bring the group back to the central issues; raises questions about where the group is heading.	"Let's take stock of where we are. Helen and John take the position that we should act now. Bill says 'wait.' Rusty isn't sure. Can we set that aside for a moment and come back to it after we . . ."
10.	Energizer	Prods the group to action.	"Come on, guys. We've been wasting time. Let's get down to business."
11.	Procedure developer	Handles routine tasks such as seating arrangements, obtaining equipment, and handing out pertinent papers.	"I'll volunteer to see that the forms are printed and distributed." "Look, I can see to it that the tape recorder is there and working. And I'll also run by the church for the chairs."
12.	Secretary	Keeps notes on the group's progress.	"I keep great notes. I'll be glad to do that for the group."
13.	Evaluator-critic	Critically analyzes the group's accomplishments according to some set of standards; checks to see that consensus has been reached.	"Look, we said we only had four hundred dollars to spend. What you're proposing will cost at least six hundred dollars. That's a 50 percent override." "Can we all agree, at least, that we must solve the attrition problem—that that is our first priority?"

▲ **Table 10.1** continued

Group Building and Maintenance Roles

Roles	Typical Behaviors	Examples
1. Supporter-encourager	Praises, agrees with, and accepts the contributions of others; offers warmth, solidarity, and recognition.	"I really like that idea, John." "Priscilla's suggestion is attractive to me. Could we discuss it further?"
2. Harmonizer	Reconciles disagreements, mediates differences, reduces tensions by giving group members a chance to explore their differences.	"I don't think you two are as far apart as you think." "Henry, are you saying. . . ?" "Benson, you seem to be saying. . . . Is that what you mean?"
3. Tension reliever	Jokes or in some other way reduces the formality of the situation; relaxes the group members.	"That reminds me—excuse me if this seems unrelated—that reminds me of the one about . . ."
4. Compromiser	Offers to compromise when own ideas are involved in a conflict; uses self-discipline to admit errors so as to maintain group cohesion.	"Looks like our solution is halfway between you and me, John. Can we look at the middle ground?"

▼ Table 10.2

usually results when two people compete for status. If that happens, one person will usually emerge in a higher status position than the other person. It then becomes the problem of both the emergent high-status person (and every other member) to help the unsuccessful bidder to accept his or her position.

Roles	Typical Behaviors	Examples
5. Gatekeeper	Keeps communication channels open; encourages and facilitates interaction from those members who are usually silent.	"Susan hasn't said anything about this yet. Susan, I know you've been studying the problem. What do you think about. . . ?"
6. Feeling expresser	Makes explicit the feelings, moods, and relationships in the group; shares own feelings with others.	"Don't we all need a break now? I'm frustrated and confused and maybe we all are. I'd like to put this out of my mind for a while."
7. Standard setter	Expresses standards for the group to achieve; may apply standards in evaluating the group process.	"In my view, this decision doesn't measure up to our best. We really haven't even set any criteria much less tried to apply them."
8. Follower	Goes along with the movement of the group passively, accepting the ideas of others and sometimes serving as an audience.	"I agree. Yes, I see what you mean. If that's what the group wants to do, I'll go along."

After Wilson, Gerald L., and Michael S. Hanna, *Groups in Context: Leadership and Participation in Small Groups*, Second Edition. Copyright © 1990 McGraw-Hill. Reprinted by permission.

▲ Table 10.2 continued

Talk that can help people feel better about themselves when they lose a status competition takes the form of positive strokes and reinforcement when the individual makes a contribution. These behaviors are the responsibility of every group member.

Self-Centered Roles

Roles	Typical Behaviors	Examples
1. Blocker	Interferes with progress by rejecting ideas or taking the negative stand on any and all issues; refuses to cooperate.	"Wait a minute! That's not right! That idea is absurd. If you take that position, I simply can't continue to work with you."
2. Aggressor	Struggles for status by deflating the status of others; boasts; criticizes.	"Wow, that's really swell! You turkeys have botched things again. Your constant bickering is responsible for this mess. Let me tell you how you ought to do it."
3. Deserter	Withdraws in some way; remains indifferent, aloof, sometimes formal; daydreams; wanders from the subject; engages in irrelevant side conversations.	To himself: "Ho-hum. There's nothing in this discussion for me." To group: "I guess I really don't care what you choose in this case. But on another matter . . ."
4. Dominator	Interrupts and embarks on long monologues; authoritative; tries to monopolize the group's time.	"Bill, you're just off base. What we should do is this. First . . ."

▼ Table 10.3

Roles	Typical Behaviors	Examples
5. Recognition seeker	Attempts to gain attention in an exaggerated manner; usually boasts about past accomplishments; relates irrelevant personal experiences, usually in an attempt to gain sympathy.	"That was a good thing I just did." "Yesterday I was able to . . ." "If you ask me, I think . . ." "Don't you think I'm right [Don't you think I'm wonderful]?"
6. Confessor	Engages in irrelevant personal catharsis; uses the group to work out own mistakes and feelings.	"I know it's not on the topic exactly, but I'm having a personal problem just like this. Yesterday, Mary and I had a fight about . . ."
7. Playboy	Displays a lack of involvement in the group through inappropriate humor, horseplay, or cynicism.	"Did you hear the one about the cow that swallowed the bottle of ink and mooed indigo?" To the only female in the group: "Hello, sweet baby, let's you and me boogie."
8. Special-interest pleader	Acts as the representative for another group; engages in irrelevant behavior.	"My friend Alan runs a company that makes a similar product. How about using his company? We might as well spend our money with people we know."

After Wilson, Gerald L., and Michael S. Hanna, *Groups in Context: Leadership and Participation in Small Groups,* Second Edition. Copyright © 1990 McGraw-Hill. Reprinted by permission.

▲ Table 10.3 continued

Learning how to manage interpersonal conflict in a group is an invaluable leadership skill.

Interpersonal Conflict

A common problem in groups occurs when individuals engage in damaging interpersonal conflict behavior. Of course, some conflict can be useful to a group. Conflict can increase involvement of group members and it can provide an outlet for hostility. It can promote cohesiveness and increase group productivity. Conflict can also increase the chances that group members will genuinely commit themselves to the group's decisions.

However, conflict can also be damaging. If conflict harms individual members or inhibits the group effort, then conflict must be managed. Conflict management is the responsibility of every group member. However, you must be thoughtful and careful about what you do and what you don't do in the presence of conflict.

Interpersonal conflict can be defined as an expressed struggle between interdependent parties over perceived incompatible goals, scarce rewards, or limited resources.[7] This definition makes clear that conflict may not have anything to do with the truth. People engage in conflict over perceptions. Moreover, conflict requires the parties to be interdependent. If people do not need each other, then they have no need for conflict. They can simply go off on their own and achieve what they want to.

When people engage in conflict, they usually aim to obstruct, damage, neutralize, or eliminate each other. The intensity of the conflict (i.e., their efforts to obstruct, damage, neutralize, or eliminate each other, and the related stress) is related to a number of variables.

First, the more important and desirable a person's private goals are, the more intense is that person's conflict experience and behavior. Second, the relative attraction of the alternatives affects the intensity of a conflict. For example, if two alternatives seem equally attractive, then the conflict is likely to be intense—especially when the parties in the conflict also attach a high degree of importance to the outcome.

A group might discover that each of its available alternatives promises both attractive and undesirable features. The perceived relative significance of these features can influence the intensity of the conflict experience.

Finally, the sheer number of alternatives available can affect the intensity of a conflict. For example, a group might have so many alternatives that it has trouble sorting them all out in its effort to arrive at the best decision.

Whatever the degree of intensity, the determination of the people in conflict to obstruct, damage, neutralize, or eliminate each other can be damaging, or it can be very useful to a group. Therefore, it can be both functional or dysfunctional. In part, the outcome depends on how well and how skillfully the individual members of a group manage that conflict.

Conflict is most likely to be functional when the conflicted parties share a common value system. This is when they value each other and the group's goals. Since people who share these common values experience a need to work through their differences, they are likely to take greater care in their choices of language and behavior. People who do not share a common value system are much more likely to engage in self-serving and self-indulgent behavior. They may go so far as to take an extreme "all or nothing" posture.

Conflict is more likely to be functional in some kinds of group activity and dysfunctional in others. For example, conflict can be highly functional when a group is searching for and evaluating information. On the other hand, conflict tends to be dysfunctional when people are trying to make choices.[8]

The idea that conflict can be functional sometimes surprises people in our society. Yet, we know that conflict can serve at least five useful functions.

1. Conflict increases involvement of group members. Clearly, when people are involved in conflict, they are more likely to voice their views. If it is managed, conflict can produce a more complete discussion of issues and ideas. People may risk expressing their positions more completely; and in doing so, they may draw others into the discussion.

2. Conflict provides an outlet for hostility. If a group can permit conflict, it can provide an opportunity for individual members to "let off steam." Sometimes, for example, individuals get their feelings hurt in group decision making. They may form negative impressions of other members, even to the point of establishing some covert agenda to get even. Such behavior is unlikely in groups that allow and manage full expression of conflict. In the case of full expression of conflict, the members hear each other out, disclose themselves more fully to each other, express their feelings and wants, and express their likes and dislikes. This kind of acceptance is bound to reduce hostility.

IT'S MORE FUN TO KNOW

Self-Esteem and Leadership

Men and women who think positively about themselves and show positive behavior in group situations are rewarded and become leaders. The strength of self-esteem helps to predict leadership, regardless of gender.

See Patricia Hayes Andrews, ''Performance Self Esteem and Perceptions of Leadership Emergence: A Comparative Study of Men and Women,'' *Western Journal of Speech Communication*, 48:1 (Winter 1984), p. 11.

Comment . . .

Positive self-esteem results in people taking leadership roles. It makes a great difference in how you see yourself. If you believe in your ideas and yourself, then you are on the way to becoming a leader.

3. Conflict contributes to group cohesiveness. The time spent in conflict becomes part of a group's history. If the members eventually realize that their group can withstand the tensions produced in conflict, then they can become more trusting. They have learned that they can be successful by working through their conflicts. In addition, conflict often contributes to productivity, with a corresponding increase in cohesiveness.

4. Conflict contributes to group productivity. The most important reason for working in a decision-making group is to come to a quality decision. A group can often make a better decision than an individual. Well-managed conflict often yields a better decision. It causes people to search for more alternatives, and it sometimes causes group members to increase their efforts to arrive at solutions.[9]

5. Conflict contributes to commitment. You might reasonably suppose that a clash of ideas would cause people to pull away from a group, and to discount its decisions. But this is not the case.[10] Indeed, such clashes can be very constructive. If a group achieves consensus after its members have freely and openly expressed their arguments and ideas, the members appear more likely to be committed to the final decisions.[11]

How, then, can we improve our personal conflict management behavior in groups?

What Not to Do

Avoid saying such phrases as "communicate more" or "cooperate more." These statements create defensiveness because they tend to sound like they are blaming the conflict on some individual. Interpersonal conflict is always mutual. Take the attitude that there are no heroes and no villains. Do not blame another person or the group for the conflict and don't attack any of the other group members. Blaming and attacking will create defensiveness, and it will almost certainly cause a counterattack. This behavior can only be damaging.

What to Do

It is much more difficult to suggest the means to effective conflict management than it is to list behaviors that generated the conflict. Even so, there are some methods that will aid in managing conflict:[12]

1. Stay in the present tense. Rather than look for the causes of conflict, search for solutions. In any case, it is not possible for a person to take back anything from the past. However, it *is* possible to make plans for the future.

2. Separate the problem from the person. It is possible to value individuals and still dislike their actions. Talk and work at keeping the problem separate from the person. For example, say, "I'm concerned that our differences on this issue may damage our relationship, and I don't want that to happen." Or, say, "I want to take this slowly. I like you, but I resent what you did. Can we focus on our differences and still be kind to each other?"

3. Talk about yourself, not about the other person. Choose language and behaviors that make it clear that you are taking a conciliatory posture. For example, say, "I am angry" rather than "You make me angry." Say, for example, "I would like you to. . . ." rather than "You will have to. . . ."

4. *Look for solutions in small steps.* Address one conflict issue at a time; don't try to manage the entire problem at once. Establish and follow a sequence one step at a time.

5. *Work for an agreement to negotiate.* The act of agreeing to negotiate places limits on the conflict and opens an exchange of ideas. Some of the following techniques for conflict negotiation can be helpful:

> **a.** *Set the ground rules.* For example, you might make a rule that no one raises his or her voice, or that no one leaves the room for a specified period of time.
>
> **b.** *Find an appropriate time and place to negotiate.* Conflict management takes time. Don't try to manage a conflict when there is not time for both parties to address the matter. Try to negotiate on neutral territory (such as a restaurant), rather than in one party's office.
>
> **c.** *Set and follow an agenda.* Make a contract to set and follow an agenda. It helps you to keep on track and assures that the conflict areas are thoroughly addressed. One researcher recommends what he calls ABCD Analysis: Antecedents—What precipitated or led up to the conflict? Behaviors—How did the conflicting parties act? Consequences—What resulted from the behaviors? Do differently—What can be done differently now?
>
> **d.** *Reward the other's negotiation behaviors.* An agreement to negotiate or any other constructive behaviors are positive steps. Reward these steps with praise and with your own positive behaviors.

Groupthink

Sometimes a decision-making group becomes too cohesive. When this happens, the group risks making poor decisions. Irving L. Janis was the first to describe this phenomenon, which he called **groupthink**.[13] Groups suffering from groupthink make unrealistic decisions. These groups come to believe that they are extraordinarily powerful and moral. They become closed-minded, refuse to entertain contrary views, and rationalize their decisions, despite warnings that they are in error. They stereotype individuals with opposing views as evil, weak, or too stupid to understand. Groups suffering from groupthink tend to minimize their own doubts, and they pressure each other to conform to a single, groupthink view of reality.

Dennis S. Gouran has studied inferential errors in group decision-making at some length.[14] He listed three ways in which group interaction promotes errors in a group's inferences. First, the groups introduce atypical information on a progressive basis. For example, a group member might describe a police officer in an uncomplimentary or negative way. Other members begin to search for similar cases in their own experience, and they may even go to a greater extreme. Thus, through their symbolic interaction the members create images that lead to inferential errors.

The second way a group's interaction can promote inferential errors involves passive acceptance of specialized knowledge. For example, a member might pass information to the group with the sentence, "I got this from Mayor Jackson, and she ought to know." The other members accept that testimony as true. Similarly, groups often cannot differentiate among dogma, conjecture, and scientific consensus.

The third way a group's interactions can promote errors in group inference occurs when the members construct scenarios and scripts. For example, a department member might propose that the work group to which they belong join forces with another group in a different department that's working on a similar task. The members begin to speculate about the advantages and the disadvantages of such a merger. As they talk, an image evolves of how they would fare in the proposed merger. Thus, they create a scenario that becomes a mind-set in which their decision making must take place.

When symptoms of groupthink occur, the group's decisions are almost always flawed. Such a group's decision making is based on incomplete understanding of the problem drawn from an incomplete set of alternatives and is based on faulty inferences. Members do not examine the risks of their preferred choices, and they process available information from the bias of their own preconceived view. Such a group rarely works out contingency plans because they believe that they are infallible.

What conditions contribute to groupthink? Janis described four conditions that promote the syndrome. First, the group experiences moderately high to very high cohesiveness. They like each other so much that they begin to believe in each other's infallibility. Second, the group tends to be insulated from the world, which includes being insulated from opposing views. The insularity keeps the members from hearing criticism or gaining new information. Third, groupthink groups lack a tradition of impartial leadership. Instead, the leadership tends to use its power and prestige to influence group members to approve the preferred decisions. Fourth, groups suffering from groupthink tend not to have norms or rules to govern their methods or procedures. Thus, they are free to follow the path of least criticism, which often goes against evidence and argument.

Risky Shift

An additional feature of group decision making that sets it apart from individual decision making is a feature commonly known as the "risky shift." In effect, the idea of the **risky shift** is that groups tend to take greater risks than individuals. Of course, this is partially because of the condition that allows groupthink. It is also probably because individuals, who would be conservative in their private decision making, share the responsibility with others in a group. The risk is also diffused among the group members, and no one individual feels the full threat of potentially adverse consequences from a bad decision.

An illustration of this idea appears in movie westerns. Individual citizens from a small western town gather outside the jail, determined to hang the bad guy from a local tree. The sheriff diffuses the tense scene when he steps out of the jail and confronts the mob. First, he silences the hot-head who is providing leadership to the mob. His next argument is usually to name individuals and to remind them of their individual value systems. Then, the sheriff tells them to return to their homes. Thus, he counters the mob fever that illustrates the risky shift.

In summary, four common problems occur in decision-making groups: membership dissatisfaction, interpersonal conflict, groupthink, and the risky shift. Each of these problems can be avoided, but only if the individual group members take it upon themselves to contribute effective leadership to the group.

Working with Group Tension

Some people seem to be natural leaders, while others seem to have difficulty asserting themselves. What makes the difference? People who provide the needed leadership in groups monitor the tension levels of the group during meetings. They determine on the basis of their observations what the group needs and what they should do.

You can sense the **tension** levels in a group meeting. Sometimes, especially during moments of conflict, the tension levels are almost tangible. At other times, especially during social moments, the tension levels are so low that they are not even noticed. Successful leaders have learned to become sensitive to the constantly shifting levels of group tension. They use their observations as a way of knowing what the group needs.

Figure 10.1 illustrates how this works.[15] The dimension at the left-hand side of the diagram is labeled *levels of tension*. Group tension ranges from 0 upward. The plus mark (+) indicates ever increasing levels of tension. The bottom dimension of the figure is labeled *time*. The line of dashes in the figure represents the group's threshold of tolerance for tension. If the

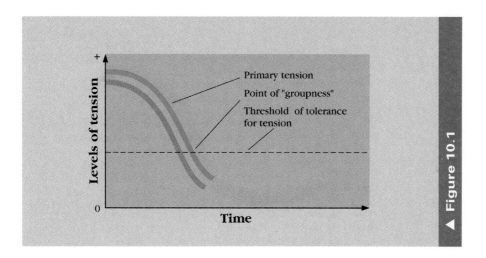

Figure 10.1

A chart of group tension. Effective group leaders monitor a group's tension level to draw out the full resources of the group.

tension stays below that threshold, then the members of any group are comfortable enough to work on their tasks. By definition, if the tension rises above that level, then the tension becomes too great because it is above the group's tolerance threshold. When tension is that high, the group must deal with the tension.

To illustrate how tension thresholds work, imagine three different groups. One group has a very high level of tension; a second group has a very low level of tension; and a third group has an optimum level of tension. (You will rarely find one group with one clearly identified tension level.) Learning to monitor tension takes patience. Don't be discouraged if it takes a while. The rewards are worth the effort. Learning to become sensitive to tension levels in a decision-making group and learning what to do about them can have a dramatic impact on the success of your group and on your own personal success as well.

Consider the case in figure 10.2. The tension levels are much too high. Follow the tension across the time dimension, beginning at the left-hand margin. The shaded area is called *primary tension*. Primary tension is common in groups. It takes a while for a group to get down to business. Members need to joke, to chat about last night's baseball game, or to gossip about some local celebrity. They do this because they experience primary tension. Primary tension is that feeling you get when you enter a room for a party, only to discover that the person who invited you is the only person you know.

In this case, the group eliminates primary tension easily and goes along for a while working on the task. Then, at point C, the tension rises above the group's threshold of tolerance. They reach a crisis. The tension levels continue to rise. If the group doesn't do something soon about the tension, one

Figure 10.2

High tension levels. High tension levels can be reduced by discussing the source of the tension. This often requires candor and tact.

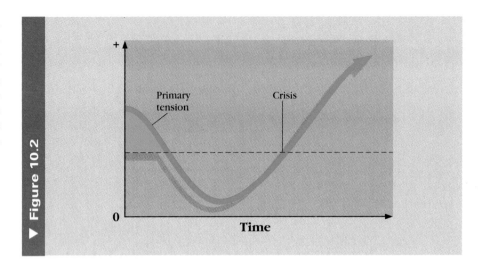

of two things will happen. First, the group may expel the member who is creating the tension. And second, the group may disband.

In any case, when a group is experiencing this much tension, the group cannot be productive; therefore, the group must do something. Here is your opportunity for leadership. When the tension levels are too high, perhaps because the group is in conflict, talk about the source of tension. Is it disagreement over a goal? Is it disagreement over a procedure? Is it social conflict? Learning to talk about the tension wisely is an important step toward dealing with it.

Consider a second theoretical group. In figure 10.3, the tension levels of the group are too low. The tension levels have steadily dropped since the group was formed. Under these circumstances, the group cannot be productive. Leadership is needed, either because the group is enjoying themselves so much that they have lost sight of the task (a group can be too cohesive), or because the group is apathetic because its members are disinterested in the group activity. Another possibility is that the members are not committed to the good of the group. In either case, this is another opportunity for you to provide leadership. The group needs to get moving on the task.

A third possibility exists. In figure 10.4, the group has eliminated primary tension without difficulty. They proceeded for a while before confronting a crisis, but they handled the crisis well. Tension rose above the group's threshold of tolerance three times, and each time the group managed to work through the crisis.

A group must experience this kind of crisis and crisis management in order to be productive. It needs to gain confidence in its ability to withstand

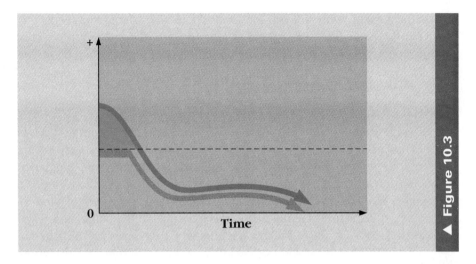

Low tension levels. Low tension levels need to be raised for a group to be productive. An effective leader will turn the discussion toward the group's procedures to reorient the group toward its tasks.

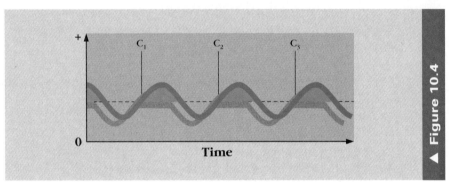

Optimal tension levels. Effective crisis management facilitates maximum group productivity. Members must be confident that their opinions will be heard and evaluated fairly.

the pressures of conflict and disagreement. Its members must feel free to say what they want without fear that the group will disband. There is a logical reason that tension is necessary for a productive decision-making group.

Any time a group is making progress, it is also making changes. All progress implies change, and change always introduces a level of tension. Repeated tension levels above the group's tolerance threshold are inevitable in a productive group. Part of what makes a group productive is that the members learn how to manage the tension. This ideal situation also provides you an opportunity to contribute your leadership skills to a decision-making group. When the tension levels are following a cyclical pattern, such as the one shown in figure 10.4, talk about the topic.

In summary, you can learn to monitor group tensions. Based on your observations, you can identify what kinds of leadership the group needs. When the tension levels are too high, the group needs to talk about the source of the tension. When the tension levels are too low, the group needs to establish a procedure that will get it back on track. When a group is experiencing cyclical tension and the release of the tension, the group has its best chance of success. When a group is working well, stay with the agenda.

Working with an Agenda for Decision

In 1910, when John Dewey published his ideas about how people think, he did not imagine that he would have such a lasting impact on the theory and research of group discussion.[16] Nevertheless, his reflective thinking pattern almost presents a ready-made agenda that any group can follow. Over the years, speech and group discussion instructors have used and adapted the pattern of reflective thinking that Dewey described. One of the most useful variations on Dewey's thinking pattern was developed by Brilhart and Jochem.[17] To help you work with reflective thinking, here is a full discussion outline based on the Brilhart/Jochem agenda:[18]

I. What is the nature of the problem we face? (present state, obstacles, goals?)

   A. What are we talking about?

      1. Is the question or assignment clear?
      2. Do we need to define any terms or concepts?

   B. How much freedom do we have?

      1. Are we to plan and take action, or what?
      2. What sort of end product are we supposed to produce?

   C. What has been happening that is unsatisfactory?

      1. What is wrong? What is the harm? How do we know?
      2. Who is affected? How? Under what conditions?
      3. How serious is the situation?
      4. Have any corrective actions been taken? How did they work?
      5. What additional information do we need in order to understand fully the nature and extent of the problem?

   D. In general terms, what is the desired situation or goal we hope to achieve?

   E. What factors seem to have caused this problem?

      1. Are we certain about any causes?
      2. What obstacles must we remove to achieve our desired goal?

   F. How can we state the problem so that it includes the present situation, the desired situation, the difference, the causes, and the obstacles?

      1. Do we all agree on this statement of the problem?

2. Should we divide our statement into "subproblems?"
   a. If so, what are they?
   b. In what order should we approach them?
II. What might be done to solve the problem (or first subproblem)? (Here the group brainstorms for possible solutions.)
III. What specific criteria should we use to evaluate our possible solutions?
   A. What absolute criteria must be met?
   B. What relative standards shall we apply? (List and rank these values and standards by group agreement.)
IV. What are the relative merits of our possible solutions?
   A. What ideas can we screen out because they are unsupported by facts?
   B. What ideas must we take out because our group members do not all support them?
   C. Can we combine and simplify our list of possible solutions?
   D. How well do the remaining ideas measure up to the criteria?
V. How will we put our decision into effect?
   A. Who will do what, and when?
   B. How will we check to be sure that we follow through on our agreements?

Of course, when the group is actually working, members seldom are able to follow such an agenda in precisely this order. Often, a member jumps ahead (a process called *reach testing*).[19]

Other members will follow. Someone may object on procedural grounds. Still another member may complain that an idea does not meet certain criteria. In short, a productive decision-making group resembles a cavalry charge in an old-time western movie. The horses are all going in the same general direction with the same purpose, but they are not moving with military precision.

Decision Emergence

Even though the reflective thinking process provides an agenda to follow while working in groups, the reality is that decisions *emerge* out of the talk of the group members. This interaction tends to follow a much different pattern of thinking from the agenda just presented.[20] Indeed, groups tend to make many small decisions that lead to consensus about the questions they are attempting to address. This process of decision emergence tends to follow through predictable phases.

Orientation

The first phase is called the **orientation phase.** This phase is identified by examining the purpose of the talk. At this time, people are trying to sort out their basic relationships and social climate. They are struggling for a "pecking order" or a "status consensus." A number of very general, tentative proposals are made, and they are confirmed or rejected during this phase.

For example, during the orientation phase one group member may say, "We need to be careful in order to examine all of the facts and features of this problem carefully before we start working on what to do." Another responds, "I agree! We've got to be as thorough as our time and talent will allow." A third says, "So we're not going to hurry into a decision until we know as much as this group can know about the subject, right?" And the first speaker supports this by saying, "I agree with that wholeheartedly." Thus, the group begins by making agreements to be thorough and tentative, to collect lots of information, and to withhold decisions until that information is collected. The orientation phase is a necessary time for group members to develop a rapport with each other and to determine their general directions and their general norms that will govern their behaviors.

Conflict

The second phase, the **conflict phase,** is marked by a change in member behavior. The group is beginning to address the issues. Some disagreement with specific proposals begins to occur. Members feel less constrained from conflict, less inhibited, and less tentative. In this phase, the members are testing their direction and their positions. They may begin to form coalitions and to seek support for their ideas. They explore each other's arguments, make counter-arguments, and attempt to discredit each other's points of view. Fisher characterized the conflict phase. "The norm is dissent, controversy, social conflict, and innovative deviance."[21]

Emergence

In the **emergence phase,** the final outcome of the group's discussion begins to form. People begin to talk in vague and ambiguous terms, as in the orientation phase, but this time, they talk for a much different purpose. They attempt to save face for each other and to reduce conflict as the final decision becomes apparent. In addition, the coalitions begin to dissolve as members begin to support the emerging decision. Any remaining objections, if they are expressed at all, don't find support. To illustrate, a faculty committee recently had to decide which student or students in the major program of their department would receive scholarship money from a newly established departmental scholarship fund. Committee members really struggled over the criteria, but finally, a decision began to emerge. One dissenter said, "I still

Group decisions go through stages. This group's members are reinforcing each other on a successful decision-making meeting.

don't like it. You are eliminating two of our best students by requiring that the recipients be from these two counties." This had been his strongest argument throughout the deliberations and it had been supported, originally, by two other members. Now, one of the other members said, "It is, and that's a shame in some ways, but don't you think this requirement is sensible? I mean . . . you know?" Clearly, this speaker was withdrawing his support for the dissenter.

Reinforcement

Even though final decisions are formed during the emergence phase, group consensus does not occur until the **reinforcement phase.** In this last phase, the specific details of the emergent decision are brought into focus. Hardly any dissent occurs. The members engage in reinforcing behavior by supporting one another's views, repeating their affirmations and commitments frequently, and encouraging others to make such statements. The process, therefore, reinforces the emergent decision and strengthens the members' commitment and resolve. As this kind of talk continues, the atmosphere noticeably lightens. Conflict has dissipated, and humor tends to be evident. The members express their feelings of accomplishment.

Presenting the Group's Findings

Surprisingly, the work of a decision-making group rarely ends with making a decision. Instead, the group must usually present their findings to someone else. Their findings may be presented to a management group, to a single executive, or to a large gathering of people assembled to consider the group's ideas. In almost every case, a decision-making group will take on some form of advocacy in order to get its proposals adopted. Sometimes this report will be written. At other times, it will be presented orally. Sometimes the report takes both written and oral forms. Regardless of its form, the goal is to present the group's work clearly and persuasively.

Written and Oral Reports

Written and oral reports of a group's findings are similar. Each begins with a brief overview, presents the group's analysis of the problem, describes the criteria the group applied to possible solutions, offers a solution, and then ends with a summary and an appeal for support of the proposal.

If the group has appointed a leader, that individual usually presents the report. If not, the group usually selects the member who has the best communication skills. If you are selected, you should approach the oral report in the same fashion that you would prepare for any other speech. Your job is clearly identified for you by the group. You will either inform and educate, or persuade, or possibly both.

State the purpose of the report early and preview its main points. Review your group's analysis of the problem and the criteria used to test the proposed solution. Describe the recommended solution. Support your ideas with the evidence and arguments that your group discussed. You may want to use visual materials as you make your presentation. Be careful to adapt to your listeners and to the context. Also, use language that is articulate, yet comfortable to you and your listeners. Finish with a summary and ask the listeners to adopt the group's recommendations.

At the end of the presentation, you may be asked some questions. Respond to those questions thoughtfully and honestly. Try not to deviate from the group's decisions during this period. Remember, you are not advocating your own personal point of view; you are representing the group's thinking.

Formats for Presenting a Group's Thinking

Sometimes a group is asked to present its ideas in a public discussion format. The remainder of this chapter focuses on the most common formats in which public discussion occurs.

Public discussions differ from decision-making discussions in a fundamental way. A public discussion is held for the benefit of the listeners, and it is not usually a forum in which group decision making occurs. Even when decision making does occur in a public meeting, the presence of the audience implies that the group will pay attention to the needs of the listeners. If you are asked to participate in a public discussion or to plan and present such a discussion, choose a basic format. The most common formats are the forum, or whole-house debate, the panel, the symposium, and the colloquium. Table 10.4 illustrates these formats and shows why and how to use them.

Forum

A **forum** is a public discussion that involves full audience participation. The most common example is the New England town meeting. People gather to propose and to debate civic issues, and to make decisions about them. In its pure form, this kind of meeting includes impromptu or extemporaneous speeches from representative citizens. People debate each other, ask questions, and make comments. Finally, a vote is taken on the issues, and decisions that affect the entire body are made.

Often, a forum centers on, and is coupled with, some other communication activity. A speech, a film, or a panel discussion may be used to stimulate audience involvement. A chairman, or moderator, keeps the discussion moving in an orderly fashion.

The leader of such a forum has a difficult job. The task is to stimulate the group further, in order to assure that everyone who wants to speak has an opportunity, and to encourage as many people to speak as possible by making sure each individual presentation is brief. That is a difficult job when the audience's emotions are aroused. The moderator's role also is to encourage, to recognize, and to clarify the various viewpoints so that the audience can make an informed and wise decision.

If you are the leader of such a meeting, you might want to suggest some guidelines. Ask that members be recognized by the moderator before they speak. Establish a time limit for each speaker and establish a method for assuring that the time limits are known and applied fairly. If a person has already spoken and others wish to speak, ask the person who has already spoken to abstain in order to allow the others a chance to speak. Try to secure floor microphones, and ask people to use them so that everyone in the audience can hear all of the speeches. Keep the audience informed about the overall time frame of the meeting and the time remaining.

Call for a different viewpoint if several of the speakers have said essentially the same thing. Finally, try to summarize the main ideas and positions presented on the various sides of the issues. If appropriate, restate what the members' actions will mean when interpreting their vote. For example, "If you move to this side of the house when I call for the vote, you will be voting to increase property tax support to the schools by $1 million. If you move to this side of the house, you will be voting to keep the property taxes where they are now. Are you ready for a division of the house?"

Basic Formats for Public Discussion

Format Called	Reason for Using
ROUND TABLE	To promote equality of feelings; maximize participation of all members; ensure as much spontaneity as possible.
SYMPOSIUM	To present a variety of views in the form of short speeches or reports for the benefit of the audience.
PANEL DISCUSSION	To conduct a semistructured discussion of issues on a topic for the benefit of an audience.
FORUM	To encourage audience participation on issues surrounding a topic.
COLLOQUY	To inform an audience through the use of planned questions designed to get unprepared responses from participants for the benefit of the audience.
WHOLE-HOUSE DECISION MAKING	To debate issues as a body, then decide, using appropriate voting methods.

▼ Table 10.4

Arrangement Suggested	Method
	Group discussion of problems and solutions for the purpose of making a good decision or sharing information.
o o o M o o o ▭	Moderator introduces the panel; provides history of the issues at hand; presents each speaker in turn; monitors time; thanks the participants; ends the meeting with a brief charge to the audience or a summary of the issue.
	Moderator introduces the panel and problem and keeps the discussion flowing; restates often; controls (somewhat) equal and fair time allocation. Members are responsible for developing points of view and have some control of agenda.
	Moderator introduces the program and speaker, who presents a brief statement and interacts with the audience. Moderator participates to encourage audience involvement. A variety of discussion formats can be used.
	Moderator introduces the speaker and panel of questioners, then regulates rotation and time. Sometimes summarizing, sometimes clarifying, moderator does not participate as a panelist.
	Moderator regulates the discussion and debate, attempting to get maximum input from both sides in order that members of the house may cast informed votes. Parliamentary procedure is commonly used to govern the event and facilitate orderly progress.

From Hanna, Michael S., and Gerald L. Wilson, *Communicating in Business and Professional Settings.* Second edition. Copyright © 1988 Random House, Inc. Reprinted by permission.

▲ Table 10.4 continued

Panel

A **panel** discussion is also carried out for the benefit of the audience, but not with direct audience involvement. Panel members are usually experts or reasonably well-informed people who share their points of view about a common question. Typically, a moderator asks a question, and the panel members interact with each other in response to the question.

The moderator's job during a panel discussion is demanding. It includes developing the discussion question outline and distributing it to the participants, along with presenting the ground rules for the discussion. It is the moderator's job to ask questions, maintain order, summarize agreements and disagreements, and keep the panel on track. The moderator also introduces the topic to be discussed and the members of the panel. In the end, the moderator summarizes the discussion, thanks the speakers, and asks for questions from the audience. This also implies that the moderator will maintain progress and order during the question-answer period.

Symposium

A **symposium** is not a discussion. It is a series of speeches related to a central topic. Its purpose is to provide material for discussion or to inform. Sometimes a panel discussion follows the speeches of a symposium. Sometimes the symposium is followed by audience questions and panel answers or by audience participation in a forum. If you are ever the moderator of a symposium, review the preceding discussion on forum and panel discussions.

Colloquium

A **colloquium** is a format for public discussion that involves a panel of experts who are asked questions by an audience. The audience knows the general topic for discussion and usually has prepared questions. Sometimes the format includes a primary question and follow-up questions. The experts respond to questions; they do not typically ask them. This format is useful for giving information, but it does not really allow the colloquium participants to interact with each other.

Each of these forms of public discussion can be used by a group to present its findings. Often these forms occur in combination. They are common enough that you may have opportunities to participate in them. In every case, public discussions are presented for the benefit of the audience. If you want to be successful in this context, try to understand and to adapt to the audiences.

Summary

Decision-making groups are everywhere, and you will almost certainly have an opportunity to participate in them. Your skill can make a significant contribution to your group's success and to your own. A decision-making group is any collection of three to eleven individuals who share a common problem or goal, who interact with each other, and who are mutually dependent.

People join groups because groups collectively provide more resources than a single individual and because groups tend to be better at controlling error. Being a participant in a group means giving your best effort, behaving rationally, playing fair, and participating fully. These things are essential to any member of a group. They imply that you must learn to be flexible and democratic, that you value group processes over individual enterprise, and that you plan carefully.

Leadership is an individual's ability to assess a communication situation and to provide the ideas and information needed by the group. Decision-making groups need leadership to identify and understand problems and solutions. An effective leader knows when to focus on task concerns, when to focus on relationship issues, and when to focus on procedures.

Four particularly common problems that decision-making groups face include: membership dissatisfaction, interpersonal conflict, a phenomenon called groupthink, and a phenomenon called "risky shift." These problems call for effective leadership.

There are also specific behaviors that are common in successful decision-making groups, and you can use them to work with the tension levels of a group. When tension levels are too high, talk about the source of the tension. When they are too low, talk about procedures. When they are just right, stay with an agenda that will contribute to effective decision making.

A group will usually have to report its findings, either in oral or in written form, or both. A report has several components and can present a group's ideas in a choice of formats: (1) forum, (2) panel, (3) symposium, and (4) colloquium. These public formats are different from decision-making groups because they are audience centered rather than problem centered.

Discussion Questions

1. Write down the name of the best group leader that you have ever known or witnessed. Name the worst group leader that you have ever known or witnessed. Compare and contrast them. Make a list of the characteristics that account for your naming them best or worst group leaders. Share your list with a group of your classmates. Do you find any significant similarities or differences in the lists?

2. If you could pick all of the members for a decision-making group, what characteristics would you want the members to exhibit in order to mold an ideal group? Make a list, specify reasons for your choices, and then compare your notes with a small group of classmates. Could your group select an ideal five- or six-member group from among people on your campus?

3. Make a list of the groups to which you belong. Try to write at least three benefits that you derive from belonging to these groups. Bring your notes to class so that you can compare and contrast your thinking with other members of your class.

4. Think of a group to which you belong and that you feel strongly positive about. A social fraternity or sorority might provide an example. Consider that group's cohesiveness. What behaviors do the members of the group exhibit that tell you that they are cohesive? What could you do (if anything) to enhance that group's cohesiveness? Does the cohesiveness level of the group ever change? Why? What causes the elevations and depressions in cohesiveness levels? Make a few notes so that you can compare your thinking with others in your class.

5. Working with a small group of classmates, role-play the following situations. As group members, identify the kinds of conflict management behavior that the role-players exhibited (or might have exhibited). What, if anything, does this experience teach you about conflict management in small groups?

- A member seems always to come late for group meetings.
- A member acts as if she/he were superior to the others.
- One of the members plays the part of a joker.
- One member tries to boss the others around, telling them what to do and how to do it to the point that another member feels a good deal of resentment.
- A group member seems unable to stay on the topic, but likes to talk. The result is that the member seems always to be distracting the group from its task.

References

[1]Gerald L. Wilson and Michael S. Hanna, *Groups in Context: Leadership and Participation in Small Groups,* 2d ed. (New York: McGraw-Hill, 1990).

[2]Randy Y. Hirokawa and Roger Pace, "A Descriptive Investigation of the Possible Communication-Based Reasons for Effective and Ineffective Group Decision Making," in *Communication Monographs* (December, 1983), pp. 362–79).

[3]Gerald L. Wilson and Michael S. Hanna, *op. cit.,* p. 182.

[4]Kenneth Benne and Paul Sheats, "Functional Roles of Group Members," in *Journal of Social Issues* 4 (1948), pp. 41–49.

[5]Gerald L. Wilson and Michael S. Hanna, *op. cit.,* pp. 154–60.

[6]R. Heslin and D. Dunphy, "Three Dimensions of Members' Satisfaction in Small Groups," in *Human Relations* 17 (1964), pp. 99–112.

[7]Joyce L. Hocker and William W. Wilmot, *Interpersonal Conflict:* 3d ed. (Dubuque, IA: Wm. C. Brown Publishers, 1990).

[8]Leonard C. Hawes and David H. Smith, "A Critique of Assumptions Underlying the Study of Communication and Conflict," in *Quarterly Journal of Speech* (December, 1973), pp. 423–35.

[9]L. Richard Hoffman, Ernest Harburg, and Norman R. F. Maier, "Differences and Disagreements as Factors in Creative Group Problem-Solving," in *Journal of Abnormal and Social Psychology* 64 (1962), pp. 206–14; Thomas Beisecker, "Communication and Conflict in Interpersonal Negotiations" (Paper presented to the annual meeting of the Speech Communication Association, New York: December, 1969).

[10]Henry W. Riecken, "Some Problems of Consensus Development," in *Rural Sociology* 7 (1952), pp. 245–54.

[11]B. Aubrey Fisher, *Small Group Decision Making,* 2d ed. (New York: McGraw-Hill, 1980), p. 239.

[12]Joyce Hocker and William Wilmot, *op. cit.*

[13]Irving L. Janis, *Victims of Groupthink* (Boston: Houghton Mifflin, 1972). Irving L. Janis, *Groupthink* (Boston: Houghton Mifflin, 1982).

[14]Dennis S. Gouran, "Inferential Errors, Interaction, and Group Decision Making" in Randy Y. Hirokawa and Marshall Scott Poole, (eds.), *Communication and Group Decision Making* (Beverly Hills, CA: Sage Publications, 1986), pp. 93–111.

[15]Ernest G. Bormann, *Discussion and Group Methods: Theory and Practice,* 2d ed. (New York: Harper & Row, 1975), pp. 181–82.

[16]John Dewey, *How We Think* (Boston: D. C. Heath, 1910).

[17]John K. Brilhart and Lurene M. Jochem, "Effects of Different Patterns on Outcomes of Problem-Solving Discussion," in *Journal of Applied Psychology 48* (1964), pp. 175–79.

[18]John K. Brilhart, *Effective Group Discussion,* 5th ed. (Dubuque, IA: Wm. C. Brown Publishers, 1986), pp. 308–10.

[19]Thomas M. Scheidel and Laura Crowell, "Idea Development in Small Group Discussion," in *Quarterly Journal of Speech* 50 (1964) pp. 140–45.

[20]B. Aubrey Fisher first described this influential idea in 1970. See "Decision Emergence: Phases in Group Decision Making," in *Speech Monographs* (March, 1970), pp. 53–66.

[21]B. Aubrey Fisher, *Small Group Decision Making: Communication and the Group Process* (New York: McGraw-Hill Book Company, 1974), p. 142.

Chapter 11

Organizational
Comnmunication

Objectives

When you finish reading this chapter you should be able to:

1. Explain the importance of organizational communication.

2. Describe the evolution of an organization.

3. Compare and contrast tall and flat structures.

4. Describe vertical, lateral, and serial flow of communication through a hierarchy.

5. Define and explain span of control and its relationship to power in the organization.

6. Compare and contrast line functions and staff functions.

7. Specify and explain the information function, the command and instruction function, the influence and persuasion function, and the integration and maintenance function of organizational communication.

8. Name, identify, and separate the scientific management, human relations, contingency, systems, and organizational culture schools of organizational leadership.

Key Terms

chain of command
command and instruction function
complexity
contingency school
culture
division of labor
entropy
flat structure
grapevine
hierarchy
horizontal flow
human relations school

influence and persuasion function
information function
institution
integration and maintenance function
line
negentropy
organization
organizational communication
organizational culture school

power
scientific management school
serial communication flow
span of control
staff
systems school
tall structure
organizational communication
vertical communication flow

Introduction

When people define what a manager does for a living, they stimulate their thinking by placing their ideas on a chalkboard one by one as they say them. The result is a list like the following one:

1. Manage people.

2. Set organizational objectives.

3. Develop and maintain the organization hierarchy.

4. Maintain organizational law and order.

5. Make decisions.

6. Lead groups of people.

7. Motivate others.

8. Manage organizational change.

9. "Run" the sales effort.

10. "Run" production.

Each of these matters is a function of communication within the context of an organization.

The purpose of this chapter is to place the study of communication into the context of complex organizations. What sets organizational communication apart from other kinds of communication? The goal is to identify and to describe useful knowledge and skills to improve your communication in the organizational context.

Some Definitions

Casual reference to organizations often refers to working and social units of various kinds and sizes. For example, we may refer to a business organization, although we may think of social fraternities and sororities as organizations, too. However, this general usage of the term "organization" is not very useful for the purpose of this chapter. What is needed is a definition that more carefully identifies the focus of this chapter and the study of human communication, but one which remains broad enough to include all kinds of organizations.

There are many definitions of an organization.[1] Some definitions point to and emphasize the goals, the role specialization, and the rules that structure people's working or social relationships over a long period of time. This definition points to a very stable, predetermined structure.

Other definitions emphasize the role that information processing plays when people's work must be coordinated and integrated to meet changing conditions. By implication, this definition points to a moderately stable structure of some kind, but one that changes occasionally as needed.

Still other definitions of "organization" emphasize the key role that communication and perception play in the continuing process of defining and renegotiating people's working relationships. By implication, this kind of definition suggests a structure that is continually evolving and changing. This chapter needs a definition that makes clear that the first purpose of any organization is goal achievement. Beyond that, the definition must make clear that human communication is the essential means by which organizational goal achievement occurs. Finally, the definition must make clear that careful management can improve both the quality of the goal achieved, and the means of achieving it.

An **organization** is a planned system of behaviors of two or more people who seek to achieve a common goal or set of goals by coordinating their efforts.

Think of an organization as being closely synonymous with human work. For instance, it would be difficult to imagine human work that does not take place within the context of some social organization. The family is an organization. The school is an organization. The corporation is an organization.

You can also think of an organization as being nearly synonymous with human communication about work. It would be difficult to imagine any organization that could exist independently from the communication that binds its members together and gives them focus and direction.

Some organizations are complex. Others are simple. **Complexity** refers to the degree of differentiation or separation in an organization, both in terms of hierarchical structure and physical distance. The complexity of an organization influences the communication that occurs within it.

For example, a young family (father, mother, baby) can be thought of as an organization. So can the giant Chrysler Corporation. The family is a simple organization. Some of its communication patterns will be formal and ritualized. This is especially true as the family communicates outside its own boundaries. However, most of its communication will be casual and informal. For example, you won't find much "going through channels" in most families.

In contrast, the Chrysler Corporation is enormously complex. Its communication behaviors and patterns will be more complex than a family's communication behaviors and patterns. Figure 11.1 is typical of a "tall structure" (i.e., a complex organization with many steps in the hierarchy).

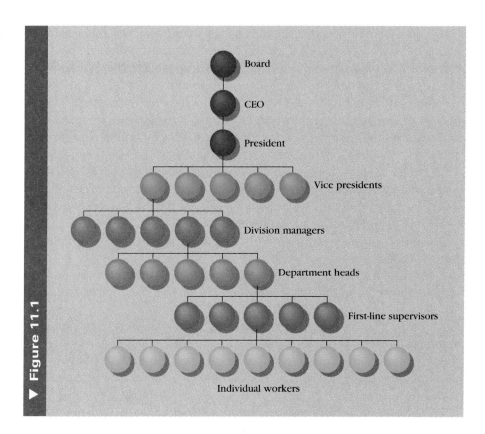

Figure 11.1

Organizational communication is communication that occurs in the context of an organization. Some of it is formal and ritualized, and some of it is spontaneous. Also, some of it is strictly rule-governed according to the norms and policies of the organization, and some of it is casual. However characterized, the organization's communication is its most important feature. Organizational communication accomplishes the job of goal achievement.

Importance of Organizational Communication

The term "institution" often conjures an establishment that serves a lofty goal, such as a school, a church, a hospital, or a court of law. An **institution** is any organization that has a social, educational, or religious purpose. By this definition, Xerox Corporation is an institution. It has all kinds of social and educational purposes. For some of its members, it may even take on religious significance. This criteria also applies to many other kinds of organizations.

Institutions always have multiple goals. The organization exists to serve those goals. In the case of business organizations, the goals can be very complex.

What organizational goals might a company like Exxon Corporation set out to accomplish? Some of the obvious goals follow:

1. Making money

2. Developing and advancing technology

3. Making the world a better place in which to live

4. Providing work

5. Providing social security

6. Distributing wealth

7. Establishing national or local policy

8. Further basic research

9. Encourage restoration of environment

10. Supply consumers with quality products and services

11. Move resources to places where they are needed

12. Take an interest in the culture and welfare of countries in which they are represented

Effective organizational communication could have made a very important difference.

Each of these is a legitimate goal of Exxon Corporation, as each one is a goal of most multinational organizations. However, what you probably remember about Exxon is the Exxon Valdes oil spill that occurred on March 24, 1989, at Prince William Sound. This is a case where effective organizational communication could have made a very important difference.

Immediately after the spill, Exxon tried to respond to meet two important goals. First, it responded to clean up the mess. And second, it responded to clean up the public image of Exxon. The response was working. Millions of dollars were spent every week. Thousands of people swept and mopped the beaches. While damaging, it looked as though the oil spill was not going to be as great of a disaster as it first appeared. However, by the end of summer, 1989, that had changed. Even though there was still a mess on the beaches, Exxon announced that the work was complete. This announcement created a furor in the news media. In response, the media complained that Exxon was ignoring its responsibility, that the leadership of the organization was making irresponsible choices, and that the Exxon organization was somehow evil.

What happened was that the responsibility for the cleanup within the Exxon organization, which is a highly compartmentalized and complex structure, had shifted to the legal department. The goals and objectives of the legal department were different from the originally stated goals. For the legal department, the critical issues were legal ones rather than social or ethical ones.

Evolution of an Organization

As a child, you went through a phase of experimenting and playing with the idea of organizations. You may have formed a neighborhood "club," complete with a clubhouse. You may have decided which of your chums would be the president, the vice president, the treasurer, the secretary, and so forth. For most children, organizational development ends here, because that's where the neighborhood runs out of children at just the right age and at just the right stage of development.

Such childhood organizations don't last very long because they aren't needed. There is no special goal other than organization for its own sake. In addition, the structure of the organization is arbitrarily imposed by the children without any understanding of the functions that a structure must perform. Therefore, the neighborhood club is nothing but a childhood game.

In the adult world, every organization evolves; that is, an organization develops gradually as the pressures and needs of its internal and external environments dictate. Its structure also evolves; and with it, an organization's purposes and goals, history, norms, themes, and so forth also evolve. You can say that every organization is created in the symbols exchanged by its members as they address the social pressures of their lives.

Organization as Culture

Every organization is a culture within a culture. Chapter 17 will discuss the whole matter of cultures and communication across cultural boundaries in greater detail. For now, **culture** means an identifiable group whose members share beliefs, customs, communication patterns and a common history by means of their communication behavior. Every complex organization fits this definition.

Anthropologist Clifford Geertz urges us to understand culture ". . . not as complexes of concrete behavior patterns—customs, usages, traditions, habit clusters . . . but as a set of control mechanisms, plans, recipes, rules, instructions . . . , for the governing of behavior."[2] He might argue, therefore, that our study of organizational communication should focus upon the control mechanisms that people use to coordinate their efforts to achieve their common goals.

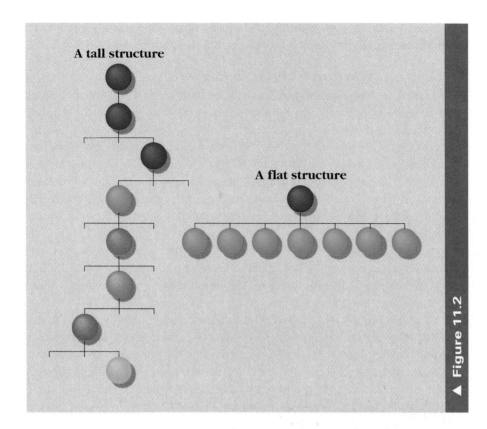

A tall structure

A flat structure

Tall structure versus flat structure. A tall structure is characterized by the number of levels in the hierarchy.

▲ Figure 11.2

The control mechanisms include such things as hierarchy, span of control, line versus staff, division of labor, and role specialization. Each of these features is an appropriate concern as we study organizational communication.

Hierarchy of an Organization

A **hierarchy** is any system that places people in rank order, one above the other. Complex organizations are often viewed in terms of a hierarchy of relationships. The president is the boss. The vice presidents answer to the president. The division managers answer to the vice presidents. The department heads answer to the division managers, and so forth. The positions in the hierarchy are power and authority relationships that exist for the purpose of governing the organizational culture.

When an organization includes many levels in its hierarchy, it is called a **tall structure.** When it has only a few levels in the hierarchy, it is called a **flat structure.** Thus, the tallness or flatness of an organizational structure is an issue of hierarchy. Figure 11.2 illustrates the difference between a tall structure and a flat structure.

Problems of communication flow in the organization come directly from the hierarchical structure. It is useful to take a closer look at this flow.

Communication Flow in a Hierarchy

Vertical communication flows up and down the hierarchical structure. What flows upward is usually job-related information, or suggestions for changes that might improve the organization's ability to achieve its goals. Thus, the upward-flowing messages are very important to the overall health of the organization. However, often such messages seem unpleasant to managers. For example, managers may not want to hear about worker dissatisfaction, and managers don't usually like to hear about their expensive errors. If managers ignore upwardly flowing messages, workers soon decide that there is no point in sending them.

In addition, there appears to be a certain "fear factor" in sending them in many organizations. That is, people seem reluctant to send anything but positive or supportive messages up through channels because they fear reprisals if they do otherwise.

At the same time, managers tend to concentrate on only certain kinds of messages. They think about things like production levels, and profits and loss. They tend to be more concerned about downward flow of communication than upward flow. Because of the greater power of people higher up the organizational ladder, and perhaps because of the fear factor, too, messages that flow upward tend to be greatly reduced.[3] For example, suppose a line worker, Benny, complains to his immediate supervisor about one of his coworkers. "He's drinking and using drugs on the job. That's dangerous, and I'm afraid. I want you to take care of it." In addition, suppose that the supervisor decides that this is a situation that they'd better handle on their own. In this case, the supervisor might not send any information about the drinking and drug use beyond their own level. Thus, management might not receive a critical piece of information needed to control drug and alcohol abuse in the organization.

Messages that flow downward tend to be greatly expanded. A CEO's casual question on the golf course directed to a vice president provides an example. "Tell me, Bill, what's going on in the personnel department to check for drugs and alcohol on the line?"

No one likes to be taken by surprise, especially when they have the responsibility for something that they know nothing about. Bill had neither heard anything specific about a drug/alcohol problem, nor had he heard anything about any activity in the personnel department to check for drugs and alcohol. Therefore, he responded in an embarrassed way, "Uh, we're looking into it, Fred. I'll check the status on things when I get back to the office and I'll call you."

Notice how the message begins to expand. At the ninth green, Bill puts out, excuses himself, and walks briskly to the clubhouse. He places a call to his assistant. "Get me all of the information that we have on drug and alcohol abuse, and set up a meeting with Dan Smith [head of personnel] for this afternoon. Tell him the president is upset about the drug problem."

In turn, Dan Smith gets the message this way, "Mr. Smith, this is Mike Snow. During their game this morning, Fred asked Bill for a rundown on what personnel is doing to control the drug problem. He's apparently quite upset about how slowly things are moving. Bill wants a meeting with you this afternoon to clear things up."

You can see that a casual question has expanded rapidly, as messages flow down through the chain of command. Although this is important for the distribution of administrative directives, it can also create problems.

Horizontal flow refers to messages sent by people who consider themselves equal. A chairman of one department calls a chairman of another department, for example. Horizontal flow is essential because it allows people to share information about methods and problems and about the political pressures in which each has to work. It facilitates task coordination and problem solving. It helps the organization to manage internal conflicts.[4] Horizontal flow, however, can also create problems.

For example, accountants and financial controllers speak one jargon, while engineers speak another. Moreover, the thrust of the engineering department is about making things and making things work. The thrust of the financial department is about budget control. Typically, the engineering department and the financial department in the same organization consider themselves opposed to each other. Two typical reactions include: "All the engineers want to do is spend money." "If those financial people would open their eyes, they'd know that they are losing dollars to save pennies."

These differences in language and perception can create distorted interpretations of each other's communication. Such differences can even create a competition between people where cooperation would serve the organization's goals much better.

Serial communication flow occurs when a message is sent along a chain of people. In its simplest form this can occur when you tell something to your friend, who turns around and tells it to someone else. Serial communication occurs without regard to the hierarchy, so it is highly efficient. Rumors spread at the office through serial communication.

You may have heard of the **grapevine,** which is a popular term for the informal networks that evolve in an organization. The grapevine is who really talks to whom. Every complex organization has one. It is the informal network that is not shown on the organization chart. It is the network of contact that actually occurs in an organization. Wise leaders must learn to use it, but research literature offers little help in learning how.[5]

The information relayed by the grapevine is often very accurate. The accuracy rate may be as high as 90 percent.[6] People also believe in the grapevine and count on its accuracy, often with dramatic effect.[7]

The problem is that, regardless of the accuracy of the key ideas, messages that flow through informal channels are always distorted and changed as they move through people. This is because each of us must take in the message, understand and interpret it, and decide its importance. This process causes the message to become influenced by our own points of view. Because each of us is limited, the message changes noticeably. The intensity level is usually changed. For example, we tend to drop strong language and strong nonverbal cues.

Other details are "sharpened." Some details are made more important in comparison to others, and they are passed on with new vigor. Those sharpened details may carry through the entire chain.

The most common problem is that much of a message that flows through a series of speakers is simply left out, forgotten, or ignored in the retelling. Therefore, the message that begins the series may not resemble the message that ends the series.

To manage the grapevine, some organizations provide a "hot line" to the personnel office so that employees can verify what they have heard. Other managers deliberately identify and feed opinion leaders with information, counting on the grapevine to disseminate that information quickly.

Power and Span of Control

Communication flow through an organizational hierarchy must be managed. The problem of managing it raises the two additional issues of power and span of control. **Power** means the ability or potential to influence others. In the context of this chapter about communication in organizations, power is a communication issue. Excluded from this discussion is any kind of power that flows directly from the use of physical force.

Thus, the use of military might is the exercise of power, but it is outside the scope of this chapter. If police arrest a worker against his or her will, that, too, lies beyond the focus of this chapter. But the *threat* of force is a consideration for us, since someone must communicate the threat.

J. French and B. H. Raven provide one of the clearest descriptions of where people get power in organizations.[8] According to them, power derives from five sources: (1) use or threat of force, (2) use or promise of reward, (3) position in the hierarchy, (4) special and essential knowledge, and (5) interpersonal liking.

Social power is always based on dependency. If someone needs you
and perceives that they need you, then you have power in that relationship.
The idea of dependency points to a key question when people use (and
abuse) power in their relationships. To what extent, if any, are you willing
to continue to depend upon the other person? To what extent, if any, is the
other willing to depend upon you?

For example, suppose you have the only gas station in town. Your friend
wants to buy gas and doesn't want to drive twenty-five miles to another gas
station. To the extent that your friend wants gas, but doesn't want to drive
very far to get it, you have the power to set the price of gas.

If someone puts a gas station across the street from your own, your
friend is no longer dependent upon you for the gasoline. You can't charge
much more for the gasoline that you sell than the person across the street
because the customers don't need you as much. Of course, there might be
other reasons that people come to your gas station. Your service might be
better. Your product might be better, or your product selection might be
better liked by the customers. You might have cleaner restrooms, might have
a convenience store in your station, or might have a good mechanic. In fact,
you might be just a very nice person so people like to do business with you.

All of these factors might negate the fact that your gas is two pennies
per gallon higher than the gas sold across the street. Regardless, these factors
are all based on a dependency of some kind.

Reward is dependency-based; you can reward someone if you have
something that they value. Hierarchy is also a dependency-based source of
power. For example, if you are the department head, you have a legitimate
right to make decisions that influence other people's choices. Your subordinates depend upon you to make those decisions.

You might be the best, or only, mechanic in town. Therefore, people
depend upon you for your knowledge because it is a source of expert power.

If another mechanic moved to town, the customer's dependence on you would be reduced, thus, so would your expert power.

You might also be a very nice human being. Being liked is a power source. If people look to you for confirmation of themselves, you have referent power. Thus, to round out the gas station metaphor, people might come to your station partly because they enjoy doing business with you. Suppose that the person across the street is always grouchy and ugly to his customers. Your referent power might be sufficient to support a slight increase in the price of your gas. That is, because people like you, they might be willing to pay a penny or two more per gallon for the gas you sell.

Power in an organization is also directly related to the tallness or flatness of the organizational structure. It is an issue of "span of control."

Span of control means the number of subordinates who report to an individual supervisor. Thus, span of control is primarily a feature of the overall power plan of an organization. Span of control limits the authority of an individual supervisor. It is closely related to the concept of division of labor. **Division of labor** refers to the decisions made in an organization about who does what. Span of control is also closely associated with the concept of **chain of command,** which is the planned power and authority relationships of an organization. These features of an organization are a major source of communication problems.

To illustrate these ideas, consider Henry Ford's major contribution to the automobile industry. His idea was to make more cars of the same quality by dividing the labor. This was accomplished by specializing the tasks that individual people must perform. Rather than having twenty workers, each trying to do every task involved in making a car, why not teach each one to specialize in the tasks involved in assembling part of a car, then send each car down an assembly line? The idea revolutionized American industry.

Some researchers believe that an individual's span of control should not be more than a dozen subordinates. Other authorities believe that it's possible to provide effective leadership to many more people than that, especially if the subordinates are given decision-making autonomy and some degree of responsibility for their own success. That kind of decision making may be the most important single determinant of what constitutes an appropriate span of control. For example, a single boss might be able to control a very large number of subordinates, if those people are all engaged in making the same product or performing similar and simple tasks. In contrast, to coordinate broadly diverse activities requires a good deal of personal attention. Thus, task diversity is directly related to an appropriate span of control.

The hierarchy of a flat structure has fewer levels. This fact yields a much broader power field. The result may be that the supervisor in a flat structure runs a loosely controlled operation. Because more individuals report to a single supervisor, individuals tend to have greater autonomy in decision making and more direct responsibility for their own success in achieving their goals on the job.

A flat structure can generate communication problems. Since the individual supervisor's span of control includes so many "direct reports," the number of messages that she/he must process tends to be greater than a manager in a tall structure. The sheer number of messages sent through channels from subordinates can create a problem of information overload. Yet, if the supervisor does not process all the messages, she or he may risk a loss of control. In addition, increased span of control tends to decrease task efficiency because it decreases role specialization.

This does not mean that a tall structure is necessarily either more efficient or more effective than a flat structure. Tall structures also create communication problems. Bureaucratization can become a problem. Distortions that occur when people must go through channels are a problem. For workers, the tallness of a structure can create a feeling of isolation and distance from the decision making, which can result in decreased allegiance to the organization and become a problem.

So, one style of structure is not inherently better than the other. Rather, the preference for one over the other depends upon a complex set of conditions. The tallness or flatness of an organization must evolve out of economic and other considerations.

The point is that the structure must be appropriate. Questions such as: Who's in charge? Who does what? and Who's responsible? (along with questions concerning a person's role definition and his/her ability to perform the tasks in that role definition) are all related to what kind of organizational structure evolves, and whether the leadership of the organization can adapt to those conditions.

Line Functions and Staff Functions

The two primary tasks of an organization are (1) to produce goods or services, and (2) to market those goods or services. Call these two functions **line** functions. All the people who produce the goods or services, both managers and workers, are line employees. The people who are directly involved in selling and the people who supervise the sales force are also line employees.

Everyone else in the organization performs a **staff** function. Thus, the staff includes all of the individuals who are involved in supporting the line operations. Although there are some exceptions, staff most often serves in an advisory capacity to the line. Staff generates the services that the line needs to produce or sell. Accounting departments, legal departments, advertising departments, and personnel departments are examples of staff departments.

IT'S MORE FUN TO KNOW

Social Competence and the Influence of Others

Researchers find a relationship between social competence and prevention of drug use. People have to feel comfortable in talking to friends and acquaintances in small groups and one-to-one. It is not enough to urge them to ''Just Say No.''

See Kathleen Kelley Reardon, ''The Role of Persuasion in Health Promotion and Disease Prevention: Review and Commentary,'' in *Communication Yearbook, 11,* (ed) James A. Anderson (Beverly Hills, CA: Sage Publications, 1988), p. 281.

Comment . . .
People who feel comfortable with their peers and feel competent about their relationships are less likely to use drugs. Social and communication relationships may be one of the keys to success in the ''War on Drugs.''

Entropy and Negentropy

All organizations have the potential to decay. What has been put together can be taken apart or can be "unglued" of its own accord. The term used to describe this tendency of an organization to disintegrate is **entropy.** When an organization recognizes that it is in danger of entropy, it acts to prevent the decay. The pressure resulting from that effort is called **negentropy.**

A major task of management in any organization is to counter entropy with negentropy. That is accomplished by means of communication behavior. To illustrate, suppose a manufacturing company is in the business of making and selling aluminum storm windows and storm doors. The people in the organization take great pride in their work. As a result, the doors and windows are well designed and well made. Because they are of such high quality, people begin to want those storm windows and doors on their houses.

The increase in demand places a strain upon the organization's ability to meet the demand. Something has to be done, but what? Raise the prices? Hire and train more help? Both?

Management must make some difficult decisions or risk the health and stability of the company. Put another way, the managers must introduce negentropy. To hire and train help is costly in both time and money. Can the company's financial structure withstand the sudden impact on cash flow? If so, who will do the recruiting and training? If not, will a raise in prices pay for the increased costs to the company that flow from recruiting and training new employees?

Should the company be reorganized in some way? For example, should the window division be separated from the door division? Will that division need new equipment and space? Who will pay for the increased costs of these things? Who will coordinate? Who will buy the materials for the two divisions?

Can the company just say "no" to the increased demand, then go about the business of making windows and doors as they always have? What would that decision do to the sales force, who want to increase sales in order to increase their commissions? What would be the long-range effects of such a decision (to do nothing) on morale? What would be the effects on the image of the company in the community? What would be the effects on the internal politics of the organization?

The managers had better talk things over. They must act to introduce negentropy into the system. Otherwise, the pressures that have given rise to the questions will begin to wear away at the stability and strength of the organization.

Organizational communication may be influenced by some of the features that are peculiar to complex organizations. How the structure (the hierarchy) evolves and the resulting power relationships that flow out of the hierarchy can both make an important difference in how smoothly and how effectively organizational communication occurs. Issues of line and staff are involved. Issues of control are involved.

To understand these variables, it seems important to consider, first, what organizational communication does, and how and in what context organizational communication occurs.

Organizational Communication Functions

More than twenty years ago, Lee J. Thayer published a book titled *Communication and Communication Systems in Organizations, Management, and Interpersonal Relations.*[9] In it he identified the four functions of communication in organizations. They were: (1) information, (2) command and instruction, (3) influence and persuasion, and (4) integration and maintenance. In 1985, Charles Conrad reduced that number to three and refocused the functions.[10] For Conrad, organization communication served to: (1) provide direction and feedback (the command function), (2) form and maintain relationships (the relation function), and (3) manage ambiguity (the ambiguity-management function).

Meanwhile, from 1971–1976 the Organizational Communication Division of the International Communication Association developed a system called "communication audit" that allowed researchers to assess the employees' perceptions of communication processes that occurred in their organizations. Then, in November 1988, Sue DeWine and Anita C. James of Ohio University suggested a refinement of the communication audit.[11] They called their instrument a "Survey of Organizational Communication." Their survey questionnaires focused upon: (1) receiving information from others, (2) sending information to others, (3) follow-up on information sent, (4) interpersonal communication relationships, (5) organizational outcomes, (6) channels of communication, and (7) sources of information. In addition, DeWine and James included questions about how the respondent experienced communication (Did it seem effective?) and about the quality of the information sent and received.

The goal of all of these efforts was to organize and to understand *internal* communication in an organization. What does communication do within an organization's boundaries?

An organization must also communicate outside its boundaries. For example, a company may want to advertise a new product, or some service organization may want to enhance its image in the community. The *external* communication of an organization includes advertising, public relations, and environmental adaptation. These external communication activities of an organization constitute entire professional areas in our economy. They use both print and broadcast media as channels.

Lee Thayer's "Taxonomy of Organizational Communication Functions" remains the most useful list for examining the functions of internal organizational communication.

Information Function

Organizations need and process two kinds of information in **information function.** External information is sent and received in order for the organization to advertise its products or services, to maintain its image in the community, and to adapt its policy to the ever-changing pressures of its environment. Internal information provides the basis for determining the organization's goals, assessing its own performance, and coordinating its individual subunits.

Information exchange is the only means that an organization has to transmit (and measure) expectations and requirements to the subunits. Thus, the information function of an organization is critical. Problems occur when errors are introduced in the information exchanged.

To illustrate, one fall term a university realized that it had many more students than parking spaces. The flow of traffic around and through the campus was a nightmare. University officials decided to build additional parking lots. Bids were solicited, contractors were selected, and work started—all without making any provisions for the impact of this activity on traffic flow.

Faculty lots were overrun by student cars, and the faculty could not get near their classrooms or offices. In response, the school administration told police to be very strict in issuing parking tickets in areas where no construction was under way, but not to put tickets on cars in areas where construction was *impeding* the flow of traffic.

An enterprising reporter on the student newspaper discovered the decision and published it in the newspaper. Students began to park anywhere they could find a place to put their cars—on the grass, in faculty and staff lots, and even in handicapped parking spaces. Soon there was a flood of parking violations followed by a noisy demonstration in front of the administration building. By now, there was no place on the campus where the construction was not impeding the flow of traffic. In time, of course, as contractors completed the new lots, the problem was resolved. However, it could have been prevented if the administration had been more careful about the accuracy of its communication.

Command and Instruction Function

The **command and instruction function** of organizational communication is the primary means that managers use to keep their organizational units working toward the organization's goals. Commands and instructions help people to stay within the organization's policy and to do their jobs well. If given correctly, commands and instructions minimize errors. Finally, commands and instructions coordinate the individual workers so that their efforts integrate smoothly. Determining what commands and instructions to give and to whom is not an easy task.

Influence and Persuasion Function

Organizations must use the **influence and persuade function** in order to exercise certain kinds of control over the behavior of individual members. Thus, influence and persuasion are closely related to command and instruction. Primarily, the difference exists in the level of commitment that an individual member has to the organization and its goals.

The greater the person's commitment, the lesser the control necessary to keep him or her working toward the organization's goals. For example, read the following conversation:

JEFF: "I love my job! Each morning I can hardly wait to get to work. In fact, this morning I was thinking about the details of my project, got an idea, and before I knew it, I was in my office. I was almost an hour early!"

HENRY: "Not me. I work to live. It's all the same to me. So I come when I have to, and I go home on time. I have better things to do with my time than hang around the office."

Jeff and Henry have different levels of commitment to the organization and its goals. A manager would have a greater need to control Henry than to control Jeff. In addition, as a means of control, Henry is more likely to receive commands and instruction; Jeff is more likely to receive influence and persuasion.

Integration and Maintenance Function

The **integration and maintenance functions** of an organization aim to accomplish five goals. The first goal is to keep the organization in operation. If marketing can't sell what production makes, then the organization will shut down. If production can't make what marketing sells, then the organization will shut down. Thus, production (line) and marketing (line), and all of the staff functions that support these two lines, must be integrated and maintained.

Some very difficult and risky decisions must be made in order to keep an organization in operation. For example, a giant chemical company decided to comply with increasing pressures from environmental protection groups. They committed over $250 million to build an aboveground wastewater treatment plant that would protect the local waterways. Such a massive commitment of cash to this project meant that the other component parts of the organization would be cash poor. Management had to make many adjustments in order to keep the organization going.

A second goal of the integration and maintenance function is to keep organization members going through channels. Otherwise, the individuals at the center of the organization's networks are unable to process all the information. Realistically, if a corporation's president had an open door for anyone in the organization, all of the president's time would be taken up with small talk instead of presidential duties.

The third goal of integration and maintenance is to sort and to cross-reference the data of the organization. Without this activity, the organization could not continue to function. For example, suppose that you own a supermarket. Your cashiers help you to maintain your inventory by dragging each item's bar code across the laser readers at the checkout stands. These data go to a computer that keeps track of the sales of the items, analyzes the demand, compares the demand against the inventory in stock, and then tells the purchasing department when and what to buy. If such inventory data were not sorted and cross-referenced on a continuing basis, the shelves would not be restocked, and your frustrated customers would start buying their groceries somewhere else.

The fourth goal of integration and maintenance is to relate the various parts of the organization to the whole and to the contexts in which they must work. Keeping the sales force and the production line in touch with the other's needs and capabilities illustrates this goal.

Suppose the marketing department sells one hundred units, but production only has enough materials to produce ninety units. The contract guarantees that money will be available to the organization to pay for the materials needed, but someone has to tell purchasing what to buy and when. In addition, someone has to tell the salespeople the delivery time frame to negotiate with the customers.

Finally, a fifth integration and maintenance goal is to confirm the individual members and the organization. People need to believe that what they do is important, and that others respect their organization. Thus, it's important that the organization's communication system reinforce the employees' sense of self-worth. Moreover, it is important to reassure employees that the organization is a good one. Otherwise, the individual members may begin to drift away to other organizations.

Communication inside an organization performs five very important functions for that organization. The information function provides the basis for determining goals and assessing the performance of the organization. The command and instruction function and the influence and persuasion function serve the control needs of the organization by assuring that the organization's departments and people keep working toward the organization's goals. The integration and maintenance function does four things. It keeps the organization in operation. It keeps the members going through channels. It keeps the data of the organization sorted and cross-referenced. It integrates all the parts so that the organizational whole can continue to

exist. And it confirms the individual members and the organization as a whole. Without these functions the organization could not continue to exist. To perform these functions well, an organization must also have effective leadership.

Leadership in the Organization

Leadership of an organization is everybody's business.[12] Regardless of the position an individual holds in the organization's hierarchy, everyone is in a position to provide some leadership. In fact, the more effectively an individual provides leadership, the more likely that person is to move into hierarchical positions where the leadership is legitimized.

Leadership of an organization is everybody's business.

Scholars have studied leadership behavior in organizations for a long time. In this century, at least five so-called "schools" of leadership have dominated scholarly thinking.

Scientific Management School

The **scientific management school** believes that people are economically motivated; they will respond with their best effort and skill if their economic rewards are tied to their performance. Thus, the most effective leadership finds ways to tie the individual's financial rewards to performance.[13] An example would be working on straight commission.

Human Relations School

The **human relations school** rejects the views of the scientific management school and replaces them with a more social orientation. They believe that attention to the workers' needs and to job satisfaction is necessary for effective leadership. They want to involve workers in decision making and to assure that peer relationships are attended to with an eye toward satisfying the social needs of the workers.[14] The management style of quality circles applies much of this approach.

Contingency School

The **contingency school** rejects the idea that any one way to manage people and organizations is best. They argue that each situation is unique.[15] Thus, the appropriate management behavior depends on some interrelationship among the task, the organizational structure, the kinds of employees, and the manager. This school would require a leader who is particularly adept at monitoring group conditions and who is flexible in choosing a course of action.

The **systems school** focuses on communication. Communication holds the organization together; communication binds the subsystems; and communication makes negentropy possible. Thus, the systems school combines much of what is effective from the scientific management and human relations schools. Both the physical and the psychological aspects of an organization work together as part of a system. They must all be taken into account. And that would not be possible without effective communication.[16] A company, such as 3M, that encourages its employees to express new ideas and that rewards experimentation with bonuses and profit sharing in cases of success might find a lot of support in the systems school.

Organizational Culture School

The **organizational culture school** believes that organization must be viewed as a culture. It sees each organization as a unique society that has its own rules, its own history, and its own values. To study these things is to understand the ways that an organization works and how to influence its members.[17] In America, the family farm represents not only a "business," but also a distinct way of life. Thus, a farm or a farming community is culturally distinct from most other ways of making a living.

These five schools of organizational leadership concern how people should communicate in organizations, and to whom. If studied carefully, they should help you to determine how to communicate in a particular context.

Summary

Organizational communication is communication that occurs within an organizational context. It is influenced by all of the features of the organizational culture that evolve over time. It is the essence of every human organization. Organizational communication is nearly synonymous with human work.

The hierarchy that forms the structure of the organization imposes itself on organizational communication in a number of ways. The upward and downward flow of messages is directly influenced by the "tallness" of the structure. The horizontal flow of messages among equals can create problems. The serial flow of messages across a chain of people can be greatly distorted. Power issues—including the consideration of the appropriate span of control, division of labor, and chain of command—are directly related to the hierarchy that evolves.

As an organization evolves, its goals become more complicated. The line and staff functions within the organization become more specialized, and entropy (the tendency of an organization to come apart) becomes a problem for managers. They must introduce negentropic forces into the organization. They do this through communication. They give and get information. They command. They instruct. They influence and persuade. They try to integrate the workers and the workers' efforts in order to maintain the organization and its drive toward goal achievement.

Part IV

Public Communication Settings

The public communication section of this text incorporates principles drawn from group communication, the nature of interpersonal relationships, the individual as communicator, and the other chapters that precede it. The materials in this section compliment the other principles. They are helped by emphasizing theoretical and practical matters read earlier.

Public communication is intimately tied to the circular nature of communication and to the role of self-image in communication. The role of language and the way each of us constructs our reality through symbolic interaction is essential to anyone hoping to be successful in the public setting. How you feel about yourself as the center of attention in a public relationship affects the level of success you anticipate for yourself. It is also crucial that your skills in critical and creative thinking help you to originate and evaluate your ideas before you present them to others.

In many ways, public talk is an extension of the ways you communicate in interpersonal and group settings. Roles are more formal but you must pay attention to your language and to the ways people react to your words. Are they listening? How could you work with them to increase their level of retention? What nonverbal messages are you sending as you prepare to talk to a group of your peers for the first time? The answers to these questions require a specific examination of the nature of the public communication event. The answers are contained partially in the content of the chapters you examined in the two preceding sections.

The public communication experience deals with a group of people listening to you speak in a formally structured situation. You may have talked in groups previously but here the rules are more formal. You will talk and they will listen. There will not be a dialogue until you are finished. While you are in control of the situation, you will use those principles and techniques that we discuss in this section to increase the likelihood of your success.

To become a successful public communicator requires hard work and an understanding of the theory and application of communication principles in a medium to large group setting. This section outlines an approach to public communication that focuses on your individuality as a speaker/human. You have the talent to be successful in this experience. The information that enables you to build upon that talent and realize success is the content of this section on public communication.

Chapter 12

Preliminary Concerns in Public Speaking

Outline

When you finish reading this chapter you should be able to:

1. Define communication effects and explain their significance.

2. Explain the importance of the speaker's attitude toward the communication situation.

3. Understand the role of communication apprehension and its effect upon communication behaviors.

4. Cite the major characteristics of effective selection and the narrowing of speech topics.

5. Explain the role of the purpose and the thesis statements in structuring the message.

Objectives

audience centered

communication apprehension

communication effects

economy of scale

general purpose

positive self-thought

self visualization

specific purpose

sustained interaction

thesis statement

Key Terms

Introduction

The terms *communication, rhetoric,* and *persuasion* are synonymous. Each of these words refers to the social process of using symbols to influence thought and action.[1] This definition is consistent with the symbolic interactionist position. Chapters 1 and 2 explained this approach that asserts that all our lives are connected with symbols. We react to words (symbols) and they become our link with conveying reality. It is not true that "sticks and stones will break my bones, but words will never harm me." Words are our way of conveying reality to others and are our method to affect and inform other people. This interactive process also relates to the definition proposed in chapter 1 where it said that communication means the dynamic and complex process of message exchange and interpretation.

This chapter explores the basis of public speaking. It looks at how people perceive public speaking and why. In the process, it examines some conceptions and misconceptions that affect the way people talk and feel about public communication. As you learn more about public speaking, you will approach public communication opportunities more realistically and effectively. You will also become more confident about your ability to communicate with your peers in a public setting.

You will see what kinds of messages are effective in public talk. One of this chapter's major concerns is the importance of a clear *thesis statement* and its effect on the development of the rest of speech preparation. This chapter emphasizes narrowing of the topic and developing materials that interest listeners. It also emphasizes the kind of topics that interest people and how you can organize and develop your subject.

Communication Effects

Whenever someone gives a speech or someone listens to one, the speaker is trying to influence the listener. The change that the speaker seeks in the listener can be an observable change, such as a decision to purchase a product or service. It also can be a mental change, such as a change in attitude, value, or belief. These changes are called **communication effects.**

Public speaking is our least frequently used form of daily communication activity that attempts to affect the attitudes, beliefs, and values of friends and strangers. Suppose a friend asks you, "How would *you* like to present your proposal for selecting the President of Alpha Omicron Zeta?" You probably would not answer "By giving a speech at the next meeting." Instead, you might choose to write each person a letter. Or you could talk to them individually. In short, you would choose the form of communication that is most comfortable for you, and you would choose the one that you thought would have the greatest effect.

Most people have little experience in speaking formally and publicly to others, because they are reluctant to choose a mode of communication that is unfamiliar. They continue to do the things that are easy and common. For example, they use the same route to go to the grocery store. They choose to eat at a restaurant that they know has good food. They speak freely on the phone to their friends and relatives. However, when it comes to less familiar matters, they are more guarded. For instance, a visit with an academic advisor demands careful language selection and strategic planning, if their objective is to get the desired results. If they decide to ask a new classmate for a date, they may rehearse many times before the conversation. These are examples of situations that people view with apprehension. When they are worried, they evaluate the situation carefully to determine if the advantages (of a visit to your advisor or a date with an attractive person) are greater than the discomfort that the communication situation creates.

Public speaking is an opportunity. It is a chance to affect other people. Influencing people, whether by our appearance or by our speech, is both gratifying and challenging. Public talk is one of the most efficient ways of getting information from point *A* to point *B*. There is a marvelous **economy of scale** in public talk. For instance, a speaker sends a message to a group of people. The same information could be communicated to them on an individual basis by conversation, but individual conversations would be remarkably inefficient. A speech gets the same message to all people at the same time. Audience members can hear and learn as much as in personal contact with the speaker. We can have the same communication effect in public speaking with many people as we do interpersonally with one or two people.

The Speaker

The speaker is a key element in the public speaking experience. Ideas that originate with a speaker must be **audience centered,** the message must be adapted to work effectively with the interests and capacities of the listeners. The speaker is a goal-oriented person. When Barry Sanders, the Heisman Trophy Winner in 1988, entered his first professional football game as a member of the Detroit Lions, he said "it felt good to get hit." He said that he expected the team to win and that he wanted to do what was expected of him and what he expected of himself. Like Barry Sanders, the effective speaker must decide what to expect. The aim should be to present ideas so that audience members understand and act upon them. The goal is to have an effect upon the audience through shared symbolic meaning.

Attitudes toward the Situation

Your attitude toward public communication is a result of your experience. Perhaps a high school English teacher required you to present an oral book report in class. Or, you might have been assigned a report on some phase of World War II by your American history teacher. These are common settings for developing attitudes toward public speaking. You may feel uncomfortable with the material and with the situation in which you present it, so you conclude that public speaking creates your discomfort.

You communicate one-on-one many times each day. However, you can probably count the number of public speeches that you have given on the fingers of one of your hands. The less frequent the experience, the greater the doubt that may accompany it. Therefore, the way you feel about public communication is actually drawn from very limited direct experience. You rely on the testimony of friends and your observations of others in public speaking situations to help you to form your attitude. Their words affect the way you think, feel, and act. Your symbolic interaction with them affects much of your behavior.

To exemplify how limited experience creates uncertainty, suppose someone asks you how you feel about race walking. You might say, "It looks silly, but I guess it must be worthwhile because it is an Olympic track-and-field event." Similarly, if a friend invites you to go whitewater canoeing next weekend, you might say, "OK, but I don't know how to paddle and I sure don't want to turn over in the cold water. I'll go if you'll show me what to do before we leave."

We have positive attitudes toward many activities, even though we may not have firsthand experience with them. A lack of information or exposure does not necessarily create a negative or positive attitude. Interpersonal communication plays an important role in helping us to resolve much of our personal uncertainty.

On the other hand, attitudes toward public speaking vary widely. You can find an entire range of reactions. Some people will tell you, "I really like it. It's exciting." Others may say, "I'm not too comfortable doing it."

This range of attitudes has a relation to the way that you feel about speaking in public. Hopefully, you will approach this topic with an open mind. Postpone a final decision. Get all of the available information before you develop a hard-and-fast attitude about public speaking. The more you understand about public speaking, the more you will be able to see it as a challenging and fulfilling experience. In various ways, we all have learned "the thought is father of the deed." Approach this activity without preconceptions. Try to gain more information about the process. It may change your attitude toward public communication.

Positive Feeling about Success

Positive experiences in public speaking and in much of human experience results from **positive self-thought.** The well-known author, Wayne Dyer's recent work *You'll See It When You Believe It,* deals with personal transformation.[2] The words personal transformation mean that you must "transform" or change yourself and become a self-believer. Sentences by Dyer have special application. He writes,

> ". . . *If you picture yourself poor, you will act out your daily life based on this image." He goes on to say, "Tell yourself that everything you visualize is already here."[3] Those two sentences capture the essence of this chapter's message. Try substituting a few words so the statements are changed to say, "If you see yourself as a poor communicator, you will behave based on that self-image." Next sentence. "Tell yourself that the good speaker that you would like to be already exists in you."*

Chapter 2 discussed the importance of **self-visualization,** the process of seeing yourself succeeding. Sales people call it "PMA," a positive mental attitude. It is the reverse of self-doubt or uncertainty. Before you speak, you "see" yourself walking to the front of the room. In your "mind's eye," you begin with confidence and interest; your words and actions are forceful, and your audience is interested. As you use examples and present proposals, the listeners nod in agreement. They smile when you joke or tell an interesting story. When you finish, you visualize the audience expressing their approval by again nodding or applauding. You have just visualized personal communication success.

You cannot succeed when you tell yourself that you will fail. A pessimist will always be able to find something wrong. However, public speaking is not simply a matter of believing that you will do well in order to succeed. (Wishing does not make everything come true.) Instead, it is also hard work and preparation. When you have completed those steps and when you believe that you can, and will, do an effective job, you will have taken the first steps towards becoming a successful public communicator.

Uncertainty about Public Communication

People are often apprehensive about the unknown. Therefore, public speaking presents an interesting paradox. Some people have an approach-avoidance conflict about talking publicly. They want to be respected, seen as friendly, approachable, well informed, and organized. At the same time, many people prefer to be unnoticed. They are reluctant to state their opinions in a group. They resist being the center of attention. They are self-conscious about their personal appearance and behavior.

People who have considerable anxiety about public speaking are **communication apprehensives.** This apprehension does not necessarily transfer into different modes of oral communication. For example, people who are afraid of speaking publicly are not necessarily afraid at the prospect of speaking interpersonally.[4]

Negative Attitudes toward the Situation

You may feel comfortable speaking with your friends one-to-one, but avoid talking to them as a group. When you talk to an audience, you may not see the people or the situation as friendly. The audience and the people may seem intimidating. That is because you set high standards for yourself. You expect a standard of excellence in your speech, which is much higher than the audience anticipates.[5] This happens when you *know* everything you intend to do. If the slightest thing goes wrong (i.e., forgetting a minor detail), then that becomes the focus of your attention. For example, if you are talking about the nutritional value of major fruits and forget to mention apples, that may worry you. You may feel that your audience thinks that you don't know your subject or skipped apples purposely. Thus, you tend to become obsessed with that one minor error. However, you need to remember that the audience never knew what you intended to say. Only you did. But your preoccupation with that one "slip" made you feel that the entire experience was unsatisfactory. This resulted in you becoming nervous about any future opportunities to speak in public.

Finally, it is normal to have concerns about public speaking. Apprehension, or fear, is common and expected. Several years ago, Bruskin Associates found that 40 percent of the population is afraid of speaking in public.[6] Only 32 percent of people are afraid of heights and 18 percent fear sickness. Therefore, if you are worried about speaking in public, you are normal. Many of your peers and the general population feel the same way.

This book and this course will not rid you of those fears. It is not a magic cure that you can take to dispel all of your concerns. In fact, it would be incorrect and untrue to say that public speaking is "easy."[7] Instead, you will learn about how to control the physical and the psychological problems that accompany the experience. Follow the steps and read the text. Listen to your instructor. Prepare and practice thoroughly. If you do, you'll find that public speaking becomes slightly easier each time. You may continue to be anxious about the experience, but you will learn how to control your apprehension. Put your nervous energy to work. Channel it into a vigorous presentation of ideas, into gestures that complement your ideas, and into the use of visual materials.

Interest in Communicating Ideas and Information

You have ideas and interests that you want to share with other people. If you had a choice, you probably would talk to each person individually. However, you realize that personal conversation is terribly inefficient as a message channel. Hence, you must select a more efficient—but equally accurate—way to transmit ideas. Public speaking is your best choice.

From a symbolic interactionist perspective, your goal is to create a cooperative event in which you and the listeners become parties to a **sustained interaction.** In this case, the sustained interaction is your public speech and your listeners' reactions to it. As a result of the message exchange, your purposes and the listeners' purposes work together.

Tony Schwartz described this process in *The Responsive Chord.*[8] For him, joining these purposes happens when a speaker "strikes a chord" that sets up a response in the receiver (listener). It is something like the "sympathetic vibration" of a violin string, when you strike a tuning fork nearby. The listener's response is cooperative. There are many cases where public speaking has this effect. For example, you ask a group of your friends to come to the "Malone for Student Body President Booth" at the Activities Fair. As you pass the campaign booth, you notice that two acquaintances are signing the list to staff the telephone banks. "This sounds interesting. Glad you suggested it!" one acquaintance says to you. Your message had sustained interaction.

President Bush declared a "War on Drugs." He called upon people and communities to act together to halt the consumption of cocaine, marijuana, and other illegal substances. He said, "If you use drugs, you will be caught. If you are caught, you will be prosecuted. And if you are prosecuted, you will be punished." This message caused sustained interaction.

People heard the president's words and looked for ways to carry out the actions that he said were necessary. Governors, mayors, school superintendents, and religious leaders asked people to step forward and to help others to stop using dangerous drugs. Congress offered funds to help eradicate the drug problem. The listeners and the speaker were partners in a cooperative event (i.e., the public speech). The resulting action was consistent with the aims of the speaker and with the interests of the listeners. Bush's message struck a sympathetic chord in some people.

Successful public speakers must have that interest in communicating ideas and information. To have sustained interaction, you need to involve your listeners in your message. The purpose of your message should be to join the listeners' motives to your own. When listeners identify with people or with values, they often identify with the cause, the philosophy, or the person

We all have ideas and interests that we want to share with others.

IT'S MORE FUN TO KNOW

Effect of Speech Practice with a Video Tape Recorder

There is little reason to conclude that the use of a video tape recorder reduced the social security (of these students). It did not reduce anxiety, exhibitionism, or reticence significantly.

See Robert W. Lake and W. Clifton Adams, "Effects of the Videotape Recorder on Levels of Anxiety, Exhibitionism, and Reticence in High School Speech Students," *Communication Education*, 33, (October 1984), p. 333–336.

Comment . . .

If you intend to use the VCR for public speaking practice, do not expect it to make you more comfortable or to make it easier for you to speak. Your anxiety and attitude toward the communication experience will not change significantly because you use a camera and recorder in practice experiences.

too. This position was first developed by Kenneth Burke over twenty years ago in his *Rhetoric of Motives.*[9] An earlier example from this chapter exemplifies this idea. The students who went to the activities booth to sign up to work also identified with the candidate for president. They shared the cause with the individual.

A message is a powerful instrument. It is powerful when it has shared meaning. As symbolic interactionists, the message must arouse feelings and understandings in the listeners' mind which are similar to those of the speaker. You then have a joint meaning and a shared message. Symbolic interaction is the goal of the public and private communicator. Sender and receiver are on the same wavelength. In a public setting, you have a single sender and

Speaker–Message–Audience –Voice–Reactions

multiple receivers. The earlier example of President Bush and his drug message illustrates this dimension of symbolic interaction. The shared meanings and intentions came from the message. The public responded to the symbols President Bush used. Attitudes were affected and actions were taken because all parties to the message understood what needed to be done.

The Message

One of the more formidable problems beginning public speakers face is choosing a topic. A student may say "But there's nothing that I can talk about that would interest this audience." That is simply not true. Nearly everything you know can be made interesting and appropriate for public presentation. The problem is in determining how to set up that identification in the listeners. Study the relationship among the elements in figure 12.1. Figure 12.1 places the role of the message in perspective. The speaker has aims and anxieties. If the speaker is going to be effective, then the message must be appropriate and attractive to the audience. The speaker decides on a goal and then selects ideas and supporting material that will align the ideas to an audience.

The focus is on the content and on the scope of the message. What comprises an effective message? How can the speaker make the subject understood and still be interesting to the listeners?

Quality of the Content

A topic for public speaking must meet several criteria. First, it must be considered *worthwhile* by listeners. They must see some value in listening to what is said. Next, the topic should be *interesting* to the audience. Put a special perspective on the subject so that it is unusual and appealing. Finally, the topic should be *important* enough for listeners to attend and for you to speak. It should be a subject that touches the lives and concerns of people generally and members of the audience specifically.

Topic Combinations

Change Color?	New Size?	New Material
Blue	Longer	Plastic
Green	Shorter	Glass
Yellow	Wider	Fiberglass
Orange	Fatter	Paper
Red	Thinner	Wood
White	Thicker	Aluminum

▼ Table 12.1

The possibilities for developing a worthwhile, interesting, and important subject are huge. Clearly, you must focus your ideas. To illustrate, look at the possible combinations in table 12.1, combinations based on Angelo Biondi's pamphlet *Have An Affair With Your Mind.*[10] It is possible to interchange terms from the categories to develop varying combinations for changing or improving objects or clothing. Pair a term from one category with a term from any of the other categories. The idea is to discover possible combinations that frequently would not occur in idle thought.

This process of brainstorming by making new combinations works for nearly any subject. Just substitute features of your topic for the categories and terms listed. Then, you have possibilities for different approaches to your speech topic.

How many times have you heard the comparison, "This is the *Cadillac* of bicycles," or "I want to show you the *Cadillac* of pickup trucks?" The comparison is used so much that it has become synonymous with quality. These types of simple comparisons emphasize the importance of a quality "standard" in products. We need to apply similar standards to the content of the ideas that we present. Ideas should last. They should wear well. They should accurately express what we mean. The same features that we expect in an expensive automobile are also qualities that we should expect in a public speech. These questions can help place a high value on the quality of speech content:

A speech must be relevant to audience members.

From Other Times	Rearrange Things	Add or Subtract Something	Table 12.1 continued
Old West	Switch parts	Make stronger	
Roaring Twenties	Turn backward	Make faster	
Next century	Combine purposes	Divide	
Middle Ages	Combine parts	Make lighter	
Cave man	Change pattern	Remove something	
Pioneer			

▲ Does the topic have social significance?

▲ Does the subject have intellectual or moral value?

▲ Does your content address basic human needs and/or wants?

▲ Have you selected and developed material appropriate for your particular audience?

If your speech content is high quality, then you should be able to answer "Yes" to one or more of the questions. Use them to decide if you have chosen a topic that is worthy of public discussion.

Interest to Audience

A speech must be audience-centered. This means that its subject must deal with the needs, wants, and aspirations of the listeners. Therefore, you must understand how your listeners feel. Become aware of how much and what kind of information they have on your topic.

Consider this situation. You choose to speak to the members of Zeta Zeta Beta about why "hazing" should be discontinued at the local and national level. One member says, "I had to go through it. I want pledges to understand that there is an apprenticeship that they have to serve." Another member says, "Sure, it's easy for you to argue that we should stop 'Hell Week'. But that's another of the traditions that we hear people tell us that we should drop. Soon, we'll just sit on the lawn, drink tea, and play croquet." It's safe to say that you may not encounter a friendly audience if you make this proposal to this audience. Lack of audience support *does not* mean you should avoid the topic. It *does* mean that you need to consider the audience's feelings so that you can present your view tactfully.

In the example, you (the speaker) have selected a topic that is socially significant and that is morally valuable. Those positive elements are present. Your listeners disagree sharply with your position and arguments. They are interested in what you have to say, although they may think the proposal is poorly conceived. This topic satisfies the criterion of audience interest.

Do not select a topic that merely reinforces what your listeners want to hear. Don't be afraid to challenge them with ideas that they might not accept. Speak to their interests. To a group of sorority members, a proposal to change their initiation system would get attention because it would be relevant to them.

Not all topics need to be sharply controversial in order to hold attention. American voters have discussed ending the use of the electoral college to choose the president. A few years ago, a constitutional amendment was introduced in Congress to require the direct election of the president. Suppose you appeared before a group of Young Republicans on your campus to advocate reintroducing the constitutional amendment. Do you believe that they would be interested? Does the membership of that group suggest that they are well informed and aware of some of the problems your plan would solve? Both answers should be "Yes!" In these cases, you are dealing with topics of interest to the audience.

If you had chosen to speak to the Young Republicans on "counted-cross stitch as a hobby" you probably would have an uninterested audience. Similarly, a speech to a campus Greek organization on financing repairs to the interstate highway system probably would be greeted with yawns. The interrelationship of audience membership, motivation, and topic choice control listener interest in your topic. Thus, we create our society and ourselves by exchanging our ideas.

Relevance of Ideas

In order to identify what is relevant, you can examine the norms and the expectations of the general population. For example, the general population has many of the same interests as the special groups previously discussed. It is possible that they would be concerned with direct election of the president. They are much less likely, however, to be interested in the fraternity initiation process, except to the extent that it becomes an issue for the general public.

The public is concerned with matters pertaining to personal needs and desires. Maslow's hierarchy of physiological needs, safety needs, belongingness and love, and esteem needs are high on the list of relevant issues. Topics that refer to these needs are appropriate topics. The general population worries about air and water quality and a better job. They are concerned with crime, the cost of living, how to improve their personal relationships, and good but inexpensive education for their children. These questions are interesting to the public and to students alike. Look at your daily newspaper or a magazine like *Time* or *Newsweek,* and you'll see the major concerns of the American public. These are the same questions that occupy your listener's mind.

When you begin the process of choosing a topic for public presentation, remember that you must select a subject that relates to your listeners. Above all, the subject and the way it's developed must be tailored to the knowledge, attitudes, and interests of your listeners.

Determine Your Purpose

A **general purpose** statement is the articulation of your goal. It is what you intend to do in your speech. In public communication, there are two general purposes for most communication: to inform, and to persuade. You should determine the aim of your speech early, before you begin to organize your ideas and collect information. The purpose will provide you with direction as you organize and collect materials.

If the general purpose of your speech is to *inform,* your goal should be to add to your listeners reservoir of information. The general purpose is a broad statement of intent, while the **specific purpose** describes more precisely your specific intention. If your general purpose is to inform, you could develop a specific purpose statement like the following one:

General Purpose: To inform

Specific Purpose: To inform the audience of the five basic steps in the development of black and white photographic film.

With this purpose statement, you have decided on what you are going to do. The statement implies that the audience understands the term "black and white film." In saying that you will discuss the steps involved in developing a black and white film, you preview the organization of the speech briefly. Chapter 11 will discuss the informative speech in detail. Another general purpose is to *persuade.* You try to affect the attitudes, beliefs, or values of your audience when your aim is to persuade. An example of the specific purpose of a persuasive speech could be "To explain to the audience why real estate is a profitable investment today." The topic may appear to be informative. However, the primary goal is to provide the audience with reasoning and evidence to reinforce or change their belief about the value of this investment instrument.

A third general purpose of speech is to *entertain*. You may think of the night club comedian as serving this purpose. The purpose of entertainment is not necessarily to get a "belly laugh." The purpose of entertainment is to create an amusing, pleasing, perhaps smiling atmosphere. Listeners are relaxed.

Not all people are entertained in the same way. That's why there are so many different comedians and so many different approaches to comedy. As a general purpose of speech, entertainment can involve a light discussion of language problems (i.e., oxymorons such as "jumbo shrimp and military intelligence"). Listeners can be amused or entertained without being convulsed with laughter.

Scope of Intended Message

When choosing a topic, be sure that it can be discussed thoroughly and clearly in the available time. Remember, you speak at approximately 140–160 words per minute. A five minute speech involves only about 800 words. When you consider some of the previously mentioned general topic areas, you do not have much time to develop and to support your ideas. A carefully selected and well-narrowed subject is one of the best insurance policies for success in public communication.

It is common for a beginning speaker to choose a topic that can not possibly be discussed in the time allotted for the assignment. A few examples can help you to understand this statement. Consider the following speech topics that students chose to discuss in five minutes:

- The theory and application of jet engines
- How World War II started
- How to play chess
- The importance of a positive balance of trade for the U.S.

It might be possible to discuss a topic from this list in only five minutes. However, if an audience knows nothing about chess, it will take more than five minutes for them just to understand the rules that govern the movement of each piece and their relative importance. The advice of sages to "keep it simple" certainly applies to people beginning as public speakers.

Choose *simple* topics, and develop them clearly and simply. Remember, an audience member should not have to struggle to understand the ideas.

A good thesis statement makes the point clearly. An example: "Automobile insurance rates are based on the accident records of the population."

Clarity of Thesis

The **thesis statement** is a statement of the central message or idea of your speech. It is one of the most important elements in speech preparation. You should develop the thesis statement *after* you determine your general and specific purposes. The thesis statement provides a direction for selecting the major and supporting ideas for the entire speech. The thesis statement tells listeners what is going to be discussed, and it gives them an idea about how those ideas will be supported. Some people call the thesis statement the central idea. Whatever its name, it performs the same function. It focuses and provides direction for the entire message.

It is important for the thesis statement to be clear because it outlines the thrust of the speech. The following is an example of a thesis statement.

"Automobile insurance rates are based on the accident records that are categorized by personal features such as age and gender."

This thesis statement indicates the primary direction of the speech. In a speech based on this thesis statement, the speaker will identify some major divisions of the population. Then, based on those elements, the speaker will show how accident records affect the calculation of automobile insurance premiums. As one option, a speech developed from this thesis statement might focus on insurance categories based on age and sex. The thesis statement tells us that, based on accident records, some groups within the general population will pay more for insurance. The speaker will expand on the thesis by picking specific groups by age or gender to narrow the topic even more, since there would probably not be time to cover *all* the demographic categories.

The result is that listeners understand what age group pays more for insurance and why. That is the direction identified by the thesis statement.

A successful speaker will accomplish the goal presented in the thesis statement. The direction and major elements of the speech are presented clearly in the thesis statement.

The speaker must then develop the topic that evolves from the thesis statement in an interesting way. Reciting insurance statistics, however, will not get or keep an audience's attention. "Two thousand men died as a result of drunken driving while 1,518 teenage women died from injuries resulting from DWI accidents." That statement does nothing to get audience attention. It is boring. It is not related to the audience and its needs/wants or related to what we know about listeners. Listeners want to hear ideas that are vivid and applicable.

A speaker may say, "In this audience of 125, two of you will likely die in an accident caused by a male driving while drunk, while only one of you is likely to be killed by a drunken female driver." The statement is specific and it is personalized. Listeners can identify themselves as one of the fatalities. The increased personalization of ideas and materials increases listener interest and involvement. Tie the factors of interest and involvement to each idea developed. This, coupled with a good thesis statement, will help listeners to understand the direction of the message and to grasp its importance.

Limit Breadth of Message

A listener's attention span to public speaking is limited. Therefore, any comments should take that attention span into consideration.

A carefully worded thesis statement will create listener interest. The statement should also limit the scope of the topic to generate *clarity* and *understanding*. General topic selection can be simple, but narrowing the subject for a brief speech can be difficult. Look at the following example:

General topic: "Allergies"

This general topic has potential, but a thorough discussion of it is impossible in an hour, a day, or a week. One way to narrow a complex topic such as "Allergies" is to ask yourself this question: "If, when the speech is over, the audience will only remember one thing, what would I want it to be?" That one thing is usually a sub-topic that will work much better in terms of presenting a clearly focused speech.

Some possibilities follow for sub-topics that stem from the general topic.

- Common methods physicians use for allergy testing
- Common seasonal allergies
- Some frequently encountered food allergies
- Life-threatening allergies

Now, there is a list of potential speech topics. The subject matter is narrow enough to identify several possible major ideas that might be developed from a thesis statement. Keeping the original broad subject of "allergies" would have defeated any speaking effort. With the narrower subcategories, the material is manageable. The speaker must now develop a thesis statement to outline the major areas to discuss.

Finally, the phase of identifying main ideas that are interesting and can be well supported is developed. The general topic of allergies already has several specific areas. For example, suppose "Common seasonal allergies" is the focus of your presentation. You could organize materials in a chronological pattern by moving from summer to fall to winter to spring. These would be the major divisions of the topic. You could then organize the topic like this:

Topic: "Common Seasonal Allergies

Thesis Statement: During each season of the year allergic people react to atmospheric or environmental substances.

I. The summer months cause grass, tree, dust, and pollen allergies.
II. During fall and winter, peoples' allergies to dust, spores, mold, and pollen may be severe.
III. In spring, patients who are allergic to trees, grasses, pollen and mold and dust have significant symptoms.

These are the major ideas of the speech. With research and preparation, you can fill in the supporting arguments, the evidence, the examples, and the reasoning. When you clearly define and narrow your topic, the steps in preparing your speech are reasonably simple. It is *critical* to narrow the topic adequately and to make the organization simple and easy to follow.

This example is as broad a topic as could be covered in a five-minute speech. The analysis is an overview of one area of allergy symptom and treatment. The chronology makes the categories easy to follow. The topic is organized simply. It is also clear that the speaker will support the major ideas of the argument with examples and reasoning.

After a topic has been selected and narrowed, the development of major ideas must take place. The sequence and patterns that can be used will be discussed in subsequent chapters. Organizing a speech takes discipline and an understanding of the basic steps. You now have that understanding; take advantage of it.

Summary

Public communication is concerned with the *effect* of the message on the listeners. That effect results from the speaker determining a specific purpose and choosing the appropriate topic for the audience. Subjects must be narrowed carefully. They should be high quality and should address the interests, needs, and wants of the target population. When preparing for a public presentation, a speaker must determine the general and specific purpose of the speech and prepare a thesis statement. The thesis statement indicates the major ideas that the speaker intends to develop in the body of the message.

It is common for people to feel uncomfortable about speaking in public. However, the key to a presentation's success is effective and thorough preparation. Speakers establish higher standards for their personal success in public performance than do their audiences.

Discussion Questions

1. When you have spoken publicly, how have you managed communication apprehension? Are your reactions common? Explain why.
2. What is the difference between a general and a specific purpose? Provide an example of each as you choose a topic that interests you.
3. Are political speeches audience centered? Explain your answer and provide an illustration of your position.

References

[1] Sonja K. Foss, *Rhetorical Criticism: Exploration and Practice* (Prospect Heights, IL: Waveland Press, 1989), p. 4.

[2] Wayne W. Dyer, *You'll See It When You Believe It* (New York: William Morrow and Co., Inc., 1989).

[3] Dyer, pp. 58, 59. Reprinted with permission of the author.

[4] J. K. Burgoon and J. L. Hale, "Dimensions of Communication Reticence and Their Impact on Verbal Encoding," in *Communication Quarterly Month* 31, (1983), pp. 302–12.

[5] Joe Ayres, "Perceptions of Speaking Ability: An Explanation for Stage Fright," in *Communication Education* (July 1986), pp. 275–87.

[6] R. H. Bruskin Associates, "Fears," *Spectra* 9 (December 1973), p. 4.

[7] Kathleen Hall Jamieson, *Eloquence in an Electronic Age* (New York: Oxford University Press, 1988), p. 21.

[8] Tony Schwartz, *The Responsive Chord* (Garden City, NY: Anchor Press/Doubleday, 1973).

[9] Kenneth Burke, *A Rhetoric of Motives* (1950; Berkeley: University of California Press, 1969), pp. 41–43, 46, and 55. Kenneth Burke, *A Language As Symbolic Action: Essays on Life, Literature and Method* (Berkeley: University of California Press, 1969), p. 301.

[10] From Angelo M. Biondi, (ed.), *Have An Affair With Your Mind* (Great Neck, NY: Creative Synergestic Associates, Ltd., 1974) pp. 12–13. (Reprinted with permission).

Chapter 13

Preparing and Delivering the Speech

When you finish reading this chapter you should be able to:

1. Explain the major steps in analyzing the audience and the occasion.

2. Name and explain the function and major organizational characteristics of a speech.

3. Define and explain the role of delivery and the use of notes as elements of effective public speech.

4. Describe the function of each of the three main parts of a speech.

5. Provide examples of the five tactics a speaker can use to secure the attention of the audience.

6. Explain two of the four patterns for organizing a speech.

audience centered
body
chronological order
conclusion
credibility
definition and example
demographic variables
example and illustration
expert sources

impression formation
  and speaker behavior
introduction
library
problem-solution
quotation
rhetorical question
signpost
spatial relationships

startling statement
statement of purpose
statistics
story
testimony
topical organization
transition
visual support materials

Introduction

Preparation is the first step of a crucial two-part activity in public communication. A successful speech and effective delivery of the message depend on good preparation. Being thoroughly prepared does not guarantee the expected results, but it does increase the chances of being successful. The *presentation* of your idea must be appealing and effective for audience members to respond appropriately.

Delivery and preparation are two essential parts of the public communication process. If you can master them, then you can succeed as a public speaker. The purpose of this chapter is to help you to master them.

Analysis of the Audience and the Occasion

Success in public talk centers on audience response. One way to measure your success as a speaker is to pay close attention to audience behavior. Two things increase the probability of getting the desired audience response.

First, you must analyze the audience. You must become aware of the general makeup of your audience by finding out about some personal information about the audience members. Such information could include the audience age, sex, socioeconomic status, cultural origin, race, wants, needs, aspirations, and knowledge of the subject. Second, you must consider the features of the speech that can influence your success. What are the unique features of the occasion and how do those characteristics affect the audience? If you want to be a successful public communicator, you need answers to these kinds of questions before you begin preparing the speech.

The Significance of Analysis

Audience analysis helps you to understand and to anticipate the values and feelings of your listeners. It is a "yardstick" to measure the target audience. That yardstick helps you to measure what to include and how to arrange the ideas in your speech.

You would not think of diving into a pond if you didn't know the depth of the water. You would be concerned about sharp objects beneath the surface and about pollution in the water. These considerations would affect your decision to go for a swim. Just as you need information about what lies beneath the surface of the water, you also need information about what lies beneath the surface of the audience. You need to know how many people will be present, as well as the attitude and how much information your listeners know about the topic of your speech.

Let's continue the comparison with the analogy about diving into a pond. Even if you know what is below the surface of the water, if you see lightning in the distance or if the temperature is below freezing, you probably will not jump into the water. Weather and temperature are conditions that apply to your swim. Likewise, speaking events include special conditions too. For example, why is the audience assembled? Is the event motivational as in a rally to "fire up" the team? Or, is the event informational as in a team meeting to introduce the season schedule? Will you be the only speaker at the rally or will there be others?

Other conditions, such as the time of day and physical location, affect the way people can feel and act. For example, you may find that as a listener that you are more alert in a midmorning class than you are in a class that takes place right after lunch—particularly if the afternoon class has comfortable seats and a room that is warm and stuffy. A speech does not take place in an isolated environment. Therefore, through analysis an effective speaker tries to anticipate conditions that can affect the speech.

Thus, analysis of the audience and the occasion is one of the most important steps when preparing to speak. Become **audience centered.** Determine how much the audience knows and how they feel before you prepare a message. It is also important to understand the environment in which the message is presented. In an **audience-centered speech,** the speaker designs and develops the message based on the knowledge and attitude of the audience and on the nature of the occasion.

Two Steps in Audience Analysis

Audience analysis can be complicated. However, you can do a reasonably thorough job without having a highly sophisticated research background by following a sequence of steps.

Step One: Research

Ask your host or members of the audience such questions as, "How many people will be in the audience?" "How old are the members of the audience?" "Will the audience be primarily male or female?" The purpose of such questions is to secure in advance as much information as possible about your audience, so you can adapt your speech to them.

Table 13.1 lists some of the important **demographic variables** to consider in audience analysis. Demographic variables include information about the sex, race, religion, socioeconomic status, and so forth. Each variable can make a difference in the choices that you make as you prepare and deliver a speech.

Important Demographic Variables

age	race
sex	educational level
occupation	geographic background
religious affiliation	political affiliation
socioeconomic status	other _____
membership in organizations	

In most cases, enough advanced notice is given to do this analysis. In those instances where it isn't, you may need to make an educated guess. Based on the composition of an audience, we can *infer* certain attitudes, information, or characteristics. For example, a predominately male group would probably have little information or interest in changing fashion styles for women, even if they are well informed on men's fashion trends.

If you speak to a group of political conservatives, it would be appropriate to infer that they hold fiscally conservative attitudes. Additionally, if the conservatives are politically active, they probably also know a substantial amount about the national debt and about federal government financing.

Age can also suggest something about audience information and attitude. Older people tend to be politically conservative, financially restrained, and unlikely to accept change in their immediate society. People between twenty and thirty years of age have an interest in active leisure, in opportunities to "get ahead quickly," or in educational opportunities that improve their work situation.

Not all of the information about an audience is necessary to analyze member attitudes or information. It is helpful to be fully informed; however, with a minimal amount of data, you can still estimate what speech approaches will "work" with your audience.

Step Two: Interpret Information

To use the information you gain from your audience analysis, decide what kinds of changes you want to make in your speech. Ask yourself questions like the following ones:

1. How are they *now* responding to my idea?

2. What do the demographic features suggest about this audience's current attitudes, beliefs, and behaviors around my topic?

3. What audience elements cause my listeners to respond as they do?

4. How do I want this audience to change as a result of this speech?

5. What audience elements and setting characteristics will help the audience change in the desired direction?

Public communication does not need to be persuasive in order to cause change. When you just intend to provide information to a group of listeners you cause change; it adds to their knowledge. Listeners can act in a more informed and rational way if they have more information. Thus, purposeful informative public talk can also cause significant change. For example, telling people about how air pollution occurs in cities may change listener attitudes about freeway construction and emission restrictions. As people realize that using their automobile contributes directly to lower air quality in their homes, they become more likely to accept increased automobile emission restrictions. As their knowledge increases, people see the implications of the ideas and they act on their newly discovered information.

Assume that you have decided upon your speech's general and specific purposes. Now, your task is to use the information that you have gained from your audience analysis to help you to achieve your goals. If your audience is uninformed and your purpose is to inform, you should provide them with a reason to listen and then present the information.

Sometimes you must provide information to affect the perceptions of your listeners. For example, perhaps you want to alter the values of an audience of college students. Your aim is to encourage them to begin a systematic savings program while they still are in college. However, they need information. Why should they save when they barely can pay their bills? Why save when they have only a modest income? The answer may be that it helps to develop a set of habits. The world is not made of money, and those students may find that they can barely pay their bills when they are employed full-time. They need information in order for their values to be modified. The kind and amount of information depends upon audience analysis.

Audience members are individuals first, and then part of a group. Think of them as individuals.

Be concerned with the audience members as individuals, not just as a group of people. Each person has individual needs, wants, values, and attitudes. When people are together we tend to consider them as a group, but we should not lose our individual perspective towards them. Try to remember their individuality and speak to their individual concerns.

Address your communication to the needs and wants of your audience. Once you determine their concerns, aspirations, and feelings, you can use the information to prepare and to structure an effective message.

Chapter 12 discussed the purposes of public communication (i.e., to inform, to persuade, and to entertain) and the role of the thesis statement in developing the message. Remember, you first determine the general purpose of the message and then you refine that goal to a specific statement of your intended purpose. Finally, you prepare the thesis statement or central idea of the speech.

Determine your direction. Remember, information is the key to affecting your audience, and listeners must be considered as individuals and not as a group.

Analysis of the Subject and Collection of Materials

The time for choices has arrived. Which option do you prefer? Which one is most *appropriate* on the basis of audience analysis and your purpose? This selection process is not simple. If you keep your aims modest and remain conservative in your goals, you will most likely succeed. Public speakers should not attempt too much. In five minutes, it is impossible for you to change the attitudes of a lifetime.

Also, remember that the constraints of a single speech will not allow you to contribute significantly to your listeners collection of information. Choose a modest goal; you are more likely to be successful.

Next, you should *collect materials.* A speaker can be a rich source of ideas and examples for listeners through personal example. Use your experience. Those experiences include work, personal observation, conversations or associations with experts, and general life experience.

The **library** is also a useful source of information, and it can provide documentation for many of your statements. Look in *The Reader's Guide to Periodical Literature* for recent materials from popular sources such as *The New York Times, Newsweek, Time, US News and World Report,* or *The Wall Street Journal.* Publications such as *Opposing Viewpoints* and *Facts on File* are rich sources for topic ideas for speeches and for argument and evidence to explain or support your statements.

You also can go to an **expert source** for information. If you intend to talk about recent developments in high-definition television, contact an engineer at a local television station. A resident expert can explain the details, advantages, and problems with HDTV. Experts, such as local business people, teachers, conservation workers, engineers and farmers, are everywhere and they are easily overlooked. They are valuable contacts for ideas and for support of your arguments. Remember that someone as familiar as your next-door neighbor is an expert in some employment field or hobby.

Write down the information that you get from these sources; do not try to memorize it. If you interview the television engineer about HDTV, take notes. When it is time to organize and present your materials, you can use direct quotations and details that otherwise would be forgotten.

You've studied the process of collecting a variety of ideas and selecting the one that is most appropriate for your audience. Expert information for presentations is available from experts in your community, as well as from traditional printed sources. Now you have the material; your next step is to organize it in the most effective way.

Organization of Materials

Preparation and organization are major predictors of success in public speaking. The way you structure the parts of your speech affects your success. There is no substitute for thorough preparation and organization. Effective speakers are well organized and thoroughly prepared. If you prepare carefully, you will be well organized. Good organization is a result of thorough preparation.

The three major organizational features in every speech are the introduction, the body, and the conclusion. You'll need to understand why these features are so important and how to organize your ideas this way.

The Introduction

The purpose of the **introduction** is to get the attention of the audience. It also prepares your listeners for your topic.

In the introduction, you should focus on the thesis statement. Your central idea should be clear from the beginning. As you structure your introduction, keep in mind the aim of your speech and develop an approach that will focus on it. The next step after the thesis is usually a preview of the sequence of your message. There are many ways to accomplish the preview.

Securing Attention

You can secure listener attention using several different techniques.

Rhetorical question.

A **rhetorical question** asks a question that the listeners answer silently for themselves. "Who here would like to die prematurely?" "Would you settle for an *A* in all of your courses this semester?" The answer to these questions is obvious. An audience does not need to answer them aloud, but the questions prepare the audience for the message.

Startling statement.

A **startling statement** is an attention getting device that speakers often include in their introduction. A startling statement should not be used alone. Instead, they should be combined with other techniques in the introduction. "Chest X rays are not useful in diagnosing lung cancer." "Americans spend more on dog food than half of the underdeveloped nations spend on foodstuffs for their people." These are two examples of attention-getting statements. One relates to a central idea concerned with lung malignancies. The other topic probably focuses on spending behavior or nutrition.

Statement of purpose.

The **statement of purpose** is a technique most commonly used in informational speeches. "Today I want to explain the basic principles of an office copying machine." "Harvesting corn is not a simple procedure." Hence, the speaker makes the direction of the speech clear. When you hear the introduction, you know what the speaker will discuss. This approach follows the maxim: "Tell them what you will tell them. Tell them. Tell them what you told them." Those three sentences describe the intention of the introduction, the body, and the conclusion of a speech.

Story.

A **story** is also another technique to secure listener attention."After Hurricane Hugo ripped through Charleston (South Carolina), devastation was everywhere. Homes were gone, water and electricity were not available, and food was in short supply. But there were heroes everywhere. Although he had seen two of his own children drown in the flood waters, a policeman stood in water chin-deep, holding a small child above his head. Power company workers labored day and night to restore power although they didn't know if their own families had survived the terrible winds and rain."

A story like this seizes the interest of the audience. It provides true specifics. The listener can visualize the horror and determination of those emergency personnel who worked to help others without knowing about the fate of their own families. The story sets the mood for a message of dedication and commitment.

If you decide to choose a story as a type of introduction, focus it on the central message of the presentation. It should also focus the attention and interest of the audience on the topic of the presentation rather than just being an interesting story that only draws attention to itself.

Quotation.

A **quotation** is still another technique to secure listener attention. As the famous economist Bernard Baruch said, "I will never be an old man. To me, old age is always fifteen years older than I am." A quotation such as this would be an interesting introduction for a speech on middle or old age. It establishes that people see age relatively. Young people see those who are fifteen years older as "old." As we grow older, we keep pushing that barrier back.

Quotations are an effective way to introduce a theme. They also help to establish credibility when the speaker indicates the importance of the source of the statement. In the example, it would be appropriate and necessary for many audiences to learn that Bernard Baruch was an internationally famous economist and writer.

The Body

The central information-carrying portion of the speech is called the **body.** The body of a speech should consume at least 80 percent of your speaking time. Because you give so much time and attention to the body, its organization is very important.

Patterns of Organization

1. **Chronological order.** One successful pattern for the body is to structure ideas in a time order. "During World War II, we rationed gasoline to be sure there was enough fuel. Then after the war and until the 1970s, we built gas-guzzling automobiles. When the Arab oil embargo reduced available fuel supplies, Americans bought small, more fuel efficient automobiles." American reliance on gasoline as a topic could be developed in a chronological way. In the example, the speech begins with the 1940s, moves to the 1960s and 1970s, and deals finally with the late 1970s and 1980s. This pattern is commonly used in informative speeches.

Spatial relationships provide a way to organize ideas.

2. **Spatial relationships.** Space represents a physical or proximal status to explain relationships. Marie White used spatial relationship to explain her rezoning proposal to the city council.

"From the west side of the city limits to 10th Street, we propose to zone the entire area for light industry. Eleventh Street, to 82nd Street will be zoned residential. A commercial/light industrial park area will run from 83rd Street to 87th Street. That leaves the area from 87th Street to the east city limits available for limited heavy industry. There will be spot rezoning possibilities for strip malls, convenience stores, and restaurants. A clear plan like this will help Monopolis to develop sensibly and progressively."

You can visualize how the zoning plan would operate from west to east. Organization like this, which is easy to understand and follow, is most likely to be understood.

It is common for speakers to also combine time and spatial organizational patterns as in the following.

"Remodeling the bedroom of a home can be complicated. First, you need to consult a builder or architect who will provide you with suggestions. Then a floor plan and a set of drawings will be prepared. Similarly, a contract between you and the contractor, specifying the costs, features, requirements, and conditions of the agreement should be executed.

When the contractor begins work, they may first remove any walls or other structural features. Then, if necessary, the plumber will run new pipe, sewer line, add fixtures, and complete this phase of the work. The electrician will run any new wires, replace or remove fixtures, and possibly upgrade the basic wiring. Next, the sheet rock workers will arrive to put the necessary walls in place and repair ceilings or walls. Then, it is time for the painters and paperhangers to do their job. Finally, the carpet installers will put down the pad and lay the carpet."

It is common for speakers to combine organizational patterns. As shown, the combination of chronological and spatial patterns offers organization strengths that neither pattern has by itself.

3. **Problem-solution.** The most common organizational pattern used in persuasive speeches is problem-solution or some variation of it. It consists of establishing the existence of a problem. The speaker then explains how the proposed solution solves the problem. Figure 13.1 is an outline of a problem-solution sequence.

The problem is identified (credit card use), as well as the solution (increased qualification levels for issuance of a card). This example is simple, but it illustrates that the solution must meet the characteristics of the problem. In this case, the problem is the lack of responsibility by creditors and the belief that if they do not pay that someone else will.

4. **Topical organization.** The nature of the topic may dictate a unique topical organizational pattern. The subject may need to be organized by using a system that works well for that arrangement but not necessarily well for others.

For example, this text is topically organized. Divisions in the discipline such as theory, listening, interpersonal communication, public communication, and intercultural communication make specific chapter topics. Instruction in the field of philosophy would be organized using topics common to its own discipline. Such differences occur because each field has a unique approach.

I. Credit cards cause many of the financial problems for young people today (for)
   A. Many people under 21 receive unsolicited invitations to apply for a credit line (and)
   B. Students often use credit cards without an initial appreciation of the debt they are accumulating (and)
   C. The users of credit cards often lack enough income to retire the debt (and)
   D. The resulting debt often must be paid by the adult cosigner (and)
   E. The credit card holder with a cosigner often is unaware that the cosigner is ultimately responsible for all charges and interest.
II. Credit cards should be issued only to persons who can qualify independently for a charge account (for)
   A. This procedure would reduce much of the mass solicitation of possible creditors (and)
   B. A thorough qualification procedure would eliminate persons who lack the ability to pay back the loan (and)
   C. Applicants would understand that their qualifications must meet standards before credit is available (and)
   D. The number of late and defaulted payments by young people would be reduced.

▲ Figure 13.1

The topical pattern applies to such diverse subjects as the organization of a university, an income tax return, the nationalities of people, or the divisions of a state legislature. This approach focuses upon the natural categories of the subject. It reflects the way people frequently think about these subjects and it is a very easy to use approach.

Credibility and Supporting Materials

Earlier, speaker **credibility** or "believability" was mentioned. For a speech to have any significant effect on an audience, the listeners must believe the speaker. One way to increase a speaker's believability is by the kind and quality of supporting materials. Supporting materials include such things as examples, statistics, testimony, and personal experience. Look at the following example.

> *"According to* People Magazine, *the wealthiest people in the United States pay more than their fair share of income tax. In fact, they are over-taxed."*

IT'S MORE FUN TO KNOW

Use of Signposts and Speech Summaries

When you include a preview or a review of ideas, there is more understanding than when no summaries are presented.

See John E. Baird, "The Effects of Speech Summaries Upon Audience Comprehension of Expository Speeches of Varying Quality and Complexity," *Central States Speech Journal*, 24:2 (Summer 1974), p. 172.

Comment . . .
Telling people what you will tell them, and then reviewing the material helps them remember. Previewing and reviewing are simple steps and make it easier for listeners to remember the message.

People is not a highly credible source. This tax argument needs to be supported by more believable sources, such as objective data from *Time Magazine, The Wall Street Journal,* or *Statistical Abstracts.* The objective is to persuade your listeners, and your goal is possible if you use sources of information that are highly believable.

Testimony or quotes from informed and respected authorities, such as the governor, the president, the National Geographic Society, the president's Council on Physical Fitness, or the U.S. surgeon general is highly believable. Many people maintain that "reputations are built by the company you keep." That notion is true for speaker credibility. The believability of ideas is a result of supporting source quality.

Effective Supporting Materials

In many ways, the central idea and main points of a speech are only as effective as the supporting material. These materials can be placed in two major categories—verbal supporting materials and visual supporting materials.

Verbal supporting materials.

When you explain ideas, you often may use **definition** and **example** to clarify and support your statements. Key words and how they operate within your speech is important to your success. Your audience must understand what *you* mean when you use the language.

Suppose you planned to talk about purchasing health insurance. A key term in the insurance business is the "type of risk" that you are considering. A person over fifty years of age is a moderate to high risk for health insurance. The term "risk" means how likely it is that a policyholder will have a claim. People over fifty years of age have a greater frequency of illnesses than do people under fifty years of age. The kind of risk is very important if you are talking about buying health insurance because policies are more expensive for older citizens.

When you define risk for this speech, you are supporting and explaining your ideas. The likelihood of hospitalization or serious illness falls into the risk category. Now, your listeners can better understand your arguments. That understanding is a result of the process of definition and explanation.

Statistics are grouped numbers that people use to merge a collection of cases. Our world is filled with statistics. We hear that "only 33 percent of the adult population still smokes cigarettes." "The PAC Ten Conference is twice as likely to win the Rose Bowl as a team from the Big Ten." We hear people make these statements to support their assertions. They feel that the introduction of statistics will make their argument more acceptable. However, we have an ethical responsibility to introduce and to present statistical information in an accurate and responsible way. We also need to tell listeners about the source of the information. Look at the way one speaker introduced and used statistical data to support a position.

"The cost of the great drought of 1988 affected both producers and consumers. Farmers in the Great Plains lost an average of $15,000 per year in income from crops. Soil erosion added another $2,500 to their bill. Consumers of wheat, corn, soybeans, and the products made from these crops saw their food costs increase by 14 percent or $284 per person in the United States. The drought was a national

catastrophe for farmers and consumers alike. This information came from the 1989 U.S. Department of Agriculture's Annual Survey of Farm Production and Consumption."

The raw statistics could be confusing. In this case, the speaker interpreted them. By explaining the statistics to the audience, the speaker reduces the chance of the listeners becoming lost or misinterpreting the information.

The speaker followed basic guidelines in presenting the information. The statistics were *rounded off*. The statistics were used *sparingly*, and their *meaning* was clear to the audience. This speaker also cited the source of the evidence. Because the source is credible, the information is more believable.

Testimony is the use of a statement by a credible source to support a position. This strategy makes use of the words of others to strengthen your arguments. "As General Omar Bradley said, 'The way to win an atomic war is to make certain it never starts.' " Testimony like this would be useful to support arguments on dismantling of atomic stockpiles. Of course, there are numerous authorities you might wish to cite. When you cite an authority, it is appropriate to cite more than one statement. A single statement/source can be found to support nearly any idea. Support your first statement with a second *believable* source that says nearly the same thing.

Much of our conclusion drawing comes from **example and illustration.** When in doubt about the meaning of an idea, we often say "Give me an example." In our daily lives, we reason from example. You might say, "I know that Carlos is skilled with machinery. He overhauled the engine of his car and last weekend he repaired the cornpicker when it broke down in the field." Another example might be, "Margarita is both popular and attractive. She was elected vice president of her class and she is now a candidate for the Miss Illinois title." In both examples, you see specific illustrations of the generalization. When you provide the example, the generalization is much more acceptable.

Visual supporting materials.

Visual supporting materials include an object, a photograph, a graph or chart, or a sketch that helps to support the speaker's message. The underlying principle of visuals is that they must contribute to the audience's understanding of the message.

There are several guidelines which govern the use of visual aids. First, they should *reduce* the complexity of the message. They should help listeners to *organize* the ideas. This suggests they should help the audience *understand* the ideas. They should *maintain* audience attention for your ideas. Finally, they should *help* your listeners to remember your ideas.

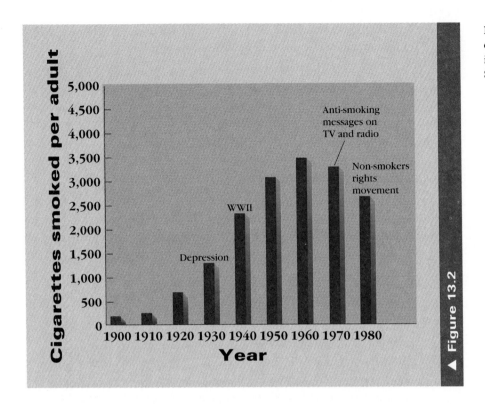

Figure 13.2

For visual support materials to be successful, they should be large enough to be seen and clear enough to be understood. Those sound like simple guidelines, but speakers often have some difficulty with them. The visual should be large enough to be seen and read by the person who is farthest from the speaker in the room or auditorium, which makes the reading process easy. Listeners should not have to struggle to read a visual. If they do, it is no longer an asset to the speaker; it is a detriment.

The visual aid should speak for itself. It should not require lengthy explanation. A chart or graph should complement the speaker's words. Look at the graph in figure 13.2. Without much explanation, it shows the smoking trend of adults in the United States from 1900 to 1980.

Here are some important guidelines to follow in order for visual aids to be successful.

- ▲ "Prepare your visual aids in advance.
- ▲ Talk with your audience, not with your visual aid.
- ▲ Introduce, explain, and then put away your visual aid.
- ▲ Practice using the visual aid.
- ▲ Don't use the chalkboard if you can avoid it.
- ▲ Don't pass objects around for audience members to study while you talk.

- Don't stand between your visual aid and your audience.
- Don't stand with your back to the audience."[1]

Your use of a visual aid should involve four basic steps: (1) introduce your visual, (2) present the visual, (3) explain the visual, and (4) put the visual away. Notice the similarity between the introduction and use of visuals and the major elements of a successful speech. Keep both simple and they are likely to be effective.

Conclusion

The **conclusion** should unify the main ideas of the speech and leave the audience with some idea or theme to ponder. The conclusion should help your audience to remember or focus on your central idea. There are several ways to conclude a speech effectively.

Summary

The *summary* is a "wrap up" of the main ideas in the speech. Here's an example:

> "And so you can see that the transducer is a vital element in the production of many defense products. This element, smaller than a cigar, reports the altitude to the control mechanisms of such vital elements as Coast Guard helicopters and the 'Harm' missile. Its success or failure in reporting the altitude of the plane or missile can result in success or failure of a mission. Properly functioning transducers make it possible for helicopters to save lives at sea. They aim missiles at proper altitudes. Faulty transducers can cause helicopters to crash or missiles to fail. This tiny component is a crucial element in our national defense."

The function and the effect of the transducer (the subject of the speech) are brought into focus again in this conclusion. A listener who lost track of the flow of ideas during the body of the speech can recapture the ideas in the conclusion because of the summary.

Call for Action

A *call for action* is a request for the audience to do something. Usually it occurs near the end of a persuasive speech. Remember, it *is not* a feature in many informative speeches. Look at this example:

> "Let's mobilize ourselves and do something for the homeless in this community. We need to stop sitting around and complaining. We must do something. Come on. Be an activist. Before you leave here this evening, sign up with Frances or Karl for the travelcade to the

state capitol next week. Let's show our state government that everyone is entitled to a roof over their head. Join the march for freedom and equality. Love your neighbor. Make your neighbor a more comfortable human being."

The action here is specific and can be carried out. In calls to action, the listener must understand what they are to do. The action also must be simple and clear. When you ask people to perform an act, make it relatively easy. Then, success is much more likely.

Quotation

When used in the conclusion, *quotations* are sometimes repetitions of statements used in the introduction. In these cases, they are a restatement of the theme or the thematically establishing statement. We could tie together a quotation with a call for action or with a reminder of a theme. Consider this example.

"As the late President John F. Kennedy said, 'Ask not what your country can do for you. Ask what you can do for your country.' That statement fits the theme of homelessness and the role you and I must play in modern society. And as Jesus said, 'The poor you shall always have with you.' "

This illustration has tied together quotations from two sources with a brief narrative statement by the speaker. The quotations are the primary focus. They create believability for the theme and they provide a powerful closing force for the speaker.

Reference to Introduction

Introductions that raise challenges, use stories, or discuss hypothetical situations often can be repeated or referred to in the conclusion. In many cases, the speaker will say, "As I said earlier. . . ," or "Remember the statement of Abner Doubleday in my introduction . . ." in the *reference to introduction*. If you use a story, a common strategy is to incorporate features of the story into the conclusion. A challenge in the introduction can be reintroduced into the conclusion in a modified form. After hearing the speech, the audience knows more of the implications of the introduction. A conclusion that modifies that introduction, based on what the speaker has told them, has an effective closing.

Transitions and Signposts

These two elements of a speech help to make the ideas clear and indicate the movement from thought to thought. A speaker who uses transitions and signposts effectively keeps the flow of thought and the major elements clear to the audience.

Transitions

The **transition** can be viewed as a bridge between major and minor ideas in a speech. Transitions tie together the speaker's primary thoughts. Some examples of transitions follow.

> *"Now that you have heard the fidelity of a Boston Acoustics speaker, let me tell you a little about the price."*
>
> *"As you move from the sprint to the middle distance race, the kind of conditioning you need changes."*
>
> *"Cost is not the only element that determines whether a shopper returns to the store. Customer satisfaction also ranks near the top."*

The second element in these examples is the next idea that the speaker will discuss. An audience wants ideas to be easy to follow. Using transitions between ideas fulfills their need for congruity. The transition may be only one or two sentences, but is an important building block in maintaining the audience's attention and understanding.

Signposts

We know that an octagonal sign means that we must STOP. A **signpost** also gets our attention. It tells us that something important is going to be said. Students know the importance of signposts. When the teacher says, "This next idea is important," or "The details of this battle will be on the final examination," paper and pencils appear. The class has been notified that important material is coming.

A speaker uses signposts in a similar way. Someone might say, "Let me outline three reasons why you should not invest in such a fly-by-night scheme." The listener knows that the reasons will follow. The points have been advertised or "signposted." Careful use of signposts helps to cue the audience about the appearance of major points. If the audience knows that important material is coming, then they'll be more likely to grasp it.

Delivering the Speech

The presentation of the verbal and visual ideas may be the most important part of your success. You may have heard people say, "I guess they had something good to say, but their voices (or physical action) were so distracting that I didn't pay much attention to their words." The message is clear. The way that you present your message is as important or more important than what you say. Therefore, consider your delivery just as carefully as you analyze your audience or organize and support your ideas. Your management of the speaking situation (and yourself) plays a major role in your success.

Pay careful attention to your delivery. You should bring a good "gift" and it should have attractive wrapping. The presentation also involves another element. That factor is how you control yourself and the speaking situation.

Managing the Speaking Situation

You are in charge. You must take control of the communication environment so that you can realize your goals. The audience listens to you for guidance. Your words and your actions should tell them that you know what you are doing. When you control the speaking situation, you insure your chances for success. Let's look at two of the important aspects of your management of the communication situation.

Impression formation and **speaker behavior** refer to what people see and how they feel about it. Impression formation is "how people see you." If you appear to be confident, you create confidence in your listeners. If you appear unsure of yourself, you create that message for the people who listen to you.

You create an impression for your audience from the time you stand up from your seat to speak. Act in control. Walk confidently to the lectern or desk. Have only a small number of notes with you and have them arranged. Look directly at your audience before you begin. Continue to look at your audience and speak in a firm voice. Stand upright, while placing your weight evenly on both feet. Integrate gestures when you feel you need to emphasize some ideas but use gestures only if they feel natural. When you finish speaking, thank your audience and return to your seat with the same confident attitude that you displayed when you prepared to speak.

This is a prescription for positive impression formation. You may not feel as confident as the prescription suggests, but you should act confident. Acting confident creates belief. If you act confidently, you will begin to feel confident about yourself as a speaker.

Positive speaking behavior and impression formation go hand in hand. If you believe positive things about your ability to succeed, you will succeed. Chapter 2 referred to the importance of believing in your ability and thinking positive thoughts about yourself. Impression formation relates directly to that advice. As the title of Wayne Dyer's book says, *You'll See It When You Believe It.* Self-belief causes you to see yourself as successful. In turn, the self-perception of success leads to successful performance. Therefore, belief is translated into action.

The *physical arrangement* is an additional important element of speech delivery. Before you speak, you need to know about the environment. You should speak from a location where you can see and be heard by all of the audience. If you cannot be heard, you need to make arrangements for a microphone. Check out all of the equipment that you intend to use (a slide

You create an impression on your audience from the moment you arise to speak. Do you think this speaker is representing himself well?

projector, an easel, a stand) in order to be sure they are in working condition. You can avoid the embarrassment of a crucial piece of equipment failing during your speech, or not knowing how to operate it, by checking it out in advance.

Go to the speech's location. Look at the room and decide if you need to make special arrangements. If so, contact the person in charge of the meeting and ask for the changes before the day or time of your presentation. Find out if there is another meeting nearby that will be held at the same time as your speech. If so, will that meeting interfere with you and your presentation? Talk to your host about possible changes or rearrangements.

If you have an opportunity, you might want to practice your presentation aloud at the location. Use all of the equipment that you plan to integrate into your speech; your visuals should also be part of your practice plan.

Practicing the Speech

Part of speech preparation is practicing the speech. You may know what you want to say, but saying it prior to the speech is the best way to feel confident that your ideas will be expressed effectively.

Familiarity with Materials

Being familiar with your materials increases your chances of success. There is no substitute for knowledge. The similarity between practicing for a speech and practicing for an athletic event is striking. Speech is a psychomotor activity. (It involves the mind, as well as the body.) We practice a speech so that we can present ideas in the proper order, feel more comfortable in the speaking situation, and develop confidence in the ability to succeed. Athletes practice for the same reason. The golfer practices so that the stance is proper, the grip is constant, the swing is "grooved," and the mental concentration is exclusively on the game. The result is a fine performance.

Many of the same things are done when you practice before a speech. You walk and talk through the introduction, and you make sure that your posture and physical movements do not distract attention from your speech. As you practice your speech, you become more familiar and comfortable with your main ideas and the supporting material. Your confidence increases and you have a clear idea of your language choice. When you use your visuals, they become a natural element of the speech presentation.

The effect of speech practice is an increase in speaker knowledge and confidence, as well as a greater fluency in the presentation of materials. Practice—but not too much. If you use the same language every time, then you should stop. Practicing the entire speech aloud four to six times is usually sufficient. With practice, the likelihood of being successful is increased.

Contact with Audience

Direct contact with audience members is vital. Look directly at your listeners. In conversational settings, we believe people are interested if they look at us. We consider a person who avoids eye contact insincere or possibly dishonest. That is a common feeling, although it may be incorrect. People equate a person who makes direct visual contact with being a "straight shooter"; someone who tells the truth.

However, don't stare at individual members. Instead, sweep the room by looking at people on your left, then people in the center of the audience, and then finally people on your right. Try to avoid spending too much time looking at your notes. Notes will not respond. The audience will. Your audience desires the courtesy of not only talking to them, but also looking at them as well. An effective speaker looks at you when they talk. Practice that principle when you are the speaker.

Summary

The first step in speech preparation is to analyze the audience and the occasion. Consider the setting and the characteristics of the audience as crucial elements when preparing materials for presentation. When the analysis phase is complete, collect the raw materials for the speech.

Next, organize the collected materials. The steps in preparation involve deciding the pattern for organization, the types of verbal and visual supporting materials, the kind of introduction, and the type of conclusion that will help the speaker reach the specified goal.

A skillful delivery enhances the effectiveness of the message. Practice involves modest use of notes, direct visual contact with the audience, and pre-planned management of speaker and possible audience responses.

Discussion Questions

1. Explain how to decide if a person has high credibility. How could you increase your own believability?
2. In what recent public situation did impression formation play a key role? What affected the result and how?
3. Which demographic variables are most important in a classroom setting? Why are they different from a general public situation?

References

[1]Michael S. Hanna and James W. Gibson, *Public Speaking for Personal Success* (Dubuque, IA: Wm. C. Brown Publishers, 1987), p. 223. (Reprinted with permission.)

Chapter 14

Speaking to Inform

Outline

When you finish reading this chapter you should be able to:

1. Identify the major elements in a speech to inform.

2. Explain how the direction of major ideas can be presented clearly and understandably.

3. Define the essential language characteristics of an informative presentation.

4. Identify and explain techniques that will increase audience retention of material.

5. Describe the most common strategies for audience participation in an informative presentation.

Objectives

acronym	mnenomic device	restatement
audience participation	participatory modules	rhetorical question
clarity	question and answer	signposts
internal summaries	segments	sizzle words

Key Terms

Introduction

Speaking to inform is a basic purpose of many public presentations. A message that informs is an opportunity for both the listener and the speaker. The speaker shares the ideas and gets a reaction. The listener receives the message, gains information, and experiences a change in feeling or value. It is what people call a win-win situation.

Successful informative speaking requires giving the appropriate attention to the preparation and organization of ideas. An effective informative speech includes complete audience analysis, clear organization, the use of techniques that increase the retention of the material, and clear, simple language. How well you manage these communication features will predict your skill in presenting an effective informative message.

Elements of a Speech to Inform

There are basic elements to follow when developing informative skills. Understand and apply these elements in order to develop and polish materials before you speak. No one element is more important than any other. Therefore, understand and use each element equally in your preparation and delivery.

Although an informative speech is the most fundamental type of speech, it is also one of the most challenging types of public discourse. Education begins with experiences in informative speaking. As early as kindergarten, teachers assign "Show and Tell" exercises. These simple activities are a basic form of an illustrated, informative speech. Like the presentations you made as a child, the informative speeches you make as an adult contain the following elements.

Adds to Existing Knowledge

When you acquire information, you build on what you already know. For example, the kindergarten student who shows and tells about the toy giraffe builds on the information of other children in the class. The other five-and six-year-old students know about the giraffe and its long neck. The message may deal with the giraffe as a favorite toy, where it lives, its eating habits, why its neck is long, or how fast it can run. Any of those pieces of information build upon a base of knowledge that the children already possess.

Similarly, if you explain the role of dietary fat in heart attacks, listeners store that information into the knowledge that they've already assembled that deals with common health problems. For instance, an audience knows that heart attacks occur and it also knows something about the most common causes of heart attacks. A discussion of dietary fat adds information to that information base and expands the audience's existing knowledge. Each successive item of information that it learns about heart attacks or dietary fat contributes further to its pool of knowledge.

The process of adding new information to old knowledge describes what happens to you throughout life. You absorb ideas that become useful because you can relate them to matters that you already know and understand. You can acquire and learn the information as long as it is presented in an intelligible way. Therefore, your challenge in informative speaking is to make the ideas understandable. Symbolic interaction can only take place if the language you use incorporates terms the audience understands. Then, they can react to the symbols and comprehension takes place. If you perform a careful audience analysis, you can build on your listeners' base of knowledge and gain understanding.

Clarifies Relationships

An effective informative presentation helps to explain or to show the nature of personal or organizational relationships.

Consider this example. School colors are an important unifying and rallying point. People have a strong relationship with their school colors. For example, if you were a graduate of Ohio State you would never be seen wearing the blue and gold of Michigan. Instead, you might wear a blouse or tie with the scarlet and gray school colors of Ohio State University. Notice the relationship. School colors are a major indicator of school allegiance. You risk social or personal reprisal if you wear the colors of your arch rival. School colors help reinforce school ties. An informative speech can build on this premise. Try testing the strength of your commitment to your alma mater by answering this question: Would you consider wearing the colors of your opponent's school to the next home game? You probably wouldn't, especially if you valued your relationship to your institution and your relationship with your peers.

Informative speaking clarifies relationships, just as school identification and colors exemplify a relationship, so does the relationship between building codes in San Francisco and the earthquake of October 1989. Tall buildings must meet specific structural requirements so they will not collapse during an earthquake, and an informative speech needs to clarify that relationship by answering the "how" and "why" questions people ask. For example, you may explain the relationship between substantial below-ground construction, limits on height of buildings, and prohibitions on balconies, all of which function as important safeguards in case of a major earthquake. The relationship of the building code to residents' welfare is clearer as the result of an informative presentation on the subject. Information has been provided, relationships clarified, and your listeners now understand and are better informed.

Your use of symbols to portray your understanding of reality is the first step in symbolic interaction. Then, the receivers' understanding and use of those words in the construction of their own reaction complete the process. We affect, and others are affected by, the symbolic interaction that occurs.

Introduces New Concepts or Applications

We are constantly searching for a new and better way to send messages. It's that elusive new idea. Speeches to inform provide listeners with such concepts or applications.

> *The new machine in modern offices is a "fax" machine. This small electronic device will copy a printed page and will transmit the contents, via telephone lines, to the recipient across town or across the country. Fax machines apply the principles from copying machines and computer modems. If you were unaware of a fax machine and how it operated, now you have a basic idea.*

You have just read an informational passage that has introduced a new application. Through the fax machine's description, you have gained a better understanding of a relatively new technology, and your knowledge base has expanded.

In an informative speech, you can introduce a concept of a new department store or a parking garage. You can propose an idea for managing employee time more effectively. Or, in a speech, you can explain how many manufacturers can make their products truly biodegradable. Each of these approaches is an appropriate focus for an informative speech.

In speaking, we *add* to the existing store of information. With that additional information, its relationship to current information becomes clear. Then, you show how this is a new concept, is a new way of looking at affairs, or is a new application of an old idea. Those are the ingredients of the effective informative presentation.

Clarity of Direction and Ideas

A good informative presentation is a model of **clarity.** Your listeners should understand you completely and be aware of your speech's direction. There is a shared meaning of language, which is our personal symbol system. Making your audience understand is your primary goal in informative presentations.

People understand best when the ideas are clear. For example, as a student you have had many different teachers. However, your most effective instructors were easy to follow and made even the most difficult concepts or theories clear and understandable.[1]

The same principle works in an informative speech. A speaker must be clear and also express the ideas in an interesting way. Speakers prepare the message for the listeners and then make necessary adjustments when they perform audience analysis.

Early Signposts

Chapter 12 stated that one frequently used type of introduction is the statement of purpose, which is followed by a preview of the main ideas to be discussed. That kind of introduction is very appropriate for an informative presentation. It is appropriate because it is an early *signpost*. It tells listeners what they can expect. The main ideas or directions are apparent from the beginning. Thus, the likelihood your audience will listen, follow, and understand is much greater.

Effective speakers should identify approaches that are both intellectually sound and functional. One functional approach that works especially well for the informative speech pattern is to "(1) Tell the audience what you're going to tell them, (2) tell them, and, (3) tell them what you told them." You preview your material, present the material, and then summarize the material. That's such a basic pattern it seems almost too simple to work. It does help people to remember the ideas.[2] However, many beginning speakers believe that the organization must be complicated to be effective. Audiences listen best when ideas are clearly and simply presented. This pattern helps them grasp and retain the speaker's ideas.

A speech should not be a mysterious expedition. Informative speeches add new information by building upon the audience's old information. This allows the listeners to have a frame of reference. When they understand your orientation they are more likely to follow your remarks. Television detectives remind witnesses that they "just want the facts." An informative speech is more than just the facts. An informative speech also contains ideas, appeals, and illustrations that help to convey the informational core of the speech.

Your audience will be most responsive if it knows the speech's intention and what information will be covered. Inform them about how you intend to approach the subject. Advertise your direction. Help them to understand. In short, make it easy. Organization and ideas that are easy to follow are more likely to be accepted. With your help, the audience will gain more information and the speech will be more successful.

Keep the structure and ideas of your speech simple.

Mnemonic Devices

Many techniques help us to remember terms or advice. A junior high science teacher once taught the basic colors of the spectrum by encouraging students to memorize ROY G BIV. Those letters stand for red, orange, yellow, green, blue, indigo, and violet. This mnemonic device assists memory. A **mnemonic device** is a mental grab bag of letters or words that are aids to memory.[3] They make sense and help you to remember.

Here's a very common one. It tells us how to turn a wrench to loosen or tighten a nut: "Lefty loosely, righty tighty." Another mnenomic device works for the organization of an informative speech. K.I.S. for "keep it simple" describes how you should structure the ideas of your speech. If you keep the structure and the ideas simple, then it will be easy for you to remember. The audience will also understand and appreciate your statements.

Examples and the supporting materials help listeners to remember the main ideas. When you have a problem understanding a statement, you often say, "I'm puzzled about that. Give me an example." Or perhaps you comment, "I don't know if I can live with that without some specific details." People want to understand, but they can understand only if they have enough information.

It would be difficult to include too many examples, especially if you choose them carefully. Because much of our life is based on reasoning from example, place examples throughout your presentation. Examples help to make the material come alive and they also help to make your ideas clearer.

Details to explain an abstraction can illuminate the audience's understanding. "A college education opens the door to a lifetime of opportunity." That is a convenient generalization. What does it mean and where is the supporting detail? If the speaker had provided details such as the following, then the listeners might have been more receptive.

1. The lifetime income of a college graduate is approximately 15 to 25 percent higher per year than nongraduates.

2. College graduates work primarily in nonphysical activities. Their minds and not their bodies determine success.

3. College graduates are in nearly 80 percent of the leadership positions in business, industry, and public service.

4. College graduates are less likely to be unemployed than nongraduates and, if unemployed, the span of unemployment is shorter.

You and your listeners can reason from these examples. Help listeners to understand you by providing them with the supporting materials and details to flesh out the abstraction or the major points. Audiences want to understand. It is your responsibility through audience analysis to identify the materials that will help them to reach that goal.

It is important to *motivate* the audience. The audience needs to listen; thus, you need to use techniques that get the audience's attention. The material and ideas need to give the listeners a reason to participate in the communication. Will it make them happier? Is it important to their daily lives? How often do most people feel that way? What will this information add to my ability to get along with people or to make more money? These are common questions, but the answers that people give will indicate their degree of motivation. Involve your audience, structure your ideas to command attention, and motivate the audience to listen. See figure 14.1 for a sample informative speech outline.

Language Selection

Words are the vehicle for understanding. Choose them carefully. Language selection is an important ingredient in achieving understanding. As one critic said, "Much . . . spoken expression these days is equivalent to the background music that incessantly encroaches on us in restaurants, stores, offices, and bars. It thumps and tinkles away mechanically, without color, inflection, vigor, charm, or distinction. People who work in the presence of background music often tell you, and sometimes with pride, that they don't hear it anymore. The parallel with language is alarming."[4]

These words relate to the matter of symbolic interaction stressed throughout this text. Words that are meaningful, vivid, and compelling get our attention. We are moved by them. When there is a constant blather of language, which sneaks into every crevice of our lives, we turn it off. Our response to symbols is our reaction to the world. The way that you understand the world is a result of your reaction to symbols. You need to interact

General Purpose: To inform

Specific Purpose: To explain the direct and indirect costs that result from a "Driving While Intoxicated" conviction.

Thesis Statement: People who are charged and arrested for driving under the influence of alcohol create large financial and personal problems for themselves.

Introduction: Assume you have been stopped by a police officer on suspicion of DWI or DUI (driving under the influence). That officer will examine your license and registration and then begin a rather standard procedure. I want to tell you about that procedure and the other things that happen if you are stopped for an alcohol-related charge.

I. **There are several procedures that usually take place.**
   A. The officer will look at your eyes, smell your breath, and look at the interior of the car.

      1. He is trying to see if there is evidence of drinking before he proceeds further.
      2. He must decide if there are illegal items in the car (e.g., an open container of alcohol, drugs, or weapons).

   B. The officer will administer a field sobriety test if there are any negative findings.

      1. You will be asked to walk a straight line, heel-to-toe, for a distance of 10 to 15 feet.
      2. You will be asked to count backwards from thirty, by twos.
      3. Based on your performance on these tests, the officer will decide if there is "probable cause" for you to be taken to the police station for a "breathalyzer" test.

   C. If the officer takes you into custody and drives you to the police station, these are some of the events that will happen.
   D. You must take a "breathalyzer" test.

      1. If you refuse, you must surrender your license and you will be charged with DWI or DUI.
      2. If you take the test, you must breathe into the machine with deep breaths.
      3. The technician will examine the results of the test. If you score at or above the state minimum for DWI, you will be charged with Driving While Intoxicated.

         a. State minimums vary but DWI typically is approximately .08 of one percent of alcohol in the bloodstream as measured by the machine.
         b. If you do not "blow" .08, you still may be charged with violation of "Blood Alcohol Content," which usually is in excess of .04. **You can reach .04 by the consumption of one can of beer.**

E. The officer in charge will place you under arrest. Your license will be taken and a towing company will be asked to tow your car.

    1. You will be taken to the city or county jail where a bond of approximately $250 will be required for your release.

    2. You will be allowed to make one call to contact someone who may post bond for you.

II. Now for the intermediate stage. It becomes expensive, inconvenient, and possibly embarrassing.

A. You must retain an attorney to represent you at the preliminary hearing and the trial that will follow. The standard cost for a good attorney is $500 if you plead guilty.

B. You must pay to get your car from the garage where it has been towed. That will cost you approximately $50 to $75.

C. Be prepared to see your name in the newspaper under "Arrests" with the charge specified.

III. The final stage is lengthy and also quite costly. It involves the trial and the two years after the trial.

A. Assume that you and your attorney agree that you cannot contest the charge with evidence.

B. You plead guilty at your trial to the charge of DWI. The following things happen:

    1. Your license to drive is suspended for 30 days, except to drive to work or school. **The state will not issue you any license (even a temporary one) to drive for two years unless you meet certain requirements.**

        a. After 30 days, you can drive only if you provide evidence of financial responsibility (i.e., expensive auto insurance) that will cost you about $80 to $100 per month if you drive an old car and are under 25.

        b. You will be assigned "points" against your license. It will take four years of "point-free" driving to return to zero.

    2. You must pay the court fine (about $250 to $300) plus court costs ($50), plus pay to attend a special school for people convicted of DWI (10 to 20 hours plus $50).

C. These are minimum charges and penalties. Greater fines and a possible jail sentence can occur if there was an accident, if you are a repeat offender, or if you were heavily intoxicated.

Conclusion: Drunk driving is costly and embarrassing. I wanted you to know the facts and the costs. Make up your mind.

Communication Interruptions

People who interview for jobs perceive interviewers as more empathic if the interviewers avoid interruptive statements.

See Karen B. McComb and Frederic M. Jablin, "Verbal Correlates of Interviewer Empathic Listening and Employment Interview Outcome," *Communication Monographs,* 51:4 (December 1984), p. 370.

Comment . . .

People tend to be bothered when their conversation is interrupted by others. If you listen without comment or interruption, you probably will be considered to be more understanding (and perhaps more receptive). Clearly, interviewers should let interviewees complete their statement before asking another question or offering an opinion. That advice applies in conversational situations.

with others in ways that are apparent and understandable. Then other people will understand and react to you. They will not treat you as they treat "elevator music"—just something to be tolerated because it is always "there." You don't want your message to mirror "elevator music." Therefore, choose your language with care. Your precision and skill in communication often determines personal relations. Some major considerations for the speaker in the use of language follow.

State Ideas Clearly

When you make statements in public, they should be stated clearly the first time. It should be unnecessary to repeat or to rephrase yourself, unless you are doing it for emphasis. Hence, you need to think in advance about how to verbalize ideas.

A recent classroom situation exemplifies this point. An instructor was teaching a class of graduating seniors. One student appeared unusually thoughtful. The teacher said, "Are you musing about what I said?" The student looked puzzled and replied, "I don't know. What is musing? I have never heard that word before." The instructor had made a mistake. Based on audience analysis, the instructor assumed that an audience of graduating seniors would have the word "muse" in their vocabularies, although most of the class did not understand the word. And although it could be argued that they should, the language choice caused temporary confusion, which is an interesting instructional opportunity in vocabulary enhancement.

These problems do not occur in easy to understand messages. A speaker should use language that can be understood without much clarification; thus, the audience will not be confused, and ideas will be clear. In turn, there will be more time to deal with the essential points of the speech. Use a five cent word instead of a $5.00 word. In the classroom example, the teacher used a $5.00 word and spent the rest of the hour explaining the language instead of teaching the material.

Use Vivid, Interesting Words

Clear, interesting, and gripping words will get and keep the attention of your audience. In sales seminars, trainers emphasize to new salespeople that they should, "Sell the sizzle and customers will buy the steak." You are selling the "sizzle" of ideas when you choose vivid and interesting language. Consider the impact difference in these pairs of words.

Dry	Parched
Funny	Hilarious
Interested	Bug-eyed
Devastating	Killer
Failed	Flunked

Unhealthy	Sick
Warm	Steaming
Stubborn	Bull-headed
Peculiar	Half-baked
Large	Towering
Full	Crammed

Your listeners will be more interested if you choose language that's more like the words in the second column. These are **sizzle words.** They are more descriptive and interesting and they create images in the listener's mind. That is the goal of sizzle words and a sizzle message. Try to keep your audience alert and interested. Choose your words so that they'll help you to reach that objective. Your ideas and your words are the tools to keep the audience involved in your message. Use both wisely and carefully.

Techniques for Increasing Retention

Ideas, proposals, applications, or techniques are all elements of informative speeches. They may be interesting and useful, but your goal is for the audience to retain the information *after* you have finished speaking. There are several techniques that will increase the audience's retention of your material.

Restatement of Ideas

Restatement is necessary in nearly all oral communication. It is not true, however, that the more times you restate a message, the greater the retention. If you restate the same idea three times and use slightly different language each time, your listeners are more likely to remember.[5] For example, if you are talking about the fall change of color in the trees, you might do this:

> *In September and October you can expect the leaves on deciduous trees to change color because there are fewer daylight hours. Falling leaves are not caused by low temperatures. Let me explain further. The daylight hours are shorter in the fall and winter, and the hours of sunlight affect the chemical process in trees. The result is that the chlorophyll to the leaves is shut off. The other chemicals continue to go to the leaves and the color changes. Because there are slightly different chemicals in each species of tree, the color for maple trees is different from the color of an ash tree. Then, finally, when the color goes virtually flat the leaves drop from the limbs. The entire process is independent of the outdoor temperature. Jack Frost has nothing to do with the change in color or the leaves dropping from the trees.*

Notice the restatement. The general message is the same, then the idea is repeated, but some detail is added. Hopefully, the result is that the audience remembers that leaves do not fall from trees because of frost, but because of a chemical process triggered by the length of daylight hours. Restatement should clarify any confusion and add some new information. The listener is not bored and gains some new detail, while the communication experience is enriched.

Memory Devices

An **acronym** is a word that is formed from the first letter or group of letters in a name or phrase. Acronyms are all about us. We use them to help us to remember ideas and to assist others in recalling and understanding materials.

The military frequently uses acronyms such as SAC (Strategic Air Command), CONUS (Continental United States), the OD (Officer of the Day), or CINCPAC (Commander in Chief, Pacific Air Command). These acronyms are economical devices for communication. It's easier to say SAC than to say Strategic Air Command, and there is no confusion about the meaning if you have an initial base of understanding with your listener(s). The best way to make sure this initial base of understanding exists is to explain what the acronym stands for the first time you use or mention it. College students are familiar with such acronyms as SAT (Scholastic Aptitude Test), GRE (Graduate Record Examination), PRO (Probation), and the LSAT (Law School Aptitude Test).

People find it easy to remember acronyms. An acronym, such as SCOPE (Student Communication Organization for Professional Excellence), sticks in the mind. CORE (Congress of Racial Equality) can easily be the focal point of an informative presentation. CORE can become the departure point for a description and explanation of the organization's function and development. An audience can follow materials more easily if it has a base such as an acronym to use as the focus for its attention.

Speakers often use **signposts** to introduce acronyms. Signposts assist retention because they point out important ideas. If you know that important material is to follow, you prepare for it. You may hear the speaker say, "I want to talk to you about GMAC, the General Motors Acceptance Corporation." You know that the material to follow will be about that organization. The first points in the presentation will probably define and describe GMAC. The signpost said GMAC is the focus of the speech. The signpost told you what to expect.

Internal Summaries

When ideas are wrapped in convenient mental bundles, they can be managed, manipulated, and remembered easily. The **internal summary** is what you call a "mini-summary." Suppose you are giving an informative talk on the basic parts of a camera. Here's an example of an internal summary.

> *"So far, I've shown you where the shutter control is located. You will remember that when you depress this control that the shutter of the camera will open and you will take a picture. The film will be exposed to the light."*

That is a brief internal summary of one major point in a speech that contains several points. Each major point should have an internal summary. The internal summary helps listeners to focus on the key part of the material that has just been presented. If listeners become confused during the explanation, the internal summary should briefly clarify the operation or information.

Internal summaries are useful organizational and retention tools. A listener who organizes the internal summaries together should have a clear idea of the major thoughts and the direction of the speech. Some speakers believe that internal summaries create too much repetition for listeners. The contrary is true. Internal summaries give a level of repetition that insures that listeners receive and understand ideas completely.

Audience Participation

Audience participation makes listeners feel like they are a part of a group. If they are given the opportunity, they will participate. Think back to some of the best speeches that you have heard. The speaker often phrased a question that the audience members answered. The initial answer may also be applied to the next three or four questions so that the audience can answer them aloud. For example,

> *"I want to ask you several questions that will help clarify your thinking about mandatory retirement. First, do you believe that everyone ages at the same rate? I suspect you answered that question 'No' in your mind. Now, try answering these next questions aloud.*
>
> *Do we have a mandatory retirement age for the president of the United States? (Audience answer)*

Do you feel uncomfortable as a passenger on a plane piloted by a person who appears very mature and 'senior'? (Audience answer)

Has medical science argued that people at the age of 60 or 65 should be separated from the work force? (Audience answer)"

Listeners could answer the questions in their minds. But, answering the question aloud reinforces the statement. The person has not only understood the answer, but also has verbalized it. It is similar to a situation where a friend may ask a question and you answer to yourself, "Yeah, that's okay." If, however, you say, "Yeah, okay," *aloud,* then you feel more involved and committed than you did to the personal thought. Active audience participation in the communication process enhances attention and assists in agreement as well. When people can be part of a group that participates actively and acceptably, they enjoy the experience. (Notice the similarity between this technique and "participatory modules.")

Rhetorical Question

A **rhetorical question** is a question raised by the speaker. The answer to the question is apparent to everyone and often the answer is implied in the question. For example, "How many of you want to die an early death?" This question might work satisfactorily, but it needs more introductory information for maximum impact. Instead, consider this example. "Think about how many days that you worked last year just to pay your taxes. If I told you that you worked from January 1 until April 17 just to pay your federal, state and local taxes, would you be surprised?" This question was used by a speaker who was providing a group of citizens with information about the direct and indirect taxes that they pay each year.

In both speeches the speaker is trying to focus listener attention on an issue. The question is designed to get initial agreement on the question and move from the agreed upon issues to a set of new questions or issues. It is essential that you get the desired answer to your question or it does more damage than good. In phrasing the rhetorical question, ask yourself these questions:

- ▴ Have I prepared the audience for this question?
- ▴ Am I certain they will give the desired answer?
- ▴ Will the correct answer help lead to major ideas in the speech?

If you can answer "Yes," then the rhetorical question fits.

Public speakers often mistakenly believe that rhetorical questions should be used only in the introduction. Wrong! They can, in fact, be used at any time in the introduction, the body, or the conclusion of a presentation. Rhetorical questions help to focus attention. They encourage a collective attitude (i.e., everyone is thinking the same way about the idea presented), and they actively involve the audience. Consider using them as interest techniques in informative, as well as persuasive, presentations. The rhetorical question is a device that has been used often and effectively by successful public communicators.

Participatory Modules

Participatory modules describe the parts of a speech where the audience becomes actively involved. People enjoy being "part of" the communication event. They want to do more than just sit and absorb sound waves. When given the chance, they enjoy filling in the blanks and becoming a significant part of the communication event. Look at this sample of a participatory module.

> *"I want to go over the major features of the new "Scuba" driving machine. Please help me fill in the blanks in these statements.*
>
> *The car that has a V6 engine with fuel injection and 16 valves is . . . "The Scuba." (The speaker paused before providing the name of the car. In succeeding sentences, the audience will participate in identifying the product.)*
>
> *The driving machine that cushions the driver while offering a 'sports car feel' of the road is. . . .*
>
> *The car that is ten years ahead in styling, has unibody construction, and unobstructed 360 degree vision of the road is. . . .*

If the listeners provide the information to fill in the blanks, it becomes a participatory module. The audience should know that it is expected to be involved. Their role should be clear. Notice how the speaker told them what to do; that is the crucial element. If the speaker establishes rapport and goodwill, then the audience will participate if they know what to do.

Participatory modules are useful because they reinforce ideas while involving the audience actively in the verbalization process. If we say the words aloud, we are more likely to remember them. That is one of the principles that underlies the use of the module. Moreover, the audience views it as "fun" because they become part of a social participation experience. Just as people shout out their school name or chant with a cheerleader, they also shout and enjoy the module. Listen to successful speakers; they use this technique to increase the audience's retention of ideas.

Question/Answer Segments

Question/answer segments call for a high level of audience involvement. Typically, a question/answer format allows audience members to ask the speaker questions about the topic. It is important that the speaker control *when* the questions are asked. Several approaches are possible.

All questions can be delayed until the end of the speech. This approach helps to maintain more control over the situation. The speaker knows that he will have the opportunity to explain all of their materials before the questions. Limit the available time or the number of questions permitted if the question period is delayed until the presentation is finished.

Tell the audience early that questions will be answered when the presentation is completed. Do it in a courteous manner. "I'll be glad to answer any questions that you have about the ideas that I present. But may I ask you to hold your questions until I finish. Then we can spend a fair amount of time and give you an opportunity to ask whatever you feel is important." Now the audience knows what to expect (signpost), and it will be easy for them to accept the format.

Question and answer *during* a presentation can be a serious distraction. If you allow the audience to ask questions during the presentation, you may become stalled on an early issue. Your interest in getting audience participation should not interfere with your goal of making an effective presentation. Some members of the audience may try to dispute your information or your conclusions. Instead of focusing on the ideas, the emphasis switches to whatever some audience members want to discuss. You can *lose* control of the situation. Therefore, there is considerable problem potential, and there are few advantages. The best avenue is to have this type of audience participation in a section *after* the close of the presentation.

Summary

An effective informative speech should add to the existing knowledge of the listener, should point out the relationship of the information to matters that the audience already knows or understands, and should introduce new applications or ideas. The direction of the message should be clearly organized and apparent to listeners from the beginning.

A speaker should choose simple, yet vivid and interesting language to increase audience involvement. One important feature of an effective informative speech is the use of repetition of material, mnemonic devices, and internal summaries to increase listener retention of the ideas. Audience participation also improves receiver retention and recall. Techniques in this area include the use of rhetorical questions, question/answer segments, and participatory modules.

Discussion Questions

1. What is a mnemonic device? What are three such devices that you use from time to time? Explain how they have been helpful to you.

2. How does an internal summary differ from a final summary? What is the primary purpose of the internal summary?

3. Explain some of the hazards of audience participation. In what ways do you believe speakers can control it most effectively?

4. Should rhetorical questions be used mainly for attention? When can they be introduced successfully into an informative presentation?

References

[1]Joseph Lowman, *Mastering the Techniques of Teaching* (San Francisco: Jossey-Bass Publishers, 1984), p. 9.

[2]John E. Baird, Jr., "The Effects of 'Previews' and 'Reviews' Upon Audience Comprehension of Expository Speeches of Varying Quality and Complexity," in *Central States Speech Journal* 25 (1974), pp. 119–27.

[3]David Blaine, *Memory and Instruction* (Englewood Cliffs, NJ: Educational Technology Publications, 1986).

[4]Edwin Newman, *Strictly Speaking* (New York: Warner Books, 1975), pp. 30–31. (Reprinted with permission.)

[5]J. T. Capioppo and R. E. Petty, "Effects of Message Repetition and Position on Cognitive Responses, Recall, and Persuasion," in *Journal of Personality and Social Psychology* 37 (1979), pp. 97–109; Raymond Ehrensberger, "An Experimental Study of the Relative Effectiveness of Certain Forms of Emphasis in Public Speaking," in *Speech Monographs* 12, No. 2 (1945), pp. 94–111.

Chapter 15

Speaking to Persuade

Outline

When you finish reading this chapter you should be able to:

1. Explain and define the terms "rhetoric," and "persuasion."

2. Describe how persuasion works from a symbolic interactionist perspective.

3. Describe Tony Schwartz's idea of a "responsive chord," and show its similarity to Burke's notion of "identification."

4. Briefly explain Hugh Rank's model of persuasion, and name the three methods for intensifying and the three methods for downplaying.

5. Describe how "message sidedness" and "primacy/recency" are strategies for adapting arguments to listeners.

6. Specify how speaker credibility is generated, and by whom.

7. Describe what motivates human beings from Maslow's perspective, and compare Maslow's hierarchy to Vance Packard's eight hidden persuaders.

8. Explain Alan H. Monroe's Motivated Sequence.

Objectives

action step
association
attention step
audience adaptation
communication effects
composition
confusion
diversion
downplaying
ego-gratification
emotional security
hidden persuaders

hierarchy of needs
identification
immortality
intensification
love and belonging needs
love objects
message sidedness
motivated sequence
needs
need step
omission
physiological needs

primacy/recency
reassurance of worth
repetition
rhetoric
roots
safety and security needs
satisfaction step
self-actualization needs
self-esteem needs
sense of power
speaker credibility
visualization step

Key Terms

Introduction

Have you ever wondered why some individuals seem to be especially able to influence others, merely through the force of personality and the use of language? That question has been at the core of human curiosity for most of human history. The study is called **rhetoric,** a term that is synonymous with persuasion. But what is persuasion, exactly? What does it take to be an effective persuader? Likewise, what does it take to be an effective receiver of persuasion? How can one individual gain influence over another?

It would be wonderful if we could turn to a single book or a chapter in a book by some authority in the discipline of rhetoric to find all of the answers to these questions, but we cannot. There aren't any easy answers to the difficult questions about persuasion, and there isn't an easy way for a student to discover them.

Instead of a single body of works, the study of rhetoric has a long tradition. Subsequently, the literature about it is often inherently inconsistent. It comes from many different disciplines that use many different methods of inquiry. We do not have one theoretical model of rhetoric that all scholars use, but there are some good, clear ideas about how persuasion works.

This chapter makes some suggestions about how you can improve your persuasive speaking. You can listen more intelligently when people are trying to persuade you. Some of the suggestions are drawn from rhetorical tradition. Some are drawn from the findings of contemporary behavioral and social scientists.[1] Remember that *rhetoric* and *persuasion* will be used synonymously. Each one refers to the social process of using symbols to influence thought and action.[2]

The purpose of this chapter is to provide a set of tools that will help you to be a more effective participant when persuasion is the goal of a public speaking event.

Nature of Persuasion

Persuasion implies change. The change can be observable, as in a decision to purchase, followed by the act of purchasing something. The change can also be mental, such as a change in attitudes, beliefs, or values. Even such a subtle thing as identifying with the images presented by a persuader (e.g., Marlboro Country) represents a change. Recall that such changes are termed **communication effects.**

Throughout history, the study of persuasion has been the study of how those persuasive changes occur. Aristotle defined "rhetoric" in chapter 2 of Book I of his *Rhetoric* as "the faculty of observing in any given case the available means of persuasion."[3]

Some Approaches to the Study of Persuasion

Traditional/ Contemporary Rhetorical Study	Social and Behavioral Sciences Study of Communication
Epistemic	Attitude change
Argumentative	Consistency
Fantasy-theme	Learning theory
Narrative	Social judgment-involvement
Performance	Mass media effects
Pentadic	Constructivism

▲ Table 15.1

In our own time, scholars from the rhetorical tradition, and from the social and behavioral sciences as well, have developed an extensive range of approaches to the study of persuasion. Table 15.1 displays and describes a few of them.

Thanks to the hundreds of scholars who study persuasion from these many perspectives, we enjoy a great wealth of information that is useful in persuasive speaking. However, so much information needs to be synthesized in order to be manageable.

The symbolic interactionist perspective provides a way to synthesize the order in order to manage the study of rhetoric. From this viewpoint, persuasion is something that people do with each other. It is not something that one person does *to* another, not in any context, and especially not in the public speaking context. Rather, from the symbolic interactionist perspective, persuasion is a process of creating **identification** through the exchange of symbols. As was shown in chapter 10, a public speech becomes a cooperative event that includes both speaker and listeners as participants in the process of creating a sustained interaction. A persuasive goal is achieved when the speaker's purposes and the listener's purposes work together. Thus, persuasion always implies choice. If a person forces another person to do his bidding, that event would not be persuasion. It would be coercion.

According to Tony Schwartz, persuasion occurs when a persuader "strikes a chord" that sets up a response in the receiver.[4] The listener's response is always cooperative. Persuasion results when the cooperative use of symbols produces and aligns identifications between people.

The communication effect, or alignment, can be easily identified as a single goal or some combination of three goals. One goal might be altered perceptions of a phenomenon. For example, a persuader might argue that a Ford is better than a Chevy because it is built better.

A second goal might be altered perceptions of one's relationship to some phenomenon. In this case, a persuader might argue, "Your decision to buy a Ford will save you money in the long run, since you will not have to spend so much money on gasoline, and since you can anticipate that your repair bills will be much lower than they would be if you bought the Chevy."

A third goal of persuasion might be altered perceptions of one participant's relationship to another. For example, the persuader might say, "Trust me; I have your best interests in mind, and I know what I'm talking about. I have owned both Chevys and Fords." Or, a political candidate might tell a group of anti-abortion advocates, "I am pro-life; I believe what you believe."

Identification functions in three basic ways. First, it can be used as a direct means to an end. ("Vote for me. I am pro-life; I believe what you believe.") Second, identification can involve antithesis, as when opposing parties unite against a third. ("My brother and I can fight, but no one else had better fight either of us.")

Third, and perhaps the most powerful way that identification functions, is when it flows from situations where it is unnoticed and unconscious. For example, when people begin to use the word, "we" to describe themselves in relationship to a work group, the identification may be unconscious. Similarly, we may be unconsciously identifying ourselves with some character in a television commercial who reminds us of a parent.

In all of these examples, notice that there is a fundamental assumption that sets up the basic motive for persuasion. In each case, the people who are identifying with each other remain essentially separate individuals. Group members may be cohesive, but they remain separate individuals. They are divided from each other. They are contained in their own separate physiological bodies. Rhetoric, then, becomes a means by which people can eliminate that division.[5]

From a symbolic interactionist perspective, the goal of persuasion is always to alter the ways people experience themselves, their worlds, and the interplay of the two in order to establish identification. The goal of persuasion is to establish alignment (i.e., a responsive chord).

Model of Persuasion

In the mid-1970s, a scholar named Hugh Rank developed a simple model of persuasion that suggested how persuaders could create the alignments that produce a "responsive chord."[6]

Rank concluded that persuaders have only two choices to help them to achieve their persuasive goals. They can either intensify an idea, or they can downplay it. They can intensify their own positive points and the opponent's negative points. For example, a television advertisement states that a particular pain killer is more powerful than any other and that it is also safer because it does not upset your stomach.

Persuaders can also downplay their own negative points and downplay the other side's positive points. For example, when trading in your used car for a new one, you might neglect to mention that your used car is probably going to need a new transmission, while finding fault with the grinding sound of the dealer's new car.

Of course, a persuader may try to use all four techniques at once. According to Rank's model, there are three strategies to intensify something and three strategies to downplay something. These strategies allow persuaders to develop the identification or alignment that they need between their own ideas and their listener's own perceptions.

Intensification

Intensification occurs through (1) repetition, (2) association, and (3) composition. Each of these strategies requires some description.

Repetition

You can intensify the good or bad points of an argument, an idea, a person, etc., merely by **repetition;** that is repeating them. Listen to any television commercial and count the number of times that the brand name of the advertised product is mentioned. In one minute you may hear the name mentioned as many as a dozen times. Advertisers know the value of repetition.

Repetition is the primary means by which Ford Motor Company makes the claim that the best built American trucks are made by Ford. In a single magazine advertisement, this idea is repeated directly six times, and referred to indirectly another twelve times.

Association

The second strategy in Rank's model for intensifying something is developing an **association** in the receiver's mind between the speaker's cause, product, or candidate, and something or someone that the receiver already likes (or dislikes).

That is why television advertisers use well-liked celebrities to sell everything from beer to bedspreads. For example, San Francisco 49ers quarterback Joe Montana pitched *Diet Pepsi* during the 1990 Super Bowl, while singers Elton John and Paula Abdul pitched *Diet Coke*. Actor Paul Newman raced a tiny scooter against a dragster for *American Express,* and athlete Bo Jackson and musician Bo Diddly pitched *Nike Shoes.*

Composition

The third strategy in Rank's model for intensifying the positive or negative qualities of something is to compare and contrast the **composition** of it to something else, not only with language, but also with design features in the "immediate environ" of the language.

Edwin Diamond and Stephen Bates illustrate this idea repeatedly in *The Spot: The Rise of Political Advertising on Television.*[7] When President Bush was campaigning for the Republican nomination in 1980, before the eight years of President Reagan's administration, Bush's advisors were concerned that he had only one percent in the polls. A series of television spots like the following one that featured big crowds and very little information were designed to intensify the candidate's popularity. The spot had Mr. Bush arriving at an airport rally:

> *The plane taxies up to the camera. It's nighttime. It's raining hard. Mr. Bush walks through the rain toward an adoring crowd. Quick cuts of Mr. Bush in the middle of this crowd, shaking hands, smiling, pressing the flesh, receiving the accolades of the cheering crowd.*

Video:	**Audio:**
Camera up on Bush in happy crowds.	Announcer [VO]: "This time, Americans have seen the opportunities of the 1980s—for the country and for the world. This time, there'll be no replays of the past. This time, there is George Bush.
Cut to audience, standing ovation; cut to Bush and his wife Barbara shaking hands with supporters.	"George Bush has emerged from the field of presidential candidates because of what he is—a man who has proven that he can do the tough jobs and lead this country.
Cut to white letters against blue background: GEORGE BUSH FOR PRESIDENT.	"George Bush—a president we won't have to train. This time."

> *Then a medium shot of Bush, who says into the camera, "Thank you. Thank you. I bring you word from across America: we're going all the way!"*

In spots like these, the persuader intensified Bush's popularity by the use of composition.

There are times, of course, when common sense tells us that we should not call attention to something. For example, if you have a shortcoming, it is unlikely that you'll intensify it for others. That would defeat your persuasive purpose. Instead, you are more likely to **downplay** it. Rank's model suggests three strategies for downplaying. One of these strategies is omission.

Omission

Omission is simply leaving something out. You can leave out one or more of your own shortcomings. You can also leave out one or more of your opponent's strengths. The risks involved in omitting your own shortcoming as a means of downplaying it is that the strategy can backfire. You're better off using this strategy only to downplay your opponent's strengths.

For example, in the 1988 election campaigns, Senator Gary Hart of Colorado, Senator Joe Biden of Delaware and Senator Dan Quayle, who became vice president, all omitted information about their own shortcomings. Mr. Hart was front-runner for the Democratic party nomination for the presidency. Of course, he did not disclose his involvement with women other than his wife. When one of his relationships became news, Senator Hart had to withdraw his candidacy.

Senator Biden's downfall came when the media claimed that he had plagiarized while he was in school. Mr. Quayle had difficulty when the media claimed that he had used family influence to avoid military service during the Vietnam conflict.

Diversion

Another way to downplay something is **diversion,** which is shifting the focus of attention away from a shortcoming or from an opponent's strengths. During his campaign for a second term, Republican President Reagan diverted attention away from the record budget deficits of his own administration by accusing the Democratic Congress of being big spenders. Reagan had generated a larger deficit in one term than the total combined budget deficits of all the previous presidents. However, he attacked Congress for its refusal to pass a "balanced budget amendment" and he attacked Congress for refusing to give him a "line-item" veto. Since Reagan did win his bid for a second term, it would seem that the strategy worked in getting the voters to focus on other issues.

Confusion

Rank's model of persuasion suggests a third strategy for downplaying something. **Confusion** occurs when a speaker introduces jargon, or inherently

**Confusion occurs
when a speaker
causes information
overload or
introduces jargon or
contradictory
information.**

contradictory information, or causes information overload. Sometimes people deliberately confuse others, as when a local political candidate said,

> *"I want a realistic appraisal of our local economy. I want an honest wage for the laboring men and women in our community. I want a fair profit for management."*

You might wonder why such a statement would be made. In political campaigning, every time a candidate takes a stand on any issue, they run the risk of offending those voters who believe otherwise. In this example, the claims are so generic and without detail that the voter has no information to go on. Suppose the candidate had said, "Our local economy is in terrible trouble. I want a 25 percent higher wage for the laboring men and women in our community. Management does not have to make such huge profits on the sweat of the little guy." What kind of voter appeal would such a statement have in an ultraconservative community? In this case, as many union members would probably vote against the candidate as for the candidate, and almost everyone else who went to the poles would vote against the candidate.

Rank's model of persuasion is simple, practical, and easy to use. As a persuader, it provides you with a powerful analytical and planning tool to work out ways in which to create identification and alignments in the minds of your listeners. As a consumer of persuasion, it helps you to understand how other people have created those identifications in your mind.

Audience Adaptation

Public speakers must adapt to the needs, the interests, and the wants of their listeners. If you want to strike a responsive chord in your audience, and if you want to create identification with yourself or your ideas, then you must adapt to the minds of your listeners through **audience adaptation.**

When Aristotle described this process in about 350 B.C., he presented a model with three kinds of artistic proofs. *Logos* relates to the quality of the logical arguments and the evidence that supports them. Questions about the quality of evidence provide examples. So do the questions about the logic of an argument. Is this information reliable? Is it current? Is this argument correct? Or, is it fallacious?

Ethos relates to the credibility of the speaker. Can we trust the speaker? Is the speaker trying to advance a hidden agenda? Does the speaker know the subject?

Pathos relates to the human emotions. For example, we sometimes respond to speakers because they have elicited a strong feeling. Is this feeling anger? Fear? Shame? Pity? Joy, or the promise of joy?

These three kinds of proof (i.e., *ethos, pathos,* and *logos*) developed by Aristotle constitute the most significant and influential contribution ever made to the study of persuasion. Scholars are still trying to understand the process of proving.

For most of us, critical thinking is an after-the-fact activity. That is, most of us do not naturally think in ordered and analytical ways. When conceptualizing ideas, we tend to think in associative leaps.[8] When information passes through our senses, feelings and thoughts related to that information are raised into our consciousness.

This general explanation of the thought process may explain such mental feats as thinking of an old girlfriend when you smell the same perfume, or of suddenly remembering to telephone someone when you hear a nearby telephone ring.[9] These types of associative leaps are not logical in the systematic and structured way that we have described the reasoning process in chapter 10.

In modern times, the behavioral and social sciences have provided insight into how the emotions and perceptions work in persuasion. Conceptualization and critical thinking are two distinct and separate mental activities that we now know are the functions of different sides of the brain.[10]

To persuade someone, you have to appeal to both sides of the brain. Since the left hemisphere of the brain is oriented toward digital, ordered, linear, and rational thinking, to appeal to the left hemisphere is to present logical analysis and evidence. (Aristotle's *logos.*)

The right hemisphere of the brain is oriented toward analogical, holistic, spatial, and intuitive thinking. This is the side of the brain that identifies and aligns itself with the images and emotions of a persuasive speech. (Aristotle's *pathos.*) The right side of the brain wants to move to Marlboro Country. The right side understands that a Chevy is not just a car—"It's your

IT'S MORE FUN TO KNOW

Humor and Self-Criticism

Speakers who have good ''standing'' with an audience can increase listeners' perceptions of their humor and wit and not damage their believability when they make fun of their own profession.

See Mei-Jung Chang, ''Audience Reaction to Self-Disparaging Humor,'' *The Southern Speech Communication Journal*, (Summer 1981), p. 426.

Comment . . .
Humor in which the speakers make fun of their own profession helps improve audience perception. People who already are believable can make themselves appear more humorous if they ''poke fun'' at their own occupation.

freedom." This side also feels a rush of vicarious affection and satisfaction when the woman in the television commercial, all grins and tears, throws her arms around the older man who has just given her the keys to a new car.

Therefore, a persuader establishes an identification in the minds of target listeners by designing appeals to both the logical and affective parts of the mind. The question of how to do that has consumed researchers for a very long time. Two questions come to mind: what side or sides to present and what the sequence of arguments should be?

Message Sidedness and Primacy/Recency

In his work, *Attitude Change and Social Influence,* Arthur R. Cohen wrote of two considerations that seem relevant here.[11] The considerations are message sidedness and primacy/recency. **Message sidedness** refers to whether it is more effective to present only one side of an issue, or to present both sides. The question is roughly related to the listeners' educational level. The better educated the listeners, the more effective a two-sided message. A one-sided message will be more effective with lesser educated listeners who are already convinced of the position.

Primacy/recency refers to the question of where to put the strongest arguments and appeals in a persuasive message. Should they come first (primacy), or last (recency)? Once again, it all depends upon the receivers. It appears that the relevant factors controlling the outcome are the listeners' attention, education, and acceptance of the speaker.

For example, if a listener isn't interested in the subject, then the strongest place for the argument is early in the presentation. When attention and motivation to learn are present, holding the best argument to the end is more effective.

Other factors can also play a part. For instance, if a person publicly states his opinion on an issue, that public expression tends to fix the person's opinion. So, changing this person's attitude is more difficult than changing the attitude of an individual who has not stated his position publically, regardless of the order of presentation.

In general, however, the evidence appears to support primacy. When other things are equal, people are more likely to identify with your best arguments if you position them early in your speech.

Speaker Credibility

Speaker credibility (Aristotle's *ethos*) involves the perception of goodwill. Credibility is not something innate in a speaker. Rather, it is something that listeners give to a speaker. For example, think of someone you trust, and then of someone you don't trust. Why do you trust one person and distrust the other person? It's probably because you established a set of criteria, then applied those criteria to your observations and determined that you could trust one person more than the other person. You have done it all. You have given credibility to one person in greater proportion than you have to the other. Listeners do that too.

Credibility is a function of the relationship that the speaker develops with the audience. Credible speakers try to make themselves attractive in their intellectual and physical approach to their audiences. Credible speakers make themselves believable because of their ideas and because of their use of supporting materials and proofs. They do this by knowing and speaking the truth. They believe that speaking is an ethical, responsible, personal, and public undertaking. They also know that their credibility is loaned to them by their listeners. In a sense credibility is a public trust.

Therefore, you must know what you're talking about if you want to be credible. But you can also increase your credibility by understanding how audiences judge the believability of speakers. Rhetorical critics believe that audiences use four criteria as they assign speaker credibility: (1) the speaker's apparent knowledge of the subject, (2) the speaker's apparent trustworthiness, (3) the speaker's personal appearance, and (4) the extent of audience agreement with the speaker's point of view.

Subject Knowledge

Give the audience reason to believe that you are well informed about your subject. Show your understanding of what the listener knows as you develop your messages. Clarify and support your ideas. You must seem to be well informed, interested in your listeners, aware of the various issues involved, confident of your success, and capable of expert judgment on your subject.[12]

Suppose that you want to give a speech about personal investments. You can just use terms such as no-load funds, put or call options, junk bonds, and zero coupon offerings. By just using these terms, it suggests that you haven't bothered to determine how much your listeners know about the subject. To be credible, you'd have to explain how a mutual fund operates, then define these terms. If you do, it helps the audience to understand, and it also sends a signal that you are knowledgeable and that you can deal with a technical subject in human terms.

Trustworthiness

If you want to be credible, you have to be perceived as trustworthy.[13] You have to be seen as someone who presents issues honestly to the audience. Notice that trust is closely linked to *ethics*. Honesty is the bedrock on which your reputation for trustworthiness rests. Honesty is vital in public speaking because your potential for influence is so much greater.

Do you have an opinion of Oliver North? Do you think the American people should trust Gorbachev? What do you think about Jimmy and Tammy Bakker? Are these people honest? Where did your ideas come from?

You may not remember when President Richard Nixon lied to the American people in an attempt to cover up his involvement in the Watergate affair. But you undoubtedly do have an opinion of President Nixon. If you do, where did it come from? If you do not personally hold an opinion, ask someone who was over twenty-five years of age during the Watergate affair what they think of President Nixon.

Another example of the importance of honesty to one's reputation may be found in your own experience with professors. When a professor tells you, "There will be an exam over the first seven chapters," your inclination is to believe that the test is limited to those seven chapters. If the exam includes items on the eighth chapter, you are likely to feel betrayed. If you point that

You might let this man fix the pipes in your kitchen sink, but would you let him operate on your windpipe?

out to the professor, asking for consideration, the professor will probably compensate for the error. But suppose the professor said, "Tough. The test stands as written." Suddenly your confidence in the professor would drop. You would take away some of the credibility you had bestowed upon that teacher.

As a speaker, you have a special responsibility to state facts and arguments clearly and honestly. Find the truth, then speak the truth to the best of your ability. Don't twist a position. Don't invent evidence to support a position. Don't try to mislead your audience. These behaviors are unethical, and if they are discovered, they can be devastating to your reputation.

Personal Appearance

Your credibility is affected by your personal appearance. For instance, you know how to dress for various social contexts. You would not wear a bathing suit and leather sandals to a formal ball, and you would not wear formal attire to a picnic on the beach. The reaction you would get if you did these things would be negative.

Similarly, your attire and your grooming must be perceived by your listeners as positive and consistent with their expectations of both the speaking occasion and your subject matter. Listeners tend to believe and accept arguments from people who seem well informed about a subject and appropriately dressed to discuss it in that particular context.

Audience Agreement

Credibility is strongly linked to how much the audience agrees with a speaker's message. However, the degree of audience agreement is not an attribute that the audience confers upon the speaker. It results from the statements of the speaker and the reactions of the listeners.

If your message is not consistent with what an audience already believes, it will have a negative effect on the listeners' perceptions of you as a speaker. For example, a professor once served as communication advisor to the incumbent candidate for mayor. The campaign was a close contest, and the opponent was attempting to turn the election into a referendum on the mayor. Part of this campaign strategy was an attempt to maneuver the mayor into a question-and-answer session held before a large audience of citizens. Even though the mayor knew that the audience was likely to be packed with supporters of the opponent, he disregarded the advice and accepted the invitation. Whenever the Mayor tried to answer a question from his point of view, audience members laughed, interrupted, openly engaged each other in disapproving conversation, and so forth. Needless to say, it was not a good evening for the mayor.

A message that is inconsistent with what an audience believes will have a negative effect on the perception of the speaker. This doesn't mean, however, that you should only tell an audience what it wants to hear. Instead, it means that you must understand both the subject matter and the listeners' points of view in order to discover the discrepancies. Then you can decide which communication strategies are most likely to bring them into alignment.

In summary, an audience is unlikely to be persuaded if a speaker does not establish a credible image with them. That image involves knowledge of the subject, trustworthiness, personal appearance, and the extent to which the audience agrees with the speaker's statements. Thus, credibility is not something that a speaker "has." Rather, it is a function of the relationship that the speaker builds with the listeners. Unless that relationship is carefully managed, persuasion is not likely to occur. Even if the relationship is managed carefully and skillfully by the speaker, persuasion may still not occur as a communication effect.

Persuasion and the Passions

In *The Tactical Uses of Passion,* F. G. Bailey argued that persuasion does not occur until the human passions come into play.[14] People are persuaded because they are aroused. But what motivates such arousal?

That question has been the focus of a body of scholarship called "motivation research." A review follows of the work of two motivation researchers whose models have been especially influential.

Maslow's Hierarchy

Abraham Maslow's model of human needs was developed in the early 1950s. It has been described in many textbooks in many different academic fields because it is simple and clear, and because after more than thirty years it is still valid in the face of continuing research into what motivates human beings.

Maslow devised the **hierarchy of needs** presented in figure 15.1 to illustrate his idea that people are driven by need states to act as they do.[15] He believed that we require the satisfaction of certain physical and psychological needs for our lives to be complete. He ordered these needs in a hierarchy to show the relative importance of the needs.

Maslow believed that human need states fluctuate continually and that they include, to some degree, one or more of the motivators in the hierarchy. However, Maslow believed that some needs are more significant than others. He said people will try to satisfy those more basic needs before they shift to the higher order needs. For example, the need for food and water takes precedence over our love and belonging needs.

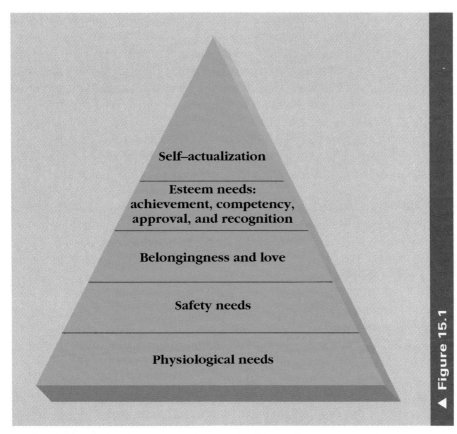

Data for diagram based on Hierarchy of Needs from *Motivation and Personality*, Third Edition, by Abraham H. Maslow. Revised by Robert Frager et al. Copyright © 1954, 1987 by Harper & Row Publishers, Inc. Copyright © 1970 by Abraham H. Maslow. Reprinted by permission of Harper & Row, Publishers, Inc.

Need states vary in strength; therefore, we make choices in satisfying them. Thus, we are motivated to align ourselves with those people or ideas, movements, and so forth that we believe will help us to satisfy our need states. Maslow described five such need states. From the most basic need upward in the hierarchy, the five need states are physiological needs, safety needs, belonging and love needs, esteem needs, and self-actualization needs.

Physiology

The **physiological needs** are the most basic needs in the hierarchy. They include the need for food, air, water, sexual release, elimination of waste, and so forth. If these needs are not satisfied, they become the most predominant motivating force in a person's life.

You can see that the physiological needs provide opportunities for a persuader to motivate identification with an idea or product. To illustrate, we all need clean air and pure water. In a speech about environmental safety, a persuader might build upon these needs to support a call for pollution control legislation at the local or state level.

During the campaign for the presidency in 1988, then Vice President Bush did just that. His opponent was the Governor from Massachusetts, Michael Dukakis. In one of Bush's television commercials, the camera showed close-up views of trash, oil slicks, and dead water-fowl in Boston harbor, while the announcer (voice-over) asked the viewer, "Do we need a president who doesn't care about the environment?"

Physiological needs can be powerful building blocks in constructing messages that will help strike a responsive chord in the listeners.

Safety and Security

The **safety and security needs** include the need for security, for freedom from harm and fear, for protection by the law, and for order in life. These needs play an important role in people's choices. They provide powerful opportunities for persuaders.

We all need to feel safe when we drive our cars in traffic or when we go to bed at night. We want to feel secure in the idea that we have enough money to buy what we need and want. Knowing this, advertisers play on our fears and on our needs for basic security and safety. That's why, for example, you see cute little babies sitting on the floor next to tires while the reassuring voice in the background says, "There's so much riding on your tires." That's why Americans spend so much money on locks, burglar alarms, and sound devices for their cars. That's why Dave Lennox, the stylized spokesman for Lennox heaters and air conditioners, asks you, "If nothing lasts forever, would you settle for a lifetime?"

Love and Belonging

The **love and belonging needs** explain why people become attached and dependent upon social groups, parents, and peers. This need includes the desire to be accepted by others, to receive attention and love from others, and to find approval. The need for love and belonging is a powerful opportunity for persuaders.

Consider how the advertiser plays on this need in a *toothpaste* ad. Clearly, the appeal is to love and belonging. The reader *must* choose to buy a brand of toothpaste or lose someone's approval. What self-respecting person could ignore a child's struggle with cavities, bad breath, and film stain?

Self-Esteem

Your image of yourself, including your personal competence, your reputation, your status, and your prestige are all part of your self-esteem. They are all tied up with your **self-esteem needs.** All of us want to think of ourselves as valuable and unique, but not all of us do. Instead, some of us have to prove, over and over again, that we are valuable, lovable, and productive.[16] In each one of us, there is a little boy or girl who needs parental approval and reassurance. Therefore, self-esteem is another powerful opportunity for a persuader.

See how these lines appeal to the continuing need in each of us for reinforcement of the self-esteem:

> *"The few, the proud, the Marines."*
> *"For people on their way to the top."*
> *"It doesn't get any better than this."*

The Phillip Morris Company confirms the reader's sense of self-worth with its Merit Ultra Lights ad: "Brilliant deduction. Why is Merit Ultra Lights one of today's fastest growing brands? It is our hypothesis that it has something or other to do with how good it tastes. What do you think?"

The Lindal Cedar Homes Company also appeals to self-esteem needs when it shows the reader a large contemporary home, beautifully lighted, and reflected in the mirrored surface of a lake. The language, a banner line, says, "Reflections of You."

Self-Actualization

The highest order of need on the Maslow hierarchy is the **self-actualization need.** This need includes the motivation to be self-fulfilled, creative, and imaginative. It is the need for novelty, ingenuousness, and originality.[17] Self-actualized people are spontaneous, uninhibited, expressive, and natural in their expression of ideas or feelings. Clearly, this need provides a powerful tool for persuaders.

The United States Army uses the tool when it says "Be all that you can be." The Marines use the tool when they say they're looking for "The Few. The Proud. The Marines." So do makers of simple products such as Channellock pliers, when they show their product under the lines, "The original. Copied but Unmatched." In each case, the persuader is attempting to "hook" into the listener's motivation to become self-actualized.

Self-actualization is the appeal behind the full-page ad in *BusinessWeek* that shows a colorful rainbow coming out of the open window in the top floor of a tall building. The line: "People who use the new Lotus 1–2–3 will create business graphics better than ever before."

Self-actualization is also the intended appeal in Canon's advertisement for its FAX-705 machine. It shows a line of people that runs across both pages. The headline: "You'd think that you had nothing better to do with your time."

In 1964, Vance Packard published a now-famous book, *The Hidden Persuaders,* that in some ways resembles Maslow's work. Packard described eight **hidden persuaders** or "compelling needs" that he had synthesized from motivational research. Those hidden persuaders are still used in radio, television, and print advertising to create identification and alignment between the target receiver and the persuader's idea. Many similarities exist between Packard's motivational model and Maslow's.

The seven hidden **need** persuaders are: (1) need for emotional security, (2) need for reassurance of worth, (3) need for ego-gratification, (4) need for love objects, (5) need for a sense of power, (6) need for roots, and (7) need for immortality. You can use these powerful persuaders both as senders and receivers of persuasive discourse.

Emotional Security

Packard believed that people are basically insecure. Inside each adult is a child who thinks of himself or herself as "not OK." Consequently, advertisers promise **emotional security.** The basic message is, "If you use this product, you won't have to worry."

Figure 15.2 illustrates this appeal in a charming way. If only the woman in the foreground had used *Sunlight* (either powder or liquid), she would not have had to worry about what Clifford's parents might think of her.

Reassurance of Worth

People want to believe they're "OK." Because this is true, persuaders sell products and services to assure customers of their **reassurance of worth;** that is, that they're genuinely worthwhile. The appeal is often to buy something special because they deserve it. "Loreal. Because you're worth it." At other times, the child in every adult is rewarded for being good. "For all you do, this Bud's for you."

Ego-Gratification

People want to believe that they are more than merely "OK." They want to think themselves special and distinguished. So advertisers accommodate them by showing how their products or services express this distinction in **ego-gratification.** For example, a man buys an expensive car to show that he is special. A woman uses expensive perfume to assure herself that she's special.

Love Objects

Love objects are things outside people that make people feel good and that assure them that they're "OK." Friends, lovers, children, toys, pets, cars, stereo systems, computers, athletic teams, and an endless list of other things can

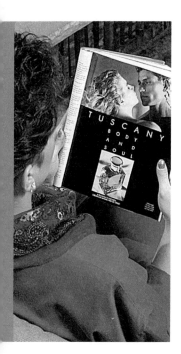

To what does this advertisement appeal?

become love objects. Advertisers know that if they can create an image of a love object with which people identify, then they can sell people almost anything. Therefore, they constantly present us with images of fancy cars, cute babies, and dogs and cats in commercial messages every day.

When American Standard, the maker of bathroom fixtures, presents a two-page photo-montage in *Connoisseur* magazine showing a young mother and her small daughter in the bathroom, it is an appeal to our need for love objects. The pedestal sink, the modern faucets, and the circulating-water tub are each shown once. The youngster is shown six times, and a close-up of the mother kissing the child's foot is shown once.

Sense of Power

The little child inside each of us wants to be assured, "You're more than a helpless child." To accommodate this need, advertisers offer big muscles, compelling beauty, powerful cars and trucks, computers, credit cards, public speaking courses, and countless other goods and services to appeal to our **sense of power.**

For example, Sharp Electronics Corporation advertised a "Survival Kit for the Information Age"—a folding portable computer that will allow the customer to "take all your personal and business data with you." The machine "plans, organizes, reminds, informs, advises, calculates . . . [and] keeps you in two-way communication with [your] computer." The language shown in the liquid-crystal display says "Knowledge is power."

For another example, one of Lotus 1–2–3's ads shows an office window being blown out. The only language: "People who use the new Lotus 1–2–3 will have more power than ever before."

Ford advertises its Motorcraft batteries by showing a bolt of lightning that leaps from the battery to the hood of its most powerful pickup truck. Chevy advertises its trucks with pictures of snarling grizzly bears.

Roots

The little child inside us wants security or **roots.** We want things to be the way they were. Change is threatening. Moreover, many of us get "homesick." We feel lost and without a sense of place. Since WWII, we have become a mobile society, and very few of us are attached to the land or the place of our parents and grandparents. This need for roots underlies the resurgence of nostalgia for "the good old days."

Advertisers use this powerful need when they offer us old-fashioned goodness, natural products, time-tested methods, and "the right thing to do." They appeal to our need for roots when they imply that our parents or our grandparents would approve.

Lincoln Log Homes sell as much for this need as for their quality. The Marlboro man and the Camel Filter man are both shown in situations that hearken back to simpler, pioneering times. Bartles and James sell their wine coolers from rocking chairs on the front porch of their farmhouse.

Immortality

We do not want to die. The little child in each of us is afraid of our own mortality. The need for **immortality** is a powerful persuasive tool, and it is used by makers of exercise equipment, make-up, health foods, and countless other products. It leads to religious and occult promises. It generates claims that a product will last forever, and that certain products and services will allow us to last forever, too.

Persuaders play on this mortality fear when they claim that their services and products will make a person remembered long into the future. Some advertisers (e.g., life insurance agencies) even offer to keep us in control long after we're dead. Why else would you need "a piece of the rock?"

As the twentieth century draws to a close, and more so than in Packard's day, advancing technology has made this need for immortality an even more powerful persuader. How must a person feel who has been replaced by a machine?

The promise of "neural network" computers—machines that will be thousands of times faster than today's best computers—must be frightening to many people. These machines are expected to be capable of interpreting speech, vision, and data in ways that are impossible with current computer technology. In addition, they are going to be able to learn from their own experience. By 1985 auto makers, oil drillers, chemical producers, and financial service companies were already experimenting with these machines, and they were having promising results. Is there a need for mere human beings if these neural computer systems become commonplace? How will a human being make a contribution then? This is the appeal to the need for immortality.

In summary, both Abraham Maslow and Vance Packard created models to explain why people act as they do. These models of motivation are useful to both senders and receivers in the rhetorical event. As a persuader, you can use the appeals to create identification and alignment between the receivers and your subject matter. As a receiver, you can use the models to understand what other persuaders are doing in their attempts to move you into an identification with their rhetorical purpose.

Remember that in all rhetorical events and especially in public speaking, there is always a risk involved in using such motivators. An emotional appeal can backfire if the audience decides the speaker is untrustworthy. Beyond that, as a speaker, you have an ethical responsibility to play fair. You must do everything that you can to construct your appeals and arguments so that they are ethical and logical, as well as emotionally compelling.

Monroe's Motivated Sequence

How can you use all of this information about persuasion? During the mid-1930s, Alan H. Monroe developed a pattern for organizing persuasive speeches that has been very influential over the years.[18] The **motivated sequence** is a method for organizing speeches in order to persuade. It works because it follows a predictable pattern of thinking that is common in our society. The motivated sequence has five steps: (1) **attention:** get the audience to focus on the topic, (2) **need:** show the audience members some aspect of their lives that is out of alignment, (3) **satisfaction:** provide a solution to realign the situation, (4) **visualization:** help the audience to see the solution working, and (5) **action:** actually give the audience specific instructions on how to implement the solution to bring about the realignment. The motivated sequence parallels the problem-solution organizational pattern discussed in chapter 11.

Summary

This chapter is a set of tools that can help both senders and receivers of persuasive messages to understand, analyze, and plan for communication effects. Persuasion results when identifications (i.e., desired communication effects) are created through the exchange of symbols.

Basically, persuaders can either intensify something or downplay something in the minds of their listeners. This chapter described and illustrated the six techniques Hugh Rank identified for doing these things.

In order to be successful at intensifying or downplaying, persuaders must attempt to adapt to the cognitive and affective needs of their receivers. In this regard, the message-sidedness and primacy/recency issues were explained. Is it better to show only one side of an argument? Or, should a persuader show both sides? Is it better to put the best arguments first? Or, is it better to put the best arguments last? These questions have consumed the attention of social and behavioral scientists for many years.

What is at stake is the speaker's credibility. If a listener does not trust the speaker, the speaker is unlikely to be persuasive. It is the listener who invests the speaker with credibility; the speaker doesn't automatically have it. Still, research has suggested that people look for subject knowledge, trustworthiness, personal appearance, and the extent to which a speaker's ideas agree with their own as measures of speaker credibility.

After the speaker gains the listener's confidence, persuasion can occur. The identification or alignment between speaker and listener depends upon the logical flow of evidence and arguments, but only if the speaker also appeals to the listeners' affective needs.

Maslow's hierarchy of needs and Vance Packard's hidden persuaders describe the basic human motives. Thus, they provide powerful tools for persuasion. Since they are used so much by persuaders in our society, they provide the reader with the tools for analysis of motivational appeals, as well.

Finally, there is the question of how a speaker can organize all this information. Alan H. Monroe's motivated sequence provides an organizational strategy that is persuasive because it follows a predictable pattern of thinking that is common in our society.

To be an effective participant in the rhetorical process implies that you know how to use the tools that are most commonly seen in your life such as identification, omission, or the use of needs to motivate.

Discussion Questions

1.   Tony Schwartz's idea of a responsive chord seems similar to Burke's notion of identification. How are these two ideas related or similar? Can you think of a television commercial that attempts to strike a responsive chord? How did the advertiser attempt to do that?

2.   Bring a magazine advertisement to class. Does it attempt to play up the advertiser's idea of good? Does it play up the other's bad points? Does it play down the advertiser's bad points or the other's good points? How does it do this?

3.   Working in a small group, spend about fifteen minutes creating a thirty-second spot for one of the following items. Use at least three hidden persuaders. Then present the spot to the class.
    a)   A five-year-old, four-cylinder, two-door Toyota Tercel with 88,000 miles.
    b)   A brand new Mercedes-Benz sedan.
    c)   A new brand of instant coffee (invent a name).
    d)   A new detergent (invent a name).
    e)   A down-scale furniture distributor.
    f)   A vinyl and carpet flooring company.
    For each of these, what did you target? Did you use any of Rank's strategies for building up or downplaying? Do you think advertisers deliberately attempt to develop such strategies, or do you think it's more likely that someone just gets an idea for a commercial and writes it down?

References

[1] To our colleagues who wish to evolve course content and textbook discussions on the basis of "meta-analysis," this determination may be a bit disagreeable. They quite rightly want the suggestions writers make to be consistent with the research they cite. But they overlook the wisdom about persuasion that has come down to us by tradition, and without empirical quantification. Rhetoric is both an art and a science. It rests upon inferences drawn from rhetorical criticism as well as from empirical research.

[2] *Rhetorical Criticism: Exploration & Practice* (Prospect Heights, IL: Waveland Press, 1989), p. 4.

[3] Aristotle, *Rhetoric*, W. Rhys Roberts, tr. (New York: Random House, The Modern Library, 1954), p. 24.

[4] Tony Schwartz, *The Responsive Chord* (Garden City, NY: Anchor Press/Doubleday, 1973).

[5] Burke's *A Rhetoric of Motives* (Berkeley: University of California Press, 1950; reprinted, 1969), pp. 21–22, 130, 150, 211, and 326.

[6] Hugh Rank, "Teaching about Public Persuasion," in Daniel Dieterich, (ed.), *Teaching about Doublespeak* (Urbana, IL: National Council of Teachers of English, 1976).

[7] Edwin Diamond and Stephen Bates, *The Spot: The Rise of Political Advertising on Television* (Cambridge: The MIT Press, 1984).

[8] Howard R. Pollio, *The Psychology of Symbolic Activity* (Reading, MA: Addison-Wesley Co., 1974), pp. 33–61.

[9] Gordon Pask, "Cognitive Systems," in Paul R. Garvin, (ed.), *Cognition: A Multiple View* (New York: Spartan Books, 1970), pp. 349–405.

[10] Geschwind, "Specializations of the Human Brain," in *The Brain* (San Francisco: Scientific American/W. H. Freeman and Company, 1979), pp. 108–19.

[11] Arthur R. Cohen, *Attitude Change and Social Influence* (New York: Basic Books, Inc., 1964).

[12] James C. McCroskey and Thomas J. Young, "Ethos and Credibility: The Construct and Its Measurement after Three Decades," in *Central States Speech Journal* (Spring, 1981), pp. 24–34.

[13] Philip G. Zimbardo, Ebbe B. Ebbesen, and Christina Mashlach, *Influencing Attitudes and Changing Behavior* (Reading, MA: Addison-Wesley Publishing Company, 1977), p. 98.

[14] F. G. Bailey, *The Tactical Uses of Passion: An Essay on Power, Reason, and Reality* (Ithica, NY: Cornell University Press, 1983).

[15] Abraham H. Maslow, *Motivation and Personality* (New York: Harper and Row, 1954).

[16] Thomas A. Harris, *I'm OK-You're OK* (New York: Avon Books/Harper & Row Publishers, Inc., 1967).

[17] James L. Adams, *Conceptual Blockbusting* (San Francisco: San Francisco Book Co., 1976).

[18] Alan H. Monroe, *Principles and Types of Speech* (Chicago: Scott, Foresman and Company, 1935).

Part V

Communication Across Boundaries

We have seen the building nature of communication in each of the preceding sections. Now, we turn our attention to special contexts in which communication plays a crucial role; namely, mass communication and intercultural communication.

In both of these settings, communication behavior has special characteristics. Many people consider themselves experts in the evaluation of mass communication. Much of the population spends a considerable portion of their leisure time viewing television, listening to the radio, or viewing films. Naturally, they believe that they have developed a usable set of criteria to evaluate each of the mass media. Among these is the response to the language (spoken and nonverbal) that we call symbolic interaction. The general public speaks loudly to the networks and to the filmmakers. They talk with their pocketbooks, and for the most part that talk dictates what you see or hear.

The mass communication unit looks at the development of each medium and the major forces in its definition. At the heart, each mass communication medium is subject to many of the same principles as interpersonal, nonverbal, and public communication. Mass communication is a special channel for the communication event. As you understand the context for the message and the evaluative criteria, the direction, the problems, and the character of mass communication will become clearer. The challenges and future of these media also will take on different dimensions.

Intercultural communication addresses matters of nonverbal messages, interpersonal relationships, and the differing ways cultures relate to each other and to themselves organizationally. The study of interpersonal communication in the context of human communication explains how people relate to people and nations to nations. The late President Dwight Eisenhower was the first proponent of what he called the "person to person" relationship between nations. His notion that nations represent people and their needs takes on special meaning as we study the context of intercultural communication in this book. Note how the culture defines verbal behavior and the reactions of people.

Consider communication contexts as an opportunity to learn and to understand the extension of communication principles to media and to cultures. These special settings have established functional rules for communication behavior. As you understand these guidelines and their application, it will become easier to appreciate the significance of discourse in modern society.

Chapter 16

Mass Communication

When you finish reading this chapter you should be able to:

1. Identify the major elements in mass communication.

2. Explain the effect of media on your life.

3. Compare and contrast the roles of the forms of media.

4. Identify the mass media technology.

5. Explain the ways media can affect the development of society in the 1990's.

cool media	hot media	prime time
economic impact	information overload	prior restraint
effects on family units	involuntary exposure	satellite transmission
film and society	media combinations	televised sports
freedom of expression	media in politics	viewing time
gatckeeping	peer influence	mass communication

Introduction

We are a nation "hooked" on mass media. We are dependent consumers of mass media. Today, we expect television networks to help us to see men walk on the moon and to read about the latest scandal in Washington or on Wall Street. We want our news only a few hours after it happens. The latest radio bulletin, the "top 20 songs," events in the middle east, a Supreme Court decision, traffic tieups, and ads for special sales are part of our daily lives and delivered to us through mass channels. We are so accustomed to these channels that a vacation from radio, television, newspapers, and magazines makes us feel that we are out of touch with the world. Computer networks link us with banks, with information sources, and with other students in different buildings, other campuses, or other countries. For better or worse, we are a "hooked up" society living in a new technological age. Are you one of the many people who must read the morning newspaper at the breakfast table to check out the sports? Do you examine the financial pages? Do you seek up-to-date news on the latest world or community happenings?

As we drive to work, we listen to traffic reports, hear music, and laugh at jokes about prominent people or unusual events. At noon we eat lunch while watching the noon news or a favorite daytime TV drama. We use the radio to determine the fastest route home. We listen to a "talk show" or music while we drive.

When we arrive home, we spend time reading the evening paper. Then we watch a favorite TV program or sport event. If we discover something broken, or if we need something not typically carried in the local department store, we turn to the yellow pages or to the want-ads of the local newspaper. Before we go to bed, we check the late news to hear the weather forecast. Our day, every day, is a series of interactions with the mass channels of communication.

Elements in Mass Communication

We need to remember that the mass media respond to audience demands. We create the media just as they create us. This symbiotic relationship between people and the media has been a major force in the development of civilization. It has been with us since the ancient Romans built signal fires on hilltops to communicate with their legions.

The gatekeeping function of the editor or media director is so important because people believe the world is exactly as the media tells them it is. Yet, the editors and media directors make errors in their human decisions.

We'll also take up the issue of media exposure. How much does daily exposure to the same newspaper or the same television station affect our reality?

This chapter is about mass communication. **Mass communication** is a process in which professional communicators (gatekeepers) design and develop messages especially for transmission through electronic or mechanical devices to large audiences. Each of the elements in this definition is intended to focus attention on some important feature of the mass communication process.

Mass communication has several distinct characteristics:

1. It has what can be called professional communicators or gatekeepers. They are the people who decide what is seen, heard, and read.

2. Mass media are involved with the dissemination of the message through mechanical or electronic means. We spread information by the printed page or display, film, radio, computer messages, and television broadcasts.

3. Mass communication develops messages that are designed for large audiences. We may believe we experience them in a one-to-one relationship, but they are designed for consumption by many other people at the same time. When we watch a movie or a televised program, we feel that we have a direct personal involvement. We may be watching it alone, but there may be millions of other people doing the same thing at the same time. The message is designed for each person in a large audience.

4. Mass communication is symbolic interaction. Message exchange and the sharing of symbols are the heart of mass communication. We are affected by the mass media because we play our role as consumers of ideas generated by radio, TV, and the press. Their use of the language and of the social interaction that happens when we receive the message is more evidence that symbolic interaction is central to mass media. You will see that the sharing of language and nonverbal messages is central to this process.

Audience as Key Element

Communication cannot occur without a source and a receiver. Publishers can prepare and distribute newspapers; but if there are no readers, the publication will be a financial failure. We all know the history of television programs that are introduced by networks. Many programs have an extremely brief life span.

The importance of the audience must not be underestimated. A newspaper or magazine is successful because it is bought and read. People enjoy "The Cosby Show," "Sixty Minutes," and "Roseanne" so they watch these programs. Because there is an audience, advertisers pay for space or time, and the media operation makes a profit. When any portion of this equation fails, that mass media operation has problems. The *audience* is the key to success. Without readers, viewers, or listeners, mass communication cannot exist. The mass media are economically driven. The mass media adapt themselves to meet the demands of their intended audiences. If they do not, the audiences go elsewhere for their information or entertainment. When audiences do that, advertisers drop away from the media operation and financial difficulty ensues.

Pre-communication Expectations

Readers, viewers, and listeners explore a medium with specific expectations. When they purchase a newspaper or magazine, they usually are looking for something specific. It may be information about some world event or about a dispute between the executive and legislative branch in Washington. They may be looking for the results of a sporting event. They may be curious about some financial or law enforcement issue. They may be interested in community news, in financial reports or projections, or in the opinion from the editorial page. They may purchase the paper because of the grocery store or discount store ads it contains. But they always have certain expectations when they pick up a newspaper.

As television viewers and radio listeners, people bring a different orientation to the medium and varying objectives. More people seek entertainment from these media than information or news. The convincing evidence is that news programs are rarely among the most popular programs on a station. News operations at a television network typically operate in the "red" and are subsidized by the entertainment division.[1] "NBC Nightly News" is not profitable. The entertainment programs such as "The Golden Girls," "LA Law," "Cheers," and many others pay the bills so the news can be telecast. Most Americans find television and radio important sources for entertainment and escape.

Gatekeepers and Their Functions

Gatekeeping is a kind of regulator. It functions to determine what we receive, when we receive it, and how we receive it. In some ways, gatekeepers are like an accelerator in an automobile that determines how fast a car will travel. They make decisions about how much and what kind of information or entertainment we receive. They determine the extent and nature of our symbolic interaction with the medium. The gatekeeping function operates in the smallest radio station and in the tiniest newspaper in the most remote region. It is not just television networks or newspapers like *The New York Times* that have gatekeepers. *The Marysville Daily Tribune* and radio station KXEO employ reporters, editors, and photographers who determine what information to include and the emphasis of certain stories. They decide what kinds of entertainment and what kinds of editorial positions are appropriate. The gatekeeping function is complex because it varies with the medium.

Newspapers

Gatekeepers play a significant role in a daily newspaper. When reporters receive an assignment, all the details are not clear. Reporters may be told to investigate a stabbing in a downtown bar. When they arrive at the scene, they make several choices. Should they include the details about the appearance of the bar? What about the people who were present when the stabbing happened? What was the race of the victim and the assailant? Answers to these questions are part of the gatekeeping function of reporters. The reporters will include the answers to some of those choices in the story.

Then, the city editor and the executive editor function as gatekeepers in deciding what stories are published and how much of the information provided by the reporters will be printed. They are involved in redrafting stories, altering published viewpoints, and placing stories in the newspaper. They operate both individually and as a team. The city editor acts as a screening (gatekeeping) element, but the decisions made at that level must later be endorsed by the executive editor. It is not an accident that a story such as the Watergate scandal received so little public attention for some time. The gatekeepers in many major publications considered the theft at Democratic headquarters a "third-rate burglary," not something that justified major attention or could possibly result in the President of the United States resigning his office. The gatekeeper decided what to let through the "gate" of publication and what to keep out of print.

Television

The decisions of these gatekeepers are strongly influenced by the corporate policy but, more importantly, by the mores of the public and advertisers. The programming produced by the Fox Network in its efforts to compete directly with the "Big Three" included suggestive materials NBC, ABC and CBS would not telecast. After success in attracting audiences during the weekend, major advertisers such as General Mills approached Fox and told them that they wanted the content modified somewhat in exchange for continued sponsorship. Those corporations did not want their names identified with strongly "nonfamily" values.[2] The symbols the viewers saw were extremely important to the major advertisers. These symbols carried a message about the values and (potentially) the motives of the companies. The gatekeepers had to respond to their advertisers that influenced the existence of the network. The general public was affecting the gatekeepers.

Professional organizations also influence the decision making of gatekeepers. The reaction of The American Nurses Association to the weekly ABC television production of "Nurses" was so strong that the network agreed to revamp the program. They agreed to portray nurses as health care professionals with a high level of intelligence, rather than as free spirits who roamed through scenes as automatons in search of pleasure.

Peer influence affects gatekeeping decisions. It is an important way for mass media industries to regulate themselves. Gatekeepers regularly associate with their colleagues at other broadcasting stations and newspapers. In their discussions about current activities, they learn about programming ideas and promotional techniques. They become aware of production approaches and special features, which they use to help them to determine choices about materials that the public will read, hear, or see. The information they secure from the reading of trade publications and the decisions of other mass media outlets in other markets also contributes to their gatekeeping process.[3] Peer influence is a strong factor in decisions about materials or approaches.[4]

Film

Film and society has had a long and distinguished history in the communication of reality and issues in America. More recently, it has reflected the characteristics of the teenage and early twenty-year-old group, which attends films more than any other single age group. The producers of some films focus on themes of breaking societal rules, anger, sex, and the violation of parental wishes. These elements—contempt for authority figures—plus the use of violence as a form of rebellion are often themes in popular modern films. *Animal House, Porkies, Rambo, Blue Lagoon,* and *Meatballs* are typical movies that fit these criteria.

However, these are not the only themes present. From the 1970s to the late 1980s, filmmakers used several other themes popular with the public. Films such as *Platoon* and *The Deerhunter* reflected the reality of horror and conflict in the Vietnam War. Successful message films, which dealt with societal problems, were exemplified by *Wall Street, Tucker, The Elephant Man,* and *Rain Man.* Other more escapist themes and sometimes amusing films included *Coming To America, Annie Hall, Big, Back to the Future, Indiana Jones,* and *Field of Dreams.* Violence, crime, and horror made an appearance in movies such as *The Godfather, Scarface, Renegades, Pet Sematary,* and *Lethal Weapon.*

**Films carry a point of
view to the audience.**

Film in the 1990s reflects society. It tends to emphasize the themes and
types of action that the public wants. Filmmakers produce works that either
mirror the reality, or mirror the fantasy of the adolescent and adult world.
Filmmakers understand the themes that arouse interest in the viewing public,
so they develop products that reflect the general themes ticketholders are
likely to enjoy. They function as gatekeepers by developing themes that appeal
to the entertainment and message needs of society. They ask themselves,
"Will the message sell?"

Finally, filmmakers develop symbols that affect listeners in desired ways.
They are successful, however, only if their symbols trigger the desired reaction. The celluloid on which they place their product must stir responses
in the viewers. When those viewers see the symbols, the filmmaker is "talking"
to them. There is shared meaning. Symbols are exchanged. The filmmaker
is a symbolic interactionist at work.

Restrictions on Media

The widespread belief that written statements of nearly any kind are protected by freedom of speech in this nation is a misconception. Although the
First Amendment provides **freedom of expression** and freedom of the press,
a presumption exists that we will use those powers responsibly. Most people
are familiar with the need to avoid libelous statements (i.e. falsehoods or
defamatory statements that are printed). Since early American history, editors
and writers have printed stories that contained material they believed was
true. In cases where known untruths were published, the print media was
subject to legal suit for the publication of false material.

The free flow of material to the public about activities of the government, especially in areas of national security, has been reduced considerably
since the 1970s. Using concepts such as **prior restraint** (i.e. the prevention

of publication of material), and "the national interest or welfare," stories about the Central Intelligence Agency, about the U.S. invasion of Grenada, and about the United States involvement in the Iran hostage situation were effectively muzzled. Some journalists believe that no one should be free to print news about the intelligence or military activity of their country. Others argue that the government's claim of national security sometimes prevents them from reporting on information the public needs to know. While the debate continues, cases of prior restraint remain common in both the press and in the electronic media. They do represent new legal restrictions placed upon the spread of information by the government.

Radio and television operations are regulated by the federal government. They must provide access to the airways for even opposing positions. Print media are less directly restricted. Their primary responsibility is to take care that stories do not slander or defame people. Radio, television, and the print media are indirectly regulated by Washington on matters dealing with national security.

Exposure to Messages

Much of our exposure to messages is **involuntary exposure.** Often, we cannot escape from messages of the media. Again, recount some of the events of your day. If you arose in the morning and did not listen to the radio, glance at a newspaper, or view even a moment of television before you went to class or work, it would be an unusual day. During the day, if you were able to avoid hearing any news, seeing a magazine or billboard, newspaper, or even listening to broadcast music, your communication experiences would be extremely odd. Not to be exposed to elements of mass communication during a day is a highly *unusual* experience.

Media Combinations

The major media today rarely exist in isolation from us. We do not just listen to the radio, just watch television, or just read the newspaper. Instead **media combinations** exist, and we combine these channels in our search for information and entertainment. This generation has more of a television orientation than any of its predecessors. The visually oriented print media publications, such as "USA Today," cater to those preferences.

We do not rely upon one medium for our information. We may hear a story on the radio and then want to "see" what happened. Television and radio provide more instantaneous coverage, but the print medium provides the detail that fleshes out the story.

It is difficult to conclude that one medium has more influence on public attitudes than another. According to Comstock, a substantial percentage of the public believes that network news is biased.[5] In some cases, the percentage of the public that feels this way is roughly one-third of the viewing population. Lichty argues that newspapers are the primary source of information for news.[6] This is especially significant in the formation of attitudes, especially if you consider that persons with more education rely more heavily on print media. These people rely on a combination of sources for their information more than any other population group.[7] Because educated people search more for information, print media are most likely to influence them.

Comstock found that people of lower socio-economic status watch more television.[8] Those figures have been affected somewhat with the spread of cable television.[9] For the average person, only work and sleep occupy more of their daily time than does television.[10] The result is that exposure to television by the less educated is higher, but those with considerable education now are viewing television more. For those who originally relied on print media, television now plays an important role in providing information and shaping attitudes.

People rely on combinations of media for their information. One recent study documented the effectiveness of a public information campaign that used television and printed advertisements as major influences in reducing public anxiety and doubts about Tylenol following the introduction of poison into some of its capsules.[11] An interaction of printed and televised materials provide people with information and help shape their attitudes.

Selective Exposure

People expose themselves more to the medium that they like and trust most. For an increasing number of people, that medium is television. Society has moved away from the printed page because, as Schwartz says, ". . . the need to read and write is *not* as urgent as it was before the electronic media."[12] People watch television but they rely on printed material for in-depth coverage of current events, political commentary, controversial issues, and opinion positions.

Radio and television are the sources for immediate information, such as late-breaking news. They are the glamour media. However, when in-depth coverage, opinion articles, and complicated issues must be analyzed, the more educated population relies on the print medium. Newspaper people often refer to themselves as the journalists who get their hands dirty. The less educated populus is satisfied with a "Headline News" approach, which provides minimal depth for stories.

Television Newscast Portrayal of Presidents

"Generally, the networks depict a silent president: viewers are two and one-half times more likely to *see* a president speaking (with voice-over provided by news commentators) than to *hear* that president."

Source: Roderick P. Hart, Patrick Jerome, and Karen McComb, "Rhetorical Features of Newscasts About the President," *Critical Studies in Mass Communication* 1 (1984), p. 268.

Comment . . .
Contrary to what we often hear, the president does not have the opportunity to use a newscast to present a point of view. The commentator (or voice over) does the talking, while the network presents a picture of the president. In most cases, the network states or rewords the presentation of the chief executive.

The Effect of Media on Our Lives

The media are everywhere, and they affect most conversations or experiences. One of the first questions a friend might ask when you meet in the morning is, "Did you see the Letterman Show last night? It was great!" Or "What did you think about the blackout that cut out five minutes in the movie on Channel 11 last night? Do you know what she said to him about the missing money?" The media bring us happiness in programs we enjoy, and they convey sadness when we hear or read about tragedy somewhere in the world. The media can influence our attitudes about the working and living conditions of others. In addition, the media can have a profound effect on our political system.

The persuasive power of the media is great. Radio was highly effective in persuading the board of education in New York to keep John Jay College open.[13] In fact, people influenced their media leaders based on what they heard. Dan Rather's interview with Vice President Bush on CBS Television in 1988 created considerable sympathy for Mr. Bush and a substantial amount of public indignation for Mr. Rather and his lack of respect for a major public figure.[14] A series of articles in the *Wall Street Journal* about insider information and the use of privileged information to make money in stock trades created suspicion about the equities market. Small investors lost confidence in some market procedures. The information triggered a wholesale series of criminal investigations and prosecutions.

Acquiring Information

The media have changed the face of society. The explosion of materials in print has made it nearly impossible to keep up in our reading. Thus, we have become more selective about what we listen to, view, and read. Some newspapers, such as the *Wall Street Journal,* provide a quick preview of the inside stories with a front page section called "What's News." The skeleton story provides the basic details and refers the reader to the specific story by page number. If you read the bare details, then you can decide if you want to read the complete story.

Television provides varied programming with several formats for entertainment and informational materials. We acquire information about nature through "Wild Kingdom." That information creates a concern for the natural habitat of seals or the effect of acid rain on fish in Canada. In this context, informational materials are persuasive. Much of the same information can appear in a network documentary on the effect of pollution on wildlife; however, the impact can be less because viewers might perceive the documentary as a less persuasive experience. Generally, the "Wild Kingdom" can be seen more as an informational report on wildlife. In both cases, information is acquired.

Panel programs such as "Meet The Press" or "Face The Nation" have reputations for political newsmaking. Readers can acquire the same information that television viewers hear when they examine their newspapers on Monday morning. However, the follow-up questions cannot be asked. In addition, the drama of the moment is lost when the confrontation is removed. Therefore, television has the advantage of being an immediate medium and has the potential for creating more controversy. When Ronald Reagan stumbled through a debate on television with Walter Mondale in 1984, the American public anxiously waited for the next debate. They wanted to see if Reagan was senile and was losing his grip. He was not. His immediate and calculated response to questions in the final presidential debate satisfied nearly all of the doubters.

We use many kinds of information from the media in our lives. Hearing about a crime committed down the street on the morning news certainly does not get our day off to a positive start. Hearing a weather forecast that calls for steady rains following two months of drought may be very pleasing. Reading about the exciting comeback of the greatest golfer of all time may be inspiring to older players.

The acquisition of information is sometimes purposeful and sometimes accidental. Much of what we retain from the newspaper, radio, or television comes from chance encounters. We happen to read a headline. In turn, it interests us and we read the story. We pick up the newspaper, intending to read the business news. We read the business news, but we also glance at the headlines in the community news section. Some of our reading is purposeful, and some is accidental. In some of these examples, we may not only acquire the information, but also use it. We may use it in conversation and in decision making, or we may add it to our storehouse of incidental personal information.

Media and the Family Unit

Media's **effects on family units** have changed. During the 1940s and 1950s, the image of a night at home involved the family gathered around a radio, listening to such programs as "The Fred Allen Show" or "Inner Sanctum." Today families sit on the couch, recline in a chair, or lie on the floor and watch reruns of "MASH," agonize through "Murder She Wrote," or laugh at "Johnny Carson." Attention to media has not changed dramatically in the last forty years. The medium of choice is different (i.e., television instead of radio) but the family still uses it for information and primarily for entertainment. Radio leaves much of the action or scene to the listener's imagination. Television limits the imagination. The scenes are explicit and opportunities for viewer imagination are more limited.

The print media play less of a role in the family unit now than a generation ago. With increased technological advances, electronic media enable children to acquire huge amounts of information with only modest reading skills. By looking at the pictures and listening to the narrative, they can become skilled observers of current events. They recognize famous people and know the landmarks of cities such as San Francisco or New York without leaving the living room.

People are more quickly informed because of the media. They have more to talk about because of their increased information. It is contradictory, but we use media to escape from tension. Conversely, when we are calm, we

often watch or read something to stimulate us. Radio, television, and the press (i.e., books, magazines, or newspapers) offer us alternatives.

Media and the Young

Today's children are products of a visually-oriented society. "Seeing is believing" is appropriate to describe them and their attitudes. Many children and often adolescents believe much of what they see or read. When questions are raised, their answer may be, "It has to be true. I saw it in the newspaper/on television." Hence, they are not critical of media material.

Children spend from twenty-two to thirty-two hours per week watching television. As they reach their teenage years, the amount of time spent watching television is about twenty-four hours per week. When evaluating the impact of television on children, remember the charge made about the current population of older adults was that it spent too much time listening to the radio. Television has a different type of impact. Children and adolescents are more active in their use of the medium. Like adults, however, children use television for entertainment. (There are many channels and choices, and people are forced to make those decisions.)

The most intriguing question is, "What effect does television have on viewers, especially children and adolescents?" Gerbner and Gross contend that people who watch a great deal of television mold their notion of the world around the programs and themes that they see on television.[14] Milavisky reports that it is not possible to predict aggression over a long period of time. He cautions, however, that there are times when aggression *appears* as a result of television viewing. These are "points" in time and not a long-term result.[15] Milavisky believes a substantial amount of television-induced violence results from cops and robbers programs, war movies, and other programs that show aggression. Television does have an effect on youth, as well as on adults. The impact is not constant but episodic. We need to become more sensitive to the fact that television has the potential for significant influences on the lives of viewers.

Media in Our Institutions

If the print medium, radio, or television were not present, how would we keep up with financial matters, the daily news, popular music, or the candidates for public office? It would be very difficult. This section examines the intimate relationship of the media to these institutions.

Political Affairs

The **media in politics** have assumed center stage in political campaigns. Candidates would not run for office without an elaborate media plan. Officeholders use the media to establish and control the agenda for discussion of current issues.

The earliest documented case of an elaborate media campaign is reported in *The Selling of the President 1968* by Joe McGinnis. He reports how Richard Nixon was "packaged," in a fashion much as modern merchandisers would sell soap flakes or soft drinks.[17] Today, television has become the medium of choice for candidates running for public office. Because the purchase of television time is so expensive, the amount of money required to conduct a successful election campaign has increased. Political campaign fund-raising begins with some 60 to 70 percent of the funds earmarked for television production and the purchase of time on television stations. Television has been successful as the most desirable political medium because it is a "cool medium" in the categories of **hot media** and **cool media** as defined by the late Marshall McLuhan. The print medium requires a low level of audience participation when compared to television so print media is considered "hot." People prefer the "cool" medium because they want the opportunity to fill in their own definitions of the candidates, so they choose television.[18] We could not imagine a state or local election campaign without commercial spots. "Vote for me; I understand how you feel. I'll clean up the mess." This is a familiar televised line, and many candidates are coached for television appearances so they will look as good as possible. The television camera is truly *The Unseeing Eye.*[19]

The executive branch and members of the Congress also use the print medium for setting the political agenda and expressing general opinions by unattributable statements. "Leaks to the press" and "deep background" stories are ways the two branches of government control issues and help to manage public opinion. Elected officials would have difficulty responding to public opinion and articulating their positions without space in the press.[20]

It would be difficult to imagine public officials running for election or conducting their offices without using the media. The media are crucial to their job. So, too, the media need political officials and their acts, for without them there would be little news and no editorializing.

Economic Activities

Among the millions of American investors, nearly all turn to the stock market quotations in the newspaper at least every few days. This medium tells them if they are making or losing money. The largest circulation daily in the United States is *The Wall Street Journal.* Information sent through this newspaper and other print publications affects our economy and has **economic impacts.**

The electronic media get that information to us quicker—but in a shorter fashion. They cannot provide the thousands of price quotes for individual stocks, but they can tell us about stock and trading trends. Radio and television shouted about "Black Monday" and kept us informed on an hourly basis about the fall in the stock market. Radio and television report on activities in the Persian Gulf and what that may mean to the price of oil. They tell us about the Alaska oil spill and then tell us that the price of gasoline will increase about 10 cents per gallon.

Sports

Televised sports live by the media. Without newspaper coverage, radio broadcast, closed circuit television, and live television coverage, sports today would not occupy such a significant role in American life. It would be difficult to imagine a newspaper without a sports section. The local television news has a special section devoted to sports. One network, ESPN, televises only sports-related programs. Television networks bid billions of dollars for the exclusive rights to televise the NCAA games.

Television has become such an accepted and desired element of sports that collegiate organizations have been developed to encourage the televising of their games. The money associated with televised sports has affected all sports. Telecasts have attracted even more people to the sports. Each year, record numbers of viewers watch the Master's Golf Tournament, the NCAA Basketball Championship, and the US Open Tennis Championship.

The sports section of the newspaper has remained a standard. Box scores, feature stories, and play-by-play analysis were present before the arrival of the electronic media. Newspapers provide the complete statistical and analytical data that only the printed page can offer. The sports section may be less glamorous than the television picture, but it can be re-read, re-analyzed, and re-thought many times. In this case, the electronic image fades quickly.

Media today have made sports a national preoccupation. The social and financial significance of sports and leading sports figures have resulted from the media coverage and image. Sports are both escape and obsession.

Media as Culture

Each medium has an effect on each of us, but it also has a significant impact on our society. Some people call this the instant gratification society. If that label is valid, it may be because we receive so much information and because we process it so immediately. A definite cause-effect relationship cannot be established between the media and changes in society. "Go for it," "You deserve a break today," "Treat yourself" are among the slogans that we read, see, and hear on the media. They urge us to act immediately, to think about the short-term acts rather than the long-term consequences. Advertisers ask us to spend now and to save later, and to charge it to our local department store. Society generally considers time as money, and the media reflects that orientation. Therefore, they provide us with one hour murder mysteries on television. Some people will watch the program rather than spend eight to twelve hours reading an Agatha Christie murder mystery novel. We would prefer to watch the video cassette version of a "How to . . . " book rather than to read the book itself.

People continue to read books in record numbers; hence, it can't be argued that media, especially electronic media, have caused cultural illiteracy. Instead, we are just interacting with our culture differently. In fact, our cultural literacy may be higher now than ever before.[21]

People also have become more sensitive to other cultures. The availability of print and visual media to explore and to explain "German customs" or "Korean familial relationships" helps us to understand the origins of some of our cultural behaviors. It also serves as a mediating influence. Americans can adopt aspects of another culture so that this country becomes an even better combination of cultural heritages.

Because our electronic media are "time oriented," our culture has become more time-bound. Broadcast and telecasts begin exactly on the hour or on the half hour. The concept of **prime time** programming is another illustration of how media affects activity. Because the most appealing programs appear during those hours, many of us arrange our schedules so that we will have that **viewing time** available. In turn, the timing of prime time programs has been arranged around the times when viewers or listeners are available. Sporting events occur more in the evening when an audience is available.

Financial Concerns as a Major Force

It is costly to develop and to present media materials/programs. Paper, airtime, cameras, reporters, editors, and producers are among the cost factors. As the number of newspapers decrease, and as the number of radio and television broadcasts increase, the financial factors become more critical. All media are forced to develop techniques or formats that will appeal to the largest number of people. This next section examines some of the factors involved in publishing and production decisions.

Thematic Development

The media use themes that have major popular appeal. These themes may reflect the fantasy world of their target audience, or they may represent the reality of modern society. In both cases, the themes must be appealing to their audience.

Violence

"Miami Vice" and "Hunter" are explicit in the amount and degree of violence portrayed. Some of the most popular programs center on the action of a car chase, the shooting out of windows, the crushing of buildings, the killing of drug dealers, or the attacking and wiping out of dozens of enemy soldiers. Networks recognize that thematic balance—including comedy, and other entertainment programs—is necessary to retain the greatest number of viewers. However, in recent years the explicit nature of much of the violence (i.e., shooting, stabbing, exploding, maiming) has increased. The entertainment channels (i.e., Showtime, HBO, Cinemax, and The Movie Channel) are more likely to show films that use violence.

Popularity versus Quality

Television programmers have been criticized for presenting what critics call "trash TV." Trash TV programs include "All American Wrestling," "Wheel of Fortune," and "Lifestyles of the Rich and Famous." Popularity is the hallmark of these programs. Quality is not. However, the viewing public is receiving what it wants. Large numbers of people want to see how the enviable wealthy live and play so the media gives them a glimpse with "Lifestyles." The classic confrontation between good and evil, formerly seen in the western movies, now appears in wrestling exhibitions. These programs offer no substantive content; they are escape.

If enough viewers watch these programs, advertisers are delighted, unless the material is blatantly offensive. If advertisers purchase the time, which supports the program, then the station or network can continue to broadcast it. Stations must have revenue to survive and advertising is a station's lifeblood. As long as a theme is successful, networks will continue to develop clones to attract viewers. Therefore, station and network programming may not be based on quality or necessarily on variety. Sometimes, it rests on what the public wants.

Program Scheduling and the Market

The force of the market (and its viewers) has a major impact on the kind of program that is shown. Programs unlikely to attract large audiences are slipped into undesirable time slots. Sunday morning features such programs as "Weight Loss in America" at 7:30 A.M., "Welcome to Pooh Corner" at 9:00 A.M., "Canadian Sportfishing" at 11:00 A.M., and "Gourmet Cooking" at 11:30 A.M. Although well-designed and produced programs, they will never have a large audience because Sunday morning is a time slot near the bottom of the preferred viewing times. Compare these programs with the following list: "60 Minutes," "Designing Women," "Roseanne," and "Growing Pains." The themes may be slightly different, but the viewing times are decidedly different. The second list consists of programs shown in *prime time,* 6:00 to 10:00 P.M. Their placement on a network at these times insures them of a much better chance of attracting a large audience than if they were shown on Sunday morning.

The success of prime time programs in the ratings determines how much the network can charge advertisers for commercial spots. For the most part, prime time programs finance the major networks. Millions of dollars are at stake during prime time. Ratings mean profits, and profits mean new program efforts. Successful prime time programs create funds to develop new programs. A network can only become profitable if it provides the public with enjoyable programs during prime time. Programs during much of the rest of the day (with the exception of the "soaps") have little effect on network finance.

Mass Media in the 1990s

The expansion or explosion in communication media is startling. Techniques taken for granted today were unthinkable only a generation ago. Live, color television pictures from remote sections of China or from the Kremlin were impossible in the 1960s, and home computers were something unthinkable. These advances are significant, but we are on the threshold of even more striking communication innovations in the next decade.

Dissemination of Materials

This is the information generation, and people seem obsessed with the need for more up-to-date information for their decision making. The technology of this decade has provided the tools to be in touch with other people at the speed of light in distant portions of the world.

Satellite Transmission

Virtually all television network programs are sent to receiving stations by **satellite transmissions** from orbiting satellites in space. Local stations can send sound and visual reports of events to the networks as needed.

Rural and city dwellers have TVRO's (Television Receive Only) or *dishes* in their yards. These outdoor antennas make it possible for the resident of Omaha to watch WTBS in Atlanta, WPIX in New York, KTLA in Los Angeles, ESPN for sports, Showtime for entertainment or movies, CNN for news, or Arts and Entertainment for drama. These are only a few of the possibilities. Over ninety stations send signals that can be received by ground satellite stations in the United States.

Major communication companies send their information from coast to coast using satellites. They rent space on these orbiting objects and, using many rented channels on the satellite, they send millions of signals, which are transmitted and received across continents or oceans.

Satellites offer a secure method for transmitting information, and it's a method that is remarkably efficient. Weather, information, and commercial satellites, as well as military satellites, are taken for granted, although they now provide an enormous array of information and entertainment.

Electronic Mail

In the business world, much of the information that one worker passes on to the next is electronic. When an employee sits down at a desk, that person may turn on a computer and check the "mailbox." An "electronic mailbox" can contain messages from the boss about various tasks to be performed, it can contain messages about new company policies on vacation and overtime, or it can contain two or three messages from other employees about problems with their joint assignments.

As soon as the message is sent, it is received. That immediacy is typical of the electronic age. Rapid sending and receipt of information gives everyone more time to evaluate the data and to make more informed decisions. No delay exists in the morning mail.

The explosion in communications media has changed the ways we live, work, and think.

Electronic mail is a highly efficient and immediate way of sending and receiving messages. It is not restricted to a single building, city, or state. It can be sent nationwide, and its use increases the efficiency of any organization or person. Electronic mail is a major contributor to improving the immediacy of communication.

Potential Influences on the Individual

Mass media and the changes in the 1990s will modify our lives in unimaginable ways. High definition television will increase the reality of viewing. The availability of information will make us better informed than any generation in history. Our choices will multiply because of more information and more options. The revolution of the 1990s glitters with these opportunities.

Depersonalization of Contact

As we rely more on electronic media, the amount of direct contact with people will decrease. If we rely solely on personal computer contact, how do we deal with people when we meet them face-to-face? A danger exists that interpersonal relationships will suffer and that more impersonal relationships will develop.

Information Overload

Some of us shout, "I just can't take any more information! There's too much for me to remember." That is a real possibility in the 1990s. If we try to absorb as much information as possible, we could suffer from **information overload.** Like the car made to operate at 80 mph, but being driven at 95 mph, we, too, could have an information breakdown. The result could be confusion and withdrawal from sources.

Difficult choices face us, and we have to be discriminating viewers. Rather than sit with our remote control, flipping from channel to channel, we need to make choices in advance. Our lives need to be better organized. Because there is so much to do, we must structure our activities more efficiently.

Increased Selectivity in Exposure

The depersonalization and information overload phenomena can be avoided with increased selectivity. Make decisions. What choices benefit you personally and professionally? Decide on your personal priorities, then select the appropriate media elements that meet your needs. Without selectivity, you will wallow in an avalanche of media messages; that is, from the information from television, from radio, and from the printed page (i.e. magazines, personal computers, satellites, and electronic mail).

Your degree of selectivity today is only a fraction of what will be necessary to be a successful and well adjusted person in the next five years. The media explosion is occurring, and the answer to its problems is to choose the information that is beneficial, as opposed to the information that is merely "noise."

Mass media are critical aspects of our lives. In many ways, our lives are governed by our interaction with the media. As the media channels increase and as we understand their influence, we (i.e. society) face difficult choices. Should the media continue to be controlled by market forces? What is in the best public interest? Is it being served by programs and entertainment that may be different than national and community norms? These two questions address the premise of the First Amendment, which the media guards relentlessly.

Summary

Mass media are essential elements in modern society. In many ways, they *define* today's world. Many forms of media gatekeepers determine what we read, hear, and see. They provide the information and entertainment, while people decide, on the basis of time, their personal preferences and needs. The media are formers of opinion and play critical roles in our political institutions, our economic world, and in the nature and direction of our society. Modern media produce programs and publications that are financially successful and reflect the needs and desires of their audiences. Satellite communication, personal computers, and electronic mail are among the media technological advances that will determine how people and societies will relate to each other in the 1990s.

Discussion Questions

1. Discuss what kinds of programs are scheduled in prime time. To what extent do the networks use similar thematic standards?
2. How does the media affect the outcome of elections? Should election results on the East Coast be announced before the polls close on the West Coast in California?
3. What major recent films have had an effect on the way you perceive history or society? To what extent was the representation accurate?
4. How would society be affected if satellite transmission were interrupted? Would it do serious harm to society?
5. Does the availability of information by the media create news and not just report it? Discuss the Vietnam War, the stock market crash, airline accidents, and the recent revolutions in Eastern Europe.

References

[1]Peter J. Boyer. *Who Killed CBS?* (New York: Random House, 1988).

[2]Dennis Keale, "Can Fox Cool Down and Stay Hot?" *Wall Street Journal* (May 26, 1989), p. B1.

[3]Samuel L. Becker, *Discovering Mass Communication* (Glenview, Il: Scott, Foresman and Company, 1983), pp. 56–57.

[4]Timothy W. Luke, "Chernobyl: The Packaging of Transnational Ecological Disaster," *Critical Studies in Mass Communication* (December 1987), pp. 351–75.

[5]George Comstock, *Television in America* (Beverly Hills: Sage Publications, 1980), p. 50.

[6]Lawrence W. Lichty, "Video Versus Print," *The Wilson Quarterly* VI (1982), pp. 49–57.

[7]Leo Bogart, *Press and Public* (Hillsdale, N.J.: Lawrence Erlbaum, 1981), pp. 76–79.

[8]Comstock, 1980, p. 30.

[9]Dean E. Alger, *The Media and Politics* (Englewood Cliffs, N.J.: Prentice-Hall, 1989), p. 16.

[10]Becker, 1983, p. 405.

[11]Alan D. Winegarden, "A Burkean Analysis of the 1982 and 1986 Tylenol Poisoning Tragedies," unpublished Ph.D. disssertation, University of Missouri-Columbia, 1989.

[12]Tony Schwartz, *Media: The Second God* (Garden City, NY: Anchor Books, 1983), p. 130.

[13]Schwartz, 1983, "The John Jay Campaign: A Case Study," pp. 61–69.

[14]Boyer, 1988.

[15]G. Gerbner and L. Gross. "Living with Television: The Violence Profile," *Journal of Communication* (1976), pp. 173–96.

[16]J. Ronald Milavsky, Ronald C. Kessler, Horst H. Stipp, and William S. Reubens, *Television and Aggression* (New York: Academic Press, 1982), pp. 481–89.

[17]Joe McGinniss, *The Selling of the President 1968* (New York: Trident Press, 1969).

[18]Marshall McLuhan, *Understanding Media: The Extensions of Man* (New York: New American Library, 1964).

[19]Thomas E. Patterson and Robert D. McClure, *The Unseeing Eye* (New York: G. C. Putnam's, 1976).

[20]"Role of the Mass Media in American Politics," *The Annals of the American Academy of Political and Social Science* (September 1976).

[21]Becker, 1983, p. 431.

Intercultural
Communication

Outline

When you finish reading this chapter you should be able to:

1. Explain why intercultural communication skills are becoming more important.

2. List at least ten of Richard Brislin's fourteen types of cross-cultural contact that Americans are likely to encounter.

3. Define the terms "culture," and "subculture."

4. Describe culture shock, and name the sources of stress that create it.

5. Specify six categories of variables that can predict how much stress individuals may experience in cross-cultural encounters.

6. Name and describe six suggestions for improving communication across cultural boundaries.

Objectives

attribution

biological factors

categorization

control issues

culture

culture shock

differentiation

ethnocentrism

geopolitical factors

global village

interpersonal factors

intrapersonal factors

space and time

subculture

Key Terms

Introduction

When the American automobile industry finally figured out that it had difficulty competing with the Japanese automakers, leaders in the industry joined forces with the Japanese. By 1985, ITT Automotive, an auto-parts manufacturer in Marysville, Ohio, had set up a 50–50 joint venture with a Japanese auto-parts maker called Sanoh Industrial Company.[1] The idea was to supply Honda in the United States, but the venture failed. Of the 126 joint U.S.–Japanese ventures to supply Honda, Nissan, and Mazda, almost all are losing money.

Problems with communication across cultural lines were at the heart of all these failures. Management styles were different, expectations were inflated, and quality and labor practices were unclear or uncertain. The two sides almost always entered into the bargains with different agendas. Americans wanted access to Japanese automakers. The Japanese were after a foothold in the U. S. market.

The problems could have been avoided if both parties had been more skillful in communicating across cultural boundaries. For example, Toyota of Japan and General Motors of the United States are currently cooperating in making and marketing Geo automobiles successfully.

As communications technology advances and international transportation shrinks the world, intercultural communication opportunities are likely to increase. Opportunities for misunderstandings can also increase. For example, one business executive considered his counterparts in Athens, Greece, to be rude. They asked "personal" questions (i.e., questions about the business executive's religious beliefs, his political views, and how much money he earned on his job) just a few weeks after his arrival.

The Greeks, of course, did not consider themselves rude. They were just being friendly. To them, such questions signaled their acceptance of the American.

Such stories are commonplace. They point to a growing challenge for all of us because our intercultural communication effectiveness is usually inadequate. In fact, the gap between our intercultural communication skills and the need for those skills is increasing.

This chapter examines the most common cross-cultural communication problems. It suggests certain skills to improve cross-cultural communication effectiveness.

In general, U.S. citizens—especially members of the ethnic majority—tend to have a chauvinistic attitude about communication across cultural lines. That is, we unconsciously assume and project that our *own* culture is correct. In doing so, we create unnecessary problems for ourselves. This chauvinistic attitude and its resulting problem is called **ethnocentrism.** The term means the attitude that one's own race, nation, or culture is superior to all others.

Importance

Contacts across cultural and national boundaries will increase. People are more mobile than ever. They travel from country to country and from continent to continent for both business and pleasure.

Richard W. Brislin has identified fourteen separate types of cross-cultural contact that Americans are most likely to encounter.[2] Not all of them require travel to other lands. Notice how increasing mobility plays a part in such contacts. Have you already experienced one or more of these fourteen types?

1. Overseas study at the college level.

Students from the United States commonly travel to other countries as part of their study. Students from other nations commonly study in U.S. colleges and universities. This pattern is reflected in tables 17.1 to 17.3, which describe the flow of international students. All of the tables come from the Institute of International Education and are used with permission. The data's conclusion are clear: students from all over the world are interacting with each other in increasing numbers.

To gain perspective on your own interaction with student exchange, ask the admissions office at your school about how many international students are enrolled.

2. A business assignment in a country other than one's own, usually as representative of an international business.

With each passing year, international business travel increases. For instance, a man whose career has taken him to the executive suite in Del Monte Tropical Fruit Company travels somewhere each month overseas. During the most recent twelve-month period, he has traveled extensively in Japan, Kenya, The Philippines, Costa Rica, Guatemala, England, and Monte Carlo.

This travel is not uncommon. As American and foreign businesses continue to expand and merge, such travel will increase.

3. Diplomats and embassy staff who represent one country while stationed in another.

4. Language interpreters who work in permanent international organizations or in short-term multinational conferences.

5. Technical assistance personnel assigned overseas.

6. Participants in organized programs emphasizing contact with people of another nation or culture (e.g., The Peace Corps).

7. Military personnel assigned as advisers to governments or defense units of other countries.

Foreign Student Enrollment and Institutions Reporting Foreign Students, 1954/55–1987/88

Year	Foreign Students	Number of Institutions
1954/55	34,232	1,629
1955/56	36,494	1,630
1956/57	40,666	1,734
1957/58	43,391	1,801
1958/59	47,245	1,680
1959/60	48,486	1,712
1960/61	53,107	1,666
1961/62	58,086	1,798
1962/63	64,705	1,805
1963/64	74,814	1,805
1964/65	82,045	1,859
1965/66	82,709	1,755
1966/67	100,262	1,797
1967/68	110,315	1,827
1968/69	121,362	1,846
1969/70	134,959	1,734
1970/71	144,708	1,748
1971/72	140,126	1,650
1972/73	146,097	1,508
1973/74	151,066	1,359
1974/75	154,580	1,760
1975/76	179,344	2,093
1976/77	203,068	2,294
1977/78	235,509	2,475
1978/79	263,938	2,504
1979/80	286,343	2,651
1980/81	311,882	2,734
1981/82	326,299	2,454
1982/83	336,985	2,529
1983/84	338,894	2,498
1984/85	342,113	2,492
1985/86	343,777	2,507
1986/87	349,609	2,518
1987/88	356,187	2,552

From Gerald L. Wilson and Michael S. Hanna, *Groups in Context: Leadership and Participation in Small Groups*, 2d ed. Copyright © McGraw-Hill Inc., New York. Reprinted by permission.

▼ Table 17.1

Foreign Student Enrollment, Institutions Reporting Foreign Students, and Percentage Change, Selected Years, 1954/55–1987/88

Year	Foreign Students	% Change	Number of Institutions	% Change
1954/55	34,232		1,629	
1959/60	48,486	8.3	1,712	1.0
1969/70	134,959	12.9	1,734	− 1.3
1974/75	154,580	2.9	1,760	0.3
1979/80	286,343	8.5	2,651	5.9
1980/81	311,882	8.9	2,734	3.1
1981/82	326,299	6.0	2,454	−10.2[1]
1982/83	336,985	3.3	2,529	3.1
1983/84	338,894	0.6	2,498	− 1.2
1984/85	342,113	0.9	2,492	− 0.2
1985/86	343,777	0.5	2,507	0.6
1986/87	349,609	1.7	2,518	0.4
1987/88	356,187	1.9	2,552	1.4

[1]Rate of increase for accredited institutions (see text). In 1981/82 the number of institutions surveyed decreased due to elimination from the Census of all institutions that are not listed in the *Education Directory, Colleges and Universities* with (1) accreditation, (2) provisional or probationary accreditation, or (3) preaccredited status by a Regional Accrediting Commission.
From Gerald L. Wilson and Michael S. Hanna, *Groups in Context: Leadership and Participation in Small Groups*, 2d ed. Copyright © McGraw-Hill Inc., New York. Reprinted by permission.

▲ Table 17.2

8. Emigrants moving from one country to another, who then establish citizenship in the host country.

9. Researchers who work on cultures other than their own.

10. International and interregional tourists.

11. Members of a certain ethnic group who interact with members of another.

12. People who participate in "arranged interethnic contact," such as legally desegregated schools.

13. Members of ethnic groups who are required to move from one area of a country to another.

14. Students who, as part of their education, live and work with members of an ethnic group other than their own.

Country of Origin of Foreign Students Within Selected Leading Host Countries

Leading Place of Origin	Host Country	
	United States[1]	*France[2]*
Iran	10,420	5,233
Greece	4,140	3,405
Malaysia	19,480	—
China	25,170	1,059
Taiwan	26,660	—
Morocco	—	25,297
Nigeria	8,340	—
Jordan	5,140	—
Hong Kong	10,650	—
United States	—	3,503
Germany, F.R.	5,730	3,776
Turkey	2,630	—
Japan	18,050	—
Canada	15,690	—
Venezuela	3,790	—
United Kingdom	6,600	2,126
Syria	1,740	3,161
Italy	2,200	—
Lebanon	5,820	5,113
Egypt	2,090	—
Algeria	—	10,535
Singapore	4,870	—
Cameroon	1,400	4,694
Ivory Coast	—	3,157
Brazil	2,950	—
Madagascar	—	4,393
Portugal	—	2,369
India	21,010	—
Kenya	—	—
Iraq	—	—
Netherlands	1,630	—
Spain	2,500	3,047
Yugoslavia	—	—
Austria	—	—
Switzerland	1,040	—
Korea	19,520	—
Total of leading senders	235,920	80,895
Percent of total foreign students	66.2	61.2
Total foreign students	356,187	131,979

[1]Source: *Open Doors 1987/88*
[2]Source: *Reperes et References Statistiques*, 1987 p. 195
[3]Source: *Basic and Structural Data 1986/87*, Federal Ministry of Education and Science Germany F.R.

▼ Table 17.3

Germany, F.R.[3]	United Kingdom[4]	Canada[5]
7,872	2,023	125
6,447	2,289	361
—	5,600	1,849
1,117	410	1,716
583	157	165
201	49	836
274	3,221	264
976	591	53
—	6,935	8,896
4,042	3,438	2,969
—	1,496	427
9,215	190	119
1,134	402	442
429	805	—
161	109	200
1,872	0	758
467	176	27
1,943	464	110
316	182	403
696	622	141
355	562	256
—	1,329	1,271
192	193	204
—	14	179
547	370	133
—	16	23
396	134	37
585	1,012	898
—	1,056	530
356	1,568	54
1,856	362	87
1,446	234	85
1,749	34	44
3,662	41	138
1,203	219	173
2,673	183	308
52,765	36,486	24,281
70.8	65.0	69.0
74,574	56,121	35,155

[4]Source: *Statistics of students from abroad in the United Kingdom 1984/85*, The British Council
[5]Source: *The National Report on International Students in Canada 1986–87*, Canadian Bureau for International Education

From Gerald L. Wilson and Michael S. Hanna, *Groups in Context: Leadership and Participation in Small Groups*, 2d ed. Copyright © McGraw-Hill Inc., New York. Reprinted by permission.

▲ **Table 17.3** continued

Thus, it seems clear that more and more contact is being made with other cultures and that this trend will increase in the coming years. As the turn of the century approaches, each of us will have to learn to improve our ways of communicating in cross-cultural events. Now, we truly are members of a **global village.**

In addition to human mobility, the United States and most other countries are also so intimately linked economically and politically that cross-cultural contact seems inevitable. The patterns of this economic and political contact are changing. In the past, our economic ties were primarily to Europe. Now, we are increasingly involved with other countries, such as China, Japan, and Korea.

The reality of economic and cross-cultural interdependence is apparent every time you read a national news magazine or turn on the evening news. For example, during the summer of 1989, every issue of *Insight,* a weekly news magazine, carried at least one (and usually three or four articles) that pointed to our economic and political ties to the world. *Time, U. S. News and World Report, Newsweek, Business Week,* and *Insight* print these articles every week.

Communication across national and cultural boundaries has become more rapid and less expensive than ever before. In part, this rapid communication has been thrust upon us by major advances in technology. T.V. news and entertainment programs bring foreign cultures into our living rooms every day, and international telephone and computer hookups are common in business. Calling home is commonplace when traveling overseas.

People of different cultures are heard every day through our communications media, and we form impressions and stereotypes on the basis of these sources. Of course, our own country uses the mass media to communicate abroad. For example, in November 1989, *Voice of America* began beaming television programs to Cuba by using a balloon anchored in the Florida keys as an antenna.

Our television news industry is having an enormous impact around the world. With the aid of technology, it will be possible to tune in English language programming throughout western Europe. The American film and television industry has become the largest importer and exporter of high and low culture programming. Dubbed versions of *Dallas* and *Dynasty,* for example, have faithful fans in Paris and Tokyo. The reverse is also true. Television programs produced in Mexico, Brazil, and Spain are finding increasing Spanish-speaking audiences in the United States.

Finally, the mobility of peoples from all over the world has greatly influenced immigration and migration patterns in the United States (figure 17.1). The West Coast, for example, is experiencing a dramatic increase in

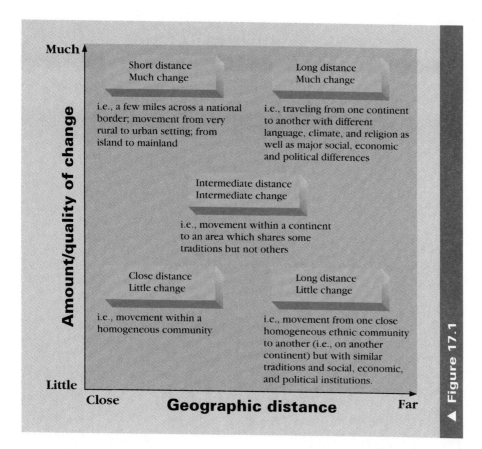

A representation
of possible
patterns of
migration based
on geographic
distance and
cultural difference

Figure 17.1

Much

Amount/quality of change

Short distance
Much change

i.e., a few miles across a national border; movement from very rural to urban setting; from island to mainland

Long distance
Much change

i.e., traveling from one continent to another with different language, climate, and religion as well as major social, economic and political differences

Intermediate distance
Intermediate change

i.e., movement within a continent to an area which shares some traditions but not others

Close distance
Little change

i.e., movement within a homogeneous community

Long distance
Little change

i.e., movement from one close homogeneous ethnic community to another (i.e., on another continent) but with similar traditions and social, economic, and political institutions.

Little

Close   **Geographic distance**   Far

the number of people from Pacific rim nations. All over America, people are moving from rural to urban centers, and from region to region.

Our northern and southern borders are practically wide open. The Canadian province of British Columbia, for example, is admitting some 10,000 new people from around the world every month, many of whom migrate, again, into the United States. The flow of people from Latin America across our southern border has reached an all-time high. All this movement increases the likelihood of needing effective intercultural communication skills.

The United States is still a melting-pot nation. Many U.S. cities—especially those that are seaports—contain international populations. These people eat different foods, speak different languages, and make different assumptions about the world. (See table 17.4.)

Therefore, there is a good deal of reason to study intercultural communication behavior. Ignoring the likelihood of communicating across cultural boundaries will create problems. However, understanding that increased contact with people from other nations and other cultures is inevitable will give you an opportunity to develop intercultural communication skills.

Top Ten Languages Spoken Worldwide by First-Language Speakers[1]

1. Chinese   (1 billion)
2. English   (350 million)
3. Spanish   (250 million)
4. Hindi   (200 million)
5. Arabic   (150 million)
6. Bengali   (150 million)
7. Russian   (150 million)
8. Portuguese   (135 million)
9. Japanese   (120 million)
10. German   (100 million)

Registration in Modern Foreign Languages in U.S. Institutions of Higher Education: Fall, 1986: (Given in percent of Students Registered)[2]

1. Spanish   43%
2. French   28%
3. German   12%
4. Italian   4%
5. Russian   4%
6. Other   3%
7. Japanese   2%
8. Chinese   2%
9. Hebrew   2%

Top Ten U. S. Trading Partners, 1988 (Exports in Billions of Dollars)[3]

1. Canada $70.9 billion
2. Japan   37.7 billion
3. Mexico   20.6 billion
4. United Kingdom   18.4 billion
5. West Germany   14.3 billion
6. China   12.1 billion
7. Korea   11.3 billion
8. France   10.1 billion
9. Netherlands   10.1 billion
10. Belgium   7.4 billion

[1]Source: The Encyclopedia of Language, 1987 Edition. Cambridge University Press, December, 1987
[2]Source: "Foreign Language Enrollments in U. S. Institutions of Higher Education for Fall 1986" by Richard I. Brod ADFL Bulletin 19:2 (January, 1988)
[3]Source: Bureau of the Census, Foreign Trade Division, December, 1988

▼ Table 17.4

You can become more effective in intercultural events if you *choose* to develop them, but you must make an active choice.

Definitions

To understand the problems that are created from having contacts across cultural and national boundaries, it is important to understand the definition of a culture. Benjamin Whorf argued that culture and language are so closely tied together they are inseparable.[3] The structure of the language determines both thinking and behavior.

Culture

When we use the term *culture,* there is no shortage of definitions. For example, the revised edition of *The Random House College Dictionary* defines culture as "the sum total of ways of living built up by a group of human beings and transmitted from one generation to another."[4] This definition is somewhat broad, but it does focus on two important concepts. First, it focuses on "ways of living." Second, it focuses on "transmission" of those ways of living.

The ways of living are patterns of behavior. These behavior patterns conform to a culture's norms. They are often unexpressed and invisible premises upon which reason is placed. In short, they are basic assumptions that "go without saying." Transmission of those norms, of course, is a communication function. A cross-cultural sojourner must learn the norms in order to have a satisfying cross-cultural experience.

Anthropologist Dorothy Lee took a symbolic interactionist position when she defined culture to mean ". . . a symbolic system which transforms the physical reality, what is *there,* into experienced reality."[5] This is very similar to Raymonde Carroll's definition. "My culture," she wrote, "is the logic by which I give order to the world. And I have been learning this logic little by little, since the moment I was born, . . ."[6] This, too, is a broad definition. It pinpoints human communication behavior as the locus of culture.

Notice, however, that it does more. It makes clear that how people use the language of their culture controls the way they experience the world. If we do not at least share the fundamental assumptions of a language, we do not (and can not) experience the world in the same way.

According to Richard W. Brislin, "a culture can be explained as an identifiable group with shared beliefs and experiences, feelings of worth and value attached to those experiences, and a shared interest in a common historical background."[7]

A culture is an identifiable group whose members share beliefs, customs, communication patterns, and a common history.

Again, the focus of the definition is helpful. Brislin points to an identifiable group, an "in group" if you will, that shares beliefs, experiences, and so forth. They operate on shared assumptions. Because they are fluent with those assumptions, they do not often consciously think of them. If they are not part of the "in group," people encounter ambiguity in our cross-cultural encounters.

Clifford Geertz understands culture to be "an historically transmitted pattern of meanings embodied in symbols, a system of inherited conceptions expressed in symbolic forms by means of which men communicate, perpetuate, and develop their knowledge about and attitudes toward life."[8] Carley H. Dodd wrote that "culture is the total accumulation of many beliefs, customs, activities, institutions and communication patterns of an identifiable group of people."[9] Thus, there are many ways to define the term *culture*. Each way emphasizes something special about the concept.

For the purposes of this chapter, a **culture** is an identifiable group whose members share beliefs, customs, communication patterns, and a common history through communication behavior.

Subculture

A **subculture** is a culture within a culture. Thus, the idea of subculture is not demeaning. A subculture is not "less than" nor "subordinate" to another culture. It merely exists within the context of a larger culture. For example, a broad range of ethnic subcultures exists within the broad context of American culture. Subcultures in the United States, in general, share language, a sense of place, and so forth.

In some ways, each subculture resembles the larger culture, but each one may be identified as unique and separate from the larger culture by certain distinct features. Race, age, geography, national origin, linguistic patterns, and a large number of vocational and avocational mores and norms identify specific subcultures. Given such a definition, it could be said that as a "college student" you are part of the "college subculture."

The implication embodied in these definitions is that if you don't share the communication behaviors, the history, the beliefs and customs, and the basic assumptions, then you cannot participate in the culture. This is the problem of intercultural communication.

We tend to take others for granted; thus, we tend to ignore the differences between ourselves and people from different cultures. Sometimes, we may assume that our culture is the dominant culture of the universe and that all other cultures are either derived from ours or inferior to it. Too often, Americans violate basic behavioral norms when they travel across a cultural boundary. Too often, they decide that people who are different from us are inferior to us.

Culture Shock

Some individuals, when they sojourn across a cultural boundary, especially for an extended period of time, experience a phenomenon called culture shock.[10] **Culture shock** is the psychological reaction of stress that sometimes occurs when an individual enters a culture very different from their own. Whether or not you experience culture shock, you may find that communicating across cultural boundaries is stressful. (See table 17.5).

At least six phenomena contribute to the stress that some people experience when they move into another culture:

1. Strain resulting from the effort required to adapt psychologically to the new culture.

2. Sense of loss of friends, of status, of profession, of possessions, and so forth.

3. Rejection by (or of) the new cultural group.

4. Confusion of role and role expectation, of values, and so forth.

5. Emotional response to striking cultural differences.

6. Feelings of impotence resulting from the inability to cope with the new culture.

Adler's Five-Stage Theory of Culture-Shock Development

Stage	Perception	Emotional range
CONTACT	Differences are intriguing. Perceptions are screened and selected	Excitement Stimulation Euphoria Playfulness Discovery
DISINTEGRATION	Differences are impactful. Contrasted cultural reality cannot be screened out	Confusion Disorientation Loss Apathy Isolation Loneliness Inadequacy
REINTEGRATION	Differences are rejected	Anger Rage Nervousness Anxiety Frustration
AUTONOMY	Differences and similarities are legitimized	Self-assured Relaxed Warm Empathic
INDEPENDENCE	Differences and similarities are valued and significant	Trust Humour Love Full range of previous emotions

Source: P. S. Adler, 'The transitional experience: an alternative view of culture shock.' *Journal of Humanistic Psychology,* 15 (1975), 13–23. Copyright © 1975 by A. S. Adler. Reprinted by permission of Sage Publications, Inc.

▼ Table 17.5

Imagine a situation in which the traveler exercises nearly complete control of the decision making. A long-awaited vacation trip provides an example. The traveler plans carefully, saves money, and then travels to an island in the Caribbean to escape the winter weather.

Behaviour	Interpretation
Curiosity Interest Assured Impressionistic	The individual is insulated by his or her own culture. Differences as well as similarities provide rationalization for continuing confirmation of status, role, and identity.
Depression Withdrawal	Cultural differences begin to intrude. Growing awareness of being different leads to loss of self-esteem. Individual experiences loss of cultural support ties and misreads new cultural cues.
Rebellion Suspicion Rejection Hostility Exclusive Opinionated	Rejection of second culture causes preoccupation with likes and dislikes; differences are projected. Negative behaviour, however, is a form of self-assertion and growing self-esteem.
Assured Controlled Independent 'Old hand' Confident	The individual is socially and linguistically capable of negotiating most new and different situations: he or she is assured of ability to survive new experiences.
Expressive Creative Actualizing	Social, psychological and cultural differences are accepted and enjoyed. The individual is capable of exercising choice and responsibility and able to *create* meaning for situations.

▲ Table 17.5 continued

In contrast, the refugees from war torn Southeast Asia, who have settled in many American cities, may have been forced by political factors into their cross-cultural encounter. Their stress levels are probably higher than those experienced by the vacationer.

IT'S MORE FUN TO KNOW

Personal Worry and Personal Success

People who worry a great deal about social problems beyond their control also probably worry more about their personal success and personal relationships. Self-esteem appears to affect reactions to society, as well as personal situations and experiences.

Comment . . .

These results suggest that people with low self-esteem (self-concept) spend a considerable amount of time worrying about both themselves and world problems that they are powerless to change. Applying this to intercultural communication, it seems that raising self-esteem could reduce self-consciousness in a new culture. With a better self-concept it could be easier to focus on the positive aspects of an intercultural experience instead of worrying about cultural differences beyond an individual's control.

See Glynis M. Breakwell, Chris Fife-Schaw and John B. Devereux, ''The Relationship of Self-Esteem and Attributional Style to Young Peoples' Worries,'' The Journal of Psychology, 122 (3), (May 1988), pp. 207–215.

Predictors of Communication Problems

Is there a way to predict the likelihood of culture shock? In the foreword of *Culture Shock: Psychological Reactions to Unfamiliar Environments,* Walter J. Lonner suggested that at least six categories of variables might predict how seriously an individual person would be affected by culture shock.[11]

Control Issues

First, individuals who travel across cultural lines, whether or not they leave their own country, may encounter certain **control issues.** That is, how much control does the individual have to decide whether to engage people from the other culture.

Intrapersonal Factors

Second, Lonner speculated that there must also be certain **intrapersonal factors,** such as a person's age, language skills, tolerance for ambiguity, and prior cross-cultural experiences that contribute to the amount of stress felt in a cross-cultural encounter. For example, students sometimes travel abroad as part of their educational experiences. A person with only one term of study in the French language, who had never before left home, and who is fairly shy, will probably experience more stress on a study tour than will the gregarious French major who spent last summer with French-speaking relatives in Quebec.

Biological Factors

Third, **biological factors,** such as overall physical conditioning and special dietary needs, can create stress problems. Imagine the strain that must result if a traveler cannot keep up with the group. Imagine the discomfort if a traveler cannot tolerate the local food or has to carry along special foods for dietary reasons.

Interpersonal Factors

Fourth, **interpersonal factors,** such as the extent of one's support group, can influence the stress a person experiences when moving across cultural lines. For example, suppose a student, Bill, decides to spend the summer traveling in Europe. The knowledge that he can call home for financial help *if* he needs it must be comforting to him as he sets off across Europe on his own.

Similarly, international students can find themselves adrift in the environment on an American campus. Some years ago, a professor's family shared their home with a young woman from Japan who had traveled to the United States to study English. Both the host family and the young woman experienced tension involving common events such as food preparation and eating habits and toilet and hygiene habits.

The trouble became apparent when the young woman began to withdraw from the American family. Rather than join the family at meals, for example, she excused herself on the grounds that she had to study. Then, later, she would prepare her own meal. Rather than study in her room, she went to the home of Japanese friends to study and to escape the culture shock that she was experiencing. She went on a buying spree, using a credit card that her father had provided, to purchase many new clothes and artwork for the walls of her room. Then, the long distance telephone bills began to arrive; she had been calling home late at night. Before the end of the academic year, the young woman was experiencing such stress that she returned home.

The Japanese woman was suffering from culture shock. She was under stress from her effort to adapt psychologically to her new environment. She was also aware that the host family was experiencing some of that stress in attempting to adapt to her presence. In addition, she obviously sensed the loss of friends, status, and possessions. Her telephone calls, her withdrawal from the American family, her rejection of the American cultural group, and her embracing of the Asian students on campus provide an indication.

She appeared to be confused about her role in the family. The family tried to make her a welcome guest by including her in the family circle, although she had difficulty with such familial intimacy.

For example, the Japanese student experimented with how she could be most comfortable when addressing the one man in the family. He invited her to use his first name, but she could not. "It would be too familiar," she said. The titles, Dr. and Mr., both of which she used for a while, seemed too formal. She tried to join the adult children, who called him "dad," but that didn't seem to fit. Japanese women develop a relationship with their mother's oldest brother, and they depend on that person for adult male understanding. She could not use the designation, "uncle," because "that is so special for me." Finally, she settled on the French *mon pere,* which translates, "my father." It was a compromise in her mind and a shortening of "my American father." She reasoned that she could not use English or Japanese for this designation because "it wouldn't be right," but the French provided her with enough distance to be comfortable.

Space and Time Factors

A fifth variable, **space and time** factors, can contribute to stress when an individual crosses a cultural boundary for a long time. A one-week visit to Rome would not be as stressful as a long trip in Italy. The nine-month winter in northern Canada would cause greater stress than a week-long visit at Christmas. A nine-month stay as a foreign student at Moscow State University in a dormitory room that is one-third the size of a comparable accommodation at an American campus can create difficulties in adapting to the foreign environment.

Geopolitical Factors

Finally, **geopolitical factors** play a part in developing stress from a cross-cultural experience. To visit a region in political strife—parts of Latin America, for example, or parts of the Middle East—creates levels of anxiety because of the unpredictability.

These six factors can serve as predictors of cultural stress. You can use them to estimate the likelihood of having difficulty with cross-cultural encounters.

Suggestions for the Cross-Cultural Sojourner

The following five recommendations are designed to help you communicate more effectively and more successfully in those events that involve people from a different culture. As you read, keep in mind that it's important both to remain free of cultural ethnocentrism and to remember where you come from and who you are. It is not possible to give specific recommendations about every culture; therefore, each of these pieces of advice is broad enough to apply to a variety of situations and each one covers a set of related suggestions.

Learn the Rules of the New Culture

As a cross-cultural traveler, you probably don't know the other person's world view. Do not assume that you know it. Instead, study. Read about the culture. Learn to ask questions.

For example, Americans are generally taught to value progressiveness. Americans are generally outgoing. There is a fundamental assumption in our society that people should compete. These assumptions of our own culture may be inappropriate in some other culture. For example, Japanese and Native American cultures both place a strong emphasis on teamwork and may be offended by the selfishness of individual competition as it is often found in majority American culture.

So study. Learn to ask questions. Ask them before you go into the other culture. Ask them while you are in the other culture. Ask for guidance about when to be direct and when to be indirect. Ask for information that will reduce your uncertainty. Ask about the norms of the culture.

Learn as much as you can about another culture before you enter it. Continue to learn while you are there.

Learning about another culture implies that you must discover the rules of behavior. Beyond that, learning about another culture means to discover, so far as possible, the prevailing attitudes and values of that culture.

For instance, there are some fundamental differences between the American culture and the French culture in attitude about one's home. Americans are open. Their homes reflect this openness in many ways. Americans are comfortable leaving their windows uncovered so that people walking by can look inside their homes. Americans are casual about separating their lawns from the street. More often than not, no fence demarks that separation. Americans, especially in suburban communities, frequently mark their territorial boundaries with shrubs and trees, not walls.

In contrast, the French home is generally considered a very private place. It is separated from its neighbors by walls and fences for privacy. French families rarely feel comfortable in their homes, especially at meal times, unless the blinds are drawn.

Therefore, try to develop a respect for another's traditions and to resist the tendency to impose your own cultural traditions on others. For example, there are broad cultural differences in the roles women play in societies around the world. American women enjoy a level of freedom that is virtually unheard of in some cultures. It's apparent that a cross-cultural traveler must be alert for any such differences and must plan in advance how to handle them.

Thus, first learn the rules about cross-cultural communication.

Assume Responsibility

A person who crosses a cultural boundary ordinarily chooses to do so. This choice implies a responsibility to serve as a liaison between your own culture and the new one.

Try to learn the language of the new culture. At least, learn as much of the verbal language as you can, given the circumstances of your situation. In addition, learn as much as you can about the nonverbal messages systems. Anecdotes about communication problems due to such differences as touching norms, posture cues, proximity, and gestures are common.

Language classes are commonly taught in colleges and universities. Courses are also available on video and audiotape, and self-study books are available. What prevents most people from learning another language seems to be the inconvenience of the regimen.

To learn Spanish or French, German or Japanese, or any other language means memorizing the words and practicing the pronunciation to use them. It requires a persistent effort that some Americans don't want to sustain, so they don't bother. This message to another culture means that Americans practice linguistic ethnocentrism, which is both offensive and unnecessary.

For example, an American citizen once approached a ticket agent in a French station. "Do you speak English," she asked in English. The Eurail agent smiled, made a sad face, shook his head, and said, "No."

"What? You don't speak English? I thought all ticket agents spoke English!" The Frenchman made a show of his apology. He was sorry, but he did not speak English. Furthermore, he was truly sorry that the American was so frustrated that she stalked out of the building.

Moments later a second American entered the room and approached the ticket agent. In halting French, this person asked the same question: "I'm sorry to ask this. Do you speak English?" This question, spoken in French, brought a smile and a chuckle from the agent, who then replied in flawless English. "Of course. How can I help you?" Subsequently, the second student's effort to learn and to use the French language sent a positive signal to the ticket agent.

Learn the language. At least, learn as much of the language as possible. Learn greetings, for example. Learn to ask and to give proper names, and learn the rules that govern using a person's name. For example, speakers of American English have come to rely upon the word "Ms." (i.e. pronounced "mzzz") to address a woman whose marital status is unknown. Does such a convention exist in a foreign language? How is a woman addressed in the country where you plan to visit?

Learn the language conventions that govern conversation. American language conventions are not universally shared by other countries. For example, to the French, a conversation is something special. It affirms and reveals the nature of the ties between the participants. If a Frenchman notices that a conversation is lagging, or that someone new has approached a conversational group, he may very well change the subject in mid-sentence. An American may find such behavior rude, especially if the Frenchman initiated the conversation by asking for the American's opinion. In addition, to the Frenchman, the American's response to such a question may seem like a lecture, may seem too long, may seem too detailed, or may seem too developed for the conversation. So learn the conventions that govern conversation.

Learn to count. Learn the money system and to recognize and name the bills and coins. Learn to tell time. Learn to ask in the other language for help with a language translation.

In addition, remember that the other person speaking English may also be translating English into another language. Speak slowly and distinctly. Offer and ask for clarifications, and learn to listen carefully.

Listen for unintentional meanings. A person translating another language into English may mistake one word for another. Be sure to respect their effort to speak English. Don't correct their English or grammar. Rather, understand the difficulty and paraphrase often. For example, you might say something like, "I want to be sure that I understand you. You would like me to. . . ."

As a liaison, it's wise to avoid talking about politics. Besides, it is difficult to understand the political situation in a host culture. Even if you did understand it, running the risk of offending someone is seldom worth it. This does not mean, of course, that you should be oblivious to such information. Try to be aware of current events. However, at the same time, you need to recognize that those events, especially if they are local ones, may be thought of in a proprietary way. That is, the people may think that the events are none of your business.

It may also be unwise to talk about money. Your assumptions about money and your attitudes about its use may be substantially different from the assumptions and attitudes in another culture. In addition, in many parts of the world the American society is seen as a society whose affluence is based on greed. We are enormous consumers of energy and resources—a fact that is often resented in many parts of the world. If you express your ideas about money, you are likely to offend someone—something that a cross-cultural communicator can not afford to do.

A story makes this point. A person once returned home to the little community where he was raised after many years. In a sense, this return was a cross-cultural sojourn. On a Sunday morning, the visitor went to church. Someone asked him what he thought about spending the church's money to repair a fine old organ in the church. Foolishly, he answered and expressed his opinion as if a regularly attending member of the church. Actually, it was none of *his* business, and some of the members of that church made that clear.

Don't talk about sexual behavior or sexual matters. Although American men and women are fairly comfortable with such conversations, and although sexuality plays an important role in the social reparte of both men and women in America, this is not usually the case in other countries and cultures.

Furthermore, dress modestly and conservatively when traveling in another culture. A walk across any American college campus will confirm that young men and women in this country dress very casually, and often provocatively. We generally accept this casual dress as normal and appropriate, and we are largely unaffected by it.

A young woman in sandals, shorts, and a tight-fitting t-shirt is out of place in most of the Middle East, in most of Latin America, and in most of Asia. Indeed, her casual attire, while commonly found on many college campuses, may even seem out of place off campus in many American cities. As a subculture, college students may ascribe to a norm of attire that is slightly different from even the majority American culture.

Casual attire, along with loose sexual behavior in many of our movies and TV programs, has been largely responsible for the commonly held belief overseas that young Americans are sexually promiscuous. Both men and women can choose to dress less casually. Therefore, a more conservative and modest style of clothing is often appropriate when you travel into another culture.

Also, to succeed in cross-cultural communication is to assume responsibility for the communication. If your knowledge and ability fail you, ask questions. Involve yourself in bridging the gaps that separate you from others before you involve yourself in their affairs.

Observe Carefully

The cross-cultural traveler should also be a careful observer. This process begins by broadening your view of cultures. For example, if you think of a different culture as "foreign," you may already be imposing damaging assumptions upon it. To some, *foreign* implies *alien, strange,* and perhaps, *irrelevant.* Instead, try to think of a different culture as a resource.

Remember, what you know from past experience may not apply in a different culture. Because it is impossible to anticipate every cross-cultural encounter, some good advice is "do as others do."

When you find yourself in a cross-cultural situation, try to look beyond superficial conditions. For example, differences in temperature and climate can contribute to differences in clothing styles, but so can differences in economic systems. Therefore, what you first observe is often only a "surface" observation. A more important question is what gives rise to the surface conditions?

Another comparison between French and American cultures illustrates this point. American and French attitudes about the relationship between parent and child are quite different. A French woman knows that the birth of her child makes her accountable to other adults for her behavior toward that child. She assumes a debt to her society. Her role—more collectivist than an American woman's role—is to transform the child into a responsible member of French society.

In contrast, the American mother assumes more of a debt to the child than to society. Thus, her obligation to the child comes before her obligation to society. Therefore, her role is not so much to teach the child the rules of society, as it is to give the child every opportunity to develop their unique potential.

The first part of learning to tolerate differences is identifying your own prejudices.

A cross-cultural traveler should find a cultural model, then follow their lead. Do as that person does. Notice such things as the comfortable spatial distances between the model and other people. Notice the cultural model's eye contact with other people. Notice when the model is formal and informal, and try to find out the underlying cultural rules that govern the behavior. Also, notice how the cultural model uses time. What is a long time to them? If you are confused, inquire about the model's attitudes and opinions concerning these things.

Tolerate Differences

This advice points directly to a person's life orientations. Everyone develops prejudices. Unfortunately, some of these prejudices reveal themselves more strongly in our relationships with people of other cultures. We can observe racial strife, religious strife, political strife all around the world merely by watching the evening news or by reading the morning paper.

The first part of learning to be tolerant of differences is to identify one's own prejudices. Do you make decisions or choose actions based upon stereotypes? Are you confident that your stereotypes are correct? Are you confident that they apply in these particular cases? Pay attention to how you feel; ask yourself why you feel as you do, and then make any adaptations that seem warranted.

Try to take an *I'm OK—You're OK* orientation to people of other cultures. Accepting others means that you are resisting the temptation to change them. Accepting others means that you are accepting their opinions, even if they do not agree with you, and that you are working to understand other points of view, rather than trying to reshape them into your own image.

You must learn the premise for situations. For example, in France a "friend" is carefully chosen over a period of time. French people don't have many friends because of the special nature of friendship in that culture. A friend is very special. A French friend will take charge of a situation for a friend, and the friend will allow it.

For example, suppose you complain to a French friend that you are not feeling well. Your French friend may take control by bringing food to your house and preparing it. Or, your French friend may announce in a preemptory tone, "I will pick you up at nine. You will go to the country with us. You need to relax and to rest. Don't make a scene about this, you can't say no."

An American would probably withdraw from such behavior because it would seem to be an imposition on the friend. Beyond that, such behavior might be seen to imply that the American is incapable of handling their own affairs.

Remember that people's views differ greatly about many things. Attitudes about work—especially those things that concern what is proper task-related behavior and social behavior—vary widely. We have already mentioned time and space differences, and the fundamental assumptions that are carried in language. Other things that differ from culture to culture include *roles,* for who does what; questions about superior/subordinate relationships flowing from hierarchy, class, and status; and basic assumptions about the importance of the group and the importance of the individual. Also, to whom do you talk? With whom do you seek interactions? In nearly every culture, the distinction between in group and out group makes an important difference. Cross-cultural travelers accustomed to being a part of the in group at home will undoubtedly find that they are part of the out group overseas. What seems reasonable to an American may seem superstitious in other countries.

All people categorize bits and pieces of information as a way of organizing the complexities of the world. However, people do not always make similar categories. Thus, **categorization** and **differentiation** can be a basis for cross-cultural differences. Moreover, people account for the existence of things according to their own cultural assumptions. Thus, **attribution** can be an important source of cross-cultural misunderstanding.

For example, consider an American naturalist who, on his afternoon walk through the woods, "discovers" a new specie growing there. In our society, we understand that the naturalist's discovery was something *already* there. The newness exists only in the mind of the naturalist.

A different culture might understand knowledge differently. Some primitive cultures, for example, might attribute the existence of the new specie to the whim of a god, who actually put the specie there at that moment for the amusement of the naturalist.

It doesn't matter who's right or wrong. The differing views are *experienced* as right by the members of the respective cultures.

Similarly, such a pervasive concept as "the week" is only a product of culture. There is nothing "natural" about it.[12] The week is merely a concept. George Lakoff devoted his monumental work, *Women, Fire, and Dangerous Things: What Categories Reveal about the Mind* to the study of alternative conceptual systems.[13] It argues that our traditional view of knowledge may be totally wrong.

Each of us carries an image of reality, of how it is and how it's supposed to be, that may not be shared by people of another culture. Their reality, if different, does not automatically become "wrong," while ours is "right."

Learning to tolerate others also implies learning to be positive by affirming others. Rather than looking for differences in a host culture, look for similarities. Try to empathize with others and to develop some patience.

For instance, America is a nation of fast things. We love fast cars and fast boats. We want to travel across great distances in fast planes. We buy fast food. We're impatient with standing in line. We assume our cars will never break down, and we like to arrive "just on time." But what does this mean, exactly?[14]

To North Americans, time refers primarily to a duration between two points. We think in units of such time, usually of about five minutes in duration. Thus, we're "on time" if we arrive within five minutes of an appointment. If we arrive ten minutes after the appointed time, we're "late" so we apologize. If we're going to be more than ten minutes late, we owe an apology and a telephone call to the person who is expecting us to be on time.

In contrast, Arabs work in units of about fifteen minutes in duration. To arrive within fifteen minutes is to arrive "on time." An Arab may apologize if they arrive thirty minutes late, but won't consider this to be offensive.

Finally, learning to tolerate others can mean learning to devalue your privacy. In the United States, we are accustomed to lots of privacy. We have private bedrooms, private bathrooms, private homes, private cars, private airplanes, and so forth. Not everyone in the world has, or even cares for, such privacy. To accept someone who comes from another culture and to accept the other person's culture may require you to accept what you may think is an invasion of your privacy.

Thus, learn to be tolerant of differences. It will not be easy, but it will be worth the effort.

Develop Flexibility

Develop some emotional flexibility. This begins with self-acceptance. To be able to adapt to new situations is to trust that you are OK, and that, therefore, the need for adaptation has nothing to do with personal inadequacy. Accept yourself, if you can. Remind yourself that you are OK just the way you are. That self-acceptance will give you permission to develop emotional flexibility.

Remind yourself that not everyone has to like you and that you do not have to like everyone. You may encounter people from other cultures who do not like you. This does not mean that you are unlikable, and it certainly doesn't mean that you are culpable in any way. Their needs may be different from your own. Their values may be different from your own. Their cultural assumptions may almost certainly be different from your own. Remind yourself that you are OK, that you are not guilty, and that not everyone has to like you.

If a conflict occurs, try to be sensitive to the values that are operating. It will probably be helpful for you to talk about any conflict or tension that you feel and to give others the benefit of the doubt. For example, you might say something like, "Hassan, I don't want you to be upset, but I still don't understand. Can you tell me more of what you see (or feel, or want)?" Then listen carefully to Hassan and be willing to respond as positively to him as you can. "I think I understand, Hassan. Can we find another option that we haven't considered?" Remind yourself as often as necessary that you are OK and that Hassan is also OK and that your conflict almost certainly flows from cultural differences. Look for a common ground.

Developing your flexibility implies opening yourself to the rich opportunities of a different culture. Try new foods. Try new sounds. Try new clothing and social activities. The more you experience these things, the more flexible and tolerant you become. As a result, your cross-cultural experiences should be more satisfying.

Don't Give Up

One last thing remains: Don't give up. If your attempt to use the language or to build the bridge between yourself and people from another culture fails, keep trying. There seem to be at least two messages involved every time you communicate with others. One of the messages is about your subject matter and the other is about you. Your attempt to communicate across cultural boundaries says a lot about you that is positive, whether or not it is a perfect or successful attempt.

Summary

This chapter identified the most common areas of cross-cultural communication problems and suggested remedies for them. It is clear that we need to improve our cross-cultural skills. Communication and transportation improvements, massive migrations, a dramatic increase in international business, and growing economic interdependence with the rest of the world have increased the likelihood of an extended cross-cultural sojourn.

The chapter defined the terms *culture* and *subculture*. Each of these definitions pointed to important problems in cross-cultural communication. Strain, sense of loss, rejection, confusion, negative emotional response, and feelings of impotence all characterize the stress of cross-cultural encounters. There is a way for an effective communicator to predict the likelihood of having one or more of these problems.

In the case of cross-cultural encounters, having this knowledge, in turn, would forewarn an individual and, hopefully, reduce the effects of the stress. Walter J. Lonner suggested six variables that might predict possible cross-cultural conflict, and these predictors were recommended to enable more effective cross-cultural communication:

- Learn the rules
- Assume responsibility for communication
- Learn to count
- Stay away from controversial topics
- Listen carefully
- Learn to observe
- Find a role model
- Develop tolerance for differences
- Remain flexible
- Don't give up

Communication across cultural and national boundaries can be frustrating, but it can also be exciting. As the world gets smaller, as you come increasingly into closer contact with other cultures, and as you travel more for work or play, the responsibility for having satisfying and successful cross-cultural experiences is mostly up to you. Like most things in life, you get out of it what you put into it.

Discussion Questions

1. Interview an international student. Explain that your purpose is to report the student's perceptions of cultural differences to your class. Ask about any interesting communication problems or anecdotes that the international student may have encountered in coming to your country. What might people from our culture have done to ease the stress of the international student entering our culture? Then report this interview to your class or to a small group of classmates.

2. Glance through back issues of *National Geographic* magazine until you find an article about another culture that you find interesting. Give a brief synopsis of this article to your class or small group. Include an analysis of the point of view of the article concerning any important cultural differences.

3. Interview someone from an ethnic subgroup. Explain that your purpose is to identify any misconceptions about their ethnic minority group. Report your findings to the class.

4. Try to secure precinct voting records from the last local election. Do those voting records suggest any attitudes or opinion patterns?

5. Working as a small group, develop a list of all of the words that you can think of for one of the following artifacts of American culture.

   ▲ money
   ▲ cars
   ▲ political campaigns

   Then discuss what it must be like to enter into our culture from a very different one.

6. Study the way that a conservative newspaper and a liberal newspaper treat the same current news item. What effect do you think the treatment of these items might have on a foreigner's opinions of people in your society?

References

[1]Stephen Phillips, "When U. S. Joint Ventures with Japan Go Sour," *Business Week* (July, 1989), pp. 30–31.

[2]Richard W. Brislin, *Cross-Cultural Encounters: Face-to-Face Interaction* (New York: Pergamon Press, 1981), pp. 8–10.

[3]Benjamin Lee Whorf, *Language, Thought, and Reality: Selected Writings of Benjamin Lee Whorf,* John B. Carrol, (ed.). (New York: John Wiley, 1956).

[4]*The Random House College Dictionary,* rev. ed. (New York: Random House, 1980), p. 325.

[5]Dorothy Lee, *Freedom and Culture* (Englewood Cliffs, NJ: Prentice-Hall/ Spectrum, 1959), p. 2.

[6]Raymonde Carroll, *Cultural Misunderstandings: The French-American Experience.* Carol Vold, tr. (Chicago: University of Chicago Press, 1988), p. 3.

[7]Richard W. Brislin, *Cross-Cultural Encounters: Face-to-Face Interaction* (New York: Pergamon Press, 1981), p. 2.

[8]Clifford Geertz, *The Interpretation of Cultures* (New York: Basic Books, 1973), p. 89.

[9]Carley H. Dodd, *Dynamics of Intercultural Communication:* 2d ed. (Dubuque, IA: Wm. C. Brown Publishers, 1987), p. 38.

[10]K. Oberg. "Cultural shock: Adjustment to new cultural environments," *Practical Anthropology* 7: 177–82.

[11]Walter J. Lonner in Adrian Furnham and Stephen Bockner, *Culture Shock: Psychological Reactions to Unfamiliar Environments* (London: Methuen & Co. Ltd., 1986), pp. XIX–XX.

[12]See Eviatar Zerubavel, *The Seven Day Circle: The History and Meaning of the Week* (Chicago: University of Chicago Press, 1989).

[13]George Lakoff, *Women, Fire, and Dangerous Things: What Categories Reveal about the Mind* (Chicago: University of Chicago Press, 1987).

[14]Richard W. Brislin, Kenneth Cushner, Craig Cherrie, and Mahealani Yong, *Intercultural Interactions: A Practical Guide* (Beverly Hills, CA: Sage Publications, 1986).

Sample Speeches

Informative Speech

Writing Professional Speeches: Seven Steps for Perfecting Your Craft

by Judith Humphrey, Public Affairs, Bank of Montreal

Delivered to the International Association of Business Communicators, National Conference, Toronto, Ontario, Canada, October 21, 1987

A recent article in *The Wall Street Journal* described the indignities of speech writing. The *Journal* quoted a writer who had just quit his job. The final straw: six days before his chief executive was to deliver a speech, this writer had received 24 separate critiques of his draft from 24 executives. The result, the writer lamented, was verbal "minestrone."

There are pleasures in speech writing, but such travails occur with unfortunate frequency. One writer I know was called to the executive suite to discuss an address he had submitted a few days earlier. Barely inside the door, he was startled to see the chief executive toss the draft unceremoniously into the trash. Another speech writer suffered just as devastating a fall from grace when the draft of a talk was returned with only one notation: a "C−" at the top of the first page.

No wonder, according to a recent U.S. study, speech writers last only a half dozen years and many pack it in after only two. The high salaries offered to these corporate "ghosts" seem well merited.

The challenges of speech writing are compelling. At worst, they may at times seem insurmountable. But to give yourself every advantage, produce well-crafted, clearly argued speeches. And that brings me to my subject today.

I'd like to suggest that there are seven steps to crafting an effective speech. If you follow these guidelines, you will produce professional addresses and probably even earn the praise of your most exacting clients.

Step one

Where do you begin? First, make sure that you know your topic thoroughly. The biggest failure of speech writers is that they too often fall in love with words and ignore the substance of their addresses. We who write speeches should begin by heeding Lewis Carroll's admonition: "Take care of the sense and the sounds will take care of themselves."

Research is often *the* major challenge for corporate speech writers. There are no shortcuts. You must be thorough and let the speech reflect this depth of your knowledge. Your clients generally are experts in their subjects, and so must you be. Otherwise, they will sound less informed than they are, and it will be your fault.

Step two

The second and, I think, the most important step in preparing an effective talk is defining the main idea. Knowing your subject is not enough. You must have something captivating to say about it.

Too many corporate speakers ramble on, as does Toad in *Wind and the Willows.* None of the animals liked his speech, but it was Rat who told him just why.

"Look here, Toad," Rat said one day. "It's about this Banquet, and very sorry I am to have to speak to you like this. But we want you to understand clearly, once and for all, that there are going to be no speeches and no songs." "Just one *little* song," Toad pleaded. "It's no good, Toady, Rat replied. You know well that your songs are all conceit and boasting."

"And gas," put in the Badger.

Many executive speakers similarly lack coherence or direction, because their address is without a central argument. As a result, they come across as having nothing—or paradoxically, too many things—to say. Such speeches are literally pointless, as is the act of listening to them.

How do you formulate the main idea of a speech? To begin with, this message must serve the corporate purpose. A speech is a corporate rather than a personal statement. The speaker represents the firm—and so should you. Excluding brief after-dinner remarks, all executive addresses should be statements from a company to one or more of its publics. Shape the argument accordingly.

The nature of the audience also will influence your thesis. You want to present a speech that is relevant and interesting to the audience's concerns. But remember that your first loyalty is to your corporation. And on occasion that means conveying unpleasant news, or speaking to a wider public than the one assembled to hear the speech.

The speech's message also must be tailored to the speaker. Writers should take their cue from the Chairman of a major financial institution who said he wanted his speeches to "soar." A CEO should speak very broadly, while those lower on the corporate ladder should confine their remarks to more restricted topics.

Finally, examine the message to make sure it comports with the facts. No matter how perfectly the argument satisfies the above requirements, if it is not borne out by your research, it must be abandoned. Not only by Keats, but for speech writers, "truth is beauty."

Once you have developed the speech's message, make sure that it appears in the text at the end of the introduction. Its placement at the doorway to the speech will tell the audience much about the rooms you will lead them through. All sections, paragraphs, sentences and words point toward this main idea.

Step three

The third fundamental step in writing a speech is developing a logical structure. Structural statements give shape and definition to your talk. They carry the speech's main idea from section to section.

To develop these signpost statements, begin with an outline. Make sure it consists of full sentences, not just "points." The main division statements in this plan will prove your overall argument, and the subdivision statements will support their respective main divisions. As you write, take the statements from your outline and put them into the body of the speech. Main division statements will appear at the beginning of each new section of the speech.

Step four

The fourth step in crafting a professional speech is using language effectively. With solid research, a main idea, and a firm structure to guide you, concentrate on choosing the best words. There are several criteria that should shape your use of language.

The speech's words and phrases should be *natural.* Good speeches seem like one side of an eloquent conversation. An excellent way to achieve this style is to read your words aloud as you write them. In doing that, you can assure yourself that the cadences and sound combinations work effectively.

If the tone is stiff and overly formal, try substituting more conversational expressions. Take a tip from Mark Twain, who as a journalist was paid by the word. "I never write *metropolis* for seven cents," said Twain, "because I can get the same price for *city.*"

In shortening words and phrases, you make your sentences friendly. But if that doesn't do the trick, break your sentences into smaller units, even one or two words. Sentence fragments provide an element of surprise. And emphasis.

Language should also be *personal.* Indeed, warm and inviting. Use the words "I" "you" and "we" freely. Expressions like "I believe, as I hope you will" immediately create a bond with those who are listening. Also use language that describes feelings—the speaker's or the audience's. In so doing you call upon the audience to share the speaker's viewpoint at the gut or emotional level. Use interactive words like "share" and "invite." For example, the statement that "I'm pleased to be here to share some of my views with you" conveys the sense that the speech is more than intellectual discourse— it is a gift, and offering.

So, as you write, get personal. The speaker, after all, is a person, and should come across as one.

Language also should be *vivid* and *concrete.* Beware of fuzzy expressions like "give and take," "management philosophy," and "employee input." Also shun abstract words like "change," "challenge" and "commitment." Some speakers ride high on this level of abstraction, and never get down to specifics. Their remarks lack credibility.

Follow the lead of John F. Kennedy. Theodore Sorensen, who wrote speeches for President Kennedy, says that Kennedy regarded words "as tools of precision, to be chosen and applied with a craftsman's care to whatever the situation required. He liked to be exact."

The language of a speech also should be *poetic*—replete with alliteration, metaphors, and other figures of speech. Such adornments, far from being superfluous, enhance meaning and emphasize relationships among ideas.

Let me suggest just a few of the figures of speech you can use to embellish your speeches.

—*Anaphora* is the repetition of the same word or words at the beginning of successive clauses or sentences. An example is Winston Churchill's famous exhortation: "We shall fight on the beaches, we shall fight on the landing grounds, we shall fight in the fields and in the streets, we shall fight in the hills; we shall never surrender."

—*Anastrophe,* less commonly known but equally effective, is an unusual arrangement of words or clauses within a sentence. For example, "one ad does not a survey make" (Puegot ad).

—*Alliteration,* or the repetition of initial sounds in a series of words is a well-known and effective device. Take the following example: "We need to return to that old-fashioned notion of competition—where *substance* not *subsidies,* determines the winner."

There are other figures of speech that can be used to enhance your writing. Use them and enjoy them.

A final note on language is that it should be *non-sexist.* This may be obvious, but most speeches that I read still demean women. Let me give you some actual examples: "The casual newspaper reader learns more about corporate layoffs than *he* wants to know." (I guess females don't read newspapers.) How about rephrasing: "newspaper readers learn more about corporate layoffs than they want to know." Or another: "In 1985 our company provided more than 100,000 *man days* of training to employees." (I guess women weren't worth training.) Why not just "days of training."

To summarize, make the language of your speeches natural, personal, vivid, concrete, poetic, and nonsexist. Keep these attributes in mind as you write the speech.

Step five

The fifth step in speech writing is embellishing the text with anecdotal material. When you write, your concern should be to develop the main idea effectively, and to use language that gives the fullest expression to your ideas. That's enough. Don't worry about punch lines and anecdotes while you are writing. But once you have finished drafting the speech, go back, and add your embellishing touches.

Humor takes more forms than "telling jokes." It consists of all those anecdotes, stories, quotations, and jokes we add to a speech to make it fun—for us, for our clients, and for the audience. Humor, says Russell Baker, "is like fine oil. It lubricates human motors and makes the difficult easier." Such embellishments help the speaker come across well.

Be careful, though. Humor can do more harm than good if it is not used properly.

To begin with, make sure that such material helps you make a point. Irrelevant anecdotes and jokes undercut a speaker's ideas. Further, your stories and anecdotes shouldn't offend anyone. Avoid all sexual, religious, and racial topics. Finally, make sure that your creative touches suit the speaker. If you quote Machiavelli and your executive wants to know "who this guy was," delete the quotation. If poorly told, humor can backfire, and the joke will be on the speaker.

Where should humor be inserted in the speech? The audience expects it—and you should deliver it—in the opening moments of an address. But try not to make this material too predictable. "I'm so glad to be here in Hometown, Canada" is a cliche. Why not turn such a convention on its head, and say, instead: "I wish I could say that I'm glad to be here, but I'm not." The speaker might then go on to say that she has been calling for educational reform for the past 12 years, and that's too long.

A light touch can also be used intermittently throughout the speech to revive interest and to underscore points. After you write a draft, go through your manuscript, and be on the lookout for factual statements that you can enliven with anecdotes. "I was shocked when I walked through the supermarket last Saturday . . ." is a much better illustration of inflation than is "according to a recent market analysis, food prices rose an estimated 37.9 percent . . ."

So, use humor throughout. But make sure it is relevant, inoffensive, well-delivered, and lively.

Now you have a speech. Print it out and send it to your executive.

Step six.

Your job, however, doesn't end here. The sixth step in the speech writing process is protecting the speech.

Those who write addresses know that the first draft is not the end. Indeed, as Isaac Bashevis Singer puts it: "The waste basket is a writer's best friend." The first draft is only your starting point for your edit. Moreover, even after you have produced an excellent draft, you cannot sit back and relax. Your executive will be reading the speech, the CEO may have to approve it, and various departmental heads will probably have to sign off on it. They all will have something to add to, or subtract from, the text. It is your job to avoid "minestrone," and make sure the speech is not destroyed.

Have confidence in yourself and your work. Although the executives getting the text may know the subject matter as well as or better than you do, you are the expert on this speech. So, resist incorporating changes that violate the integrity and purpose of the speech. Make sure that the speech's structural statements stay intact. Executives often prune these sentences, without realizing their essential role. Also make sure that the revisions do not pull the speech away from its main idea. Speakers sometimes feel a speech is a grab bag for any and all of their views. Fight any changes that clutter the text, or the speech will not develop its argument effectively.

As a speech writer, you are managing the process. Don't argue with the executive, but behind the closed door of your office, "edit" executive changes and minimize them wherever appropriate. You will be doing the speaker a favor if you use your judgement in this way. Most executives I have worked for seem relieved that I did not use all their suggestions.

Step seven

Your seventh, and final, task as a speech writer is managing the delivery and distribution of the speech. Take time to prepare the text for the podium. Large type and lots of white space on the page make the remarks easier to deliver. You may also want to work with the speaker on podium skills—either by listening yourself, hiring a speech coach, or both. You should also assist the speaker by marking up the text for delivery.

When the applause dies, you've done most of the work, but you've reached only a small portion of your potential audience. So, market the speech aggressively. Make sure that it gets full distribution to the media, to the business community, and to government. Your department may have a media relations specialist, but it's your job to work with that individual, to make sure that the speech is "delivered" to this broader audience. Your executive will be grateful to you, and will think still more highly of the speech, if it gets media attention.

Don't stop there. Rewrite the speech as an article. Send it to the trade press. Then turn it into an op/ed piece for local and national newspapers. Finally, transform the speech into an article for your employee magazine.

Now you are done, and can breathe more easily, until the next assignment arrives on your desk. In fact it's probably already there, awaiting your fine touch!

Who said speech writing is easy? Certainly not the guy who received the C−. In the best of circumstances, you may not be able to avoid entirely the indignities of the craft. But if you follow the fundamentals I have sketched in today, you will have the pleasure of knowing you have done a masterful job. And you very likely will please your master.

Persuasive Speech

Investment for the Beginner

Boyd Johns, student

Most of us want to have a comfortable life, a good job, and a promising future after we finish college. We think that these things are possible because we have a college education.

Oh, yes, we should get ourselves a good job. At least it should be one with a chance for advancement and it should be a challenge for us. Because we have spent several years without some of what we call the "advantages" that our high school friends have had for several years, we want those too. By "advantages," I mean a new car and a nice apartment.

But what about the long run? Suppose you have that "good job." Suppose you have a nice apartment. What's next? Where is the money going from your check except to cover your living expenses?

I want to talk to you today about a systematic savings plan that can help you have the money you need when you decide to buy that house or send your children off to college.

Let me paint a picture for you. You have your steady job and you receive a check every two weeks. You've worked out your budget and there is some flexibility in your spending after you've paid your monthly bills. Consider this choice. Become an investor.

No! You're not going to be a Wall Street tycoon, but you can have some of the same advantages the big investors enjoy. Let me tell you about it. This is one of the most interesting and promising ways that you can invest in your future. Here's an interesting and sophisticated way to provide money for your future needs.

Each month, you invest $10 or $20 in a "no-load" mutual fund. Your money is combined with the investments of thousands of other people like you. They don't understand much about what stocks to buy or sell, but they know that the stock market usually rises faster than inflation. So, they put their money in a mutual fund. Let me explain how a no-load mutual fund operates.

A mutual fund is run by what is called a "regulated investment company." That means it is regulated by law and must give its investors a complete record of its investments and the performance of those stocks and bonds. In other words, every calendar quarter they must tell you, the investor, how your investment is performing. So you're not left in the dark about the gains or losses in your investment during the quarter. You also can check on the value of your fund (we could call it your investment) by looking at the financial pages of any major newspaper.

The mutual fund "pools" your money with other investors' money. Suppose that Paul, Mary, Jane, and Frank each invest $30 a month in mutual fund XYX. Their $120 is invested by the managers in several stocks. Of course, there are many other people also investing so the managers may be investing thousands and thousands of dollars in twenty or thirty different attractive stocks. In our illustration, Mary, Jane, Frank, and Paul each own a "share" or piece of the mutual fund. If the stocks that the fund owns go up, the value of their investment goes up. If the stocks go down, the value of their investment goes down.

What investors do with mutual funds is what professionals call "pool their risk." That means they spread their investment money around. They don't put all of their eggs in one basket. If they had put all their money in one month in General Motors stock and the stock decreased in value, then they would have a loss. With a pooled risk, an entire group of stocks (often twenty to forty) would have to fall for them to lose part of their investment. Mutual fund investors do not "make a killing" but they profit from the traditional slow, upward movement of the stock market.

At the end of a year, if you have invested $20 each month, your total investment would be $240. What would the value of your mutual fund be? It depends on how the market performs. Let me give you some examples. Some of the best performing no-load mutual funds during the last ten years have returned about 20 percent per year on investment. Let me put that in perspective.

If you had invested $240 during the year and you had a 20 percent return, your $240 would have increased to $288. Compare that amount to the same sum in a savings and loan or a bank. In those institutions, your $240 would be worth about $255. It's easy to see that your money will grow much faster if you invest it. And, if you need the money for an emergency, you always can withdraw it.

One caution. The stock market can go down and your investment can lose some of its value. But you benefit because you have pooled your risk. The loss of value in your mutual fund would probably be less than the loss of a single stock. Again, that's an advantage of spreading your money across several investments.

Finally, your money is professionally managed. The mutual fund management spends its time looking at the best investments and making decisions for you. They spend their full time studying the market and changing investments when it seems appropriate.

So, you have professional management of your money, you get a better return on your hard earned dollars, and you can withdraw your investment when and if you want. Last, there is no charge for using a no-load mutual fund. That's where it got its name, "no-load," which means no charge.

So, if you want your money to work for you, if you want a professional to make your investment decisions for you, if you want a "nest egg" available for future events, and if you want it to grow as rapidly as reasonably possible, check out mutual funds. Remember, there's no commission for this service so isn't it worth at least investigating?

There's an old saying in the investment community, "Let your money work for you as hard as you worked to earn it." Think about your choices. Do you want to live without savings? Do you want to get the best return on your hard-earned money? Could you spare only $20 a month to start you on a career that makes a home or a college education for your children affordable?

I've brought along some brochures and prospects from two of the most successful and prominent no-load funds. Please take a look at them. I think you'll see that they are the conservative and wise approach to investment for the beginner. They offer one route to financial security for the college graduate.

(Reprinted with permission of Boyd Johns)

Special Occasion Speech

Measuring the Value of a College Education: How It Changes the Common and the Not So Common in Life

by Thomas E. Bellavance, President of Salisbury State College

Delivered to the Pocomoke High School Annual Honors Awards Dinner, Pocomoke, Maryland, May 11, 1985

The special occasion speech is included here, although it is not covered in the text. You will probably want to be familiar with this because it is a commonly used speech type.

ABOUT six months ago my eighth grade daughter came to my office after her school let out and asked if I could give her some ideas for a topic she had to write on for a paper that was due the following week.

Now as we all know, the male ego has been under siege these last fifteen years, but thankfully for us, the aged and beleaguered, fourteen-year-old daughters have not as yet been totally inducted into the ranks of the on-coming hordes. So with macho bravado I seized the moment for reborn glory and assured her there was absolutely no problem; just tell me your topic and we'll have this thing sewn up in a matter of minutes. And so with wide-eyed confidence in old dad, she let fall on me her topic: the meaning of a college degree—is it worth four years?

Suffice it to say I have survived my fall from deification in her eyes, and despite her use of some of the hackneyed phrases I provided her (out of pity, I suspect), she did manage to turn in a report on her own and net a "B+" for her efforts.

Now to be confessional with you, I'm going to try it again but this time without a total reliance on clichés.

What indeed is the value of a college education and is it worth four years of one's youth; four years of tuition payments; and four years without earning power?

(By the way, you'll notice I altered the question a tad, replacing "the value of a college degree" with "the value of a college education." Anyone with a modicum of intelligence, a lot of persistence, and plenty of time can usually amass the right combination of credits and eventually emerge with degree in hand. There is a little more to it if you're after an education.)

So what is the value of a college education?

On the quantitative, or measurable side, the answers are numerous and readily available.

1. Generally speaking those with a college education have open to them more job opportunities than those without.

2. Salary ranges during the course of one's career are higher (not always at the beginning but certainly over the long haul).

3. Such individuals, because they have mastered certain mathematic and/or language skills, are more adaptable to the needs of a rapidly changing technology and, therefore, will be more marketable in their own future.

4. And certainly such individuals find their social status enhanced by belonging to the degree club,—as a matter of fact, the degree has almost become a requisite for maintaining membership in the middle class.

Now, these are measurable values which, if you'll notice, have to do primarily with money and job security and, of course, constitute a legitimate argument for value.

But on close scrutiny, perhaps not that much.

After all, some could likewise argue that the same may be attained by joining the army (or if you want to play it safe, the Merchant Marines) for a thirty-year stint.

You can't beat it for job security, plenty of opportunity for advancement, free training in a skill, guaranteed income for the rest of your life at the approximate age of forty-seven, and at the same age, free to take on a new life if you want to.

On the other hand, what used to be considered the primary value of a college education—when it was reserved for the well-to-do and elite—had little to do with money or job security.

I am, of course, referring here to the qualitative dimension of a college education and its value to the individual's understanding of life.

It is on this count that I fell flat on my face with my daughter because I took the easy way out and fed her the clichés, all of which, I am sure, you have heard a hundred times: that is, a college education

Expands your horizons.

It broadens your perspective.

It enriches your life.

It deepens your awareness,

and

It cultivates your mind.

But what does that mean *really*—to broaden one's perspective or deepen one's awareness?

Well, what it means to me is having the ability to experience life on many levels at once and having the ability to grasp the fact that life is multi-faceted, not unidimensional; and the first and foremost value of a college education is not the financial edge, but the gift of seeing and understanding that.

Let me provide you with the simplest example I can think of, to give you some idea of what I'm talking about.

When I was a senior in high school, a tree to me was a tree, whether it was a pine tree, an apple tree, or a maple. Normally trees were things that obstructed my view. When I was younger, I climbed them and that was nice; when I was older I was required to rake their bloody leaves and that was not so nice—and, oh yes, in the summer now and then they were there for a little bit of comfortable shade. But on the whole, a tree was a tree. If you've seen one you've seen 'em all.

A college education changed that for me, along with a myriad of other common and not so common things in my life.

I took an art course, for example, and suddenly everything around me began to take on a new dimension, including my old friend the tree. It now stood as an example of form, of mass, dimension and perspective, not to mention color and shade; leaves were not just leaves but a spectrum of varying tints—an exercise in appreciating the psychologically cool and therefore calming effects of the silver-grey leaves of the Russian olive and the warm and stirring effects of the red and yellow autumn leaves of the maple. And the whole world of texture was also there, from the deep, rough bark of the dark and massive oak to the soft baby-like skin of the white, willowy birch.

Trees are interesting to me now when I look at them. They're an economic force, and in an earlier day elemental to survival; for they were then and continue to be lumber and fuel, telephone poles and railroad ties, bridges and boats. They're the reason we have paper, and the reason we have martinis. Thanks to trees we have turpentine, charcoal, acetone, cellulose, resin, tanning chemicals, rosin, potash, and a number of other important industrial compounds.

Some of the most fundamental laws of physics are brought to mind by the trees now, with its careful attention to leverage, supportive angles, and distribution of weight—not always apparent to the eyes when we consider its root system, which is a miniature twin of its crown; the flow of its sap alone from season to season, a brilliant feat of engineering and certainly no man-made instrument, tracks the path of the sun so simply, as does the leaf itself.

When I take the time to notice a tree, I think also of poets and tellers of tales—of Robert Frost's "Birches" and Kilmer's "Trees," of Shakespeare's "Royal Tree and Royal Fruit" and "The Last Leaf" of O'Henry. And there are any number of other staples of great literature that rustle my memory and stimulate my thoughts, like the graceful flexibility of Sandburg's Lincoln in adversity as the easy bending of the palm in a Florida gale.

Geometrically, the leaf in and of itself with its rib-like configurations, constitutes nature's prototype for man's octagons, pentagons, hexagons, and other polygonal structures.

Linguistically, it provides us with all sorts of metaphorical crutches to explain our human condition, from the tree of life to the tree of knowledge. We sometimes find ourselves up a tree or out on a limb; we nip things in the bud, and then go to the root of the matter. Success is often a matter of the proverbial acorn growing into the mighty oak. Recently the television serial "Roots" was aired, resulting in a great deal of interest in family trees.

Philosophically, the four seasons of our life are reflected in the life cycle of the tree:

The first bursting bud of spring,

The lush production of our summer fruit,

The falling leaf of our later years, and the

Stark lifelessness of the winter branch.

In the realm and religion, this is taken one more step, and the spring that follows the dead winter is the life that will blossom again after death.

And where but in the tree do we see better the fundamental principle undergirding most logical structures, from literature to computer science; from industrial organizations to demographic projections?

The genera and the species from the trunk to the limb,

From the limb to the branch,

From the branch to the twig.

This is the Bollean matrix underlying computer science, and the administrative flowchart of General Motors. No outline, no matter how detailed, is anything more than a thesis-statement trunk and a series of interrelated branches. In the nineteenth century, this very logic justified the political sway of Victorian England and the branches of her far-flung empire.

Thanks to a course in biology, the tree is also for me a world unto itself—a whole city of life, from the birds, squirrels, owls, and insects that inhabit it to literally an entire universe of seething microbes interrelating and vying with each other.

It is the source of oxygen and moisture in our atmosphere; it is the detective—through the science of dendrochronology—that tells us when an ancient culture lived, how long it existed, and when it disappeared. And for those of us, the living, it is a lesson in the natural propagation of the species. Those of you afflicted with allergies might find it interesting to know you are the victims of a wild sexual orgy going on right now within the plant world. And all of this just begins to scratch the surface when we talk about broadening one's horizons and enriching one's life.

If such a simple thing as a tree can be so interesting and complex, consider how this applies to that bewildering and paradoxical phenomenon known as man.

Certainly we have plenty of examples of what can go wrong when we fail to see man in all of his varying levels of existence; when we refuse to detect, comprehend, and appreciate that life is a variegated and complicated affair.

You know, the essential characteristic of an ignorant man is his compulsive insistence on simple answers to complex questions. Life to him is flat and two-dimensional; everything is reduced to a simple duality:

Them and us

Right and wrong

Good and bad

Friend and foe.

There's no in-between. There are no other levels open for consideration. These are the standard bearers and phrase-makers.

I recall 1970, the height of the Vietnam war, a war which was, as you all know from recent specials on T.V., one of the most complex and politically questionable engagements this nation has ever involved itself in, with the right and wrong of it still unresolved. Yet it was not uncommon to hear the uneducated person's simple view of it all—all the political issues, all the economic issues, all the military issues, all the historical issues, and all the moral issues summed up and concluded in one little phrase: America—love it or leave it. That on one side of the spectrum, and on the other: better Red than dead—simple answers to complex questions.

Let's go back a moment. It is the sixteenth century. The peoples of the Western World find it economically convenient to view the inhabitants of another continent as sub-human and therefore exploitable for economic reasons. Unlike oxen, however, they are found to be dangerous and must be chained and beaten into submission before they can be used for production. In time, and over this heinous practice, one nation is split asunder and civil war comes, and after that there is the careless and callous freeing of the "animals" in an alien land to fend for themselves. Because they are easily identifiable they are segregated, restricted to menial labor, socially confined and culturally stunted, with economic advancement and educational development categorically denied. For those who dare question or react, there is the cross, the mob, the hanging. A century of such conditioning on a people, a half-century of social unrest, a quarter of a century of some visible progress, yet much still remains unresolved: a situation with a five-hundred-year history, so complex that multi-million dollar institutions have been created to study and comprehend it. For the ignorant, however, the entire phenomenon is all very simple: They're "niggers."

Less than fifty years ago, we experienced a world-wide economic collapse. Crippling retributions of one nation exacted by others further exacerbate the financial implosion and subsequent unemployment and poverty in that country. Humans turn on humans; people are forced from their homes; places of business destroyed.

Ultimately families are ripped apart: the young and healthy packed in cattle cars and transported to work sites; the old and sick to another place. In time, there are hideous experimentations on human beings and finally the wholesale gassing and burying of bodies.

The why and wherefore of this thumbnail sketch fill thousands of volumes of research.But for the ignorant at the time, one word sufficed to explain and justify it all: Jew!

Just thirty years ago, if you lived in America, education was a liability. To think, to make distinctions, to act differently, to tolerate different lifestyles, to criticize the government—these things were dangerous; for the ignorant, during a brief span of time, held sway over the entire nation. And like it or not, everyone was labeled as either *us* or *them*. Either you were a real American or you were on the other side—a fellow traveller, a sympathizer, or a bona fide commie.

Beatniks were commies, strikers were commies, movie directors depicting America as something less than perfect were commies, professors were commies. In other words, whatever failed to fit a very narrow mold had to be *them* and therefore was sentenced to the commie side. And that's how the whole complex political aftermath of World War II was explained. And do you know what it took to bring people to their senses and admit, perhaps, that things were not quite so simple? The final and most bizarre accusation of them all—in the Senate hearing room—live and on national television—that the U.S. Army was a communist conspiracy.

The ability to detect and comprehend life as a variegated and complex phenomenon—that's what makes life interesting; that's what makes it worth living; and that's where I find the real value of education to be.

Be wary of the dogmatic, particularly in yourself. Remember there is usually no one single right answer or standard, only workable proximities. And this is trebly true when the subject under consideration is not a tree, but your fellow man.

Glossary

absolute present Principle that we can only live in the present and that our relationships are therefore always in the present.

abstraction Process of moving in language farther from a referent; of perceiving and making sense of language; of translating experience into language. A general concept that partially represents some whole.

accentuation Use of nonverbal messages to emphasize, heighten, or strengthen words.

accommodation Process of adjusting the frame of reference to integrate new information and experience.

acronym A word formed from the first letter or group of letters in a name or phrase, used as a mnemonic device.

action step Fifth step in Monroe's motivated sequence. Involves call for audience behavior.

active listening Technique that includes the skills of concentrating, frequent internal summarizing, interrupting, and paraphrasing what another has said.

adopter Movement or gesture displayed to alleviate psychological tension.

affect display Movement or gesture that reflects a feeling or the intensity of feelings.

affection Fondness or devotion to someone or some thing; liking. One of three interpersonal needs identified by William Schutz. In this context, affection is the desire to be liked by others and to develop loving relationships. Schutz identified three personality types related to the interpersonal need for affection: (1) overpersonal, (2) personal, and (3) underpersonal.

agenda for talking about relationships A list of all components of a relationship presented in an order that is convenient to follow in an interpersonal encounter. Included are observations, inferences, feelings, wants and expectations, intentions, openness, images, and check out.

aggressive Interactive style that is self-enhancing, belittling, controlling, and hurtful or damaging to others and to relationships.

ambiguity Quality of message that permits more than one interpretation.

analyst, the Mnemonic device to assist in remembering a behavior that punishes talk about negative feelings ("You fell that way because . . .").

approach-approach conflict Conflict over outcomes that are both desirable and undesirable. The actor is attracted by one and put off by the other.

argument A set of statements that makes a claim, offers support for the claim, and seeks acceptance for the claim.

argument by analogy A pattern of reasoning that claims that because two things are known to be similar in some particular ways, they will be similar in other ways, as well.

447

argument by authority A pattern of reasoning that claims that statements by an expert, or by some known person, are sufficient grounds for acceptance.

argument by cause A pattern of reasoning that claims one event, set of events, condition, or set of conditions brings about another event, set of events, condition, or set of conditions.

argument by example An inductive pattern of reasoning that claims something true of one case in a class or category is also true of some other case in the same class or category.

argument by generalization An inductive pattern of reasoning that claims what is true of certain members of a class or category will also be true of other members of the class or category, or of the category as a whole.

argument by sign A pattern of reasoning that claims the presence of some feature, artifact, characteristic, or condition is evidence of the presence of a related feature, artifact, characteristic, or condition.

art The disposition or modification of a thing by human skill.

artifacts Things people collect about themselves.

assertive Interactive style that is self-enhancing, expressive, and self-supportive, while protective of the choices of others. Not aggressive and not shy.

assimilation Process of changing what is perceived to fit a frame of reference.

association In persuasion, one of Hugh Rank's strategies for intensification by developing a connection in the receiver's mind between the speaker's cause, product, or candidate, and something or someone that the receiver already likes or dislikes.

attending In listening, the selective act of attention.

attention Process of responding to stimuli.

attention step First step in Monroe's motivated sequence. Designed to gain listener attention.

attitude "Mental and neural state of readiness organized through experience, exerting a directive or dynamic influence upon behavior, the individual's response to all objects and situations to which it is related." (Gordon Allport) Predisposition to respond.

attraction See "interpersonal attraction."

attribution Assumption that events and phenomena are caused. In cross-cultural communication, the belief that the existence of things may be accounted for according to the notions of one's own particular cultural assumptions.

audience adaptation Process of identifying and accommodating the needs, interests, and wants of an audience.

audience analysis Process of identifying and understanding the characteristic features of an audience.

audience participation Presentation technique that involves audience activity or expression.

autocrat One of three personality types identified by William Schutz with regard to the interpersonal need to control. Autocrats feel a need to dominate, to rise to the top of a hierarchy.

avoidance-avoidance conflict Conflict that results when avoiding an undesirable outcome will yield a different undesirable outcome.

avoiding Stage in relational deterioration characterized by overt efforts to break off contact and end the relationship.

b

balance State of emotional calm that results when perceptions seem consistent with expectations or our image of reality.

belief Statement about what is, developed from information outside the realm of personal experience. Three categories: primitive beliefs, surface beliefs, and derived beliefs.

bonding One of five stages in a relationship in which the partners make a special, voluntary, ongoing commitment, usually, but not always, in a public ritual.

c

categorization Process of grouping bits and pieces of raw information as a means of organizing the complexities of the world.

certainty Defensive behavior characterized by a rigid viewpoint and by both verbal and nonverbal suggestions that the speaker is correct and the receiver is incorrect. Closed-mindedness that creates defensiveness. Behavioral opposite of provisionalism.

chain of command The planned power and authority relationships of an organization.

channels The means of transmission; the vehicle or pathways through which messages are sent.

check out Colloquial term used as mnemonic device to help remember the importance of getting and giving feedback when talking about relationships.

chronemics Study of the human use of time.

circumscribing Stage in relational deterioration characterized by avoidance of topics and intimacy that might lead to self- disclosure.

claim An opinion or conclusion for which acceptance is desired.

claim of fact Statement about some past or present condition or relationship.

claim of policy Statement that calls for a course of action. Characterized by "ought" or "should." (e.g., "You ought to stop smoking.")

claim of value Statement about the value or worth of some idea or object, or some policy or practice.

clarity State or quality of being clear and intelligible.

closed questions Questions that limit and focus the response.

closed-to-open pattern A sequence of questions arranged from very specific to more open and general questions.

closing phase Closing stage in an interview. At this time, a review and clarification of agreements and key ideas should be discussed and goodby pleasantries should be initiated.

closure Process of adding information to perceptions of otherwise incomplete events.

code Set of symbols and signals used to convey messages. (See "language.")

coercive power Power that derives from ability to remove another's actual choices or perceptions that choices are available. Power that derives from force or the threat of force.

cohesiveness Sense, feeling, or property of wholeness, unity, or togetherness.

colloquium Format for public discussion that involves a panel of experts responding to questions from an audience.

command and instruction function Communication function of an organization that keeps units working toward goals, helps people stay within policy, and coordinates individual workers.

communication Process of transmitting and interpreting messages.

communication effect Any mental or behavioral change that results from communication.

compatibility Ability to coexist in harmony.

competence Perception that an individual is knowledgeable and able to perform in a given area. Language competence is knowledge and ability to use the elements and rules of language. Communication competence refers to social skill and interpersonal effectiveness.

complementary relationship Relationship, or view of a relationship, in which one person is superior and the other is subordinate, as in parent-child.

complexity In organizations, refers to the degree of differentiation or separation in an organization, both in terms of hierarchical structure and physical distance.

composition In persuasion, one of Hugh Rank's strategies for intensification in which the persuader compares or contrasts the product, cause, or person to something else, not only with language, but also with design features in the "immediate surrounding" of the language. (e.g., "I love NY" was first spelled with a heart for the o. Later, the heart symbol was used without the surrounding letters.)

compromise Conflict management strategy in which parties look for a position where each gives and gets a little, splitting the difference if possible; no winners and no losers.

conditioning Process of teaching or controlling behavior by making rewards and punishments contingent upon specific behavior.

conflict, interpersonal Form of competition. Situation in which one person's behaviors are designed to interfere with or harm another.

conflict, intrapersonal Condition or status of emotional tension. (See approach-approach conflict, approach-avoidance conflict, and avoidance-avoidance conflict.)

conflict phase Second phase in group decision emergence identified by B. Aubrey Fisher, in which group members address issues and test the direction and the positions they will take.

confrontation and problem solving Conflict management strategy in which energies are directed toward defeating a problem and not the other person. Parties look for a mutually beneficial solution.

confusion One of Hugh Rank's strategies for downplaying by introducing jargon, gobbledygook, information overload, inherently contradictory information, and so forth.

connotation The personal meaning of a word. Affective associations that an individual brings to a word. Connotation imbues language with value (right/wrong, good/bad), potency (hard/soft, hot/cold), and action (fast/slow).

consistency Perceptual process that causes us to perceive what we expect to perceive and to be uncomfortable when this is not the case. In attribution theory, the expectation that an individual will exhibit the same behaviors in similar situations. We respond to consistency by attributing the behavioral cause to the individual, and to inconsistency by attributing the behavioral cause to circumstances outside the individual.

content dimension Part of a communication event having to do with topics, objects, and events outside the relationship.

context Physical, social, psychological, and temporal environment in which a communication event occurs.

contingency school School of organizational leadership that rejected the idea that any one way to manage people and organizations was best. Rather, they argued that each situation is unique, and requires special and flexible consideration.

contradiction Denial. A statement in opposition to another statement. Use of nonverbal messages to negate verbal messages.

control (noun) Defensive behavior characterized by manipulation in an attempt to impose an attitude or viewpoint on another. One of three interpersonal needs identified by William Schutz. The degree of desire to exercise power and authority. Schutz identified two personality types related to the need to control: (1) abdicrat and (2) autocrat. Behavioral opposite of problem orientation. (verb) To exercise restraint, dominance, or direction over; to command.

control issues A predictor of communication problems in cross-cultural encounters. Questions of how much control an individual has in deciding to engage people from other cultures.

cooperation Process of working or acting together for a common purpose.

creative outlets One of Vance Packard's hidden persuaders. Involves desire to express oneself aesthetically.

creative thinking The process of developing new ideas or solutions, or recombining things already known into something different.

critical listening Part of the listening process in which four questions are asked to discover closed-mindedness or bias: (1) position, (2) agreement, (3) feeling strength, and (4) importance.

critical thinking The process of making judgments about the truth or merit of an idea.

cue Message that is not symbolic.

culture An identifiable group whose members share beliefs, customs, communication patterns, and a common history by means of their communication behavior.

culture shock The psychological reaction of stress that sometimes occurs when individuals enter a culture very different from their own.

d

decision emergence Phenomenon identified by B. Aubrey Fisher that describes how group decisions occur.

decision-making group See group.

decoder Mechanism or agent that decodes. In interpersonal events, each individual decodes the messages sent by the other.

deduction A reasoning pattern that moves from a general statement about a class or category to the conclusion that the statement applies in a particular case.

defensiveness State of having assumed a position or attitude to protect against attack. In interpersonal communication, manifested in such behaviors as evaluation, superiority, certainty, control, neutrality, and strategy. Behavioral opposite of supportiveness.

definition To mark the boundaries of some named thing. To state or describe the limits of meaning.

democrat One of three personality types identified by William Schutz with regard to the interpersonal need to control. Democrats are balanced and capable of taking charge or allowing others to be in control when appropriate.

denotation The dictionary definition of a word. Meaning of a word, as agreed to and shared by a speech community.

derived beliefs Beliefs derived from other beliefs.

description Supportive behavior characterized by factual information, absence of judgmental language, and straightforward questions.

differentiating Stage in relational deterioration characterized by focus on the individual and perception of self as separate from the other person and the relationship. In cross-cultural encounters, the process of perceiving differences between one's own and another's culture.

direct questions Questions that ask for specific information.

disconfirmation Process of ignoring or denying another's self-disclosure.

dissonance Emotional discomfort resulting from conflict between related elements in the attitude-value-belief structure. In extreme form, dissonance and guilt are synonymous.

distortion In the perception process, the actual changing of content to fit the frame of reference.

diversion One of Hugh Rank's strategies for downplaying by shifting the receiver's attention away from the thing to be downplayed.

division of labor Decisions made in an organization about who does what.

downplaying One of Hugh Rank's methods of persuasion in which one's own bad points or the opponent's good points are minimized. Strategies include *omission, diversion,* and *confusion,* each of which are defined elsewhere in this glossary.

dyad A two-person unit.

 e

ego gratification One of Packard's hidden persuaders. Basic appeal: "Your decision to act/buy/vote/accept, etc., expresses your special distinction."

ego states In Transactional Analysis, patterns of behavior reflecting the self-concept. There are three ego states: parent is the source of rules that govern behavior, adult is rational and conceptual, and child is emotional.

emblem Deliberate movement that can be directly translated into words; discrete, categorical behavior that is generally known and accepted.

emergence phase Phase in the evolution of a group decision in which final outcome of discussions begins to take form.

emotional security One of Packard's hidden persuaders. The basic appeal: "If you use/buy/select/act as persuader suggests, you won't have to worry."

emotions Words that we use to describe our physical feelings as they occur within particular contexts (e.g., fear, anger, joy, sorrow, shame).

empathic listening Part of the listening process; process of identifying one's observations of another's feelings, wants and expectations, intentions, openness, and images, and bringing them to the level of talk when they seem paramount or important.

empathy Supportive behavior characterized by identification with experiences, feelings, and problems of others and affirmation of another's self-worth.

employment interview Interview in which participants exchange information in order to make an employment decision. Sometimes called "job-search" and sometimes called "selection" interview.

encode To translate information from one form into another.

encoder The component of the communication process that translates information from one form into another; in speech, that which translates ideas into spoken words. A telephone mouthpiece serves as an encoder when it translates spoken words into electronic impulses.

entropy Tendency of an organization or system to disintegrate.

episode A sequence or set of messages that have both beginning and end, and is understood as a unit.

equality Supportive behavior characterized by shows of respect for another, and efforts to minimize differences in ability, status, power, and intellectual ability. Behavioral opposite of superiority.

ethnocentrism The emotional attitude that one's own race, nation, or culture is superior to all others.

evaluation Defensive behavior characterized by judgments, assessments, and questions about another's viewpoint or motive. Behavioral opposite of description.

evidence Directly observable facts and conditions, beliefs and claims that are generally accepted as true, and previously established conclusions.

exit interview An interview conducted by managers to secure information about why a valued employee has decided to leave the company.

expectation Anticipation of an occurrence; prediction; assumption that an event is likely to occur. Anticipated response of another.

experimenting One of five stages in interpersonal relationships in which an individual explores another and searches for common areas of interest.

expert power Power that derives from knowledge.

extrovert A person who is primarily interested in things outside of himself/herself. Extroverts enjoy speaking with others; expressing their opinions. Opposite of introvert.

f

fact-inference confusion Process of making an observation, drawing an inference about the observation, and acting on the guess as though it were a fact.

fallacy An argument that is damaged, thus invalid, due to inadequate evidence, invalid reasoning, or faulty expression.

feedback Messages sent from a receiver to a source that correct or control error.

feelings Physical, bodily experiences.

field of experience Sum of an individual's experiences, plus all connections drawn among them, that allows a person to talk about and interact with the world. Some theorists believe that people cannot interact unless their fields of experience overlap.

filtering screen model Model used to explain the process by which human selective behavior occurs.

flat structure An organization that has few levels in the hierarchy.

forcing Conflict management strategy that uses power to cause another to accept a position.

forum A public discussion that involves full audience participation.

frame of reference Interlocking facts, ideas, beliefs, values, and attitudes that give form to perceptions. The psychological "window" through which people see the world.

g

game In game theory, a simulation with rules that govern the behavioral choices of players. Game may be played as win-win, win-lose, or lose-lose. In Transactional Analysis, a game is a dishonest, ulterior transaction in which the participant hides true feelings while manipulating another into providing a payoff.

gatekeepers Professional communicators (editors, publishers, television news directors, public relations practitioners, etc.) trained as mass media communicators.

General Semantics Movement that began with the publication of *Science and Sanity* by Alfred Korzybski in 1933. Studies relationships among language, thought, and behavior.

geopolitical factors Political or geographic determinants of stress in cross-cultural encounters.

gestures Body movements that express an idea or emotion.

goodby pleasantries Last part of the closing phase of an interview designed to leave a positive impression.

grapevine Popular term for the informal networks that evolve in an organization. Who really talks to whom.

greetings Part of opening phase of an interview designed to establish rapport.

grievance interview Interview initiated by employee to focus on some matter of employee discontent.

group Three or more people. There is no theoretical upper limit to a group, but we typically think of groups as numbering from three to eleven. Six members may be the optimum number for a decision-making group. Synonymous with small group and decision-making group.

groupthink Term first used by Irving L. Janis to describe what happens when a decision-making group becomes too cohesive. Results in decisions that have no apparent basis in reality.

h

hidden persuaders Model of motivation developed by Vance Packard. Includes the need for emotional security, the need for reassurance of worth, the need for ego gratification, the need for creative outlets, the need for love objects, the need for a sense of power, the need for roots, and the need for immortality.

hierarchy In an organization, any system that places people in rank order, one above the other.

hierarchy of needs Model of human motivation developed by Abraham Maslow. Includes, in order: physiological needs, security/safety needs, love/belonging needs, self-esteem needs, and self-actualization needs.

honesty In interpersonal communication, freedom from deceit or fraud; characterized by truthfulness, sincerity, and candor.

horizontal flow Movement of messages in an organization among members who consider themselves equal.

human relations school School of organizational leadership that held that attention to workers' needs and to job satisfaction would motivate workers best.

identification In persuasion, the process of creating in the listener a sense of feeling, interest, action, or alignment with the object of the persuasive message.

identity aspiration Desire to be recognized as a particular kind of person.

ideology A particular point of view, combined with a set of rules for acting and a set of assumptions about how the world is and how it ought to be.

illustrator Deliberate movements used to reinforce and enrich verbal messages.

image Mental representation, idea, or form. Description or conception of something.

immortality One of Packard's hidden persuaders. Basic appeal: "If you act/buy/choose/accept, etc., then your life will be extended, either physically or symbolically."

inclusion One of the interpersonal needs identified by William Schutz that includes an individual's desire to be accepted, to feel wanted, and to be a part of groups. He identified three personality types: see "undersocial," "oversocial," and "adaptable-social."

indiscrimination Failure to recognize the uniqueness of a person. Interacting in terms of some class or category stereotype.

induction A reasoning pattern that moves from evidence about certain members of a class or category toward a conclusion about some other or all other members of the class or category.

inference Guess, conclusion, based on personal observation of evidence or facts.

inflection A change in voice modulation during speech.

influence and persuasion function Communication function of an organization that exercises control over the behavior of the members.

information In information theory, available data. The more available data, the more information and the greater uncertainty. More commonly used to mean anything that reduces uncertainty.

information function Communication function of an organization that provides the basis to determine goals, to assess performance, and to coordinate individual subunits (internal), and to advertise products or services, to maintain its image, and to adapt to the environment (external).

information interview An interview designed to secure information.

information overload Condition in which the complexity or amount of available information is too great to manage effectively.

information sharing meeting Regular meeting of an organization characterized by a predictable agenda and a clear set of procedural traditions.

initiating One of five stages in interpersonal relationships in which an individual observes another and decides whether to invite interaction.

institution Any organization that has a social, educational, or religious purpose.

integrating One of five stages in interpersonal relationships in which partners move closer, talk more, and think of each other more as a unit, using the terms "we" and "our" in reference to their relationship.

integration and maintenance function Communication function of an organization that keeps the organization in operation, keeps members going through channels, sorts and cross-references the data of the organization, integrates the parts of the organization into a whole, provides continuous self-confirmation.

intensification Process of intensifying. In Rank's model of persuasion, one of two methods of persuading. Strategies include *repetition, association,* and *composition.* In interpersonal relationships, one of five stages in which intimacy and trust increase as partners commit more fully to each other.

intention Will or determination to act or achieve some end.

interchangeability Characteristic of language that makes it possible for individuals to function as both source and receiver.

internal summary A brief summary of what has already been said or written that occurs within a long message. Often used as transition from one main idea to another.

interpersonal attraction Willingness to communicate and develop a relationship with another.

interpersonal communication Transactional process of exchanging messages and negotiating meaning to convey information and to establish and maintain relationships.

interpersonal conflict Expressed struggle between interdependent parties over perceived incompatible goals, scarce rewards, or limited resources.

interview Interpersonal communication context, typically face-to-face, in which questions are asked and answered to achieve some goal.

intimacy Characterization of a close, familiar, and usually affectionate relationship that results from self-disclosure and mutual acceptance.

introvert A person who is primarily concerned with their own thoughts or feelings. Opposite of extrovert.

irreversibility Feature of communication process that makes it impossible to take back what has been said. Once a communication event has occurred it cannot be "uncommunicated."

j

Johari Window Illustration designed by psychologists Joseph Luft and Harrinton Ingham to explain the relationships between self-concept and self-presentation. Includes four sections: (1) open self—things about the self that are known both to self and others; (2) blind self—things known to others but not to self; (3) hidden self—things known to self but not to others; and (4) unknown self—an area inferred to exist but not known to self or others.

judge, the Mnemonic device used to help remember one way that clear talk about negative feelings is punished in our society. ("You have no right to feel that way.")

l

language A system of signs and symbols. A body of words and symbols governed by rules that ties people together into a speech community.

leadership An individual's ability to assess a communication situation and to provide the ideas and information that a group needs.

legitimate power Power that derives from position.

leveling Process of message distortion by omitting details from what is perceived.

life script A set of assumptions, expectations, and rules for our lives that are established for us by our parents or significant others. (See "script.")

liking To regard with favor. To have kindly, friendly feeling for someone or some thing. Related to "affection."

line Refers to all of the people who produce goods or services, and who market those goods and services, including both managers and workers.

linguistics Study of language that focuses on the rules of word usage and the relationships between words, meanings, and behavior. Sometimes subdivided into semantics (study of meanings), syntax (study of rules), and pragmatics (study of language-behavior relationships).

listening Active process of receiving verbal and nonverbal messages. The process of receiving, attending to, and assigning meaning to aural stimuli.

listening, active Voluntary participation in the process of receiving information from a speaker, characterized by frequent summary and paraphrasing of what the speaker has said.

listening, appreciative Listening for the purpose of stimulating our minds and senses; listening for enjoyment.

listening, comprehensive Listening to understand the material presented.

listening, critical Application of a set of standards to evaluate what we hear.

listening, empathic A form of active listening that focuses upon the relationship dimension of communication. The listener attempts to identify, to understand, and to reflect the feelings, needs, and intentions of the speaker.

listening, naive Opposite of critical listening.

love and belonging needs Third level in Maslow's hierarchy of needs. Includes the desire to be accepted by others, to receive attention and love from others, and to find approval.

love objects One of Packard's hidden persuaders. Basic appeal is to a replacement or substitution for a loved one.

m

map-territory confusion Substitution of language for experience. Treating a symbol as an object that can be manipulated. Sometimes called *reification*.

mass communication Process in which gatekeepers design and develop messages for transmission through electronic or mechanical devices to large audiences.

material me Part of self-concept that focuses on body, home, and physical objects.

mean, to Agreement between two or more people that they will recognize what they represent by a sign or symbol.

means to member satisfaction (1) perceived progress toward the group goals, (2) perceived freedom to participate, and (3) status consensus.

message Any sign, symbol, or combination thereof that functions as stimulus material for a receiver. Information sent.

message sidedness Refers to the question of whether it is more effective to present one or both sides of an argument.

metacommunication Communication about communication.

mnemonic device A rhetorical device designed to assist memory. A mental "grab bag" of letters or words. (e.g., "**A**ll **C**ows **E**at **G**rass" is a mnemonic device that helps children learn which notes are indicated by the spaces between the lines in the treble clef of the musical staff.)

model Physical representation of something. A metaphor that allows examination of some object or process in a particular way, but also limits what can be observed in that way.

motivated sequence Pattern of organization for persuasive speeches developed by Alan H. Monroe. Includes: attention step, need step, satisfaction step, visualization step, and action step, each of which is described in this glossary.

motivation segment Part of the opening phase of an interview that attempts to secure cooperation.

n

naming Assignment of labels to objects, phenomena, events, and people.

need step Second step in Monroe's motivated sequence. Purpose is to develop a problem in the mind of the listener.

negative reinforcement Removal of an aversive stimulus to strengthen behavior. Removal is contingent on the behavior.

negentropy A system or organization's deliberate acts of intervention in the process of entropy.

neutrality Defensive behavior characterized by treating another as an object, having only one or a limited set of functions or without showing concern for that individual's problems or viewpoint. Behavioral opposite of "empathy."

noise Any interference or distortion in message exchange. Noise exists in the communication process to the extent that message fidelity is damaged. Three broad categories: (1) physical, or channel, noise, (2) semantic, or psychological, noise, and (3) systemic, or system-centered, noise.

nonassertive Interactive style characterized by self-denial, which allows or encourages others to choose and to receive what they want, even at the expense of self. Sometimes called "shy."

nonverbal communication Communication by means other than words.

o

observations In interpersonal communication, the results of noticing or perceiving the behavior of others. Process of taking in information about another person. One component of the relationship dimension of communication.

omission One of Hugh Rank's strategies for downplaying something by leaving something out.

open questions Questions that invite a broad interpretation and response.

opening phase First part of every interview. Functions to secure attention, put the other person at ease, and to prepare the way for what is coming.

openness Willingness to receive and consider ideas from another. Sometimes called "latitude of acceptance."

open-to-closed sequence A pattern of questions in an interview that begins with broad items, then moves to more and more specific items.

operant conditioning Process of strengthening or weakening behavior by making rewards and punishments contingent upon the change desired.

optimist, the Mnemonic device used to help remember one of the ways to punish clear talk about negative feelings. ("Everything will be all right.")

organization A planned system of behaviors of two or more people who seek to achieve a common goal or set of goals by coordinating their efforts.

organizational communication Communication that occurs within the context of an organization.

organizational culture school School of organizational leadership that believes we must view an organization as a culture.

orientation phase First part of the process of group decision making identified by B. Aubrey Fisher, in which group members are negotiating the nature of their relationships and their social "climate."

orientation segment Part of the opening phase of an interview designed to absorb uncertainty.

overpersonal One of three personality types identified by William Schutz regarding the need for affection. Overpersonal people take special pains to avoid being disliked by anyone. They may spend great amounts of time talking about their feelings or inquiring about the feelings of others.

oversocial One of three personality types identified by William Schutz regarding the need for inclusion. Oversocial people continually seek to join and feel a part of many groups.

p

panel Form of public discussion carried out for the benefit of the audience, but without audience involvement, in which moderator asks a question and expert panel members interact with each other in response to the question.

paradox Any statement that is inherently contradictory.

paraverbal cues Variations in rate, pitch, force, and formation of suprasegmental elements of language that constitute "how" a word is spoken.

participatory module Refers to the part of a speech in which the audience participates. (See *audience participation*.)

passive listening Attending to what is being said without actively providing feedback. Does not interrupt the speaker, but may provide subtle, nonverbal feedback.

perception Process of becoming aware of sensory stimuli which we select from available information.

perceptual accentuation Feature of perception process that distorts perceptions in the direction of wants. For example, we tend to see people we like as smarter and more beautiful than those we do not like.

performance appraisal interview Work related interview in which supervisor gives feedback to employee about performance and consults with employee to establish performance goals for the future.

personal One of three personality types identified by William Schutz regarding the interpersonal need for affection. Personal people can balance situations to be liked when affection is desirable or maintain distance when it is not desirable.

personal evidence Forms of evidence that come directly or indirectly from people, as opposed to real evidence. Categories include: specific information, testimony, definition and explanation, illustration and example.

personalizing Using language that places responsibility for judgments and opinions upon oneself.

person perception Process of perceiving another, characterized by mutuality, clarity, and number of expectations. Derives from summary evaluation and includes—and is influenced by—feelings about self and others.

persuasion Process of influencing attitudes and behaviors.

persuasive interview An interview in which one party seeks to change the thinking or behavior of another.

persuasive power Power that derives from ability to argue logically and persuasively.

physiological needs Most basic needs in Maslow's hierarchy of needs. Includes the need for food, air, water, sexual release, elimination of waste, and so forth.

polarization Use of language in pairs of opposites without allowing any middle ground. Reference to the world as having only two values.

positiveness Behavior that is sure and constructive, rather than skeptical and doubtful. Emphasizes the hopeful, the good, and the affirmative.

positive reinforcement Process of strengthening behavior by making reward contingent upon that behavior.

positive self-talk Process of thinking positive thoughts about oneself, creating positive images of self in the mind.

posture Carriage or position of the body as a whole.

power Ability or potential to influence others. J. R. P. French and B. H. Raven identified six bases of power—referent, expert, legitimate, reward, and coercive—each of which is defined in this glossary. One of Packard's hidden persuaders. Basic appeal: "Your decision to act/buy/choose/accept, etc. will render you powerful."

primacy/recency Refers to the question of where to put the strongest arguments and appeals in a persuasive message.

prime time The period of time from 8:00 to 11:00 P.M., eastern standard time, or 7:00 to 10:00 P.M., central standard time, six days a week, and 7:00 to 11:00 P.M. or 6:00 to 10:00 P.M. central standard time on Sundays.

prior restraint Censorship, frequently by the government.

problem orientation Supportive behavior characterized by a desire to collaborate with another in defining and solving a problem. Behavioral opposite of control.

problem-solving meetings Decision-making meeting that focuses upon a single concern. Usually follows a loose agenda. Can occur on *ad hoc* basis.

problem-solving questions Questions that ask respondent to describe how to solve a problem. Sometimes called "hypothetical" questions.

process Ongoing activity. Continuous changing in pursuit of a goal.

productivity Feature of language that makes it possible to create original sentences that will be understood and to talk about new ideas.

projection Process of attributing one's own feelings, attitudes, values, and beliefs to others.

provisionalism Supportive behavior characterized by willingness to be tentative, to share informations, to suggest that additional information might change one's mind, and to work jointly with another. Behavioral opposite of certainty.

proxemics Study of the human use of space.

proximity Nearness in space that makes it possible for two people to develop a relationship. Part of interpersonal attraction.

punctuation Arbitrary assignment of beginnings and endings in the continuous process of communication, thus identifying separate sequences. One means of interpreting events.

q

question-answer phase Second major section of an interview in which questions and answers are exchanged.

r

real evidence An artifact used as evidence.

reasoning Mental process by which people move from evidence, through claims, to acceptance or rejection of a conclusion.

reassurance of worth One of Packard's hidden persuaders. Basic appeal: "Your decision to act/buy/adopt/accept, etc. renders you worthwhile."

receiver Person or thing that takes in messages.

referent Object, phenomenon, person, or event to which a symbol refers. The subject of a communication event. Part of the triangle of meaning developed by C. K. Ogden and I. A. Richards.

referent power Power that derives from liking.

reflective thinking Process of identifying an idea or problem, applying standards to evaluate its worth, and arriving at a judgment about keeping or rejecting the conclusion.

reflexiveness Feature of language that permits it to be used to refer to itself.

regulator Body movement that fosters interaction. Gesture system that controls turn-taking in the flow of communication.

reification Treating a symbol as if it were a real thing, an object that we can manipulate. (See "map-territory confusion.")

reinforcement Strengthening of another's behavior or self-concept. Feedback. An observable consequence of behavior (e.g., Baby coos and gurgles, so mother smiles and cuddles baby).

reinforcement phase Last phase of group decision emergence identified by B. Aubrey Fisher, in which group members bring specific details of emergent decision into focus, and in which members affirm their commitments and encourage others to do so.

relational definition Perception that each person expresses through language to describe a relationship at a particular moment.

relational deterioration Disintegration or wearing down of a relationship resulting from loss of attractiveness, unfulfilled needs, and inability to manage differences.

relational growth Result of maintaining a satisfying, interesting, and meaningful relationship.

relational rules Societal assumptions and interpersonal agreements arrived at through self-disclosure that allows the prediction of behavior.

relationship dimension Part of a communication event, usually nonverbal, that allows interpretations about the nature of the relationship.

remembering Process of recalling by an effort of memory. Fourth component of the listening process.

repetition The process of reinforcing verbal messages through redundancy (e.g., Holding up two fingers to reinforce the word, "two"). In persuasion, one of Hugh Rank's techniques for intensification.

response Any behavior that results from stimulation.

restatement Redundancy in speech for the purpose of emphasizing the point repeated.

reward power Power that derives from ability to mediate another's rewards through possession of something valued.

rhetoric Use of language to persuade. Persuasion. "The art of discovering all the available means of persuasion."—Aristotle

rhetorical question A question raised by the speaker for special effect. Rhetorical questions usually imply their own answers.

rigidity in naming Process of fixing or hardening a label to some person, object, phenomenon, or event.

rip-off artist, the Mnemonic device used to remember one way that clear talk about negative feelings is punished in our society. ("This happened to me.")

risk Exposure to a hazard, danger, or loss.

risky shift Phenomenon that allows tendency of groups to take greater risks than would individuals.

role Behavior evidenced by an individual and sanctioned by others. Expectations of someone's dual behavior. Pattern of behavior. Routine associated with an individual in a particular context.

roots One of Packard's hidden persuaders. Basic appeal: "Your decision to buy/vote/act/accept/choose, etc., will return your sense of place."

rule Pattern of behavior expected from a certain role situation or context. A belief about what behaviors may or may not be performed in a given situation in order to achieve a particular goal.

S

safety and security needs Second in Maslow's *Hierarchy of Needs,* including freedom from fear, protection by law, and order in life.

satisfaction step Third step in Monroe's motivated sequence. Purpose is to show solution to some problem.

science Method for discovering some systematically arranged body of facts or truths about a thing that shows the operation of general laws governing the thing observed.

scientific management school School of organizational leadership that held the idea that people are economically motivated.

script In Transactional Analysis, the life plan an individual feels compelled to act out. Characterized by four basic themes, or life positions: (1) I'm O.K., you're O.K. (2) I'm O.K., you're not O.K. (3) I'm not O.K. you're O.K. (4) I'm not O.K., you're not O.K.

selective attention Process of choosing one or more of the stimuli to which we are exposed.

selective exposure Process of choosing certain stimuli while disregarding or avoiding others.

self-actualization Fifth order in Maslow's hierarchy of needs. Includes the motivation to be self-fulfilled, creative, and imaginative.

self-awareness Self-concept, coupled with perceptions of other's attitudes and opinions of oneself.

self-concept Sum of perceptions, ideas, and images about oneself. How we feel about ourselves.

self-definition Part of self-concept, expressed and modified when people talk and receive feedback.

self-disclosure Revealing one's thinking, feelings, beliefs, and so forth to another.

self-esteem Value of oneself. Self-love. Self-respect. Fourth in Maslow's hierarchy of needs. Includes the image of oneself regarding personal competence, reputation, status, prestige, etc.

self-expression Feature of language usage by which word choice reflects the status of speaker. Sometimes strong language that was not intended literally.

self-fulfilling prophesy Process of making a prediction come true. Occurs when we let our expectations control our outcomes.

self-trust Trust in one's own competence and judgment.

semantic noise Any distortion that occurs when one's use of language differs from another's.

sensing Receiving stimuli through the five senses.

serial flow Movement of messages along a chain of people.

Shannon and Weaver model Model of the communication process.

shared beliefs Beliefs derived through experience and acknowledged by others.

sharpening In perception, process of focusing on details that reinforce the frame of reference while discarding the rest.

shy See "nonassertive."

sign Token, indication. Something that stands for or announces the presence of something else when a natural relationship exists (e.g., footprint announces that a person has been there).

significant other Person who influences the formation of the self-concept. Person to whom one looks for information about appropriate behavior.

signification A use of language to point to something. The act or process of making something known by using signs and symbols.

signpost A preview of ideas to come. A marker of an important idea. An immediate indication of something important.

silence Absence of sound. Background upon which all spoken language is structured. Thomas Bruneau identified three forms: (1) psycholinguistic (part of the temporal sequence of speech), (2) interactive (pause or interruption used for decision making), and (3) sociocultural (culturally sanctioned or mandated silences).

similarity Perception that someone is like ourselves. Part of interpersonal attraction.

small group Any collection of three or more individuals who share some problem or some common goal.

smoothing Conflict management strategy of minimizing differences and emphasizing positive, common interests or of avoiding issues that might cause conflict.

social comparison Comparison of oneself to others.

social me Part of self-concept that focuses upon how others perceive and experience oneself.

source Location of an idea. Originator of a message.

span of control The number of subordinates who report to an individual supervisor.

speaker credibility Same as Aristotle's *ethos*. Perception in audience members of the speaker's goodwill, knowledge, trustworthiness, personal appearance, and the extent of agreement with audience.

special events meeting An infrequently held meeting that focuses attention on some particular occurrence (e.g., a "sales meeting" or a professional association's annual conference).

speech acts Units of talk that convey intention.

speech community A group of people who use language in the same way. Thus, they understand both the words and the rules for their use, and share a common orientation to the world in which they live.

spiritual me Part of self-concept that focuses upon awareness of oneself as a thinking and feeling person.

spontaneity Supportive behavior characterized by the candid, straightforward, and uncomplicated presentation of the self.

staff All the individuals involved in supporting the line operations of an organization.

stagnating Stage in relational deterioration characterized by inactivity, verbal silence, discomfort, and negation of one's partner.

stereotype Application of a fixed set of beliefs about a group or subgroup to an individual that ignores the uniqueness of the individual.

strategy Defensive behavior characterized by attempts to trick others into thinking that they are making a decision that in fact has already been made, or that their best interests are being considered when they are not.

subculture A culture within a culture.

substitution In communication, the use of nonverbal messages to serve for verbal messages.

summary In an interview, the review and clarification of the agreements and key ideas generated in the question-answer phase. Part of the closing phase of an interview.

superiority Defensive behavior characterized by suggestions that another is inadequate or inferior and thus unable to entertain feedback or share in problem solving.

supplementation Use of nonverbal messages to change slightly the words they accompany.

supportiveness Interpersonal behavior characterized by description, problem orientation, spontaneity, empathy, equality, and provisionalism, each of which is defined in this glossary.

surface beliefs Flexible beliefs. Least central of all elements in the belief structure, such as those dealing with matters of taste.

symbol Something that stands for something else when no natural relationship exists. A symbol represents or takes the place of, or points to ideas, to objects, or to events. In language, words, phrases, and sentences that stand for thoughts (e.g., loyalty).

symmetrical relationship Relationship, or view of a relationship, in which partners are essentially similar in status, power, responsibility, and so forth.

symposium A series of speeches related to a central topic for the purpose of providing material for future discussion, or to inform.

systems school School of organizational leadership that focused on communication. Both physical and psychological aspects of an organization work together as part of a system; they must all be taken into account.

tall structure An organization that includes many levels in its hierarchy.

tension Mental or nervous strain, or strain in relationship.

terminating Result of relational deterioration. End of a relationship. Severance of contract, sometimes codified, as in a divorce decree.

territoriality Tendency for individuals to claim, "own," and use space as an extension of their own personal space. Lyman and Scott described four categories: (1) public (area that individuals may enter freely), (2) interactional (area marked by participants as theirs while they are interacting), (3) home (private space occupied by legal sanction), and (4) body (space immediately surrounding one's physical person).

thought Result of mental activity. Perception and interpretation of a referent, including feelings, past experiences, and related perceptions. Mental image of a referent.

time Cultural system of temporal and sequential relationships between and among events that has message potential. Some cultures are monochronic because they use time arbitrarily. Others are polychronic because they emphasize people and interactions rather than an arbitrary understanding of time.

time binding The feature of language that makes it possible for us to tie ourselves to history.

touching behavior, friendship/warmth Casual and spontaneous touching that signals mutual acceptance and positive regard (but excluding love or sexual touching), as in congratulatory back patting.

touching behavior, functional/professional Touching to deliver professional service, as between a physician and a patient.

touching behavior, love/intimacy Touching that signals a special, or bonded relationship, or that assumes or confirms intimate access to be appropriate, as in handholding or lap sitting.

touching behavior, sexual arousal Touching that is pleasant because of the sexual meaning it conveys or the sexual stimulation it produces, as in petting and sexual intercourse.

touching behavior, social/polite Ritual touching to acknowledge someone's personhood or essential humanity and/or acknowledge or neutralize status differences, as in handshaking or kissing a cardinal's ring.

transactional Mutual negotiation of meaning. Mutual influence.

Transactional Analysis System developed by Eric Berne for analyzing relationship behavior as it is occurring.

triangle of meaning Figure developed by C. K. Ogden and I. A. Richards that depicts the relationship among words, their referents, and thoughts.

trust Feeling of comfort that derives from ability to predict another's behavior. A belief that the other can be relied on.

turn-taking Process of passing initiative for talk back and forth between or among participants in conversation; signaled by various nonverbal cues.

two-valued orientation Behaving or tending to experience a phenomenon or event in polarized terms, but without allowing any middle ground. (See "polarization.")

u

underpersonal One of three personality types identified by William Schutz regarding the interpersonal need for affection. Underpersonal people have little need for affection and avoid giving it to others.

undersocial One of three personality types identified by William Schutz regarding the need for inclusion. Undersocial people have little need for inclusion, isolating themselves from group involvement.

understanding Third component of the listening process; interpretation and evaluation of what is sensed.

v

values What a person considers important, composed of wants, goals, and guidelines. Characterized by statements of what should be.

vertical flow Movement of messages up and down the hierarchical structure of an organization.

visualization One method of positive self-talk, in which we imagine or visualize ourselves being successful.

visualization step Fourth step in Monroe's motivated sequence. Purpose is to develop an image in listeners of the consequences of their decisions to act/vote/purchase/accept, and so forth.

vocalics Variations in rate, pitch, force, and formation of suprasegmental elements of language that constitute "how" a word is spoken.

w

wants Wishes, needs, and desires that one holds of a relationship.

withdrawal Conflict management strategy of retreating from the conflict.

Credits

Photos

Table of Contents

Page vii
© Jeff Spielman/Stockphotos, Inc.
Page ix
© Larry Gatz/The Image Bank.
Page xi
© Butch Martin/The Image Bank.
Page xiii
© Ed Wheeler/The Stock Market.
Page xvi
© Felicia Martinez/PhotoEdit.

Chapter 1

Opener
© Jeff Spielman/Stockphotos, Inc.
Page 7
© Carl Frank/Photo Researchers, Inc.
Page 13
© David Young-Wolff/PhotoEdit.
1.5
© Bob Daemmrich/The Image Works.
Page 19
© Comstock, Inc.

Chapter 2

Opener
© Bob Daemmrich/The Image Works.
Page 29
© Mieke Maas/The Image Bank.
Page 32
© Owen Franken/Stock Boston.
2.1
© Gary Chapman/The Image Bank.
Page 41
© Richard Hutchings/InfoEdit.

Chapter 3

Opener
© Erik Leigh Simmons/The Image Bank.
Page 50
© Comstock, Inc.

Page 178
© Comstock, Inc./R. Michael Stuckey.
Page 181
© Janeart Ltd./The Image Bank.

Chapter 9
Opener
© Butch Martin/The Image Bank.
Page 208
© Steve Niedorf/The Image Bank.
Page 216
© Giuliano Lolliva/The Image Bank.
Page 219
© Tony Freeman/PhotoEdit.

Chapter 10
Opener
© Lou Jones/The Image Bank.
Page 231
© Gabe Palmer/The Stock Market.
Page 242
© Dick Luria/Photo Researchers, Inc.
Page 255
© Bob O'Shaughnessy/The Stock Market.

Chapter 11
Opener
© Marc Romanelli/The Image Bank.
Page 269
© David Woo/Stock Boston.
Page 275
© Michael Salas/The Image Bank.
Page 284
© Comstock, Inc.

Chapter 12
Opener
© Ed Wheeler/The Stock Market.
Page 297
© Jon Feingersh/The Stock Market.
Page 300
© Richard Cash/PhotoEdit.
Page 305
© Obremski/The Image Bank.

Chapter 13
Opener
© Richard Pasley/Stock Boston.
Page 315
© Bob Daemmrich/Stock Boston.

Figure 1.3
From *Human Communication: A Symbolic Interactionist Perspective* by Julia T. Wood, copyright © 1982 by Holt, Rinehart and Winston, Inc., reprinted by permission of the publisher.
Figure 1.4
From Gerald L. Wilson, Alan M. Hantz, and Michael S. Hanna, INTERPERSONAL GROWTH THROUGH COMMUNICATION, 2d ed. Copyright © 1989 Wm. C. Brown Publishers, Dubuque, Iowa. All rights reserved. Reprinted by permission.

Chapter 6
Figure 6.3
From Gerald L. Wilson, Alan M. Hantz, and Michael S. Hanna, INTERPERSONAL GROWTH THROUGH COMMUNICATION, 2d ed. Copyright © 1989 Wm. C. Brown Publishers, Dubuque, Iowa. All rights reserved. Reprinted by permission.

Chapter 10
Figures 10.1, 10.2, 10.3, & 10.4
Copyright © 1988 McGraw-Hill Book Company, New York, NY. Reprinted by permission of McGraw-Hill, Inc. From Michael S. Hanna and Gerald L. Wilson, *Communicating in Business and Professional Settings,* 2d ed.

Chapter 13
Figure 13.2
From *Selling Smoke: Cigarette Advertising and Public Health,* 1986. Copyright by the American Public Health Association. Reprinted with permission.

Chapter 15
Figure 15.2
Illustration by Stephen C. Blevins.

Chapter 17
Figure 17.1
From Adrian Furnham and Stephen Bochner, *Culture Shock: Psychological Reactions to Unfamiliar Environments.* Copyright © 1986 Methuen & Co., London, England. Reprinted with permission.

Illustrator Credits
Precision Graphics
Figures: 1.1, 1.2, 1.3, 1.4, 3.1, 4.1, 4.2, 4.4, 4.5, 6.1, 6.2, 6.3, 6.4, 6.5, 6.6, 8.1, 8.2, 9.1, 10.1, 10.2, 10.3, 10.4, 11.1, 11.2, 12.1, 13.1, 13.2, 14.1, 15.1, 17.1.

Chapter 10
Text art page 259: From Hanna, Michael S., and Gerald L. Wilson, Communicating in Business and Professional Settings. 2d edition. Copyright 1988 Random House, Inc. Reprinted by permission.

Index